Slaves Who Abolished Slavery

Slaves Who Abolished Slavery

BLACKS IN REBELLION

RICHARD HART

UNIVERSITY OF THE WEST INDIES PRESS
Barbados • Jamaica • Trinidad and Tobago

University of the West Indies Press
1A Aqueduct Flats   Mona
Kingston 7   Jamaica   W I

©1985, 2002 by Richard Hart
All rights reserved. Published 2002

Originally published 1985 by the Institute of Social and
Economic Research, University of the West Indies, Mona, Jamaica

ISBN 976-640-110-1

06 05 04 03 02   5 4 3 2 1

Cataloguing-in-publication data for this book is
available from the National Library of Jamaica.

Cover design by Robert Harris.
Cover illustration: J. Bourgoin, *Maroons in Ambush on Dromilly Estate, Trelawny*.
Reproduced by courtesy of the National Library of Jamaica.

Printed in Jamaica by Stephenson's Litho Press.

*A tribute to my late father;
an encouragement to my
children and their generation;
and
a memorial to the freedom fighters
who gave their lives in the struggle
against slavery.*

PREFACE

The Slave Rebellions and Maroon Wars of Jamaica began to interest me in or about the year 1940. Soon afterwards I commenced the research on which my second volume is based. These were the years in which the militancy of the workers, which had come to the boil in all the widely scattered colonies of the British West Indies in the late 1930s, and the new nationalistic upsurge, were taking organisational form.

Early in the 1940s I began to speak from political platforms about the resistance of the slaves to their enslavement, about Sam Sharpe, Tacky and other participants in the many slave rebellions and about Cudjoe and other leaders in the Maroon wars. After an initial period of surprise, my colleagues in the trade union and political movements began to understand my purpose.

One of the problems confronting the pioneers of the new popular movements was the formidable historical legacy of a widespread lack of racial self respect. Garvey's oratory, in the late 1920s and early 1930s, had struck a responsive chord and the experience of participation in his movement had provided many thousands of people with a foundation for self assurance. But even so, the task of inspiring national self confidence was a formidable one.

This historical legacy of self denigration was only partly attributable to the objective circumstances of generations of enslavement and cruel exploitation. It was also the contrived effect of a system of education and indoctrination deliberately designed to promote a loyalty to the prevailing imperialism and an acceptance of the domination of whites over blacks.

Many peoples who have been subjected to alien domination have been able to draw strength and inspiration from their own legends and history. The Jamaican people were at a disadvantage. The imperial power had largely succeeded in erasing from their memory their African cultural heritage. Jamaica had no legends, but it did have a history. And there were aspects of that history which, if brought to the people's attention, could provide abundant inspiration for future struggles against oppression.

My initial interest in the subject of my book was unashamedly political. But the subject of the struggle against slavery is such an absorbing one that its pursuit develops in the researcher a momentum of its own. This is the only explanation I can offer for having pursued it in such detail for so many years.

As originally conceived, my book was to have consisted almost entirely of the subject matter of the second volume — material relating to the prolonged struggle of the slaves in Jamaica against their enslavement. Subsequently I decided that, in order to give the background and place these struggles in context, a companion volume would be required.

In Volume One I have sought: to examine how the enslavement of Africans by Europeans came about; to give an account of how Africans were enslaved and transported to the West Indies; to describe the disciplinary systems of plantation slavery under the Protestant British and to make some comparisons with enslavement under the Catholic Iberians; and, to account for the growth and eventual legislative success of the anti-slavery movement in Britain. Also included in Volume One is the story in brief of the victorious revolution of the slaves in Saint Domingue.

Volume Two, being confined to but a single territory is, unavoidably, a descent from the general to the particular. Jamaica, the largest and most populous of the British islands, was one of the arenas in which large numbers of slaves struggled for their freedom with unflagging determination. Their successes, initially partial, were finally crowned by the achievement of the abolition of slavery at a considerably earlier date than would have been possible without their intervention.

Jamaica was not the only sugar colony outside of Saint Domingue in which the slaves fought for their freedom. There were few islands or mainland colonies in the Caribbean area which did not produce their counterparts of the Jamaicans Cudjoe, Tacky and Sam Sharpe, their embryonic Toussaint Louverture. In limiting my account of slave revolts and Maroon wars to those occurring in Jamaica, I do not claim that this island was entirely typical of the sugar colonies. Nor do I deny that the scope of the work would have been improved by accounts of parallel events in other territories. Possessing neither the knowledge nor the research facilities to enable me to draw a rounded picture of black struggles against slavery over the entire region, it seemed prudent to confine my attention primarily to events in the land of my birth.

Revelling in Britain's liberal image earned by the abolition of the slave trade and slavery, most historians have paid little or no attention to the frequent and formidable rebellions and conspiracies of the slaves, or the extent to which these events influenced the British decision. The suspicion is unavoidable that this is only partly to be explained by ignorance of the facts. The reluctance to investigate and assess the role of the blacks suggests a desire, perhaps sub-conscious, to erase the record of their decisive participation in the anti-slavery struggle.

The focal point around which the political history of the West Indies revolved for upwards of two centuries was the refusal of large numbers of the involuntary migrants from Africa passively to accept their enslavement. European opposition to slavery was aroused and grew over the years not only in response to the class interests of the rising bourgeoisie (discussed in Volume One, Chapter 7) but also because the slaves in the sugar colonies were continually offering and conspiring to offer violent resistance. The idea, sedulously disseminated, that the enslavement of Africans was part of the natural order of things, was challenged again and again, as much by the casualties among the whites engaged in the trade and employed on the plantations as by the disclosure of the sufferings endured by the blacks.

It is no doubt an elementary principle of economics that,

given conditions in which a sufficient supply of labour is otherwise obtainable, slavery is a relatively inefficient system of production. Were it possible to imagine a servile society isolated from outside influences, a point of time would probably be reached in due course when it would best serve the interests of the propertied classes to replace slavery by a system based on material incentives. This, however, was not the state of affairs in the British sugar colonies at the end of the third decade of the 19th century.

Not only were the majority of the plantation owners, other than those in Antigua, convinced that the abolition of slavery would deprive them of the cheap labour they required, but, with few and very localised exceptions, they were probably correct. The activity of the slaves was of vital significance in the general sense that the anti-slavery cause could not have been so successfully sustained had its most obvious beneficiaries failed forcibly to demonstrate their dissatisfaction. It was also decisive, as the evidence of contemporary opinion clearly showed, in making indefinite delay and prevarication on the abolition issue impossible.

My manuscript has been drafted and re-drafted several times and expanded as new material was discovered. Over the years I have had the benefit of the comments and criticisms of a number of persons to whom I am grateful. None of the persons I shall mention below, however, can be held responsible for any errors I may have made, either of fact or evaluation.

The first, immature, draft of my manuscript was read and criticised by Eric Williams who had then recently published his classic *Capitalism and Slavery*. Subsequently, in 1950, he published, as an article in his *Caribbean Historical Review*, my chapter (as it then stood) on "Cudjoe and the First Maroon War". A later draft which had by then grown to about 120 foolscap pages, was submitted to the late Leo Huberman and Herbert Aptheker. Both made suggestions which I was able to adopt. But the inadequacies of these early drafts were glaring and mercifully, with the exception mentioned above, they were never published. For the next ten years the MS. was seldom taken out of storage, and then only to assist me in preparing occasional lectures.

In 1964 Robert Moore at the University of Guyana read the MS. and asked me to let him make copies on a duplicator for the use of his students. The University gave me some spare copies which I sent to the Institute of Jamaica and two or three university librarians. This resulted in a couple of references in print and some encouraging comments and I decided, when I came to Britain in 1965, to finish the work for publication. Among those who encouraged me in this was Robert Hill, whose suggestion it was that I include an account of how I came to write it.

I would like to mention the assistance and inspiration I received, in more ways than I can possibly explain, from my late father Ansell Hart. His excellent collection of books about the West Indies (subsequently donated by him to the library of the University of the West Indies in Jamaica) provided me with the opportunity to start my research.

From my references and chapter notes it will be readily apparent that I am indebted to the authors, past and present, of the many works, published and unpublished, which have been consulted. Likewise, I am grateful to the persons at Accompong and Moore Town who gave me oral information and to others who gave me the benefit of their advice. Wherever possible their names have been mentioned.

I must express my appreciation of the facilities afforded to me by a number of libraries and institutions, and the permissions generously given to reproduce passages from manuscripts, correspondence, newspaper collections and rare books in their possession. Special mention must be made of the assistance afforded me by the governing bodies, librarians and staff of the Institute of Jamaica, the Public Records Office (London), the British Museum, the Royal Commonwealth Society, the Institute of Commonwealth Studies (London University), and the Surrey Record Office. The staff of the Guildford Public Library were helpful in securing for me the loan of rare books from other libraries.

I am grateful to Major General E. H. Goulburn for permission to reproduce extracts from correspondence in the Goulburn family papers relating to Amity Hall estate, and to Mrs. B. D. Rennison for permission to reproduce extracts from the personal correspondence of Sir Charles Edward Grey.

Some explanation and apology is required for the fact that four years have elapsed since the publication of Volume One *(Blacks in Bondage)*. Though it had been intended to publish this second volume soon after the publication of the first, earlier publication was not achieved for a variety of reasons quite beyond my control. Fortunately, the struggle against slavery is not a subject which becomes historically less interesting or important with the passage of time.

Judging from the number of enquiries received, Volume One appears to have aroused considerable advance interest in the publication of Volume Two. The appearance of this volume also coincides with the publication of the work in Spanish translation by the Casa de las Americas in Cuba. Appreciation of the significance of slavery and the anti-slavery struggle now extends well beyond the boundaries in which slaves fought for their freedom.

Richard Hart,
January 1985

CONTENTS

1	The Beginning of Black Resistance	1
2	The First Maroon War	32
3	Nanny Town	60
4	"The More Honourable to Them"	84
5	The Black Gendarmes	118
6	Tacky's War	130
7	The Second Maroon War	157
8	Of Peace and Perfidy	191
9	The Perils of Freedom	207
10	The Conspiracies of 1815 and 1823-24	221
11	Sam Sharpe — Organiser of the Emancipation Rebellion	244
12	"Kensington on Fire"	274
13	20,000 Slaves in Rebellion	291
14	The Cost of the Rebellion	312
15	The Rebels reset the Time Table	325
	REFERENCES	338
	INDEX TO PERSONS	345
	GENERAL INDEX	351

CHAPTER ONE

THE BEGINNING OF BLACK RESISTANCE

Jamaica is an elongated island. It stretches for about 145 miles from east to west and its width from north to south varies from 20 to just under 50 miles. Its total area is 4,450 square miles. There are fertile plains stretching inland from the sea shore, some of them extensive. There are also smaller plains and valleys inland. But the most noticeable feature of the island's geography is its mountainous spine, rising to over 7,400 feet at its eastern end.

The foothills rise steeply out of the plains. At some points the mountains come down close to the coast. Much of the high ground is steep and precipitous. In the 17th and first half of the 18th century the mountains were thickly wooded. The cultivation of sugar cane, established at first on the coastal plains, spread inland, particularly in the second half of the 18th century.

The Spaniards began to settle in Jamaica in or about 1509. The Amerindian population, identifiable by similarities of language and pottery styles as migrants of Arawak stock from South America, may then have been as numerous as 60,000.[1] Recent speculation suggests a considerably smaller number [Vanderwal 41]. A century later, in 1611, the Abbot of Jamaica recorded the presence of only 74 Indians born on the island. It is probable that there were Amerindians living in the mountains outside the control of the Spaniards. An unsuccessful expedition was sent into the Blue Mountains in eastern Jamaica in 1601 in pursuit of Arawaks alleged to have taken refuge there [Morales 25 p. 267]. There may have been others of whom the Spaniards were unaware. Nevertheless, the decline in numbers is startling.

In 1644, in a letter to the king, a Spanish resident describing himself as "Priest, Pontonotary and Apostolic official a native of the island", wrote: "This island is very rich in gold and silver mines that by-gone inhabitants worked with much profit. This has not been continued through lack of the native Indians of whom for many years past there is not even one left" [45 Vol. 1, No. 1 (June 1945), pp. 106-12].

The writer of this letter was not the most reliable of witnesses. There do not appear to have been either gold or silver mines in Jamaica, where only a small quantity of alluvial gold was washed. He was concerned about the shortage of labour, complaining as he did in the same letter that Negro slaves had been taken off the island for sale in Cartagena and Havana. Was he, perhaps, in speaking of the disappearance of the Amerindians, directing his mind only to the question of whether any were available to the Spaniards as labourers?

There may still have been, at that date, small numbers of survivors in inaccessible retreats. Perhaps, too, there were surviving Amerindian women who had become the wives of Spanish settlers. Even so, a population decline on the scale that took place in Jamaica during the century and a half of Spanish occupation is so amazing that, had the same thing not occurred elsewhere in the Caribbean, it would have been difficult to believe.

The causes of this phenomenon were no doubt the same in Jamaica as in Española. Those who offered physical resistance perished by the sword. Resistance in Jamaica may have been greater than is generally appreciated. Amerindian hostility provides a credible explanation of why the Spaniards abandoned construction of Sevilla Nueva near St. Ann's Bay.

But many more deaths were attributable to disease. Some diseases, endemic among Europeans, became epidemic when the Amerindians were exposed to them. Even the common cold became a killer when contracted by peoples who, never having been exposed to it, lacked natural powers of resistance.

A parallel cause of decline was the inability of the native peoples in the Caribbean to make the psychological adjustments necessary for survival under the regimentation of the encomienda. But it seems equally probable that, lacking the space for retreat in depth as in South America, many of the Amerindians left the island in their canoes, perhaps to meet a similar fate on other shores.

That there were Amerindian survivors living in Jamaica during the first 80 years of the English occupation is a matter of record. The Inventory of the slaves on Worthy Park estate in 1731 disclosed the presence there of six "Indians" [Craton 6 p. 54n (23); J. Arc. Inv. (1729-1836) 15 p. 147]. In 1733 the Assembly, engaged in a war with escaped African slaves, resolved on a strategy of "rooting up and destroying all the Indian and negro provisions in or near" a rebel settlement in the north-eastern mountain range [*Journals* 3 p. 120]. Whether these "Indians" were natives of Jamaica cannot be positively established. The possibility that they had been imported from Central America cannot be discounted. Describing the habits of the English log cutters in the Bay of Honduras around 1675, the pirate William Dampier wrote: "they often made sallies out in small parties among the nearest Indian towns, where they plundered and brought away the Indian women to serve them at their huts, and sent their husbands to be sold at Jamaica" [Dampier 8]. The importation of Amerindian slaves was not prohibited until 1741.[2] But whoever they may have been, there was a note of finality for all the Amerindians in Jamaica in the Assembly's resolution.

During the closing years of the Spanish occupation there were believed to have been about 1500 persons of African descent in Jamaica. What was their status? Almost all of them must have been imported as slaves but no doubt, as in other Spanish possessions, there had been many manumissions. In 1611, when there were 523 Spaniards and 558 slaves, there were 107 free blacks. Juan de Las Cabezas Altamirano, Bishop of Cuba, reporting to the king on 23 August 1608 on his recent visit to Jamaica, mentioned seeing "the brown folks playing games of ball" [45 Vol. 1, No. 1 pp. 102-6]. Whether he was referring to mulattoes and mestizoes[3] or to Arawaks is not clear.

There were self supporting villages in the rural areas populated by escaped black slaves, some of whom had probably mated with Amerindian women. Julian de Castilla, a Spanish captain who wrote of the fighting against the English in which he had participated, stated: "these slaves have withdrawn from their owners and reside in strong places which they call palenques."[4] In contrast to its liberal attitude to the manumission of slaves, the Spanish monarchy was uncompromisingly hostile to those who had illegally freed themselves. But the settlers had had no alternative but to adjust themselves to their existence.

During the fighting for possession of the island between 1655 and 1660 the Spanish leader Cristoval Ysasi was able to enlist the aid of some of these blacks against the English. No doubt he convinced them that the latter, if victorious, would seek to re-enslave them. In a letter to the Maestro de Campo dated 3 April 1656 Ysasi wrote: "I assembled from Guatibaco thirty men, Spaniards, and fifteen negroes from the palenque of the Rio Juana." But he complained that the slaves of one Hernan Peres, whom he had expected to join him, had not come [45 Vol. 2, No. 2 pp. 22-25]. Writing to the Duke of Albuquerque in August 1657, Ysasi reported: "I have to inform your Excellency that all the fugitive negroes are under my obedience" [ibid]. No doubt he exaggerated the extent of his authority. Allies of the Spaniards these blacks may have been, but almost certainly they fought under their own leaders.

In a letter to Cromwell dated 5 November 1655, Major R.

THE BEGINNING OF RESISTANCE

Sedgewicke wrote of the danger from "Blacks and Mulattos" who "meet with our English in the woods, and every now and then kill three or four of them together." A communication from Vice-Admiral Gordon and Sedgewicke dated 24 January 1656, stated:

> The Negroes ... live by themselves in several parties, and near our quarters, and do very often, as our men go into the woods to seek provisions, destroy and kill them with their launces. We now and then find one or two of our men killed, stripped, and naked, and these rogues begin to be bold, our English rarely, or seldom, killing any of them ...

In a letter to Thurloe dated 12 March 1656 Sedgewicke again referred to the damage done to the English by these blacks: "The Spaniard is not considerable, but of the Blacks there are many, who are like to prove as thorns and pricks in our sides ..." In the following months he complained that "in two days more than forty of our soldiers were cut off by the Negroes." [5]

The Rio Juana, referred to by Ysasi, has not been identified. But though the inhabitants of the palenque there were allies of the Spaniards, there were other palenques whose members remained aloof from the struggle between the contending Europeans. Referring to an expedition of a hundred soldiers to Great Pedro Point in St. Elizabeth on 4 February 1656, Edward Long wrote:

> There had been a Spanish village at Paretty ... From one or two Negroes whom they chanced to meet with here, they learned that the blacks had entirely detached themselves from the Spaniards, and were resolved to maintain their footing in the island so long as any cattle remained for them to kill [24 vol. 1 p. 252].

By 1660 the Spaniards had withdrawn from Jamaica, "leaving about thirty of their Negro slaves behind, who secreted themselves in the mountains, and afterwards entered into alliance with the other unsubdued banditti" [24 Vol. 1, p. 278 ff]. It would never have occurred to Edward Long, who wrote these words, that this derogatory term might with greater justification have been applied to the English invaders.

The English, too, had been successful in making an

alliance with the leader of one of these palenques, though whether this occurred before or after it became apparent that the Spanish cause was hopeless is not clear. His name, Lubolo, they corrupted first to Juan Luyola, then to Juan de Bolas. With some 150 followers he had settled in the Luidas Vale where they farmed extensively.

Edward D'Oyley, military governor until 1661 and thereafter, for a short period, civil governor, was instructed to "give such encouragement as securely you may wish to such negroes, natives and others, as shall submit to live peaceably under his majesty's obedience and in due submission to the government of the island" [*Journals* 1 app. 3].

On 1 February 1663 Lyttleton, the new English governor, proclaimed:

> That Juan Luyola and the rest of the negroes of his Palenque, on account of their submission and services to the English, shall have grants of land and enjoy all the liberties and priviledges of Englishmen... That Luyola be colonel of the black regiment of militia, and he and others appointed magistrates over the negroes to decide all cases except those of life and death [CSP 1663 p. 122].

A grant was made to them of 30 acres of land for each man.[6] The majority of the free blacks did not approve of Lubolo's alliance. William Beeston, one of the large land owners, recorded in his journal: "On the first day of November the out-lying negroes met with Juan de Bola, and cut him to pieces" [1].

Among those with whom the English were unable to make permanent peace were the inhabitants of the palenque south of Cave Valley, near the border of Clarendon and St. Ann on the Vermahollis savannah.[7] Peace was established with the inhabitants of this palenque in 1667-68 but it did not last for long [Cl. Min. February-March 1668]. In 1670 rewards were offered of £30 for the head of their leader, known as Juan de Serras, and £20 for that of each of his followers. The killing of a number of white men in Clarendon, mentioned in the minutes of the Council on 2 May 1670, was no doubt the work of the inhabitants of the Vermahollis palenque.[8]

The regular military and naval forces were subject to the control of the British government and were often required for service in the wars between the rival European powers which were an ever recurring feature of Caribbean history. The suppression of rebellious slaves only became their principal responsibility when a rebellion, as happened from time to time, assumed the proportions of a threat to white domination and the plantation system. From the very fact that their presence was as necessary for the promotion of imperial adventures as it was for the protection of local property rights, arose a perennial problem. The question of how much the local tax payer should contribute towards the cost of the British military and naval presence was a cause of perpetual friction between the Assembly and the imperial government.

The militia and the mercenary parties, on the other hand, were under local control. The raising of money to maintain them was the responsibility of the Assembly and the vestries. The militia, formally established by statute in 1681, consisted of all free men between the ages of 16 and 60. Originally all the members were white, but it does not appear that, as regards the ordinary privates, there was ever a racial barrier to membership. Free mulattoes and blacks who became liable to service were never comissioned as officers, even when the privates were segregated into separate companies. Nor were they ever admitted to the Horse Militia, the preserve of the most socially elevated whites.

When things were quiet the militia, which mustered once per month, did not cost very much to maintain. But in times of emergency the governor could call them into active service by a proclamation of martial law. Needless to say, the plantation owners found prolonged periods of active service most inconvenient. Apart from the inconvenience of personal attendance for duty, the normal routine of the plantation was disrupted and they were deprived of the services of their supervisory personnel and indentured servants, many of whom were skilled tradesmen.

For this reason most of the property owners were willing to bear a certain amount of extra taxation for employing mercenaries to combat the rebellious slaves and pursue those who escaped from the plantations. Sometimes mercenary parties were engaged for a campaign against a particular settlement of escaped slaves or band of runaways or to suppress a particular rebellion. At other times they were kept on active service, roaming through the woods for months on end, killing and capturing runaways.

The mercenary parties usually consisted of a commissioned officer, a sergeant and from 12 to 18 men. In the late 17th century their rate of pay was five shillings per day for officers, two shillings and sixpence for sergeants and one shilling and sixpence for privates. They also received incentive rewards of 40 shillings for every rebel or runaway killed or captured [Cl. Min. 19 Feb 1686]. Under the "Voluntary Parties" Acts it was also possible for groups of whites, accompanied if they so wished by slaves serving as baggage porters or 'black-shot', to go off into the woods in the hope of earning the rewards.

With the promotion of the commercial production of sugar in the 1670s, a heavy influx of African slaves into Jamaica commenced. Many of the slaves delivered by the English slave traders were known in the trade and on the plantations as Cromantees or Coromantees, a word spelled in a variety of ways. They were often assumed to have belonged to a single nation of that name, but there was in fact no such nation or tribe. Not all the so-called Cromantees spoke the same or related languages. The one thing that they did all have in common was that they had been shipped to the New World from the Gold Coast.

Writing in 1742 James Knight[9] stated:

> The Gold Coast Negroes, though they generally go under the denomination of Cromantus, are of different Provinces or Clans; and not under the same Prince or Chief, nor do they speak the same language. Of these, the Coromantines, Fantuns, Shantus and Achims are mostly esteemed [BM: Ad. MS. 12419, 23-4].

Edward Long [24], first published in 1774, wrote:

> The negroes who pass under this general description are brought from the Gold Coast, but we remain uncertain, whether they are natives of that tract of Guinea, or receive their several names of Akims, Fantins, Ashantees, Quamboos, etc. from the towns so called, at whose markets they are bought.

A resolution introduced in the Assembly in Jamaica as a consequence of the rebellions and conspiracies in 1760 and 1765, in which Cromantees had played the leading part, referred to: "Fantin, Akim and Ashantee Negroes, and all other commonly called Coromantees." [24 Vol. 2, p. 470].

In some recent writings[10] the Cromantees have been classified as Akans, a name used to describe a linguistically and ethnographically related group of West African tribes or nations whose principal constituents are the Ashanti, the Fanti and the Akims. Slaves drawn from the Akans were indeed described as Cromantees, but the description was also applied to non-Akan slaves whose point of departure for the Atlantic crossing was on the Gold Coast. Prominent among these were slaves of Ga origin, the homeland of the Ga nation lying to the east of the Fanti territory. It is also probable that slaves drawn from the Ga-Adagme and Ewe peoples were similarly described.

The term Cromantee was probably taken originally from the name of the Fanti coastal settlement, now a town called Kromantine, where the English built their first slave trading fort on the Gold Coast in 1631.[11] For some 30 years thereafter this fort was the principal point from which the English traders shipped their human cargoes. On sale in the Caribbean colonies these slaves were presumably identified by their point of departure. Later, when the English transferred their slave trading headquarters to Cape Coast, captured from the Danes, and established other points of embarkation, they appear to have applied the description originally used for slaves shipped from Kromantine to all slaves shipped from the Gold Coast. No doubt this was because the description was already established in the trade.

Among the African names of slaves in Jamaica it is possible to identify and distinguish between the Akan and Ga names. The Akans had a system of obligatory names, for males and females respectively, which depended upon the day of the week on which the person was born. Table 1[12] shows the day names used by the Ashanti and Akims (which are the same) and the Fanti, in accordance with the spelling used in modern Ghana. These names are compared with their corresponding phonetic counterparts found in 17th and 18th century Jamaican records.

The Ga had an entirely different system of obligatory names for everyday use. Each male lineage has two sets of male and two sets of female obligatory first names. These sets of names are used alternatively by succeeding generations. Thus the children of a man whose name has come from the first set of names will take their obligatory first names from the second set. But the man's grandchildren by one of his sons will take their names from the same sets as their grandfather. Table 2 contains the obligatory first names belonging to members of two prominent Ga lineages.[13]

These sets of obligatory first names each run to 10 or 12 names, but in practice strict requirements are relaxed after the fifth or sixth child, male or female, has been born. The parents are then free, at their fancy, to choose other names for succeeding children, including names on the lists of other lineages. In such cases the name is sometimes chosen to honour a relative or recognize a family relationship.[14]

Among the African names appearing in 18th century records and publications in Jamaica there are several Ga names whose bearers have been described as Cromantees. The most famous of these was Tacky, the leader of the rebel slaves in St. Mary in 1760. He was reputed to have been a Chief in his native land, and indeed his name identifies him as having been a member of the Ga royal family. Another prominent person to bear a well known Ga name, also of the Tackie royal lineage, was Adou, the leader of the Maroon

THE BEGINNING OF RESISTANCE

group to which the famous Nanny and her husband were attached.[15] Another prominent person bearing a Ga name was Clash, who is mentioned in the peace treaty signed with the Windward Maroons in June 1739. His Jamaican name was, without doubt, a corruption of the distinctively Ga name Aklashi.[16] Kishee could be a corruption of the Ga name Kushi.

TABLE 1

MALE NAMES

DAY OF BIRTH	Ashanti and Akim	Fanti	Jamaica
Monday	Kwadwo	Kojo	Cudjoe, Cudjo
Tuesday	Kwabena	Kobina	Cubina, Cubbenah
Wednesday	Kwaku	Kweku	Quaco
Thursday	Yaw	Ekow	Quao, Quaw, Yaw, Quayhoo
Friday	Kofi	Kofi	Cuffee, Cophy, Coffee
Saturday	Kwame	Kwamina	Quamin
Sunday	Kwasi	Kwesi	Quashie

FEMALE NAMES

	Ashanti and Akim	Fanti	Jamaica
Monday	Adwoa	Ajua	
Tuesday	Abena	Araba	Beneba
Wednesday	Akua	Ekua	
Thursday	Yaa	Aba	Abba
Friday	Afua	Efua	
Saturday	Ama	Ama	
Sunday	Akosua	Esi	Quasheba

TABLE 2

TACKIE (ROYAL) LINEAGE

	Sons	Daughters
SET 1		
First born	Tackie	Afi
Second born	Adu	Akyreko
Third born	Adama	Ashong
Fourth born	Ayerh	Adei
Fifth born	Ayigyaku	Anowa
SET 2		
First born	Teiko	Amele
Second born	Amah	Amokor
Third born	Tetteh	Amakai
Fourth born	Mensah	Amachoe
Fifth born	Okaigya	Amafo

QUARTEY LINEAGE

	Sons	Daughters
SET 1		
First born	Kwartey	Kwarley
Second born	Kwartei	Kwarkor
Third born	Kwarkwei	Kwarkai
Fourth born	Kwarboye	Kwartsoe
Fifth born	Kwartekwei	Kwarfo
SET 2		
First born	Kwartei	Oyoe
Second born	Kwartelai	Kwartiokor
Third born	Kwartukwei	Kwartekai
Fourth born	Kwarteboye	Kwartetsoe
Fifth born		Kwartefo

THE BEGINNING OF RESISTANCE

The name Juba, though of Akan origin, was used mainly, if not exclusively, by a group who long ago came to regard themselves as Ga and speak the Ga language. According to oral tradition, their ancestors migrated from Akwamu and settled at Ottublohum in Ga country in the vicinity of Accra, retaining nevertheless their Akan names. They were not the only groups to do this. The Tabon people, probably of Yoruba origin, became Ga in the same way.

The Akan, Ga and other West African linguistic groups also have family names from which it is possible to identify the region from which a person, or at least his or her ancestors, came. The complete absence of these family names in plantation records and other documents during the period of slavery cannot be adequately explained as an indication of the contempt shown by the white establishment for the slave population. A more probable explanation would be that the slaves gave incomplete information about their names in order to avoid any adverse reflection on their lineages.

No sooner had the English begun to import slaves of their own than they were faced with a rush of escapes from their plantations and the formation of new bands of rebel slaves in the mountains. These newly established settlements lacked the stability of the older self-supporting palenques. Necessarily, during their formative stage, they were largely dependent for their survival on raiding the plantations. Already, in the 1670s this had become a serious problem for the English settlers.

The first recorded slave uprising during the English occupation occurred in the central part of the island in or about 1673. An account of it, is contained in a letter addressed to James Knight, an unsigned copy of which is among the papers donated by C. E. Long, a relative of planter-historian Edward Long, to the British Museum:

> In the time of S[r] Thomas Lynch[s] Government about the year 1673 there was a rebellion in St. Ahnes parish where the Slaves of a large plantation belonging to Major Lobby[s] Father being most of them Coromantines (a Warlike nation in Guinea) Murdered their Master and about 12 white

people besides & that part of the Island being but thinly inhabited they were not pursued for some days in which time they plundered Severall little neighbouring Settlements gott arms & amunition and before a party Strong Enough could be made upp to attack them they to the Number of about 200 retired to the Mountains & secured themselves in difficult places betwixt the parishes of Clarendon, St. Elizabeths and St. Annes from whence they never dislodged [BM: Ad. Ms. 12431].

When the whites did organise a force to go after them, the anonymous writer explained, the rebels:

being armed and knowing their punishment if taken fought desperately and almost destroyed the first parties that pursued them which not only discouraged other parties from going against them but also Encouraged many other negroes to rise, comitt barbarities, & then fly to them severall instances of which Soon followed [ibid].

Thirty-five slaves were executed in 1675 for participating in a conspiracy to rebel [CSP 1675 no. 690]. In 1676 a rebellion in St. Mary, led by slaves named Peter, Scandenburg and Doctor, caused a declaration of martial law. Several participants were executed [CSP 1676 nos. 793, 822].

In 1678 the notorious pirate Henry Morgan served as governor of the island for four months. During most of his term of office, wrote Gardner [14 p. 60], the country was under martial law: "first on account of an apprehended attack from France, and secondly, in consequence of mutiny among the slaves."

The mutiny referred to by Gardner occurred at Caymanas. In the 17th century Caymanas was not comparable in area, or in the size of its labour force, to the estate as it is today. But its proximity to the old capital at Spanish Town was cause for considerable alarm. An unpublished manuscript history, written in 1722, gave this somewhat inconsistent account of the event:

a Rebellion of Negroes happen'd at Capt. Ducks Plantation at Camanners, in the Parish of St. Kathrines about 4 miles from St. Jago on the other side the River Rio Cobre; the Negroes getting Drunk of a Sunday, which is Generally their Commonest wont of Mischief, they observing the River was very High and unpassably by Great Rains, they set upon the Family and Killed Madam Duck ... & Desparately Wounded Her Husband Captain Duck, but he recover'd of his Wounds.

On this estate was the inevitable slave who had remained

THE BEGINNING OF RESISTANCE

loyal to his owners. This man "Swam over the River and Alarm'd the Town of St. Jago & a Trop of Horse, was order'd Immediately & with much Difficulty Got over the River and Soon Dispossed them, Killing Some, & Takeing Others who were put to Examplary Violent Deaths." [Barham 3].

In June 1683 a plan for rebellion on Colonel Lucy's plantation in Vere, involving about 180 slaves, was disclosed by a slave who was given his freedom for betraying the conspirators [Taylor 31 Vol. 2 pp. 549-550; Schafer 27 p. 34].

In August 1685 slaves to the number of 150 on four estates in the Guanaboa Vale rose in rebellion. Armed only with the few guns they found on the estates, they engaged a detachment of 70 soldiers sent against them. In a letter to Whitehall the governor reported [17] that seven rebels had been killed and 50 taken alive. Sixty-three made good their escape, eluding the Amerindian trackers employed to guide their pursuers [PRO: CO 138/5, fol. 87].

These Guanaboa rebels may have been the nucleus of a body of escaped slaves who, under a leader named Kofi, carried out a series of daring raids during 1685 and 1686 on plantations on the Liguanea plain and in the adjoining parts of the parishes of St. Catherine and St. Thomas in the Vale. Attempts to supress Kofi's band having proved unsuccessful, the Council in November 1685 authorised the employment of three parties of 20 men each for one month to go in pursuit of them. Members of these parties were to be eligible, in addition to their pay, for the special rewards which at this time were offered to all comers: "to any that will take or kill those negroes, viz. for the negro Cophy £10, for five others of the chiefest, £5 a head, for any others £2 a head." [Barham 3]. Inducements were offered to all who would betray their comrades: "Any rebel negro discovering his accomplices shall receive not only a pardon, but the rewards aforenamed." This offer was announced to the slaves at Guanaboa in the expectation that word of it would get through to members of Kofi's band. At the same meeting the

Council [18] approved a payment of £20 to a doctor "for curing five persons wounded in the late expedition against the negroes" [CSP 1685-8 p. 114, no. 445].

But the depredations continued and the rebel band grew in strength. On 2 February, 1686 a meeting of the Council was called: "to advise as to the means of suppressing the rebel negroes who are now more formidable than ever before." The minutes recorded that "On the advice of the Governor, it was ordered that twelve parties be forthwith raised out of the several regiments, each of eighteen men with suitable officers... that every party have a good gang of dogs, and be empowered to impress hunters and dogs." The incentive rewards were substantially increased: "Every man killing a negro to have £20 or, if a servant,[19] his freedom; every man taking a negro to have £40; any party killing a negro to divide £20 round; which rules shall be heartily commended to the next Assembly for confirmation" [ibid p. 147, no. 560].

The strategy of employing 12 parties simultaneously appears to have enjoyed some success. The minutes of the council meeting held 8 April, read: "In consequence of the killing of the rebel negro Coffee, it was ordered that the parties be reduced to three." These were to be recruited from the "Liguania" (Liguanea), St. Catherine and Clarendon regiments, "the rest to be discharged, but the officers to be ready to raise them anew in case of emergency" [ibid p. 172, no. 632]. The Council also recommended that the Assembly be summoned to meet in June when it would be asked "to meet the expenses of the rebellion."

Within a few months the lieutenant governor was reporting trouble in the adjoining area to the north comprising parts of St. Mary, St. George and St. Thomas in the Vale. In a letter dated 28 September, 1686, to a member of the Privy Council committee,[20] he gave information about yet another band of rebels:

> The numbers of these rebel negroes is variously reported at from forty to one hundred. They are supposed to have been formed first by negroes

THE BEGINNING OF RESISTANCE 17

> saved from a shipwreck, on the easternmost part of the Island sixteen or seventeen years ago, who, having associated with themselves other runaways, have made themselves plantations in the mountains from which they descend into the plains in great numbers for provisions, often doing much mischief in obtaining the same.
>
> Three parties are constantly abroad out of the parishes of St. Mary, St. George, and St. Thomas to prevent this, which is so hard a duty and so discouraging to the poorer sort of people, that those of St. George's, unless relieved, are prepared to desert their settlements [ibid p. 251].

In his letter the lieutenant governor complained of the unwillingness of the Assembly, which he had dissolved four days earlier, to pay the full cost of the military operations. But he thought he had found a way to deal with their parsimony. Reciting the fact that he had placed the country under martial law, he was hopeful that in the new Assembly to be elected: "the most obstinate will be convinced, after a little smarting under martial law, that it is better to pay, by way of tax, others to do this duty, than to have our servants, horses, and even our persons commanded away at the will of an officer without contradiction."

But to return to the body of rebels in the central parts of the island, who had made their entry on to the historical stage following the rebellion in St. Ann in or about 1673, let the anonymous author of the manuscript with the Long papers continue their story:

> at first they were contented to... hide themselves & if they could privately live they avoided doing mischief butt itt was otherways hereafter when they saw they could maintain themselves in their fastnesses by open force for att Mr. Suttons plantation in Clarendon 400 Rose att once and having gott arms were very difficultly reduced after many of them were killed. Severall others gott to the Mountains and join'd the Rebels and greatly Strengthened their party having good arms and plenty of amunition [BM: Ad. MS. 12431].

Writing to the committee of the Privy Council on 31 August, 1690 the new governor made this report:[21]

> ... On the 29th July last all the negroes on Mr. Sutton's[22] estate in the mountains in the middle of the Island broke out in rebellion, to the number of more than five hundred, forced the dwelling house, killed the caretaker and seized fifty fuses and other arms with quantities of ammunition. They marched to the next plantation, killed the overseer and fired the house, but

the slaves therein would not join them.

> They then returned to the great house, loading their great gun with nails, and ambushing a skirt of wood next the house. The alarm being given, about fifty horse and foot marched against them and there was a slight skirmish. Next day more foot came up and the negroes left the house for the canes, where the foot came in on their rear, killed some, wounded others and captured their field guns and provisions and put them to rout [CSP 1689-92 pp. 316-7, no. 1041].

The governor added that in the pursuit through the woods 12 rebels had been killed, and that 60 women and children who had come in to surrender had reported that many had died in the woods and that those who remained had few good arms. Fresh parties had, he said, been sent after them: "but I am afraid that so many will be left as to be a great danger to the mountain plantations." Summing up the situation he concluded: "This rebellion might have been very bloody, considering the number of negroes and the scarcity of white men. There were but six or seven whites in that plantation to five hundred negroes, and that is the usual proportion in the island, which cannot but be a great danger..." Finally, in a postscript, the governor said: "Since my writing, two hundred negroes have come in altogether so that, what with killed and wounded, we look upon the rebellion as over..."

The Suttons rebellion [23] added perhaps as many as 150 recruits, some of them well armed, to the rebels in the central parts of the island. Others, in smaller groups and in ones and twos, escaped from the plantations every year to join them. Incidents like this one, recorded by the author of the manuscript referred to, were to be expected on all the frontier plantations: "a parcel of New Negroes belonging to Capt. Herring in St. Eliz also rose & he being from home murdered his Lady & some of his children & being joined w^t other malcontents gott to the mountains to the great Gang" [BM: Ad. MS. 12431].

But some of the escaping slaves were headed in a different direction. The lieutenant governor complained bitterly, in a letter to the members of the Privy Council committee in February 1699,[24] that a refuge was being offered to them by the Spaniards:

> I have also now further to lay before your Lordships that they secure all our Negroes that run away from us to Cuba and set them free; Some time since about twenty runaway in one boat and landed at Trinidados on Cuba, the owners having notice sent thither to Enquire after them who were answered that being fled thither for protection they could not in Justice returne them...
>
> That in the year 1680 or 82 the King of Spain like a great and Merciful Prince... Ordered that all Persons that fled to him or his territories for Protection should have it and be wholly emancipated from any Pretenders; So that by this rule they may robb us of all our Slaves; for Cuba is to be seen from the North side of this Island in fair weather, and therefore there needs not much Navigation for them to rune thither..." [PRO: CO 138/9, fol. 318-19].

Twenty years later the same complaint was being voiced. Long records that in that year the governor of Jamaica demanded the return "of several Negroes, piratically taken from the island." The Cuban authorities replied that these and other fugitives having been "brought voluntarily to their holy church" and "received the water of baptism," the proposal for their return was out of the question. Long gave this account of what usually happened to such fugitives:

> A Negroe, flying from our colony to Cuba, or kidnapped thither, becomes the property of the Spanish crown, that is, of a Spanish alcalde. The stupid, illiterate wretch is presently admitted into the bosom of holy mother church...' He continues, however, in a state of servitude, and earns a weekly sum for his master, who must pay a certain proportion of it into the royal coffers, or give him up to labour on the fortifications, until the confederate gang of Negroes there can make up a purse for him.
>
> He then goes before another of these officers, and intimates that he has the wherewithal to purchase his freedom. The owner is summoned; and, the sum being fixed at a certain moderate rate, his master is obliged to take the money and grant a manumission. By this easy method, these deserters soon acquire their freedom, and with very little pains are able, by cultivating tobacco, breeding poultry and hogs, making chip-hats, segars, and other trifling articles, to earn a comfortable livelihood...

Long, the slave-owning planter, was outraged. "What are we to think," he scornfully added, "of a society of men, who are capable of committing such pious frauds under the mask of pretended righteousness" [24 Vol. 2, pp. 86-7].

The expansion of the sugar estates led to the importation

of ever increasing numbers of African slaves. At the same time many Europeans who, encouraged by royal patronage of the privateers, had been engaged in piracy with Jamaica as their base, left the island when piracy fell into disfavour. The growing disproportion between blacks and whites had caused the latter, even before the Suttons rebellion, to realise that their position of domination over the blacks was becoming less secure. The Assembly therefore never ceased to give attention to ways and means of increasing the white population.

In the late 17th century the so-called *deficiency laws* were enacted requiring every plantation owner to keep in his employment one white person for every five blacks. This ratio was later modified to one to ten, but even that proved difficult to maintain. The plantation owners soon found that it was cheaper to pay the fines for defaulting than to employ the required number of whites, and the *deficiency laws* came to be regarded in time as just another form of taxation.

Efforts were nevertheless continually being made to increase the white population. In December 1696 the Council of Trade and Plantations, the then current name under which the Privy Councillors responsible for colonial affairs operated, considered a proposal that more men of military age should be sent to Jamaica.[25] They had before them an alarming report, recorded in the minutes of the governor's Council, of the decline in the numbers of whites serving in the various militia regiments. The muster rolls disclosed the following picture:

Regiment	August 1695	July 1696
St. Catherine's	523	350
Port Royal	530	200
St. Andrew's & Kingston	385	200
Clarendon & Vere	375	200
St. Thomas Ye Vale & St. David's	77	30
St. Elizabeth's	248	200
North side (estimated)	100 scarce	60
Regiment of horse	202 scarce	150

THE BEGINNING OF RESISTANCE

The Council minutes containing the table lamented that:

> in one year we are to be reduced by 1050 men. Moreover all our privateers and seamen (who were a great guard and strength to the Island) have left us and most of this has happened by the harrassing... of the men-of-war,[26] who have frightened away not only our own people but also those of the Northern Colonies from bringing us provisions" [CSP 1696-7 pp. 41-2, no. 97].

The Lords of Trade and Plantations made their recommendation to the king that "the island is in a dangerous condition, and not less than 1,500 men more will be sufficient to defend it against a foreign enemy or secure it from a domestic one if the slaves should make any attempt... the slaves number close on forty thousand" [ibid].

A year later, in December 1697, the merchants and planters of Jamaica sent a memorial to the Council of Trade and Plantations:

> The planters and traders have asked the King to send 1500 soldiers to Jamaica to encourage the inhabitants to stay there, and you have proposed to send thither some poor weavers and tradesmen... The sending over of such poor tradesmen will be of great use to re-people the Island... White men are so scarce that they will easily find employment with good wages, and their employers... will use them as overseers on the plantations, whereby they may in time rise to wealth...
>
> Nothing but force can repel force in time of war, and we must ask for the whole of the 1,500 soldiers requested... [ibid p. 257, no. 508].

In a letter to the Council of Trade and Plantations dated 25th August, 1702, Peter Beckford, planter and lieutenant governor, warned that many of the former runaway slaves were no longer running away. Instead they were taking the initiative against the frontier plantations:

> They have mightily increased in their numbers these 12 months past and have been so bold to come down armed and attack our out settlements to Windward, and have destroyed one or two, which if not prevented would prove of fatal consequence and endanger the Island, for if the settlements to Windward should be so discouraged that the inhabitants should be forced to quit them, the enemy possessing themselves thereof might annoy, if not render themselves masters of the remaining part... [CSP 1702 p. 562, no. 912; PRO: 137/5, no. 80].

On 22 September, Beckford again reported on the situation at the eastern end of the island,[27] this time with greater optimism:

> Since the passing of the late Act for reducing of rebellious negroes, who have been a great body for these ten years past,... one of the partys of 20 odd men came up with their main body of 300 whom they engaged for 5 or 6 hours and routed at last. The negroes faced our men so long as they had any ammunition left and wounded three of the party. We killed and took several.
>
> They had posted themselves in the mountains between the North and South-east point of the Island, had a Town and above 100 acres of land well planted with provisions... but we have burnt their settlements, and I have ordered one of the parties to post themselves there, and the other three to pursue, and if I can they shall not rest till they are totally destroyed or reduced...'these rascalls have destroyed some of the out-settlements, and killed several white people, and if not quel'd may prove more dangerous... [CSP 1702 pp. 600-1, no. 978; PRO: CO 137/5, no. 83].

Thomas Handasyd, the new governor, reported more trouble in July 1704:[28]

> We have had a small insurrection of negroes, about 8 days ago, but both horse and foot are after them. They attacked two or three places, burnt only one house and wounded one man; there were more than 30 negroes, several of which had got firearms plunder'd and took out of houses. We have taken and destroyed 12 of them, and are still in pursuit of the rest.

But the governor was uneasy:

> I must own that I am more apprehensive of some bloody design from them, than any other enemy... Their numbers being so very great and the whites so few, makes me wonder they have not before this destroyed us all, there being in some plantations 200 or 300 negroes to one or two white men. [CSP 1704-5 pp. 223-4, no. 484; PRO:CO 137/6, no. 60].

Seven months later however[29] he was pleased to be able to report: "The Insurrection... is quite quelled, some of the Ring Leaders were taken and executed, the rest were sent off the Island..." [CSP 1704-5 pp. 393-4, No. 902].

The inducements offered by the Assembly to attract more white settlers do not appear to have produced the desired results. Commenting on the situation as it was in 1708, Thomas Southey wrote: "Various endeavours were used to procure a reinforcement of white people at Jamaica, but without success" [30 vol. 2 p. 202]. The problem was still a serious one when, in July 1713, the Lords of Trade and Plantations received a letter from Lord Hamilton, governor of Jamaica,[30] proposing a solution:

> ... ye insolence of ye negroes has been very great ... and I cannot but ... propose to Yr. Lops. thoughts ye necessity of continuing some regular forces here at least for some time after a peace[31] or until wee can reap ye benefit of it by an addition of white people amongst us, or otherwise this Island may be lyable to some very unlucky disaster by an insurrection: and I mention this matter thus early ... before a resolution be taken to recall this regiment ... [CSP 1712-4 pp. 61-6, no. 94; PRO:CO 137/10, no. 9].

Perhaps, with a war on, their lordships had other things on their minds. Though the letter was received in London in March, five months after it was written, they did not consider it until July. But they were impressed. In the following year they requested[32] that the king be advised that when the regiment was recalled from Jamaica, "two or three independent companies be left there" [CSP 1712-4 pp. 313-4, no. 606; PRO:CO 137/46, no. 6].

In 1715 the Council of Trade and Plantations considered two recent Jamaican laws forwarded for the royal assent. One related to indentured servants, the other to free settlers. The former provided that for being drunk or committing various other minor offences a bonded servant could have his term of service prolonged. The Lords of Trade considered this to be too severe and likely to discourage voluntary bondsmen. In a letter to the governor in April[33] they offered a suggestion for attracting immigrants:

> ... if a fund cou'd be found for paying the passage of people that wou'd go thither, those people to be free on arrival, and to have a certain portion of land granted to them to make a settlement, it might be a means to draw people ... And we think that if all persons as shall be deficient in their number of white men, were obliged to pay a fine of £6 per annum for every such deficiency, it might be a considerable help towards such a fund [CSP 1714-5 pp. 151ff. no. 339].

To the slave owning members of the Assembly and Council of Jamaica a proposal to increase the fines was not attractive. They found it cheaper as things stood to pay the fines rather than employ free whites beyond their minimum requirements. They had had a better idea, which the Council explained to the Lords of Trade in a memorial dated 13 March, 1716:[34]

> By this act every planter is obliged to keep one white man for his first 10 negroes... and two for his first 20, and one for every 20 after the first and in like manner for the first 60 head of cattle horses etc: the passage of these men are required to be paid by the Receiver Generall and are to be plac't upon the planters according to such deficiencys, and they are oblig'd to reimburse the Receiver Generall again who is to apply that mony towards paying the passages of others, so that this is a perpetual fund and only wants a sum of money to enable the Receiver Generall to make the first disbursements for which £500 was appropriated by that Act [CSP 1716-7 pp. 111ff. no.203(i)].

But even this clever scheme, they complained, had not produced the desired number of indentured servants, though "by the proportion of white men to black at this time wee compute at least 2000 men might be provided for by this deficiency."

The planters were never surprised when some of their slaves attempted to run away to join the rebels in the mountains. Nor was it unexpected on the frontier plantations that from time to time they would be raided for food or even for arms and ammunition. But from a letter [35] read in the Assembly 27 September, 1718 it appears that the raiders were taking an interest in loot of a rather different nature. The letter stated significantly "that the rebellious negroes of late appear at many plantations to windward, and have taken several negroes from thence" [*Journals* 2 p. 266].

A petition to the Assembly complains that the petitioners, the owners of a plantation at Plantain Garden River in eastern Jamaica, "were robbed by a great gang of rebellious negroes" who deprived them of "thirteen able seasoned men, four of whom were sawyers, six seasoned negro women, and one girl, three new negro men and four new negro women, none of which ever returned or were brought back... [*Journals* 2 p. 657].

One of the main purposes of the abduction of slaves from the plantations was to compensate for the disproportion of the sexes in the settlements of escaped slaves, a pre-requisite for their stability and expansion. "In all their plunderings," wrote James Knight's informant, "they were Industrious in procuring Negroe Women, Girls & Female Children" [BM:Ad. MS. 12431].

There were other developments of interest taking place among the rebels, a record of which is to be found in the letter to James Knight above referred to:

> ... a parcel of Negroes belonging to Mr. Downs who was Deputy marshall went away under the command of a Madagascar [36] resolute cunning Fellow and formed a New Partie behind Deans Valley & enveigled away many discontented negroes from that and other plantations and became considerable about 1720.

The letter further recorded that at that time:

> after many disputes betwixt this gang and that of the Coromantines Settled a little higher & after some bloody Battles the Madagascar Capt. being Slain the body of his partie join'd and were incorporated to the Coromantines & so arose the Great Body of the Leeward Rebells Chiefly but greatly encreas'd from time to time by frequent additions of negroes who often Singly and Sometimes a few together fledd from the plantations to join them.

James Knight, in his own unpublished history follows this account, adding that out of the merger "arose that great Body of Negroes... now under the Command of Captn. Cudjo"[37] [Knight 18; BM: Ad.MS. 12419 fol.93].

The letter to James Knight also told how, at about this time, the original settlements of blacks established during the Spanish occupation, which had hitherto maintained a separate identity, decided to admit recruits. Slaves running away from the plantations had previously found a more welcome refuge with the inhabitants of the newer settlements, "they not using them w^t the same severity that the Spa. Negroes (who desired to live concealed & w'out offence) used att first to do."

But with the passage of time:

> However innocent the Spa Negroes were att first yett when their posterity found how that the Rebellious negroes to Leeward and Severall Small gangs in their Neighbourhood Supported themselves with arms, women, & many necessarys, which they were in great want of they associated with the little

parties next to them received them under their government & followed the same Customs with them in Abating of their severitys to the negroes who fledd to them from plantations.

The benefits were mutual:

these on the other hand guided them divided into different parties unto the Severall plantations from whence they fled & every road and Lurking place about such plantations being known to the Deserters as well as the Strength of the people on itt their custom & places of lodging they Generally came in the night time & Surprized the Masters or Overseers in bed & directly knowing where they were keept Seized the arms and amunition of the Estate and then deliberately took whatever else was for their purpose and retired...'[BM:Ad. MS. 12431].

Early in 1720 the Assembly, in a new *Deficiency Law*, increased the amounts payable in default but at the same time reduced the required ratio of whites to blacks. In February the new governor stated in his report:[38]

In this bill all persons . . . are obliged to keep a white man or woman for every thirty slaves . . . they possess, and also for every 150 horses, mares, mules, asses or neat cattle . . . in case they are deficient . . . they are obliged to pay to H.M. 7s. 6d. per week [CSP Jan. 1719-Feb. 1720 pp. 328-9, no. 540].

The Act also provided that anyone having more than the required number of whites on his property should have "for his incouragement 7s. 6d. per week for every supernumerary white servant"...[39]

When the governor had broken the news to the Assembly in 1718 that slaves were being abducted in the eastern parts of the island, he had urged them to devise "proper remedies,... to prevent any mischief that may attend the island; the measures lately taken by the parties having proved ineffectual" [*Journals* 2 p. 269]. All that the Assembly had been able to propose was more of the same medicine. In October of that year they had approved yet another bill "for the encouragement of voluntary parties to suppress the rebellious and runaway negroes." But in mid 1720, despairing of their repeated failures, a bright new idea commended itself to them.

On 24 June, 1720 the governor signed this written authority by which he authorised a ship's captain to go on ar

THE BEGINNING OF RESISTANCE

important errand to Central America:

> ... I have this day, with the advice of his majesty's council, and at the request of the Assembly, treated and agreed with Jeremy, king of the Mosquito[40] Indians, for fifty of his subjects to repair to this island, and to go into our woods in pursuit of the rebellious and runaway slaves; and also have agreed with you ... for transporting them in your ... sloop, at twenty shillings per head ... [ibid p.331].

Enthusiasm for this project ran high in the white community. In August the governor reported[41] that: "this has been judged both by the Council and Assembly a better and cheaper expedient than the sending out of parties to suppress them..." [CSP March 1720-Dec 1721 p.126, no.213]. On 13 November he wrote again:

> The Indian King has been very punctuall in sending hither the number of Indians I agreed with him for to scour our woods from rebellious negroes, they are allready fitted with everything necessary and are gone into the woods in pursuit of them, and I hope they will answer our expectations in the service we propose for them [ibid pp. 194-5, no.288].

The Mosquitos, expert trackers, would have had little difficulty in locating the black rebels. But, as they without doubt discovered, defeating their quarry in battle was quite another matter. In the governor's correspondence there is no further mention of them. In 1722 everything was back to normal. In his speech to the Assembly on 14 June the governor did not discuss the fate of his Amerindian allies. The information he did give on the rebels had a familiar ring: "I ordered out parties in pursuit of them, but want of money to pay the men who venture their lives for our safety, is a great discouragement to that service"[42] [CSP 1722-3 no.215].

Three years later Jamaica had a new aristocratic governor, but his task was unchanged. Reporting on his activities since his arrival at the beginning of the year he wrote:[43]

> What I of late have chiefly been employ'd about, has been in the care of sending out partys to destroy if possible the runaway and rebellious negroes. It is surprising that to put this in execution, sho'd be attended with so much trouble and so many difficultys ... [CSP 1724-5 p. 357, no.565].

FOOTNOTES

[1] Bartholeme de Las Casas [20] estimated the Amerindian population of Jamaica at 600,000, but this is generally regarded as a clerical error, in one sense or another!

[2] D.B. Davies [9 p. 200] citing Pitman [39, XI 509], says that the Jamaica Assembly prohibited such importations in 1741 from fear "that the shipment of Indian slaves from the continent was detrimental to other commerce."

[3] The term 'mestizo' in the Spanish colonies meant a person of mixed Amerindian and European parentage. Originally the term 'mulatto' defined a person born of African and European parents.

[4] Captain Julian de Castilla, "An Account of what happened in the Island of Jamaica from May 20 of the Year 1655 when the English laid seige to it, up to July of this Year 1656" [46 no. 15 (December 1956)]. This account, together with other documents, was extracted from the archives of the Indies at Seville, Spain, by Irene A. Wright and translated by J.L. Pietersz.

[5] D. L. Schafer [27] reproduces these interesting extracts from the earliest English correspondence from Jamaica, from Thurloe [33, vol. 4, pp. 154, 455-6, 604].

[6] These lands may not have been in the area of their original palenque. By the 1680s patents of lands at Luidas Vale were being granted to white settlers, among them the founder of the Worthy Park plantation which today dominates the entire valley. The nearby Juan de Bolas Mountains and the village of that name in St. Catherine preserve the memory of Lubolo.

[7] Probably a corruption of the Spanish "Los Vermejales."

[8] The parishes established in Jamaica were considerably larger than English parishes, corresponding in size to the modern English local government units known as Rural Districts. The first parishes were established in 1664 by decision of the Assembly in January of that year.

In 1670 there were, outside of Port Royal, 11 parishes. The number rose to 19 by the mid 18th century and to 22 by 1845. Subsequently the boundaries were re-drawn and the number reduced to 14. St. George's was divided between Portland and St. Mary. St. Thomas in the Vale was incorporated into St. Catherine and Clarendon. Vere was absorbed by Clarendon, St. David's by St. Thomas in the East and Port Royal by Kingston.

[9] James Knight was the author of an unpublished work *The Natural Moral and Political History of Jamaica ... to the year 1742* by J.K. [18], which is preserved in manuscript form with the Long Papers in the British Museum.

[10] The view that all Cromantees are Akans is implicit in Monica Schuler's study entitled "Slave Resistance and Rebellion in the Caribbean during the Eighteenth Century" which she was commissioned to do by the University of the West Indies. She has been followed in this by a number of others.

[11] This town appears on some maps as Kormantine, but the preferred spelling

in modern Ghana is Kromantine.

[12] This table was compiled by the author in 1972 on the basis of an interview with Joshua Amartey, Public Relations Officer at the Ghana High Commission in London, a Fanti, and correspondence with S. A. Amaning of the Ghana High Commission staff, an Ashanti. The assistance of both is gratefully acknowledged. Mr. Amartey shared the author's view as to the probable origin of the term Cromantee. Mr. Amartey also thought it possible that the name Accompong, borne by one of the principal leaders of the Leeward Maroons, could be a corruption of Nyankopon, one of the names for the deity. According to Akan customs it would not be profane to give this name to a child but it would be unusual, the more usual name for the deity being Nyame. Another possibility is that Accompong was a corruption of the Ewe name Quarcoopone or the Ga name Kwarpong.

[13] For his information on the naming system employed by the Ga, the author is indebted to Na Anowa Tackie (Mrs. Myers), the present Na Afi or Queen Mother of the Tackie lineage, whom he interviewed during her visit to London in 1976. He is also indebted to Feli Quartey, (Mrs. C. Taylor), who arranged the interview and acted as interpreter and who supplied information on the name lists of the Quartey lineage and other Ga names.

[14] Among other familiar Ga names may be mentioned: Ayitey, Ayikwei, Ayah, Kweitia and Laryea for males; and, Dedei, Korkoi, Adaku, Tso-tsoe and Fo-foe. All names in the Tackie lineage are used with the prefix Nii for males and Na for females which, roughly translated, mean respectively Prince and Princess. The Ga also have day names similar to the Akans but not for everyday use as with the Akans.

[15] See Chapter three n.15.

[16] The story of Clash, who subsequently settled at Bath, St. Thomas with his splinter group, is documented by Barbara Klamon Kopytoff in her doctoral dissertation *The Maroons of Jamaica*, [19].

[17] Molesworth to Lords of Trade.

[18] Minutes of the Council of Jamaica, 6 November, 1685.

[19] This refers to white indentured servants.

[20] Molesworth to William Blathwayt, 28 September, 1686.

[21] Earl of Inchiquin to Lords of Trade, 31 August, 1690.

[22] The version of this letter printed in the *Calendar of State Papers* reproduces this name as 'Salter's' instead of Sutton's, an obvious error. The district in Clarendon is still known as Suttons after the 17th century owner of the plantation.

[23] Edward Long also wrote an account. He said that there were "between three and four hundred" rebels and gave their original haul as "a large store of fire-arms, powder and ball, and four small field pieces, with some provisions" [24 vol. 2, p.446].

[24] Sir William Beeston to Lords of Trade, 8 February, 1698/9.

[25] Board of Trade, Jamaica 8, nos. 11 and 79, pp.10-11.

[26] The official policy of expelling the pirates from their base in Jamaica was part of the English *quid pro quo* for the agreement of the King of Spain, in the Treaty of Madrid of 1670, to recognise English proprietorship of such territories as they then held in the Americas.

[27] Beckford to Council of Trade and Plantations, 22 September, 1702.

[28] Handasyd to Council of Trade and Plantations, 28 July, 1704.

[29] Handasyd to Sir Charles Hedges, 27 February, 1705.

[30] Lord A. Hamilton's letter to Council of Trade and Plantations dated 10 October, 1712 was received 28 March, 1713.

[31] The war against France and Spain, in progress since 1702, ended in 1713. Writing in October 1712 the governor was anticipating the peace.

[32] Council of Trade and Plantations to Lord Bolingbroke, 9 March, 1714.

[33] Council of Trade and Plantations to Hamilton, 25 April, 1715.

[34] Memo of Council of Jamaica to Council of Trade and Plantations, 13 March, 1716, enclosed in Hamilton to Lords of Trade, 12 June, 1716.

[35] Letter from Colonel John Clarke.

[36] R. Dallas [7 vol.1, pp. 31-2] made reference to 'Madagascars' who had joined the settlements of escaped slaves. He described them as "another tribe of negroes, distinct in every respect; their figure, character, language, and country, being different from those of any other blacks." Their skin, he said, "is of a deeper jet than that of any other negroe," and their features "resemble those of Europeans." Their hair was "of a loose and soft texture like a Mullato's or Quadroon's" and their stature and build were shorter and slighter "than those of the people they joined."

It would appear from this passage that these were persons from the island of Madagascar off the east coast of Africa, who were sold as slaves in Jamaica. The Malagasie people are numerically dominant on Madagascar and the presence of some of them in Jamaica would explain the vernacular word 'malagasie', which was once used to describe a person of black complexion with wavy rather than tightly curled or 'kinky' hair.

[37] Cudjoe, leader of the leeward Maroons in the First Maroon War - see Chapter Two.

[38] Sir N. Lawes to Council of Trade and Plantations, 2 February, 1720.

[39] Under the *Deficiency Acts* more than mere residence appears to have been required to 'save deficiency'. Writing to his employers in England in 1803, about a man they had sent out as a carpenter who had turned out to be quite useless, the Attorney-Overseer at Amity Hall sugar estate in Vere explained: "With regards to Mr. Riley he is of little use to the Estate further than saving a defficiency which is £50. No person is allowed to save defficiency unless they receive a salary of £50 from the Estate yearly and do duty in the Militia . . ." [Gbn. Papers] – (Thos. Samson to Mrs. Goulburn, 27 January, 1803).

[40] The Mosquitos inhabited the coastal region from Nicaragua to Honduras. In 1687 they made a treaty with the English, accepting 'protection'. The chief who made this alliance appears to have used it to found a dynasty. Thereafter, for many years, successions to the kingship were approved by the governors of Jamaica, who no doubt stood ready to assist their nominees against rival claimants.

[41] Lawes to Council of Trade and Plantations, 24 August, 1720.

[42] Lawes to Council of Trade and Plantations, 9 July, 1722.

[43] Duke of Portland to Council of Trade and Plantations, 12 April, 1725.

CHAPTER TWO

THE FIRST MAROON WAR

By the beginning of the 18th century the rapidly growing European demand for sugar had made a West Indian plantation an enormously profitable investment. Within the British empire Jamaica, with its available undeveloped land, offered investors a more favourable opportunity than the more fully developed smaller islands of the eastern Caribbean.

In November 1728 General R.O. Hunter, the new governor of Jamaica, wrote enthusiastically[1] of plans for opening up the north-eastern parts of the island:

> The new Settlements at Port Antonio are going on with a good prospect . . . I am thro'ly Convinced that a good Settlement there will very much add to the Strength and Security of that part of the Island, not only against a Foreign Enemy but also against the Insults of the rebellious negroes [PRO; CO 137/53, no. 43].

As is apparent in this assessment there were two discouraging factors. The foreign enemy, of whom there was considerable apprehension at this time, was Spain. An attack was regarded as imminent and the excuse the Spaniards were expected to use was a legalistic quibble that recognition of English proprietorship of Jamaica could not be justified under the treaty of 1670.

By that treaty the King of Spain had ceded all his Caribbean possessions then in English occupation. But having previously granted Jamaica to the Duke of Veragua, so the argument ran, the king could not lawfully have encompassed that island in his generosity to England.[2] As an excuse for recapturing it this would have been as good a pretext as political morality required.

General Hunter's report to the Lords of Trade and Plantations on 17 July, 1729, on the capacity of the available military forces to resist an invasion, was not reassuring, "The Militia consisting of hired Servants who are not to be depended upon and the Country thin peopled tho' full of Slaves, you'll think it strange but it is true, my chief Dependence, in case of an Attempt, was upon the trusty Slaves for whom I had prepared Arms..." [PRO: CO 137/47].

The arming of slaves, even trusty ones, was not without its problems. General Hunter felt that for the defence of the island he had no alternative but to train some of them in the use of firearms. Most of his 'trusties', however, carried weapons which would have been less lethal had they subsequently turned them against their masters. On 3 May, he had written advising their lordships: "I have form'd the trusty Slaves into Small bodies to be Commanded by some reform'd Officers, And have Order'd a thousand Lances to be made for Arming more, who cannot be provided with Fire-Arms, And have all hands at work in making & mending carriages for Guns" [PRO: CO 137/53, no.71].

London merchants engaged in the West India trade were equally alarmed at the possibility that, for want of an adequate defence force, Jamaica might be lost. On 17 June, 1729, they had petitioned the queen urging measures "for the preservation of an Island so valuable and so great Consequence to Great Brittaine" [PRO: CO 137/47]. Another of Governor Hunter's letters, on 4 July, 1730, had underlined the gravity of the situation:

> ... considering the male proportion our White People bear to the Black not being, as far as I can compute hitherto, that of one in twenty, the Exemption by Law of Great Numbers from ordinary Military Duty ... and what I think worst of all, the Number of White Servants, of

whom much the greater part is not to be trusted with Arms, This Island is utterly insufficient to defend itself... [ibid].

He complained that the Assembly could not be expected to vote enough money even to repair the existing forts, and stressed the necessity for assistance 'from home'.

To the great relief of the establishment, local and metropolitan, the anticipated invasion did not materialise. But their internal enemies, the escaped slaves, were growing increasingly formidable, and the governor was haunted by the fear that his internal and external enemies were working in concert. He had suspected this when he wrote the letter above referred to. By September 1720 he knew for a fact that the rebel slaves had approached the Spaniards and that the latter were not averse to giving them encouragement. He sent a copy of an affidavit by one John Tello to London which told an interesting story.[3]

Tello swore that he had recently been at Porto Bello on the Isthmus of Panama where he had conversed with the Spanish governor's father-confessor:

> That among divers other things they talked of... that there were 30,000 rebellious Negroes in this Island... that a Letter was sent from the said rebellious Negroes to the Governor of Caicas[4] desiring the said Govn: to let His Majesty the King of Spain, know, that if he would be pleased to grant them their Freedom and let them enjoy the same liberties as the rest of his Subjects, that in such case they would without any charge or trouble put the Island into his possession...

According to Tello, the talkative father-confessor said further:

> That the said Governor of Caicas not knowing by what means or conveyance the said letter came to hand called a Council to Consult thereof at which Consultation there came to them an cast[5] Indian Negro Man, who formerly had been in this Island and offered the said Governor and Council if they would give him a Sloop and letters that he would engage to bring an Answer from the Rebellious Negroes.

The Spaniards appear to have been anxious to make contact with the rebel slaves but, according to Tello's informant, they were disappointed:

> ... the said Negro was landed on some part of this Island and the Sloop... stood off... for a certain time appointed, but the sd Negro

> Messenger not appearing to the time, the Sloop stood off and on again for some considerable time, and at last went away leaving the Negro Messenger behind who has never been heard of since... [PRO: CO 137/47].

Communities of escaped slaves in different parts of the island varied considerably in numbers and strength. In some areas they could be successfully contained by the voluntary parties who went after them to gain the statutory rewards. A committee report in the minutes of the Assembly for 31 July 1729, gave a picture of how a typical group of these adventurers operated:

> The committee... do find, that Varney Philip... commanding officer of the regiment in Clarendon and Vere, finding that some rebellious negroes came down to Porus... did... empower... Simon Booth... to raise and head a voluntary party to pursue and destroy... according to the direction of... 'an act for the encouragement of voluntary parties to suppress rebellious and runaway negroes'.
>
> That... Booth... did raise a voluntary party, and went in pursuit... and did kill one man and two women, who were marked TS: with a heart, which was old colonel Sutton's mark, and supposed to be in Suttons rebellion, which happened about forty years ago, and out ever since; they also killed two other negro women, said to be rebellious, and found amongst them...

This party also made some captives:

> Booth and his said party brought home alive... four negroes; viz. One negro man, belonging to the said colonel Varney Philip,... and a negro woman belonging to Mr Rippon, who was out about seven years; one... negro woman of colonel Sutton's, and out since that rebellion; besides seven children, the eldest not above seven...

Finally the committee dealt with the matter of the rewards: "... the said Booth and party are, by virtue of the said act, entitled to the said seven children, and to 450 £ from the country, for the five negroes they killed and four they brought in alive..." [*Journals* 2 pp. 682-3].

In the following year this same Booth was rewarded with £650 on a claim for killing some blacks in Clarendon. On that occasion he brought in a mulatto girl whom he had captured in the woods. The *Journals* of the Assembly [2 p. 714] record the committee's recommendation "that the said mulatto wench, inasmuch as she was born in the woods, should be given to the said Booth and his heirs as a further encouragement."

Effective as these small parties of adventurers may have been in capturing and killing old men, women and children, and even for dispersing small settlements of runaways, they were of little use in isolation against the larger Maroon communities.

Some of these communities supported guerrilla forces large and strong enough to present a serious barrier to the establishment of plantations in their proximity. Not only did they prevent the whites from planting much of the fertile land at the western end of the island, but their activities in the north-east threatened to frustrate the whole project for the development of the area inland of Port Antonio.

Perhaps it would be as well to remind ourselves of the relatively undeveloped state of Jamaica at the end of the third decade of the 18th century. This was reflected in the official population returns contained in a report prepared for the Duke of Newcastle 15 July 1731: "The Number of White People, including Men, Women, Children and Indentured Servants, was 7,648, and the number of Black Slaves 74,525, Exclusive of the free Negroes who were then Eight Hundred & Sixty five" [PRO: CO 137/47, fols. 107-10]. The total number of persons on the island was 83,038 — a density of less than 19 persons to the square mile.

The steady increase in the numbers and strength of the settlements of escaped slaves over the first three decades of the 18th century had gradually produced a consensus among the resident planters and officials that these could no longer be regarded as separate localised obstacles to development. The problem had obviously reached all-island proportions and the continued existence of these free black communities was too infectious an example to the enslaved majority to be tolerated. Absentee landlords and merchants and the Privy Councillors concerned with colonial affairs were easily persuaded to the same opinion. A concerted attempt to re-enslave or annihilate all the escaped slaves and their offspring had clearly become the official policy by the latter half of 1729, an attempt which was to occupy the resident whites and the British government for the next decade and has come to be known historically as the First Maroon War.

The word 'Maroon', which was not in use in Jamaica prior to the middle of the 18th century, was derived from the Spanish 'cimarron' meaning wild or unruly. One of the earliest official usages of the word cimarron was in relation to Cuba in a royal order dated 11 March 1531. In this order the Spanish queen, replying to a report of the previous September from the governor, said: "I am very pleased with your tidings that the island is almost devoid of cimarron Indians . . ." [Franco 38]. With the decline of the Amerindian population the term was later applied to escaped African slaves and their descendants.

The first English writers to adopt the word rendered it, with their characteristic phonetic spelling, as 'simeron'. It appeared in this form in Richard Hakluyt's notes on the voyage of Andrew Baker of Bristol in 1576. Hakluyt reported his informant as saying:

> wee landed 10 of our men [at the mouth of the River Chagre], who travelled up into the woods three or foure daies to seek the Simerons (which are certaine valiant Negros fled from their cruel masters the Spaniards, and are become mortall enemies, ready to joyne with the English and French against them) [Hakluyt 15 vol. 7, p.70].

Similarly, in Robert Dudley's account of his voyage to Trinidad in 1594, he says, "The Simerones of the Yland trade with me . . ." [ibid p.164].

In later years some English historians, following the lead of Bryan Edwards and overlooking the fact that the original Spanish word commenced with the letter 'C', suggested a derivation from the Latin 'simia' (Spanish 'simio') meaning an ape. Perhaps they were attributing to the Spaniards the Anglo-Saxon theory that the African was sub-human? Others have shown an equally erroneous preference for Edward Long's theory that the word Maroon was derived from the Spanish 'marrano', meaning a hog. The Maroons, as he explained, hunted the wild hog.

The establishment's first objective, in the initial stages of the war, was to clear the rebels out of the mountains to the north-east overlooking Port Antonio, an area regarded as particularly desirable for the development of new plantations. At the beginning of May 1730 an expeditionary force of 95 armed men with 22 baggage slaves, the largest single party that had ever attempted an assignment in such a mountanious terrain, was assembled at Port Royal. Arriving by sea at Port Antonio they sailed thence on 28 May, landing at Plum Tree Bay. Marching inland through the mountains for nine days, they sighted their objective, the principal rebel 'town', on 7 June.

In his message to the Assembly on 17 June General Hunter said:

> The slaves in rebellion, from the increase of their numbers by the late desertions from several settlements, or from the bad success of common parties, are grown to that height of insolence, that your frontiers are no longer in any state of security; and must be deserted; and then the danger must spread and come nearer, if not prevented.
>
> By an act of your last session, the parties in several districts must be at this time in motion, according to the routes prescribed, or on their return. I have had as yet no account of the success of any of them, except that of St. Mary's and St. George's, who have killed four and taken two rebels.

The governor then reported on the expedition which had been sent to windward:

> The grand party, consisting of ninety-five shot and twenty-two baggage negroes, chiefly volunteers and detached men from the militia on this side, was with all possible expedition, sent round to Port-Antonio in pursuance of your request and advice to me towards the close of the last session: They arrived safe there; but, by the rains, and other unforseen events, could not march till the 28th of last month, when they marched by a route least suspected ...

What he had to tell the Assembly about the grand party's first engagement with the rebels was not, however, very encouraging:

> Yesterday, about five in the evening, I received by express a letter from major Ashworth, with an account of that party's being defeated by, or running away from, the rebels, when they were in the very entry of their principal settlement. Two white men and twenty-one negroes, who were returned to Port-Antonio, gave the narration contained in that letter; and with that you have also the examination of the negro who brought it

hither, and was one of the party returned.

> If these accounts are verified by succeeding ones, it appears to me the effect of something worse than cowardice: the next express will undoubtedly clear up the matter; and until I have received that, I shall trouble you no further with my thoughts of this affair... [*Journals* 2 pp. 708-9].

The governor's message also disclosed that while the grand party had been busy in the interior, "a party of the rebels have fallen upon a settlement to the windward of Port-Antonio, plundered and burnt it, and carried off a negro woman and her child."

The examination of Nicholas Plysham, one of the officers who accompanied the expedition, taken subsequently by the governor in Council on 18 June 1730,[6] is worth looking at, illustrating as it does the rough nature of the country in which the rebels had established their settlement and the guerrilla tactics they employed against a military party with overwhelmingly superior fire power:

> ... on the 7th about Noon they Enter'd the Rebels plantation, but about a Miles distance from it they fell in with some broad roads particularly one leading up the Mountain which they took to be a Road for bringing down their Timber and they march'd on till three of the Clock through the Bushes... where he saw some stragling Negroes digging provisions and Cleaning Ground...
>
> Captn Soaper getting up upon a Tree saw the Town in a Bottom upon a River about a quarter of a Miles distance... This examinant Lieut Tudor and some others ask'd Mr Soaper if it would be more convenient to lie perdue till midnight and then surround it and Enter before day.
>
> Upon which they lay quiet for about... an hour, when they heard Children Crying out Buckarrah come,... which occasioned Mr Soaper & this Examinant to go up the same tree again, when they discover'd Negroes mostly Women to the number of about a Hundred running away with Loads and a great many Children following them up the Opposite Mountain... upon which Mr Soaper order'd them to March down to the Town which they did and going thro' an Odder piece they came to the Edge of the precepice just over the Town...
>
> Soaper thinking there might be some difficulty in getting down (it being just dark) – ordered them to stay there that night and about 8 o'clock att night he order'd them to fire of the pieces... which they did in three Volleys, each Company a volley... (the Rebels Continuing Beating their Drums)...

Their presence thus discovered and unable to risk making the steep descent to the town in the dark, the attackers had to spend the night where they were. Describing the events of the next day Plysham continued:

> ... in the Morning about dawn of Day Capt Soaper Order'd about twenty men to March down the precepice to the Town as an advanc'd party and upon their getting down the Negroes that lay in Ambush fir'd upon them, upon which Soaper call'd to them to return and fir'd att the place from whence they saw the Rebels fire, and then those who had got down return'd...
>
> Immediately this Examinant perceived they were Surrounded by Negroes, who fir'd from all parts Whereby several were wounded & two kill'd which fire the party return'd and they continued firing att each other for about 2 hours and Seeing the Negroes got ground of them Soaper order'd the wounded and lame to retire down to a River... which they attempting to do were surrounded by other Rebels which he believed lay there in Ambush, upon which ye wounded returned to the Body (But twenty of the Negroes belonging to the party made their Escape that way) and with the rest of ye party retir'd into the Bushes after which the firing ceas'd on both Sides and the Rebel Negroes pursued no further but fir'd volleys and Hurra'd... and this Examinant verily believes the Arm'd Rebells that attack'd them were near to the number of 300
>
> Sworn in Council this 18th of June 1730 [PRO: CO 137/53, Nos. 123-6].

Captain Soaper also gave evidence concerning this engagement. He told the Council that he had ordered a slave to call to the rebels telling them that if they would surrender and promise not to "trouble the Backarras nor suffer any more negroes to join them", they would be given land, but that if they did not he would destroy them. To this, he said, they had replied that he would be unable to do what he threatened and that they did not want the land he offered but were resolved to remain where they were [ibid].

Reporting to London on the fate of this expedition, in his letter of 4 July, the governor wrote: "they were discovered by break of day, surrounded and routed, fifteen killed or taken away wounded and the rest returned to Port Antonio... in my humble Opinion that Partie is not sufficient considering the Numbers, Arms and Situation of the Rebels..." [PRO: CO 137/47].

Another account of this ill-fated expedition was sent to the secretary to the Lords of Trade and Plantations by a gentleman describing himself as "a true and Loyal

Subject ... and honest Debtor to his Credrs and a reale friend of Jamaica ... who has a good Estate in it to loose ..."[7] In his account the casualties suffered by the whites were put at "killed about twenty" and it was stated that "By this defeat the Rebels also acquired thirty two Guns more, and are since become so insolent, as to come down almost to the very town Settled at Port Antonio, notwithstanding they see the Kings Ships ride there. We are now fitting out another party of Three Hundred Men ..." [PRO: CO 137/47].

The same document spoke of another expedition in the spring of 1730, in an unspecified area, by a party of "fifty six stout people ... led by Stout and Skillful Officers who were also good woodsmen." They were said to have 'performed well' but:

> on the third day were in a short narrow Pass surprised by a Strong Ambuscade of the Rebells and Almost all cut off without being able to return the Injury. By this defeat the Rebels were not only much Encouraged, but took some Ammunition and Severall good Arms of which we fancied them in great Want ...

This correspondent also mentioned fighting in the west: "Some of our parties have had Success in the Leeward parts of the Island, where by Surprise they have got the better of two or three small rebellious Settlements, but never when they have met any Considerable Body of the Rebells together, for they have then always been worsted ..."

Finally, this 'true and loyal subject' appealed for the sending to Jamaica of at least 2,000 effective men from England.

When news of the defeat of the grand party led by Captain Soaper reached the Assembly, they wasted no time in arranging for another attack by an even larger party. Determined to rid the planters of the Port Antonio area of their unwelcome neighbours, the Assembly offered on 20 June, "20£ reward for every negro man, and 10£ for every negro woman the party in the said bill mentioned shall kill or take alive, with all pickaninies they take as a further encouragement" [*Journals* 2 p. 711].

Money had to be raised quickly to finance the new expedition. A committee of the Assembly approved the following suggestions which the House adopted on 23 June:

> 1. Resolved, it be recommended to the house, that the sum of 6,000£ be raised:
> 2. Resolved, that the most effectual and speedy method for raising the same will be a tax on the Jews, negroes, cattle, trades and offices: [*Journals* 2 p. 712].

Britain's response to the request for military aid was immediate and favourable. And small wonder. As an economic asset no colony exceeded the value of Jamaica. Between 1714 and 1773 one-twelfth of Britain's total imports came from Jamaica [Williams 36 p. 152]. Nor should the political influence of the wealthy proprietors of Jamaican plantations living in England be ignored.

A letter to General Hunter, date-lined from Windsor Castle on 12 October, 1730, assured him that Britain would participate fully in the war to suppress the blacks:

> His Maj^{ty} was extremely concerned to find ... the defenceless Condition of the Island under your Government ... has been pleased to order the Two Regiments of Foot ... which are now at Gibraltar, to be forthwith sent ... which you are ... to take under your Command and make the best provision you can for their Reception and Subsistence at Jamaica, in the manner that has been formerly praçtised on the like occasions: [PRO: CO 137/47].

This news, reported to the Assembly on 26 January 1731, was joyfully received.

At about this time it appears that the realisation was spreading among these former slaves that the whites were organising their campaigns against them on an all-island scale. Negotiations between their various bands, necessitated by the common threat to their survival, resulted, as the historian Dallas recorded, in the important decision to co-ordinate their operations. Dallas wrote:

> Previous to this they had no general leader of chief of the body, but wandered in gangs under the direction of different leaders; but now finding ... that parties were fitted out to attack them wherever they could be found, they concentrated their force and elected a chief, whose name was Cudjoe,[8] a bold skilful and enterprising man, who on assuming the

command, appointed his brothers Accompong and Johnny leaders under him and Cuffee and Quaco subordinate Captains [7 vol. p. 28].

If James Knight, author of the unpublished history of Jamaica up to 1742, was correctly informed, Cudjoe was born in Jamaica. Referring to the leeward Maroons, Knight [18 p.54] wrote, "Capt Cudjo who Commands Them, is the son of one of Mr. Suttons Negro's, who was at the head of that Conspiracy and Governed the Gang to the time of His Death."[9]

After the election of Cudjoe, wrote Dallas: [7 vol. 1 pp. 34-5]

> They began at that time to pursue a more regular and connected system of warfare, and in their frequent skirmishes with the troops sent out against them, acquired an art of attack and defence, which, in the difficult and hardly accessible fastnesses of the interior of the Island, has since so often failed the best exertions of disciplined bravery.

By about the year 1730, according to Bryan Edwards [10], the Maroons:

> were grown so formidable under a very able general named Cudjoe, that it was found expedient to strengthen the colony against them by two regiments of regular troops, which were afterwards formed into independent companies, and employed with other hired parties, and the whole body of the militia in their reduction.

An account of the wartime military administration established by Cudjoe among the western or leeward Maroons was given to James Knight in the letter from his unnamed informant:

> As the Gang in time increasing... the Chief Commander occasionally appointed as many as were necessary, of the Ablest under him as Captains and divided the rest into Companies, & gave each Captain, such a Number as he thought was proportionable to the merit he was possessed of. This Distinction made these Captains Ambitious to excell in whatever might contribute to the Good of the whole.

> The Chief Employment of these Captains was to Exercise their respective men in the Use of the Lance, the small arms after the manner of the Negroes on the Coast of Guinea, to conduct the bold & active in Robbing the plant^s. of Slaves, arms, ammunition Etc.

These captains, the correspondent continued, also had authority in relation to the important matter of providing the community with food. They were to lead their men in

"Hunting wild hogs and to direct the rest with the Women in Planting Provisions and managing Domestic affairs" [BM: Ad. MS. 12431].

Prior to the beginning of what has become known as the First Maroon War there were, as has been said, numerous settlements of escaped slaves and their descendants in parts of the island to which the plantations had not been extended. They varied considerably in size and militancy. Some maintained guerrilla forces for purposes both of defence and attack. Others were concerned merely to keep out of the way of the voluntary parties and to avoid capture or annihilation.

The roving activities of the bounty hunters operating under the Voluntary Parties laws had probably caused many of the smaller settlements to throw in their lot with the larger Maroon settlements by the late 1720s. There were by that time Maroon communities, both to leeward and windward, numbering several hundreds of members. The war had naturally accelerated the process of consolidation as more and more fugitives placed themselves under the protection and command of the strongest leaders.

But although there is evidence of liaison between the main bodies of the Maroons to leeward and to windward, it is by no means clear whether the connection was in the form of an alliance between independent commands or whether the windward Maroons had actually acknowledged Cudjoe, leader of the leeward Maroons, as commander in chief of all the Maroons fighting to maintain their freedom.

Oral tradition has it among the Accompong Maroons that the famous Nanny, after whom Nanny Town in the Blue Mountains at the eastern end of the island was named, was Cudjoe's sister. Whether this was a blood relationship it is impossible to determine. Nor is it known to what extent if any Cudjoe exercised control over the military operations of the Maroons in the north east. All that can be said with certainty is that the liaison, whatever its form, was close.

The Maroons appear to have developed an intelligence

system with the assistance of slaves of the various plantations. Dallas acknowledged the effectiveness of these slave informers:

> by these Cudjoe was always apprized in time of the parties that were fitted out, and knowing the routes they must take, prepared some ambushes accordingly. As he frequently defeated his assailants his success was one means by which he supplied his men with arms and ammunition ... The Maroons, too, were more provident of their ammunition than the troops were, seldom throwing a shot away ineffectually [7 vol. 1, pp. 34-5].

Writing to the Lords of Trade on 11 February 1731 the governor showed little faith in a force recently dispatched against the rebels to windward: "On the first of this Month One Country Party, fitted out for another attempt on these Slaves, set sail from Port Royal for Port Antonio under Convoy. I have heard nothing of them since, & expect little good for them" [PRO: CO 137/47 fols. 98-9]. His Excellency's pessimism may have been because the trusted officer appointed to command this party had been murdered shortly before it set out. Or perhaps he realised that a very much stronger force was required for the task.

The favourable response from Britain to their appeal for more troops put the Assembly to the necessity of making provision for their maintenance. In the same letter the governor reported on their deliberations:

> The Assembly, now sitting, are come to some Resolutions towards providing for them viz That Twenty Shillings p. week be paid to the Commission'd Officers & five to private Men, after the Provisions brought hither with them be expended, for the Officers from the Day of their arrival here. They have also resolved that Ten Pounds p. head be paid to Officers and Soldiers for every Rebel Slave by them kill'd or taken ...

The two regiments from Gibraltar arrived in Jamaica on 4 and 7 February 1731. A bundle of papers in the Public Record Office labelled "Abstract of Letters ... 1731 & 1732" contains some information about them. From the abstract of a letter from the commanding officer Colonel Hayes dated 9 March and a report signed by Hayes and two of his senior officers, it is apparent that they held the black rebels they had been sent to suppress in contempt. The letter reveals a commanding officer who "Looks upon the War with the Rebellious Blacks to be over." The report recorded that a detachment had been sent immediately "to that part where the Rebels are", adding contemptuously: "The Affair of the Rebellious Blacks a Trifle — They have been defeated & their Town burnt — Never more than 30 of them seen together" [PRO: CO 137/47, fols. 191ff].

The conceited over-confidence of these officers may no doubt be attributed to their unfamiliarity with guerrilla warfare. They interpreted the fact that the Maroons did not choose to meet them in pitched battles and positional warfare as evidence of their demoralisation and defeat. Colonel Hayes did not live long enough to learn how mistaken he had been. A victim, probably, of the 'fevers and fluxes' of which he complained that his men were suffering, he died on 20 March.

The regiments from Gibraltar did not come up to expectations. One of their captains[10] who returned to England in June 1731, told a committee of the Board of Trade on 2 July:

> That the Regiments are dispersed all over the Island; That they may be of use to destroy the Rebels in the Vallies, but cannot follow them into the Mountains: That the Rebels are more insolent and dangerous than formerly; but could be of no use to an Enemy but by serving as Guides [PRO: CO 137/47/fols. 192-3].

On 15 July the Board of Trade gave it as their opinion that the fears of an invasion from Spain being over, and:

> The regiments being of no other Service for the Reduction of the Negroes than by keeping the Black Slaves in order at home, His Majty may be pleased to order one or both . . . to return home, especially as the people of Jamaica are unwilling to contribute for any continuance to their Support.

They recommended, however "That such of the Soldiers should be disbanded, as are willing to stay in the Island, and the two Independent Companys be filled up out of the Regiment or Regiments ordered home."

The governor was opposed to the withdrawal of the regiments. Whilst he did not maintain that they had defeated the Maroons in battle he explained, in a letter dated 13

November that "the arrival of the two Regiments was providential. The plantation Negros are made more tractable by them. The recalling the Regiments would be of fatal Consequence by encouraging the present Rebels, and others to rebell" [PRO: CO 137/47/fols. 195-6].

The governor's message to the Assembly on 4 January 1732 was a sobering one:

> You were called together sooner than was intended upon the news of the bad success of the party sent out against the slaves in rebellion, on the north side of the island. Upon this news, by the advice of his majesty's council, I ordered the troops to be drawn together at two places of rendezvous, Port Royal and Port Antonio, for the defence and security of the inhabitants and planters of the latter, and to be in readiness for putting into execution such measures as shall, by the legislature, be thought necessary and practicable for the safety of this island and the reduction or extirpation of the rebel slaves...

Stressing the grave danger the governor said further:

> There never was a point of time which more required your attention to the safety of this island than the present: Your slaves in rebellion, animated by their success, and others (as it is reported) ready to join them on the first favourable opportunity, your militia very insignificant, the daily decrease of the numbers of your white people and increase of the rebel slaves; these circumstances must convince you of the necessity of entering upon more solid measures than have been hitherto resolved upon for your security; all former attempts against these slaves having been either unsuccessful, or to very little purpose.

The governor then made mention of an idea which appears to have originated among the absentee proprietors:

> It has been suggested at home to his majesty's ministers and the lords commissioners of trade, that a treaty with the rebels, by which they are to agree to be transported to some of the Bahama islands, or the employing again the Mosquito Indians against them may be of use: I only mention this, and leave it to your judgement and consideration whether either of these methods be practicable [*Journals* 3 pp. 46-7].

Replying to the governor two days later, the Assembly said:

> The defeat of the regular forces under the command of captain De Lemelier has given the inhabitants here great uneasiness, and put them under just apprehension of a general insurrection of the slaves; as all or most of them want but a favourable opportunity to withdraw from their servitude, and that they may be properly spirited to such a disposition by the success of the rebel slaves from whom they may expect more ease and freedom than

we can allow them.

> In this crisis, we hope your excellency will, with your wonted goodness, make the best use, for our advantage of the two regiments and the independent companies, while they continue together, and order such detachments out of them as your excellency will think sufficient to reduce the slaves in rebellion, particularly those in the north-east parts of the island, where, by all accounts, they have formed themselves into formidable bodies. [*Journals* 3 p. 49].

That same week the Assembly decided that any slave who killed a black rebel should have his freedom [*Journals* 3 p. 51]. On 13 January they heard a proposal from one Mr. Cameron "for bringing over highlanders to go out against the rebellious slaves", and set up a committee to consider it and work out the cost [*Journals* 3 pp. 55, 59]. Apparently the Scots were thought too expensive, or unruly, for nothing came of the proposal.

Though the Assembly had so recently shown reluctance to continue to pay for the maintenance of the two regiments which had proved so ineffective, generous settlement grants and terms of employment as mercenaries were offered to those who were willing on disbandment to settle in the island:

> Four pounds a Month to any Soldier that will offer to go after the Rebellious Negros, besides ten pounds a Head for every Negro they kill or take. If any Soldier goes out & has a Wife or Family, his Wife or Family to be maintained while he is out. If any Soldier shall be killed, Provision to be made for his Wife and Family. If any Soldier be hurt or disabled in the Service, that he be provided for.

> If any Soldier engages, to have five Pounds as Bounty Money in hand & a month's Pay advanced before he marches. If any Serjeant will enter into the Country Service to have £20 Bounty money & to be recommended by the Assembly to be made Officers to command in the Partys.

> If 20 Soldiers will settle in a Body, every one to have 100 acres of land given him, a Negro Boy, a Negro Girl, three Barrels of Beef and one Barrel of Flower & every Woman that belongs to them, & goes with them to have three barrels of Beef & one Barrel of Flower, & every Man to have an acre of ground cleared for him at the Country's Charge.

> That at every Settlement where 20 go & Settle, there is to be built a strong House with Flankers at the Country's charge, with a Gang of Dogs, & a Guard to protect them, out of the two Independent Company's of Spanish Town and Port Royal [PRO: CO 137/47 fol. 125].

On the day, 15 January 1732, that these terms were approved, Lieutenant Colonel Cornwallis, who had succeeded to the command, reported that the complement of the two independent companies regularly stationed on the island had been made up to full strength again by transfers from the Gibraltar regiments. He also said that he believed the terms offered by the Assembly would induce most of the remaining soldiers to become settlers. On 16 March the governor reported that "What remains of the 2 Regts (not amounting to 100) imbark for Ireland this day and tomorrow" [PRO: CO 137/47 fols. 195-6].

In January 1732 the Assembly adopted the report of a committee set up to consider a plan for a new attack on the principal town of the windward Maroons. The report stated:

> ... they seem confident to secure themselves from ambuscade in the route they propose to take; and that, as the number of rebels are reported to be very considerable, your committee conceive the parties should not be separated, lest a lesser number than both parties consist of should not be sufficient to encounter them and force their entrance into the town [*Journals* 3 p. 56].

Two military forces were organised for the proposed attack and in the event it was considered wiser to separate them. One, under the command of Christopher Allen, was ordered to move northwards into the mountains from the Liguanea plain. The other, led by Thomas Peters, was sent round to the north coast by sea to march southwards into the Blue Mountains. There were the usual complements of slaves to carry baggage and supplies. Both forces also contained a number of persons described by Governor Hunter as "armed Negroes" [PRO: CO 137/47 fol. 129] commonly referred to as 'blackshot'. Some of the blackshots were free men, like the establishment's most competent black mercenary Sambo who commanded a party with the rank of captain. Others were slaves. According to Dallas: "those only were allowed to serve whom their masters chose and vouched for" [7 p. 218].

Both Allen and Peters kept journals.[11] Their accounts of their advance into the mountains graphically illustrate the roughness and difficulties of the terrain. Allen recorded that on 27 February his force reached a place called "Distance Mountain". There he discovered that one man had deserted, and he himself became "ill with a ffeaver & ague". On 1 March four others, "not being able to perform the Journey" were left behind. That day, he wrote, one of the blacks was "taken ill as we rais'd the mountain, left him behind." Another "deserted with a bag of provisions." But the remainder "march'd & kept the River Course all this day and came to a halt on the side of the River ... where we Cut Boughs and made our Hutts."

Next day, said Allen, they marched "up the sd. River, & over 3 hills & the ridge of a damn'd Iron bound Mountain which was not 5 Inches wide in some places & came to a Halt on the back of a mountain." Here they had expected to find a rebel settlement but "were disappointed." On Friday 3 March they crossed this mountain "but found no town". They "came to a Halt in the heart of Yallows [Yallahs] River." That day they ate well as "Capt. Sambo Shott a Wild Boar." But several of the men were "sick with the ffeaver & ague, and several sprain'd their arms and ancles in climbing the rocks and water ffalls, some cut their shinns."

Next day they continued up the Yallahs River and "came to a Halt in Negro River." Continuing up this river on the following day, "the Doctor's Chest had a ffall & sevl. things broke & lost." But although the terrain had been very difficult, up to this point they had, at least, had fair weather. On Tuesday 7 March they "Rais'd a very high ridge of the blue mountain & came to a Halt on a ridge." From this point they could see both the western harbour of Port Antonio to the north and Port Royal to the south. But the weather was as "foggy & cold," said Allen, "as ever I knew in England."

Still on this mountain on the following day, having been "without water these 36 hours", they found a pool which was "a vast refreshmt". But they had run out of provisions. On Thursday 9 March they shot two pigeons, hardly enough to satisfy their requirements, and again they ran out of water. What water they found, Allen noted, "was not sufft. to serve all our men." By the Saturday their food supply may have been supplemented in some way, Allen's complaint being confined to recording the fact that they had had "no water this 24 hours." That night they got more water than they wanted. Allen recorded that they "had very hard rains & blowing weather all this night, which was enough to perish us all." But when morning came they "saw the three towns which seem'd just under us."

This reference to three rebel towns in such close proximity to one another is interesting. Allen, at the end of his journal, gave the names of two of them — "Molly's Town" and "Dinah's Town." Two of them appear to have been very close to each other and the third, according to Peters, was about two miles away. In the following year, according to the captured Maroon spy Sarra,[12] the Maroons began to use the name "Nanny Town", but whether this was applied to the area covered by the three sites above referred to or to one or two of them is not clear.[13]

Allen calculated that he and his men "could get there to dinner." No doubt they expected to dine well on the small stock and growing provisions of the Maroons they proposed to attack. But although they "marchd all this day very hardly to get there", they failed to reach their destination and were "oblig'd to lay all Night for fear of ffalling." To add to their discomfort it rained all night. Next day, Monday, they "March'd into a River calld Back River[14] & kept the River Course all this day", but still had not reached their objective. Meanwhile it "rain'd very hard which", commented Allen, "was a great Detriment to our arms."

On Tuesday 14 March they "March'd still up the sd. river." As Allen recorded, it was a day of misfortunes. The terrain was particularly difficult and "by climbing up & down the Water ffalls & hills several of our pieces went off." The first misfortune occurred when "Mr. Glines Primus shott Col. Norris's Negro mans thigh, & mashd his bone to pieces 6 Inches above the knee, he being left in the place where it happen'd." Then "another Negro receiv'd two Shotts in his buttock by the same piece," and one of the whites shot another in the calf of his right leg. He too was left behind. One slave "dyed on the road," though Allen disclosed no cause of death. But that day they did at last sight their objective, and "came to a Halt within half a mile of the town."

The force led by Peters had meanwhile been approaching the towns from the opposite side. Delayed by the late arrival of the ship which was to take them to the mouth of the Swift River, their point of departure for the march inland from the north coast, they had made a late start. When they reached Stringers Penn, Peters requisitioned "two beefs" which provided them with a good supply of meat and enabled them to conserve their rations. On 13 March they proceeded through heavy rains to Hobbys plantation where they dried out their powder and provisions. Leaving Hobbys on 15 March they "took up this night on Hope Ridge, the weather being fair."

On 17 March Peters and his men reached the abandoned site of the Maroon town at which, two years previously, the so-called "grand party" led by Captain Soaper had suffered defeat.[15] Thence they proceeded "down a gully into the right hand arm of the Back River of Grande." Crossing the river they reached a place where, on a previous expedition, Peters had found a rebel settlement of 11 huts. Next day they continued along the right arm of the river till they came to "the foot of the Blue Mountains." There they breakfasted, resting in some abandoned rebel huts.

Meanwhile, seeing no sign of Peters and his men, Allen had decided to attack the rebel settlement. In his journal entry for 16 March he recorded:

> In the morning made a party of 50 Shott to drive them from the lower town, but they ambushed our men & there engaged our men in ambush very hotly for 2 hours & kill'd on the Spott Mr Glines Primus, Mr Halls Titus, Col. Bennets Crantin, Col. Bennet's Primus, a Negro man Dover & wounded at the same time Lieut. McClausand Shott thro' the thigh,

Mitchell George shott in his right arm, James Dent Shott in his back & in his left shoulder.

He added that:

the Negroes that were Shott the same day, Captain Philip Shott thro his right thigh, Mr Glen's Mingo 4 shots thro' his lef arm, Mr Clark's Charles Shot thro his right shoulder, Mr Hudson Grey's Quashee Shot thro his left leg, Mr Griffins Hanniball Shott standing just above his navel, a Negro man Jack Shott in his left leg, and all this night they have been pouring Volleys on our center guards.

But despite these heavy casualties Allen claimed that during this, the first day of the fighting, "we burnt down 25 houses on the outside of the town & left 60 standing in the two towns in our possession."

On Friday 17 March Allen recorded that the rebels, although they had withdrawn from these two towns, were "Still between whiles ... fireing of Volleys." On the next day he wrote: "Between whiles a small ffireing, fair weather, but a great many of our men sick & swelld legs".

Peters, in his journal entry of 19 March, recorded that his force marched further along the ridge, descending to "within a mile of the north river (which river runs by the side of the rebels cocoa piece into the left hand arm of the Back River Grande)." There they too were ambushed, "in which ambuscade Captain Lee was mortally wounded in his belly beside other wounds of which he died." Also killed at this time were a slave named Hercules who Peters described as "one of our pilots" and "some other negro named Cuffee." Peters was certain that his men had killed "several rebels" but alleged that "their numbers being so great they carried them away and hid them so that we found but one whose head and ears Ive cut off."

Peters and his men "followed with all haste that was possible the rebells down the same river to the town." This he recorded, they "found on fire about 4 of the clock." The town, wrote Peters, consisted of 120 houses. The rebels had set them on fire but Peters' men saved the last seven by "stopping the fire." That night, "being fatigued," they "kept a good guard and rested in the town."

Earlier that afternoon, hearing the sound of shooting, Allen recorded that they had "answer'd, according to our agreement, & Shew'd our Colours." But Peters and his men "being dubious of us as we were of them" did not attempt to make contact. Next morning, however, Peters sighted Allen's white flag "two miles farther up" the left arm of the river and hoisted an answering flag. The sites of the three associated towns having been occupied by the soldiers, they joined forces.

That day, still under sporadic fire from the Maroons in the surrounding bush, the soldiers buried Captain Lee, their highest ranking casualty, "in the middle of the great town in the presence of all the officers."

Many of the whites were nervous about the armed blacks, but it was hoped that the special privileges they enjoyed would ensure their loyalty to the establishment. The baggage porters, though perhaps less reliable, were of course less of a potential danger. In his message to the Assembly on 5 April 1732, the governor, whilst rejoicing at recent reverses suffered by the Maroons, nevertheless felt obliged to sound this sobering note:

> What gives me at present some solicitude, is the desertion and backwardness of the baggage slaves; an account of which you will find in major Ashworth's last letter to me: there must be some immediate remedy for that evil, lest the whole affair should, from so slender a cause, prove abortive [*Journals* 3, p. 77].

The Assembly took the matter sufficiently seriously to appoint a committee to consider it. On 25 April they received a second missive on the subject from His Excellency, citing further advices from Major Ashworth, from which "it appeared about a hundred of the shot and baggage slaves had deserted, or left the parties" [*Journals* 3 p. 83]. Blackshot recruits with their weapons, would no doubt have received a cordial welcome from the Maroons.

The deliberations of the Assembly in November 1732 concerning an indentured servant recommended by the governor as worthy of reward, throw an interesting side-light on the social relationships of the period. Appearing before the Assembly this man, whose field of military operations was in St. Ann and the parishes further to the west:

> gave an account of his march, and taking the town, and his party's killing and wounding several rebellious negroes, and that the town he took was Wiles's Town, at or near Mountain-Spring, and, as he thought, about twenty-eight miles from Montego Bay:
>
> And the house desiring to know what he had been bred to, and how long he had to serve, he informed them, he had been bred to a merchant, came a servant, and was bought by Mr Williams for twenty-two pounds, and had served him about three years as a school-master to his children ...

The *Journals* of the Assembly on 9 November 1732 [3 pp. 103-4] record that "the house taking it into consideration, that the said Mr Lambe had been serviceable to the public; it was Resolved, that he should be set free, and that a recompense should be allowed his master for the remainder of his time, at the public charge".

The services of Lambe and others like him were much in demand by the establishment. In the following year the Maroons, having lost one of their 'towns' to leeward, had succeeded in recapturing it. The minutes of the meeting of the Assembly held on 29 March 1733 [13 p. 120] recorded that:

> Mr Arcedeckne presented to the house ... a bill for raising and fitting out one or more parties, under command of Henry Williams and Ebenezer Lambe, to retake the great negro-town, lately taken by the rebellious negroes, and for rooting up and destroying all the Indian [16] and negro provisions in or near the said town, and the great plantation-walk.

In the early part of 1733 a rebel band, commanded by a leader named Kishee, recaptured the 'town' or 'towns' in the Blue Mountains that the government forces led by Allen and Peters had occupied in the previous year, driving out the military garrison stationed in the area. Charges of negligence preferred against Major Ashworth in connection with the loss of this town were enquired into by the Assembly on 26 April of that year. Defending himself, Ashworth put in evidence a letter he had sent to the officer in charge of the garrison on

22 January, 1733. This letter had warned, "We have intelligence that Kishee, lately routed by Cornish in Cotter-Wood, is gone with their wives and children over Snake-River. It is the opinion of some persons, that they are gone in expectation we have left the negro-town, and so to re-enter without opposition."

"It would be a lucky thing for you", Ashworth had written, "If they should attempt to come amongst you." If Kishee did attempt to re-enter the town, he had said, the garrison with "forty-five shot" was in his view of sufficient strength to capture him. Nevertheless he had ordered certain precautionary measures: "you are every other day to exercise them, and examine their arms and ammunition, and to patrol the ground, so that you could not miss taking them . . . to prevent any surprise, make the men . . . to cut all those bushes down close to the ground, musket-shot distance round from the barrack-house." Finally the letter had promised reinforcements and supplies: "to-morrow I send Sambo's party, with fifty shot . . . I send you ten bags of bread, which will serve thirty men sixteen days . . ." [*Journals* 3 p. 154].

Despite these warnings and reinforcements Kishee and his guerrillas recaptured the town. Four parties of blackshot were then sent out in an attempt to re-establish control of this rebel settlement. Three of the parties were under white officers, the fourth under the command of the same black mercenary Captain Sambo who had taken part in its capture in March 1732. But whatever inducements Sambo may have had to persuade him to place his services at the disposal of the establishment, the slaves who made up the parties do not appear to have shared his enthusiasm. So many of them deserted that the attack was a total failure [*Journals* 3 pp. 79-82].

Reporting to the Assembly on 14 March, the governor said:

> The late bad success of your parties against the rebels, and the defeat of some of them, by their own negligence more than the force of their enemies, made it necessary to make further attempt, lest, encouraged by

success, they should disturb the frontier settlements, and be joined by other slaves of the same disposition:

I with some difficulty fitted out a fresh party, of such of the former as were able to march, some raised by the three adjacent parishes, and the ablest of the pioneers, which I armed for service:

These parties, consisting of about two hundred and fifty men, completely armed and victualled, marched off by different routes; and if my orders and their officers engagements are observed, have on Thursday last at noon fallen upon the rebels from opposite quarters; and I expect every hour an account of what success they have had.

And then the governor paused. He paused to read a letter which had been handed to him. When he resumed his report all his optimism had evaporated: "there has been just now put into my hands", he continued:

a letter from lieutenant-colonel Ashworth to a member of your house, which I think necessary to be communicated to you: As it gives rather a sad prospect than any hopes of success from our parties, it must induce you to concert and fall upon some speedy effectual method of reducing those rebels, than have hitherto been thought of. I have as yet received no other advice or account of this affair [*Journals* 3 p. 110].

That same month, on 29 March the Assembly received a committee report on the rewards payable to slaves in military service with the whites:

Your Committee appointed to inspect the acts and resolutions for giving encouragement to such of the party negroes as have behaved well, do find, that the rewards . . . are as follows: viz.

ten shillings per month to each negro; and ten pounds per head for every rebellious negro man, eight pounds for every rebellious negro woman, and four pounds for every rebellious negro boy or girl under the age of ten years, that should be killed or taken alive, to be distributed between them in shares proportionable to their respective pay, and that what should fall to each slave's share should be his own proper use [*Journals* 3 p. 121].

Next day, on the recommendation of the committee, the House approved rewards for slaves specifically named, whose services to the whites deserved in their view special recognition. Its minutes recorded that some received "£3 and ten yards of oznaburghs each over and above the rewards allowed by the several party laws." Others were given "£4 with a like quantity of oznaburghs each." The most favoured received, "£5 a common silver laced hat, a good blue baize coat, with a red cross upon the right breast, and ten yards of oznaburghs, each negro; and that such coat and hat, with ten shillings, should be given each of them, on the 20th December yearly . . ." [*Journals* 3 p. 122].

FOOTNOTES

[1] Hunter to Lords of Trade, 9 November 1728.

[2] Ibid, Nos. 63-6 — Document with back sheet entitled "The Affair of the Jamaican Embargo", 1728-9.

[3] The Deposition of John Tello, aged 27 or thereabouts . . . enclosed in Hunter to Board of Trade, 29 September 1730.

[4] It seems unlikely that the Spaniards had a governor in the tiny Caicos islands. This is probably an erroneous transcript of a common English mis-spelling of Caracas. In the deposition of Capt. Wm. Quarrell, forwarded under cover of the same letter, this official is referred to as "the Govn. of Cracas."

[5] In the copy of this deposition at the Public Record Office this word is difficult to decipher. The scribe appears to have written it as 'cast'. Then he, or possibly someone else at a later date, added a squiggle above the initial letter to make it look like a capital E. As the term "East Indian" would not have made sense in the context in 1730, it has been restored as 'cast'. But this too raises a question — why the indefinite article in the form 'an' before the consonant 'c'?

[6] The Examination of Nicholas Plysham.

[7] "A paper received from a Correspondent of his" in Jamaica by "Our Secretary Mr. Popple," enclosed in letter from Board of Trade, 12 October 1730.

[8] Cudjoe is too well known a historical figure for the spelling of his name to be restored to the recognised Akan form of Kojo. The contemporary spelling of his name has therefore been retained throughout.

[9] James Knight is alone in asserting that Cudjoe was the son of the leader of the rebellion at Suttons, Clarendon, in 1690. There is, unfortunately, no means of testing the accuracy of this statement.

[10] Examination of Captain Dent, 2 July 1731.

[11] Copies of the journals of Allen and Peters are preserved in the West India Reference Library of the Institute of Jamaica [MSS file 1731/32 (March)]. A letter from Governor Hunter to the Lords of Trade and Plantations dated 28 March 1732 [PRO: CO 137/47 fol. 129] refers to the journal of "Sergeant" Allen, enclosed therewith, as being "plain but true." But, curiously, the document now preserved with the copy of the governor's letter at the Public Record Office is not the same as the copy of Allen's journal at the Institute of Jamaica. The

THE FIRST MAROON WAR   59

document in London consists of only three days' entries, none of which coincide exactly with the corresponding entries in the full journal. The document reads as follows:

Feby 27th – Marched to Distance Mountain. After many hardships in climbing over Mountains passing Rivers, and the loss of Several Men by Accidts & Sickness.

March 15 – Arrived at the Rebells – chief Settlement – this day of ye 16. The Rebells fought briskly – Some fire [indecipherable word].

March 19th – When Capt. Peters came up – The Rebells then set fire to most of their Houses and fled.

This document is presumably an abstract from Christopher Allen's journal. The reference to him as Sergeant Allen probably means that he held his captain's rank only in relation to his work as a mercenary in Jamaica, having been a sergeant in the regular army.

[12] See below pp. 63-65.

[13] We do not know why these towns were named after women. In Nanny's case it is known, from the examinations of Sarra, that she was not the chief. Were these, perhaps, elderly women who combined the functions of spiritual advisers (obeah women?) with those of trustees of Maroon property?

[14] This 'Back' river was probably the upper reaches of the Rio Grande.

[15] See above pp. 37-40.

[16] There appear to have been both free and slave Amerindians in Jamaica at this time. The presence of Amerindian slaves is confirmed by a reference to six of them in the Inventory of the possessions of Charles Price, owner of Worthy Park estate in 1731 [J. Arc. – *Inventories* (1729 to 1836) No. 15 p. 147], cited in Craton and Walvin [6].

CHAPTER THREE

NANNY TOWN[1]

By the middle of 1733 the plantocracy could not but view their situation in a gloomy light. Relying on contemporary reports when he wrote of these events some 50 to 60 years later, Bryan Edwards [10 pp. ix-x] gave this account of the progress of the war:

> The Maroons had, within a few years, greatly increased, notwithstanding all measures that had then been concerted and made use of for their suppression; in particular ... they had grown very formidable in the North East, North West, and South Western districts of the Island, to the great terror of his Majesty's subjects in those parts, who had greatly suffered by the frequent robberies, murders, and depredations committed by them;
>
> that in the parishes of Clarendon, St. Ann, St. Elizabeth, Westmoreland, Hanover and St. James's, they were considerably multiplied, and had large settlements among the mountains, and least accessible parts whence they plundered all around them, and caused several plantations to be thrown up and abandoned, and prevented many valuable tracts of land from being cultivated, to the great prejudice and diminution of his Majesty's revenue, as well as of trade, navigation and consumption of British manufactures, and to the weakening, and preventing further increase of strength and inhabitants, in the island.

On 3 July 1733 an urgent message from the governor, acquainting them with the outcome of the most recent expedition against the Maroons to windward, was delivered to the Council and the Assembly:

> On the 27th of last month I received advice by letters from Port-Antonio, ... that the party ordered out against the rebel slaves had got possession of what is called their towns. On Sunday last, about noon, I

received advices from the same persons, that the parties were beat, or frightened, out of that place, by the slaves, without any loss that I have as yet learnt, except it be of arms and ammunition, and had fled back to the breast-work...

Reporting on the remedial action taken, the governor said:

Immediately... I ordered a fresh supply of provisions and other necessaries to be sent round, as also some arms and ammunition from the magazine at Port Royal, together with such a detachment as could be spared from the two independent companies, and omitted nothing within the compass of my power, that might contribute to secure or improve the advantage gained.

But the contents of these last advices require the assistance and immediate attention of the whole legislature, unless you are resolved to submit and suffer your slaves to become your masters [*Journals* 3 p. 175; PRO: CO 137/20, fol. 120].

Three days later the Assembly learned that, disturbed at the latest reports, the governor had "sent an express to the commodore, to desire one of the king's ships might, without loss of time, be sent round to Port-Antonio, to keep the people there is countenance" [*Journals* 3 p. 176]. The Assembly and Council then addressed a joint appeal to the commodore of the naval station at Port Royal "for two hundred or more of his men, if they could be spared, with such officers as he should judge proper to command them" [*Journals* 3 pp. 176-7].

On 16 August the governor sent three letters "lately received from Port-Antonio... giving some account... of the rebellious negroes having taken possession of Hobby's plantation" [*Journals* 3 pp. 195-6].

A report on the situation, to be sent to the Board of Trade, was approved by the governor in Council on 17 August. First came the familiar lament about the "misfortunes that have of late Years Attended us" and then the statement that "our chief, and our greatest, arises from the trouble and danger which our Rebellious Slaves have created us". Their lordships were further informed that:

We have been at very great Expence of Men and money to Suppress them, but our constant ill Success has only convinced us of our own Weakness, and their Strength. This Evill is become too great for any cure we can apply, and we are in daily Apprehensions of a General Defection of our Slaves, To whom, without some Speedy relief we must fall a Sacrifice, and this once valuable Colony be made useless to His Majesty.

Continuing, the report described the recent defeat of the party sent against the rebels in the north-east and "the Attempt of some of our Slaves to join them upon that Success". It told of the appeal for help to the navy. And then came the information that the governor in Council had turned down certain proposals of the Assembly "for Building Barracks and sending out Flying Party's". The reasons for this decision, taken at a Council meeting on 17 August 1733, are revealing. They disclosed that, even in the midst of the establishment's adversities, a struggle over the respective powers of the Assembly and the governor in Council was in progress:

> Several of the Schemes proposed were Impracticable, And it tended in General to wrest the power out of the hands of the Governor and fix it in Commissioners who consisted chiefly of members of their own House... Vested with Authority to hold Court Martials and to Try for Capital cases... And to direct Routs and Marches... And this without the knowledge or direction of the Commander in Chief, and in no case Accountable to him for their Proceedings.

The dispute was obviously a sensitive one:

> We cou'd mention several other Instances where in the Council have been Obliged to Submit to the Obstinacy of Assembly's from the necessity of the times, and to Pass some Bills in many Particulars against their Judgement for fear of exposing the Country to too much hazard... [PRO:CO 137/47, fol. 182].

In August a Maroon spy was captured who was willing to talk. At his first examination his name was recorded as 'Syrus' though this was changed to "Sarra otherwise called Ned" at a second examination. What he had to say[2] gives an interesting insight into how the Maroon intelligence service operated, how they obtained some of their requirements and how they organised their ambushes:

> He says he came from the Negro Town 4 weeks agoe to See what Partys were fitting out that the rebels told him of their design in robbing Spark's & Hobby's Plantations, & which last place he left them at on Thursday the 9th instant... if he found the Partys in Titchfield Town not too Strong on his return to them they would come & take it, that on... the 11th Instant

he went from this place to Hobby's (in company with 3 rebellious negroes more, who had been in this town near a week making their remark undiscovered...) where they found the Rebels just going off with their Plunder. They told them that there was Men of War, Soldiers and Party Men enugh come; that the Rebels answd let them come.

Describing the rebel force that had captured Hobby's the witness said, "there were at Hobbys 2 Gangs of Men a 100 in each Gang & Several Women which they had brought to help carry the Spoil: that they left one Gang in the Negro Town to guard the rest of the Women & Children, the names of those who Commanded at Hobby's were Pompey and Coll Needham's Cudjoe..."

The rebels, this witness confirmed, got their powder and shot not only by plundering their enemies but also by purchase:

that on Thursday Morning an Indian brought a Cagg of Powder to the Rebels, – which they sent up to their Town... He says that the way they got Powder is, they have with them 2 white Boys, one named Jnº Done or Dun, who belonged to blind Ffletcher of Passage Fort, the other Charles (his other name he knows not) that these two boys writes Passes in Coll. Needham's name And one Quashee goes to Kingston with it to one Jacob a Jew in Church Street, that he went once last month and brought with him two large horns full that they have now, he believes, 200 horns full, but very little Shott, tho' Guns and Launces enough...

Disclosing what he knew of the rebels future plans the talkative prisoner said:

they had determined on hearing of these Partys coming to Ambush them in the River Course, that a Gang of 100 was to lay on Carrion Crow Hill & 100 more Hobby's Way, that a Drum was to be placed on the Ridge over the Town to View the Partys and the Women in the town to burn the Houses in case the Party should be too strong, if not the three Gangs to surround them on the beat of the Drum, All under the Command of Scipio [PRO:CO 137/47 fol. 172].

The second examination of Sarra, made over a month later at the direction of the governor, contained the earliest account, however sketchy, of Nanny Town at its original location, its inhabitants and how they were organised:

He says that the old Town, formerly taken by the Soldiers goes now by the name of Nanny Town, that there are now, or were when he was there three hundred Men, all armed with Guns or Launces, that they have more fire Arms than they use, that the number of the Women and Children far exceed those of the Men.

Describing their rudimentary system of government he said: "the Rebels have one head Man who orders everything, and if a Man Committs any Crime he is instantly Shott to Death". The witness appears, however, to have here construed the term 'crime' somewhat narrowly, explaining that "there is hardly any thing esteem'd a Crime with them but lying with one anothers wives". When speaking of the manner in which the women were disciplined he said: "the Women are whip'd for most of the Crimes they committ", using the same word with an undoubtedly wider meaning.

A high standard of conduct was expected of the leader: "if the head Man Should be Guilty of any great Crime, his Soldiers (as they are call'd) shoot him, and appoint another in his Place". How, one is compelled to wonder, did the witness know this? Had such a thing actually happened at Nanny Town? Or was this a principle proclaimed by the inhabitants in some sort of ceremony at which they chose their leader?

According to Sarra, "Their present head man is call'd Cuffee, and he is distinguished by Wearing a Silver lac'd Hatt and a Small Sword, no other daring to wear the like". All this information about the name of the leader and the power and responsibility exercised by the holder of the office leads inevitably to speculation as to the functions exercised in the community by the legendary Nanny, a subject to which we will return at the end of this chapter.

Like the inhabitants of other settlements, the residents of Nanny Town engaged in subsistence farming. Sarra stated that the women, "and such of the Men as are least noted for their Courage perform all such work as is necessary for the raising of Provisions". It was, he said, their custom "to work one day and play the next".

The prisoner also gave information about another Maroon settlement: "The Rebels have another Town... on the top of Carrion Crow Hill call'd Gay's or Guy's Town from the Name of their head man commanding there... there is a great deal of Open Ground about it in which is plenty of Cow, Sugar Canes, Plantains, Mellons, Yams, Corn, Hog and Poultry". As regards population he reported that "the number of men in that Town is about two hundred, and a greater number of Women". But their armament, he said, was inferior to that of Nanny Town: "the men Choose to arm themselves with Launces and Cutlashes rather than Guns, and never go to meet the Partys unless to defend the Paths which leads to their own Town". When such defensive action was necessary, he added, "they were joyn'd by those of Nanny Town who are Esteem'd the best fighting men".

According to further evidence given by Sarra[3] there appears to have been the closest co-operation between these two towns, the one helping the other with provisions and shelter when the necessity arose:

> He further Says that the Rebels when they were first beat from Nanny's Town went to Gay's or Guy's Town, and remain'd there till the Provisions began to be Scarce, and then they return'd and made themselves Masters of their old Town again, and that they (the Rebels) upon hearing that there were Stronger Partys to be sent against them, Sent and Search'd the Woods for about Seven or Eight miles round to See for other Settlements, that they might unite their Strength, but could find none.

He added:

> That there is no Town at long Bay, but that they have all their Salt from there, and have made a Convenient place for boiling it. They give Encouragement for all Sorts of Negroes to join them by an Oath which is held very Sacred among the Negroes, and those who refuse to take that Oath, whether they go to them of their own accord or are made Prisoners, are instantly put to Death, and they have a Guard Night and Day over the Women who for their Defence carry about them each two or three Knives.

Sarra also corrected some statements made at his first examination and called some more names:

> He says the name of the Wild Negro that goes to Kingston for Powder is Cuffee and not Quayhoo as mention'd in the examination taken by Mr. Ashworth, and by the Description of the Place where the Jew lives that Sold the Powder it must be Jew Ally and not Church Street:

> He Says that it was a Cag of Powder and a Crony Bagg of Ball that the said Cuffee had from the Jew, and that it was Quashee and Cudjo who were the Spys at Port Antonio: He further Says that the Indian carry'd with him a Horn of Powder, and Ball in a Bagg, and that Quashee and Cudjo ... were

mostly entertain'd while at Port Antonio by Col. Needham's Negroes, particularly by one nam'd Sam [PRO:CO 137/21, fol. 42].

Whether Major Ashworth had had time, after his examination of Sarra in August, to inform the officers commanding the force which set off into the mountains towards the end of that month that the Maroons were expecting them and planning an ambush, is doubtful. In any event, the very size of the expeditionary force probably made them feel confident that the ragged, inadequately armed, band of rebels they were determined to destroy would be unable to resist their advance.

The composition of this force, the largest ever assembled for an expedition into the mountains, and what happened to it, was recorded by a planter named John Smith residing in St. George who was in Port Antonio at the time and "received it from the Mouths of the Several Officers the Day after their return": [PRO:CO 137/21, fols. 216-7]. There were more than 400 armed men, 200 of whom were seamen sent by the commodore of the naval station. With them went 200 slaves to carry the expedition's baggage.

After the first day's march "about 100 of the Country Party" were detached to occupy a high point overlooking the route of the main body, a point from which the rebels had done much damage to former parties sent against them. As the main body advanced towards their objective, with the seamen leading the column, they were advised by their 'pilot' to "uncover their Arms and fresh Prime, wch was done". But before they had marched on more than another 50 paces: "the Pilot perceived (by a teer of Gun muzles on each Side thro' the thicket) that they were in an Ambuscade" [ibid].

Chief Naval Lieutenant Thomas Swanton, in charge of the seamen and apparently in over-all command of the expedition, wrote to the governor on 4 September on his return to Port Antonio:

> I am Sorry to Acquaint your Excellency of the Misfortune which happen'd on Wednes[d]. last about 4 in the Evening, We being within half a Mile of the N E River... not above 2 miles from Negro Town; The Advance Guard

Commanded by my brother was fir'd at from a new Ambush... Several were kill'd on both Sides, the Pylate by me was kill'd, & myself wounded at the same time [PRO:CO 137/47, fol. 176-7].

According to Swanton's account, the rest of his sailors and the soldiers behind them, terrified by the sudden appearance of the rebels and demoralised by a rumour that he and most of the officers had been killed, fled in panic. That night, when they had reached a safe point:

The sailors and Soldiers then fell to plundring & destroying every individual bag & box & threw away all the Surgeons Instruments & Medicines and pull'd the Beef & Bread all out of the bags & hove them down the Precipice & to prevent our rallying, broke open some of the Amushion boxes and threw away the Powder & Ball, Drank what Liquor and cou'd & all the rest they started.

"At this time", continued Swanton:

I was in the middle of ye ambush for some time Alone, but soon join'd by three of my own Officers with some private Men, the whole number being 11 of which 7 only had Pieces that were Serviceable. The rebels saw us in this Condition, and order'd a Party to take us Alive, but we had got under a large rock where they did not Care to come.

All this time the Negroes continued Surrounding us & had left only one Pass open which by the Cover of the Night, and a Shower of rain, we got thro' into the Woods, & fell in with... several Officers & a few Men; We agreed that Night to rally in the Morning & sent positive Orders for our men to come down but they Absolutely refus'd:

Continuing his tale of woe, Swanton said:

At dawn of day all Mr. Allam's Men had deserted him and most of them with me were wounded. We then went up the Hill to the baggage in hopes to find the people there, but they were gone. By chance Mr. Cox Surgn... his Medicines were not entirely destroy'd who assisted to dress the wounded which are about 14. & 10 kill'd on the Spotts... & we are forced to come back after having got thro' the greatest difficulty....

The losses sustained by the defeated sailors alone were subsequently certified to the Assembly[4] as follows:

the arms... belonging to the two hundred and two Seamen... viz. Firelocks, 52; cartouch-boxes, 52; twenty-six of which were occasioned by the death of eleven, and fifteen wounded, and the rest, in our opinion, broke in the engagement, and dropped by the people who were taken sick in the woods [*Journals* 3 p. 213].

The victorious Maroons no doubt secured a number of these muskets. Reporting to General Hunter on 4 September, the officer who had interviewed Swanton and other survivors on their return to Port Antonio wrote[5] that while the latter were lying concealed: "they saw 30 of ye wild Negroes go by them with two or three Muskets apiece". One of the guides "also Saw of another body Ninty Six arm'd in ye same manner pass very near them" [PRO: CO 137/47, fols. 178-9].

In the same letter the officer informed General Hunter that he had proposed that another attack on "ye Negro Towns" should immediately be made. But apparently the seamen had had enough: "Lieut Swanton made me no Return to my proposal but ... has order'd his men to March early in ye morning to be put on board the Deal Castle Capt. Aubin said he would Sail ye morning after he receiv'd them on board".

The account of planter Smith, referred to above, mentioned a 'tall Mulatto' among the rebels "whom they observed had done more Mischief than any of the blacks, having Several Men to load the Muskets for him". None of the officers referred to such a person in their official reports, but according to Smith he was shot dead by a seaman. He added that "Upon this there was a great outcry among the Blacks, that Assado was killed ... carry off Assado, after which they fired no more, but drew off" [PRO:CO 137/21, fols. 216-7].

Smith then made the supposition that this man was 'a Spanish Mulatto' and suggested the possibility of a liaison between inhabitants of Cuba and the Maroons, alleging that in the case of an earlier rebel victory the Spaniards in Cuba "were acquainted with the Action before the News of it reached the Government at Spanish Town".

Writing from Titchfield near Port Antonio on 4 September Ashworth, then a lieutenant colonel, informed the governor that 'the outsettlers' whose plantations had been occupied or were threatened by the rebels had moved with their families into the town. He reported general apprehension of an attack on the town and pointed out that with the departure of the naval contingent "We shal then have no other assistance than from the Hulk now Moor'd near the Pass". Ashworth proposed that "a Wall who'd soon be rais'd Cross the Isthmus[6] of stone to Secure the Town from any attempt on that side", and that the commodore be asked to station a ship in the eastern harbour [PRO:CO 137/47, fols. 180-1].

Fears of a rebel initiative in the area were well founded. Planter John Smith's narrative continued the story:

> About 4 Weeks after this, a Body of the Rebels consisting of about 80 or 90 came down and took Possession of a Plantation and two Pens or Cattle Pastures, all 3 Joyning together, on notice of which, 50 Soldiers were sent to dislodge them, who killed one, but being beat off and again being reinforced with 50 others (which were all the Commanding Officer would venture to Spare from the Guard of Portland) they also return'd without attacking of them, Saying they yet wanted more Strength. Thus the Enemy were left in Possession of great Plenty of Cattle and Provisions.

Planter Smith's assessment of the property owners' prospects in his part of the island were low indeed:

> No Man at North Side can be said to be Master of a Slave, Many of them not doing half their work that they used to do, nor dare their Masters punish them, for the least disgust will probably cause them to make their Escape and joyn the Rebels, as many from Sev l Plantations frequently do. Therefore many of the Inhabitants, especially those at the North Side talk of and intend to draw off and quit the Island for North America, unless there be a Speedy prospect of Relief.

Over in the western parishes the planters were no happier with their lot.[7] In October 1733, on the governor's advice, a bill was introduced in the Assembly to provide for "building barracks in the western division, cutting and clearing roads therein, and for raising and fitting out parties for the more speedy and effectual suppressing rebellious and runaway negroes" [*Journals* 3 p. 207].

The preamble to the new Act warned that: "the western Parts of the Island will soon become the Seat of an intestine War, as well as the Eastern". It recited the fact that:

> the rebellious Slaves in the Parishes of Clarendon, St, Anne, St. Elizabeth, Westmoreland, Hanover and St. James's have greatly increased in Numbers, and have considerable Settlements in the Mountains and least accessible Parts in the said Parishes, as well as betwixt Clarendon and St. Anne who commit frequent Robberies and Murders ... and have occasioned several

> Settlements to be abandoned... by the Owners and Possessors; and thereby... prevents vast Tracts of valuable Land from being settled... to the great... Diminution of his Majesty's Revenue in Great Britain... [Acts 1681-1837/177ff.].

Under this Act barracks were required to be built "at the head of the Great River", north-west of Barbados Valley and between "Cargill's Plantation" and "Drax Crawl". Each barrack was to be provided with a gang of dogs, to be paid for by the church wardens out of moneys to be levied by the local vestries, but the barracks would be built by the government.

The Assembly also, at this time, accepted a recommendation "that the Selling or disposing of powder to any free negro, negro slave, Indian, or mulatto, be made a felony without benefit of clergy" [*Journals* 3 p. 199]. They hoped by this means to ensure that, with the threat of a possible death penalty hanging over their heads, persons who had been willing to risk selling powder and ball to the rebels in the past would be discouraged from doing so in the future.

In December 1733 a group of slaves rose in rebellion in Hanover at the western end of the island where, according to Governor Hunter, the Whites "had least expected it" [PRO: CO 137/21, fols. 16-17].

On 15 February, 1734 a correspondent in Jamaica wrote to a merchant in London:[8]

> We received Advice yesterday from Port Antonio, of 22 Plantation Negroes and some which belonged to the Party having deserted and gone over to the Rebells; and from St. Thomas in the East, We have an account of above 40 able Cormantine Negroes having deserted their Masters and it is supposed are likewise gone over to them...
>
> We forgot to mention that 29 Negroes belonging to his Majesty, and employed in Clearing Lynches Island, which forms Port Antonio Harbour, were likewise going to the Rebells, but were intercepted by a party sent after them, and are now in Irons on Board one of the Men of War [PRO: CO 137/47, fols. 223-4].

Another letter from Jamaica written a week later[9] stated:

> ... we are in terrible circumstances in respect to the Rebellious Negroes, they got the better of all our partys, Our men are quite despirited, and dare not look them in the face in open Ground or in equal Numbers...

... Its Gods Mercy they are not joynd by Our own Slaves, if that should happen, this Country must be cut off. If this Country be worth preserving to Great Britain, they will take some speedy Care of us [PRO:CO 137/47 foL 219].

On 19 February the Assembly considered reports of rebel activity in St. George and of the burning of the 'house and works' of one John Brooks, himself severely wounded in the attack. In a message to the Governor they drew attention to "the great distress the people of St. George's lay under and the constant depradations that are daily committed by the rebellious negroes in that parish", and urged their immediate relief [*Journals* 3 p. 224].

The governor replied on the same day advising the House that "as soon as he had heard of the depradations" he had:

sent orders to the commanding officers there to detach numbers of the militia to Buff-Bay, or Edward's Fort, to make stand against the rebels, till such time the legislature had raised sufficient funds to answer the expense of such parties, as he should think necessary for such a service [*Journals* 3 p. 225].

On 21 February 1734 the Assembly made this plea of desperation to Britain for more aid:

We do ... apply to your Majesty to implore your most gracious assistance in our present dangerous and distressed condition ... the danger we are in proceeds from our slaves in rebellion against us. We have, for several years past, been at an extraordinary and almost insupportable expence, in endeavouring to suppress them; and, whilst we had any reasonable hope of succeeding, we declined being too importunate for relief: But our attempts against them having been in vain, only convinced us of our weakness; so great, that, instead of being able to reduce them, we are not in a condition to defend ourselves.

Graphically describing the slave owners' predicament the Assembly's plea continued:

The terror of them spreads itself every where: and the ravages and barbarities they have committed have determined several planters to abandon their settlements. The evil is daily increasing: and their success has had such influence on our other slaves, that they are continually deserting to them in great numbers: and the insolent behaviour of others gives us but too much cause to fear a general defection: which without your majesty's gracious aid and assistance, must render us a prey to them ... [*Journals* 3, p. 227].

Two days later the Assembly approved a petition to the British government. They told of the defeat of the 200 sailors sent "to act in conjunction with 100 men drawn out of the two independent companies, and three hundred others the best that could be raised for that service", and said:

> These constant successes have emboldened the rebels to that degree, that they now despite our powers, and instead of hiding themselves, as they formerly did, in those mountains and covered places, they openly appear in arms, and are daily increasing, by the desertion of other slaves, whom they encourage and entice over to them, and have actually taken possession of three plantations, within eight miles of Port-Antonio and the sea, by which means they may at any time cut off all communications by land with that harbour and town...
>
> They have also, within a few days past, made an attempt on a place called the Breast-work, where a considerable number of armed men were lodged, to guard the workmen employed in carrying on a defensible barrack in that place to prevent their incursions...

Dealing next with the incapacity of the whites to defend their property and persons the petitioners continued:

> ... the white inhabitants are by no means capable of defending so large a compass of land, our numbers not being more than eight thousand and of which not above one thousand are masters of families, or have any property, and the negroes, by the exact computation, exceeding eighty thousand, besides those in rebellion, whose number we cannot get any certain account of, but, we believe, are not less than two thousand, in the several parts of the island.

Citing other matters to impress upon the secretary of state how hopeless would be the situation of the slave owners if further and adequate aid were not immediately forthcoming from Britain, the petition concluded:

> Your grace will from thence perceive, how impracticable it will be for us to suppress them, or even to defend ourselves, should the defection become more general; which we have too great reason to apprehend, from the encouragement they meet with, the affinity between them, and above all, the hope of freedom; which has shaken the fidelity of our most trusted slaves [*Journals* 3 p. 229].

Meanwhile the Board of Trade had, by letter dated 22 February 1734, reported to the Duke of Newcastle on a meeting they had held with "several Jamaica Merchants residing in London". At the Board's request the merchants' 'discourse' had been reduced to writing, with extracts from the letters of their planter correspondents in Jamaica annexed. It read in part:

> We are sorry to Observe, that Negroes daily leave Our Plantations to joyn those in Rebellion who, flush'd with the Advantage they have had in the four last Rencounters with the Party's sent out against them, have already made themselves Masters of a Plantation and of two Penns or Cattle Pastures near Port Antonio.
>
> It is to be feared, they will not stop here, that they may make some further Attempts, and probably meet with Success, from the Dread the Island seems to be in upon this occasion [PRO:CO 137/47, fol. 207].

On 7 May the acting governor [10] reported to the Assembly what at first appeared to have been at least a temporary success: "Captain Swanton, with his party from windward, had attacked the rebels in their town, and kept it in possession for some days, but, for want of a supply of ammunition, and a reinforcement, was obliged to quit it..." [*Journals* 3 p. 241].

The Assembly immediately appointed a committee "to enquire into the causes of Mr. Swanton's quitting the negro-town". But although the Assembly appear to have accepted Swanton's explanation and to have been willing to let him have another try, the Council were far from satisfied. Instead of holding the town for some days, as had been reported, the Council found that Swanton's party had not dared to attack it:

> they had got into that place called the Negro-Town, and were within sight of the houses, continuing forty-eight hours under a continued hard rain, and durst not attempt the rebels; and, being at last reduced to the necessity of retreating towards Port-Antonio, they found the rivers so swelled that it gave the negroes an opportunity of setting upon them, so that they at last fled, and threw away their arms and ammunition, with the loss of twenty of their best men; so that this last expedition in all appearance hath thoroughly furnished the rebels with as much powder and arms as they have occasion for [*Journals* 3 p. 267].

Convinced beyond all doubt of the gravity of the situation, the British government, on receiving the Assembly's petition, responded immediately. By 6 August the acting governor was able to say to the Assembly:

> His Majesty, being much concerned at the distress of his people, hath graciously ordered six independent companies of one hundred men each, to be drafted from his troops at Gibraltar, to be immediately embarked and sent for our relief; and has also directed the lords of the admiralty to send the proper orders to Sir Chaloner Ogle to give us all the assistance he can from the squadron of his majesty's ships under his command [*Journals* 3 p. 254].

His Majesty also took the opportunity to point out that these reinforcements, "with the two independent companies which you have there already, will make a body of eight hundred men, besides officers" [*Journals* 3 p. 255].

On 24 August 1734 the Assembly, considering a report on "the desertion of several settlements in the leeward district", learned that 27 properties had been abandoned because of frequent attacks involving the "burning of houses, wounding some of the inhabitants, and killing of others". The House was told that some of the settlers were willing to return to the area "if they had a sufficient guard of men for their protection" [*Journals* 3 pp. 266-7].

On 1 October the acting governor informed the Assembly that:

> the rebellious negroes have had the boldness to attack one of the plantations in the parish of St. Georges, and have taken away some of the negroes, and burnt the mansion-house, and most of the canes growing, and that they have also threatened to destroy several of the neighbouring settlements in that parish [*Journals* 3 p. 274].

The expected reinforcements from Gibraltar arrived towards the end of 1734. In December of that year a large force equipped, in addition to their usual armament, with swivel guns, set out to make yet another attack on Nanny Town in the Blue Mountains. The actual size of the attacking force is not recorded. Colonel George Brooks, the commanding officer, whose approach was along the ridge of the Blue Mountains, would appear, from his subsequent letters, to have had about 400 to 500 men. Major Mumbee, approaching from a different direction, probably had a smaller number.

The attackers approached their objective with great stealth

in weather conditions which favoured their concealment. The Maroons, on the other hand, appear to have maintained an insufficient look-out and to have permitted their attackers to get within a mile of their objective during the night preceding the attack. Describing their advance, in a letter to the acting governor, Colonel Brooks wrote:

> On Monday the 16th, 1734 We marched from the Blew Mountain Ridge... and at night gott within a Mile of the Negro Town after being the whole day in the Rain was forced to Sitt upp all Night in our Wett Cloaths without either fire or Candle, for fear of being discovered by the Rebells, the Rains Continued all Night, that it was so dark, we could not attempt them till ten a Clock the next day, at which time I ordered Captn Barbery, Capt. Stoddard Capt Wynders and Mr Dunston, who I appointed to Command Major Swantons Company, to march into the Negro Town with their proper officers and their Companies, they gott in sight of the Town before they were discovered [PRO:CO 137/21, fol. 198].

Despite their initial negligence, however, the Maroons appear to have made a quick recovery. Realising that it was too late to defend the town they quickly rendered their houses unusable to the enemy. Describing the attack upon the town Colonel Brooks continued, "as soon as the Negroes discovered them, they sett most of their Houses on fire and then fired a Volly at our People, which ours returned and Entered the Town, and took one of their ambuscades, but they kept the principall one, and fired at our men all the day".

Explaining his own activity, or rather inactivity, during this time Brooks wrote: "I stayed on the Hill on which I lay all Night and guarded the ammunition and provisions with the rest of the men, it being our whole dependence, did not think proper to trust it to any Body Else." He added, "hearing them pritty smartly Engaged, sent a detachment of fifty men, under the Command of Lieut. Garland, Lieut. Witter, and Ensign Allen, to their assistance, who immediately joyned them".

The battle was still raging next day and the soldiers found themselves under pressure. Colonel Brooks continued his account: "next morning Capt Stoddard Sent to me to come to their assistance and bring the Suivle Guns, to drive them out of their ambush, and I immediately went, but before I gott in, Eight or ten of our men run in with their guns and pistols and came Muzzle to Muzzle". These soldiers, wrote Brooks: "beat them out of their ambush with only the damage of one man wounded: I gott in soon after, we had two men wounded, in taking the Town, and one by taking the ambuscade". The resistance of the defenders was however not yet at an end: "they continued firing at us all day, from the top of the Hills and do so still; we have killed several, but have gott none, for they carry all of".

Concerning the other part of the attacking force which was to have approached the town from a different direction, Colonel Brooks added:

> I have not heard of Major Mumby, yett, nor Cannot spare men to send for him yett, our men being many of them Sick, and many deserted and the Negroes continuing showing themselves on the Hills round us, and often firing on us in the Night, as well as day, and Endeavouring to suppres us but our men are all on constant duty: so that we have no Body to Spare.

Brooks then made an urgent plea for supplies and replacements:

> Our provisions are all out, and Spoiled, and having Nothing for the men to Eat but the Cocoa's, and as we have no men to spare, to send, Desire Your Honour will send a Detachment, with some Rum, Sugar, butter, Rice, Oatmeal and flower and other provisions for our people, and some ammunition for ours groes scarce.

He would, he said, send some men to meet the provisions if it was possible to do so, but he warned of the danger of a rebel ambush: "I . . . beg your Honour will send a sufficient Guard with what you send us, or they may be Intercepted." And he expressed the hope that fresh soldiers would speedily be sent to garrison the site of the captured town. Many of his men, he said, had left home at short notice and wished to return. As for those who would have to stay, he complained that they were "much in want of Shoes, Stockings and warm Cloathing".

In conclusion, Brooks mentioned his depleted numbers: "I think it proper to acquaint you that our men are deserted so from us, that we have not above three hundred Shott White and black left now". As for his labourers, the so called "pioneers", they were now of little use as they had "lost their bills & Axes most of them". He therefore planned to send them back as soon as he could spare a guard "to return them with safety".

Another letter from Colonel Brooks to the acting governor, written on 29 December, showed how well founded his fears had been that the supplies for the troops at Nanny Town might be intercepted: "our hearty thanks... for the seasonable supply of Provisions sent to us; tho we lost great part of them, which the Negroes made away with in the Road, and Especially Rum & Sugar" [PRO:CO/137/21 fol. 199].

This letter also disclosed the fact that no appreciable success had been achieved by the troops who had been sent in pursuit of the former residents of the town. Brooks reported that he had sent out three detachments simultaneously "who on their return acquainted me that ... they saw no sign of the Rebells, but only twenty hutts in the open Ground behind a hill, which they believe the Negroes lay in a night or two after we took the Town". These troops had also "found where they had been digging of provisions a day or two before". So successfully had the retreating Maroons reaped their crops, wrote Brooks, that the soldiers had found "only two days provisions to be gott".

The information given by Brooks on the losses suffered by the Maroons during the fighting for the town was not very precise. He wrote: "Our people have found several of the Rebells dead and about fforty or ffifty fire arms that were burnt in their Houses, and some were found in the bushes as also some small quantity of gunpowder."

Indeed everything that Brooks had to say in his letters to the acting governor confirmed the accuracy of the comment by the historian Dallas when he wrote: "It is not clear that the Maroons were always to be considered as defeated when they retired and left the ground of action to their enemy: for surprise and ambush were the chief principles of their warfare" [7 vol. 1 p. 39].

Brooks stressed the need for sawyers and carpenters to prepare the timber, available on the spot, for building the proposed barracks. On the matter of the size of the garrison that it would be necessary to station in the area he gave his opinion that: "after this place is fortified, one hundred Effective men will be Sufficient to keep it, and one hundred and fifty men more that are fit to travel through the woods to be sent in flying parties, will be sufficient to drive all the Negroes out of these parts" [PRO:CO 137/21, fol. 199].

A garrison was established at the site of Nanny Town and maintained there until some time in 1736. One of the soldiers stationed there apparently felt that their presence deserved a permanent monument. He selected a suitable boulder and on it he carved a crude inscription: "Decem 17 1734 This Town was took by Coll Brook and After kept by Capt Cooke till July 1735".

For over 230 years this monument lay forgotten in the bush. In 1968 a Forestry Department ranger of Maroon descent guided a surveyor and a party of explorers to the ruins of the Nanny Town garrison and pointed it out to them. This wild and almost impenetrable region of the Blue Mountains, long uninhabited, is normally visited only by the hunters of wild hogs. Few had visited the site of the ruins and it was generally believed that dire consequences would befall any person not of Maroon descent who, by going there, disturbed the ghosts of those who had died long ago.[11]

The earliest published account of the capture of Nanny Town is that of Charles Leslie, a somewhat romanticised version in which William Stoddart featured as the establishment's hero:

> Strong Parties were ordered out under proper Commanders; that under Captain Stoddart attacked Nanny Town in the Blue Mountains, which had been built by the Rebels, and was so situate, that a few Men might defend it against Thousands. The Captain was therefore obliged to carry along with him several small Field-Pieces, and likewise to make his Approach with the greatest Caution, and without the least Noise.

> He got before Night to the Foot of the Hill, and while it was yet dark, scaled the narrow Passage with a few of the most resolute of his Company and having, with the utmost Difficulty, got the Field-Pieces mounted on the Eminence, began to play upon the Negroe Town. The Pieces were loaded with Musket-Bullets, which killed and wounded a vast Number of the Rebels, who offered to make a Defence.
>
> They did not long sustain the Attack, but in less than Half an Hour fled with the utmost Precipitation. The brave Captain pursued the Rebels, and gained a compleat Victory. Several hundreds of Negroes were killed, and many taken Prisoners. Their Town was demolished, their Provisions destroyed, and more real Hurt done them on that Day, than in 20 Years before, and with little or no loss of the Party who attacked them [Leslie 21, pp. 310-313].

Published in 1739, Leslie's account, with all it inaccuracies and exaggerations, no doubt reflects the contemporary jubilation in establishment circles at the capture of what must have been the principal Maroon town in the north-east at that time. Edward Long, writing perhaps some 30 years later, more or less followed Leslie, adding a few touches of his own. Describing the field-pieces as "portable Swivel-guns" and describing the approach taken by the soldiers as "the only path leading to their town ... steep, rocky and difficult", he concluded:

> Many were slain in their habitation and several more, amidst the consternation which this surprize occasioned threw themselves headlong down precipices ... Captain Stoddard pursued the advantage, killed numbers, took many prisoners, and in short, so completely destroyed or routed the whole body, they were unable afterwards to effect any enterprize of moment in this quarter of the island [24 vol. 2 p. 340].

Three and a half years after the event, on 13 July 1738, the Assembly, on receipt of a petition from Stoddart, considered 'the question of special reward and compensation. The committee set up to consider the petition reported that Stoddart, himself a slave owner, had taken with him on the expedition "several of his choice negro shots, who probably may have done the public some service". They also found that Stoddart's "private affairs must have suffered by the loss of their labour". On the committee's recommendation the Assembly gave Stoddart £300 [*Journals* 3 p. 448]. They awarded Colonel Brooks, his commanding officer, £600.

The site of Nanny Town in the Blue Mountains may never again have been occupied by the Maroons, even after the military garrison there was abandoned in 1736. In later years, when a part of the windward Maroons established a town at a new site in Portland, they again called it Nanny Town. To have received so signal an honour Nanny must have been a person of considerable importance, but what exactly was her role in Maroon affairs?

Nanny's fame is legendary among the descendants of the Maroons. The late Henry A. Rowe, Maroon colonel at Accompong, claimed in 1936 that Nanny was "a sister to Accompong" [Williams 37 p. 388]. But old Colonel Rowe, as the author had good cause to recall, exercised a particularly fertile imagination when recounting historical events.[12]

In Maroon oral tradition Nanny has a reputation of being not only a great military tactician but also personally invulnerable. She is alleged to have turned her back to the fire of her adversaries and, bending over, to have attracted the bullets to a portion of her anatomy where they were caught and rendered harmless. Explaining to the Catholic priest J.J. Williams how Nanny did this, Colonel Rowe showed a touch of delicacy: "Nanny takes her back to catch the balls". He added that she "had a lot of science about her" [37, p.388]. But Rowe was less inhibited when he later described the process to the author! At Moore Town Maroon leaders interviewed in the following year gave much the same version as Rowe, but some attempt was made to offer a rational explanation.[13]

Nanny was reported dead after the capture of the principal settlement of the windward Maroons by Allen and Peters in 1732.[14] A black man named William Cuffee, who had fought with the whites in that attack, was described as "a very good party negro — having killed Nanny, the rebels old Obeah woman" [*Journals* 3 p. 121]. But unless the rebels had more than one famous obeah woman of that name, it is

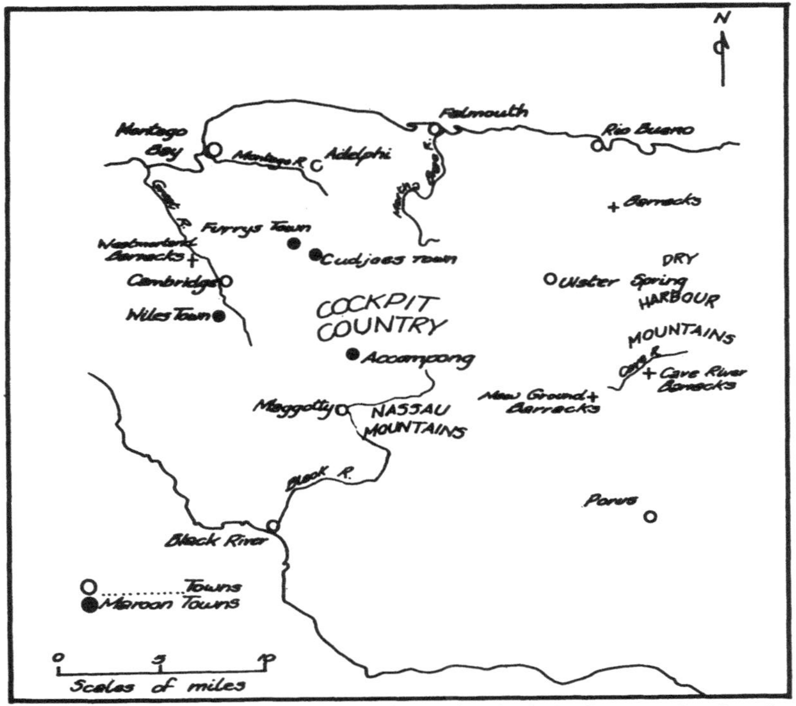

"Leeward" (Western) Jamaica centred on the Cockpit Country showing the major settlements in the mid 1730s.
Map by Alan Teulon

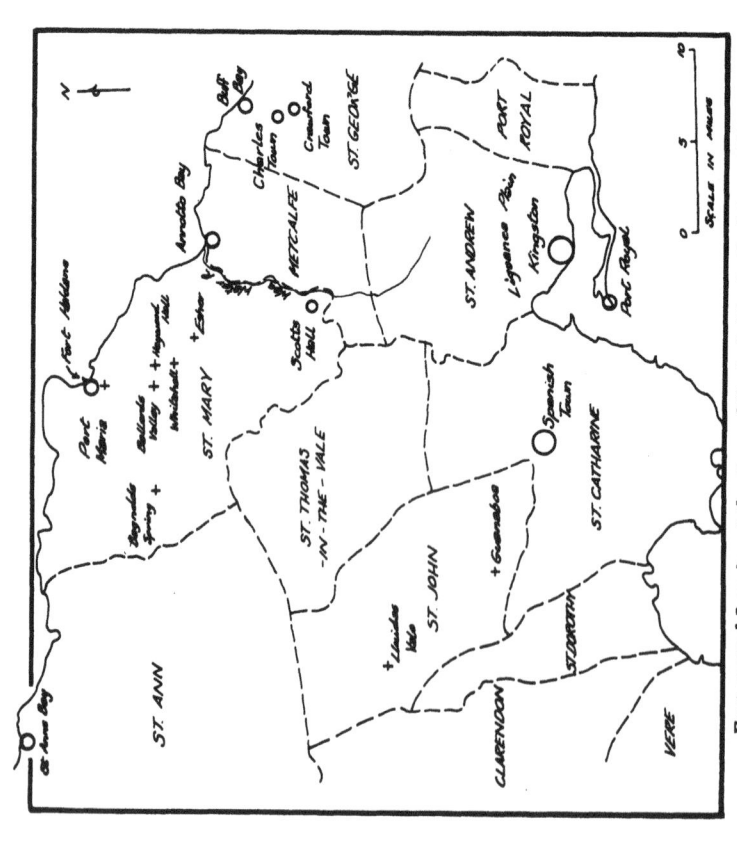

East-central Jamaica at the time of Tacky's War in St. Mary, 1760.
Map by Alan Teulon

Site of Nanny Town from the air overlooking a sheer 50 ft. drop to the Stony River below, now covered in a secondary growth of trees and creepers.

Photo by Alan Teulon

This artist's impression, popularised since Nanny was named a Jamaican national heroine, may not be a good likeness. The description by Thicknesse (if indeed he was describing Nanny, since he did not name her) is far from flattering. But by then she was well past her prime.

Stone monument discovered by Leopold Shelton at Nanny Town in 1968 reads: "DECEM 17, 1734. This Town was took by Coll. Brook and after kept by Capt. Cooke till July 1735"

Aerial view of the Grand Ridge of the Blue Mountains in Portland looking west. The peak of the mountains is 7,402 ft. above sea level and Nanny Town is in the valley on the left arm of the Back Rio Grande (now the Stony River) beneath the ridge at an elevation of about 1,900 ft.

Photo by Alan Tuelon

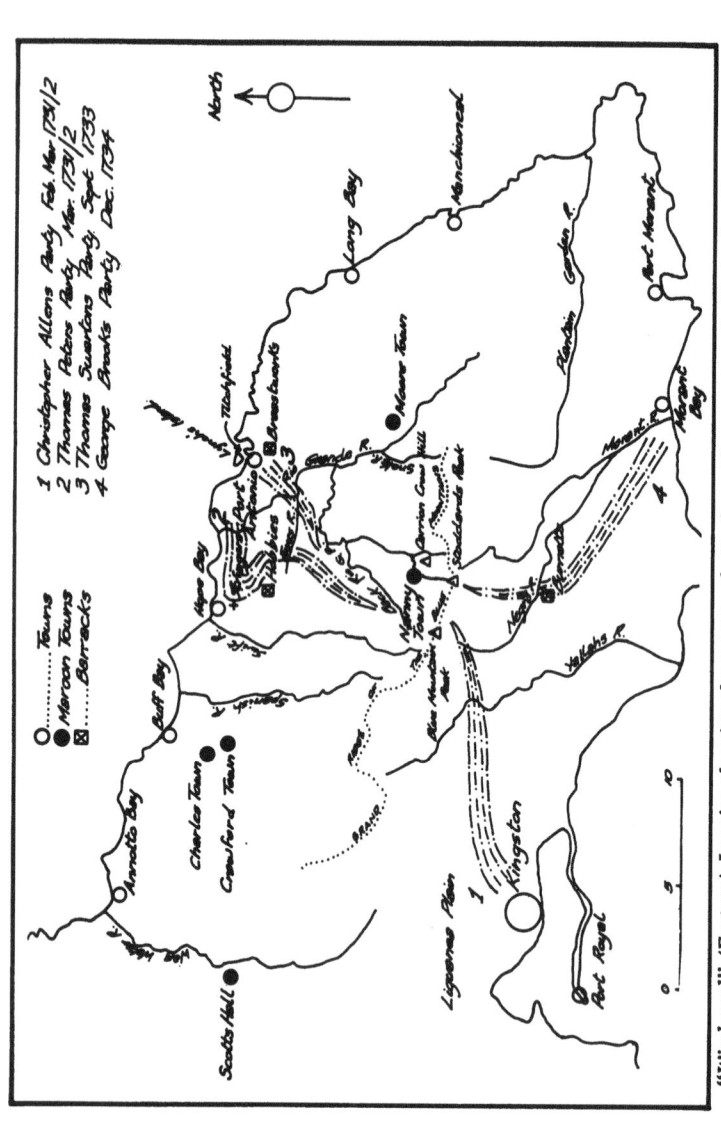

"Windward" (Eastern) Jamaica showing the routes of attack on Maroon strongholds in the Blue Mountains
Map by Alan Teulon

The main mountain ranges of Jamaica

Map by Alan Teulon

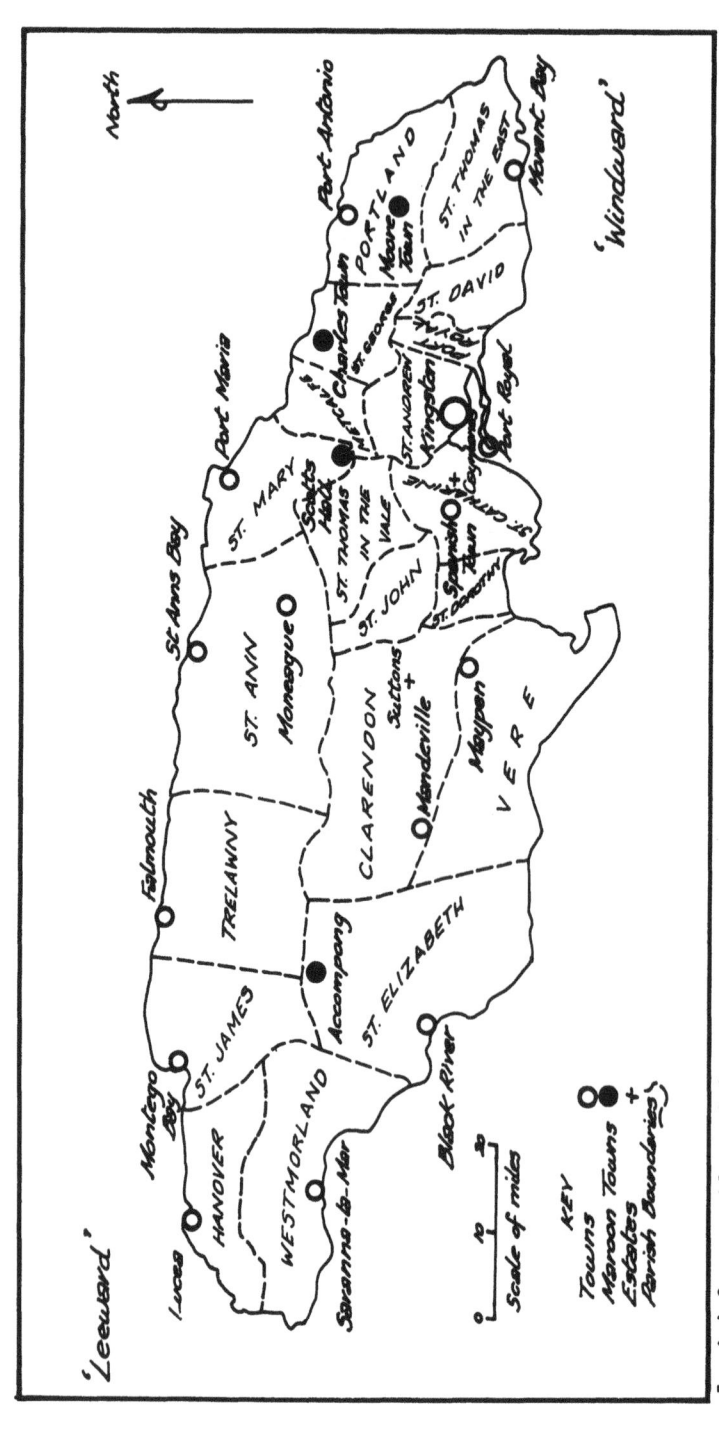

Jamaica's former parishes excluding Manchester (created from Clarendon and Vere in the 1820s) but including Metcalfe (1847) now part of St. Mary. Map by Alan Teulon.

unlikely that Nanny succumbed fatally to William Cuffee's weapon. It may, indeed, have been her survival of an attack, which at the time had appeared to be fatal, that gave birth to the legend of her invulnerability.

Sarra the captured Maroon spy, who in 1733 had disclosed that the Maroons had, on recapturing the site of their former stronghold in the Blue Mountains earlier that year, named it Nanny Town, made no mention of her as a person. The fact that he gave the name and described the functions of their chief might suggest that the story that Nanny was dead was true. Other evidence, however, strongly contradicts this supposition. There is reference to Nanny and her husband by an informer named Cupid who was examined in January 1735.[15] Cupid credited her with putting three captured white men to death [PRO:CO 137/21, fol. 207]. A reference to the windward Maroons' obeah woman in the memoirs of a contemporary of the events of 1739 could conceivably refer to her.[16] But most persuasive of all is a reference to Nanny by name in an official documentary transaction in 1741[17] [J. Arc/Patents 22:16-7; Kopytoff 18].

Though there may now be little possibility of ascertaining, with any degree of certainty, the role Nanny played among the windward Maroons, the fact that she inspired their warriors to courage and resistance in their fight for freedom is certain. In 1975 the nation saw fit to declare her, posthumously, a National Hero!

FOOTNOTES

[1]Nanny Town, the principal town of the windward Maroons in the early 1730s, appears to have acquired its name in 1733. The settlement had originally

consisted of three associated 'towns' (Molly's Town, Dinah's Town and another the name of which is not recorded). These sites were captured by the attacking forces led by Allen and Peters in March 1732 and reoccupied by the Maroons, under Kishee's leadership, early in 1733 (above pp. 52-3. 55-6).

[2] "Copy of the Confession made by Syrus a Negro belonging to Mr Geo Taylor" in Hunter to Lords Comm. of Trade, 25 August 1733.

[3] "The Further Examination of Sarra alias Ned, taken by order of His Excellency" 1 October 1733.

[4] Certificate of Mr Pratter 4 November 1733 presented to the Assembly, 17 November.

[5] Letter from Lieut. James Draper (date-lined from "Breast work") 4 September 1733.

[6] This must be a reference to the isthmus at Titchfield.

[7] The parishes in western Jamaica where there had been the most intensive development of plantations by the Europeans up to this time were Westmoreland and St. Elizabeth. In the former there were, in 1734, 9,081 slaves and in the latter 7,046 as compared with only 2,297 in St. James (which then included most of Trelawny) and 3,339 in Hanover. In that year St. Catherine with St. Thomas in the Vale had a total of 12,800. Clarendon and Vere, which on the basis of the number of slaves was probably the most intensively farmed area, had a total of 14,351. St. Andrews had 7,631. St. Mary had only 2,938 [Long 24 vol. 2].

[8] Extracts from letter from Jamaica dated "15 Feby 1733" enclosed in Richard Harris to Bd of Trade, 29 April 1734 and forwarded by them to Lord Harrington, 1 May 1734.

[9] "A Paragraph in a Letter from Jamaica" bearing a pencilled date "22 Feb^r 1733/4 Am & W Indies".

[10] On the death of General Hunter the task of acting as governor fell upon John Ayscough, the president of the Council.

[11] Leopold Shelton, the ranger who guided the party, defied very strong taboos and superstitions in doing so. Alan Teulon, the surveyor from whom the author obtained this information, made a careful listing of the ruins and artifacts found in the area and took a number of photographs. In 1973-74 he returned with a scientific expedition to explore the area and make a documentary film. Among their finds was a 17th century Spanish coin.

[12] In 1943 the author told Colonel Rowe (then recently retired from office) the story of General Walpole's rejection of the reward offered to him at the end of the Second Maroon War in 1795, when the governor and the Assembly violated the treaty by which it had been ended. Some years later Dr. and Mrs. David Lewis, visiting Accompong, heard the story from Rowe, but with one important difference. He had transferred it from the second to the first Maroon War!

[13] The author discussed Nanny's supposed supernatural powers with several leading residents of Moore Town in 1944. Captain Downer, who appeared to recognise the need to explain Nanny's invulnerability in scientifically acceptable terms, suggested that she might have achieved it by the use of herbs in which she

may have been skilled. By way of comparison he spoke of his boyhood recollections of one "Badja' Harris, whom he recalled having seen stick a knife into himself without coming to any harm. Harris did this, said Downer, when he was "in his liquor" (i.e. intoxicated with rum).

[14] Above, pp. 49-54.

[15] The examination of Cupid by one Bryan Roark mentioned a body of the windward Maroons under the leadership of Adou and referred to Nanny's husband as one who was "a greater man than Adou but never went in their Battles".

[16] Philip Thicknesse who accompanied the party sent to offer peace terms to the windward Maroons in 1739, after the treaty with the leeward Maroons had been signed, was left as a hostage in one of the Maroon towns while the treaty was being negotiated. In his memoirs he described their obeah woman.

[17] A grant of 500 acres of land to "Nanny and the people residing with her".

CHAPTER FOUR

"THE MORE HONOURABLE TO THEM"

Among the descendants of the Maroons now living at Moore Town in Portland the oral tradition concerning the fighting at Nanny Town, is about a great Maroon victory. The story that has been passed down from generation to generation among them is associated with their traditional skill in the art of camouflage. According to this legend,[1] the Maroons were aware of the soldiers' approach and concealed themselves in the bushes. Passing close to the camouflaged Maroons without detecting their presence, the soldiers entered the town and, finding the huts deserted, decided to shelter there for the night.

When the soldiers were asleep, the legend continues, the Maroons threw strips of condia, also known as 'lightening wood', onto the roofs of the huts. As the huts blazed the soldiers rushed out in utter confusion. The Maroons closed in for the attack and the surprised soldiers fled before them, most of them falling over a nearby precipice. Next morning the Maroons found all save one, of those who had fallen over the precipice, dead. The sole survivor, who had broken a leg, fashioned a pen out of 'candar skin', the bark of a kind of palm, and, using his blood as a substitute for ink, wrote a note which he gave to his captors. This note the Maroons affixed to a tree by a path leading to Nanny Town, at a fording of the Rio Grande, where they knew it would be found by the whites.

The account of this battle in Maroon oral tradition is so very different from the account contained in the letters of Colonel Brooks to the acting governor that it seems probable that quite different events were being described.

The capture of Nanny Town in December notwithstanding, a letter written by Aysough on 11 January 1735 to the Lords Commissioners of Trade and Plantations confirmed that the government was proceeding to explore the possibilities of an idea which had originated some time in the previous year with the Lords Commissioners. Ayscough advised that an Officer would be setting out on the following day "to carry in Person Terms of Peace and Freedom to the Rebells". This mission, said the acting governor, was: "agreeable to a proposal recommended by your Lordships to the late Governor Hunter, of capitulating with the Rebellious Negroes, to the End that they may be made Either useful to the Country, or shipped off to some other of his Majesties Dominions" [PRO:CO 137/21, fol. 202].

The mission of Lieutenant Bevil Granvill, the officer who had undertaken to endeavour to contact the rebels, appears to have been rewarded with little success. In a subsequent letter dated 27 February, Ayscough reported: "This Enterprize at present has had no Effect". Since the officer's return, however, a man taken in the woods had reported "that one of their Captains named Goviner, born in the woods, and a very stout fellow, would come in, with all his men, which Consists of about fforty or ffifty, if they Could be pardoned".

'Goviner', or 'Gummor' as his name was transcribed in the Public Record Office copy of a document headed "The Examination of two Negro Men both Named Cudjoe..." taken on 10 February 1735 [PRO:CO 137/21, fol. 206], was reported to have led an independent group of escaped slaves. He found himself caught between pressures from both sides. "Cudjoe and his Gang troubled him very much, and for fear of him and the Backarara [sic] Partys he... could not sitt down in one place but was forced to goe Every day to a New one". Faced with this predicament, he was apparently exploring the possibility of making a separate truce with the whites.

Ayscough reported further:

> I accepted of this offer, and have sent the same Gentleman to Endeavour to find that Captain out, to treat with him, upon the Terms of his pardon and ffreedom; how he was succeeded I have yett no account, as soon as I shall hear from him, shall take the first opportunity to Communicate the Success of this Negotiation to your Lordships [PRO:CO 137/21, fol. 206].

The lieutenant does not appear to have made contact with any of the rebel leaders, and even the hopes of coming to terms with Goviner and his band seem to have evaporated. Possibly the latter made his peace with Cudjoe instead.

In the same letter the acting governor reported that "since their Chief town has been taken from them" the former inhabitants of Nanny Town had "been forced to disperse themselves into severall Bodies". Cupid, an Ibo slave who alleged that he had involuntarily joined the rebels and had, in January 1735, "found means to make his Escape", gave information about two of these bodies.

The larger body Cupid described as "a great party" led by one Adou. Others in this group were "Mr. Orgills Scipio[2] Cesar and Adubal" and also "Nanny and her husband". Nanny's husband, said the informer, "is a greater man than Adou but never went in their Battles". The other body consisted of "about fforty Rebellious Men and a far greater Number of Women & Children". They were "under the Command of Quarentine or some such Name", other leading members being "Coll^o Nedham's Cuffee, Tomboy and Mr Samuel Orgills Apollo and Duko" [PRO:CO 137/21 fol. 203].

Adou's "great party", said the informer, "keeps still to windward Viz. about Edwards, John Brook's, and Hobbeys". But the smaller group had decided "to proceed on their March to John Cuffees Town, somewhere to Leeward". In his letter to the Commissioners dated 27 February 1735 the acting governor stated that this group "consisting of about one hundred and forty men Women and Children, is making the best of their way to the parish of St. Elizabeths, the Leeward part of the Island, to find out some remote place to settle in, or to join John Cuffee, Capt of another Gang of Rebells, that way". Who then was John Cuffee? The name is such a common one that it would be unsafe to identify him positively with the Cuffee subsequently named in clause 15 of Cudjoe's treaty (see below p. 120) as his successor third in line. But his town being in St. Elizabeth, it is more than probable that its inhabitants were subject to Cudjoe's authority.

Referring to this latter group led by Quarentine, the acting governor stated that he had "ordered flying parties ... to intercept them in their way". If these did not succeed in their mission, "another strong party" would pursue them into the place where they were going to settle.

The difficulties encountered by this group of rebels, the privations they suffered, the resourcefulness they showed and their heroic determination not to surrender their freedom no matter the cost, is all recorded in graphic detail in the informer Cupid's examination. They had, he said, "fire arms Macheats and Launces Sufficient as also plantation Tools but very little powder, Some a charge or two but the Major part none at all". They were, Cupid said, entirely dependent upon their enemies for powder and shot; "he never knew of any Supply of ammunition they had but by Robbing plantations and what former parties left them in their flights". But they had no food: "they had along while lived on the wild produce of the woods alone whence they died very fast in their Marches, and within three days killed four of their Men who were so weak with hunger that they Could not keep pace with the rest". On Wednesday 29 January, said the informer, they

> lay ... at John Townsends penn on wagg water three miles up the River from Mrs Mercer's ... they crossed the River ... the next morning in order to fall upon some adjacent plantation for provisions Cloaths and ammunition to Enable them to proceed on their March ... to Leeward, which they could not Do from their Weakness thro Hunger and ffluxes without some relief of provisions in particular.

Travelling across hostile territory with such limited fire power and so desperately short of supplies, they had to take every precaution to avoid detection. Being "so much afraid of being discovered... they filled up or smoothed their tracks when they went over sand or soft Earth". Discipline had to be rigidly enforced, lest anyone should desert and, falling into the hands of the enemy, give them away. When one "Broadgates or Edward's Pompey deserted them" they became so apprehensive of further desertions that "they putt Queen and her two Children to Death being Negroes they Carried away from Edwards's at the same time with Pompey".

Despite all disadvantages this band of rebels proved more than a match for their pursuers, as may be inferred from an entry in the Journal of the Assembly in the following year. The Assembly was then considering a committee recommendation that a man be given a reward.[3] He deserved this, said the committee, as "one of the party that was sent from the parish of Clarendon, under the command of lieutenant Rule, to intercept the body of rebels in their march from windward to leeward". His particular merit was that he had killed two, and that he and his commander: "although their endeavours could not prevail so far as to make them [their soldiers] fight the rebels, yet they were the means of keeping them together, and prevented them from throwing down their arms, which they were inclined to do, which would have supplied the rebels . . ." [*Journals* 3 p. 359].

On 16 April, Ayscough confirmed to the Lords of Trade and Plantations that the Maroons marching from the east had joined the rebels in the west [PRO:CO 137/21]. Presumably they had been accepted by the leeward Maroons under Cudjoe's command.

Meanwhile, on 7 April 1735, the Assembly, which had not been in session since towards the end of the previous year, had reassembled. Justifying the imposition of martial law while the House had been in recess, the acting governor said:

"it has in great measure answered our end, in routing and dislodging them from their strongest hold, and in distressing them so far as to force them to disperse into several bodies, and to seek another part of the country for their refuge and subsistence" [*Journals* 3 p. 286].

Later that year the new governor reported[4] on the westward movement of the leeward Maroons. They are, he wrote, "Settling themselves in some Strong fastness and when that is done, will begin their ravages again, in Such parts of the Island, as may be of more Mischievous Consequences than they have hitherto attempted" [PRO:CO 137/22, fol. 40].

Dallas gave this account of their westward movement:

Cudjoe, finding his haunts accessible to the rangers, who were stationed at the barracks east of him, and the communications of his foraging parties with his old friends in the back parts of Clarendon cut off, resolved to change his position, and to seek a situation of greater security for his quarters, as well as a more extensive field for his operations.

He accordingly removed to a place in Trelawny near the entrance of the great cockpits to the north-west, the first of which, called Petty River Bottom, now well known, was accessible by a very narrow defile. This cockpit was considered a very large one, containing about seven acres of land and a spring of water.

Dallas gave this account of their westward movement:

Cudjoe displayed great judgment in choosing this position, as in case of alarm he could easily throw himself into the cockpit, whence no valour or force could drive him and at the same time he placed the great range of cockpits between him and his former annoyers. The choice of position was equally judicious in respect to predatory incursions; as the parishes of St. James's, Hanover, Westmoreland, and St. Elizabeth's lay open to him and presenting more extensive and less defensible frontiers, affording him opportunities of acting with smaller detachments, and of obtaining abundant supplies from different quarters [Dallas 7 vol. 1 pp. 43-5].

From his new stronghold, wrote Dallas, Cudjoe "sent out parties in various directions to a great distance, in order to deceive the Government, and even kept up an alarm in the neighbourhood of his old position". It was at this time, according to Dallas, that the principal towns of the Maroons in western Jamaica were established: "Cudjoe now augmented the body he had placed under the command of his brother Accompong, and established them on the northern borders of St. Elizabeth ... This station was above the mountains of Nassau, a place where there is still a town called Accompong after his name".

Dallas also gave a good description of the guerrilla tactics developed by the Maroons under Cudjoe's leadership. They did not risk battles in open country but, relying on information from out-scouts of the routes being taken by their attackers, excelled in the laying of ambushes in the mountainous defiles. They would allow the soldiers to "advance towards the mouth of the defile, through the track obscured by trees and underwood, in an approach of many windings ... occasioned by the irregularity of the ground, or designedly made for the purpose of exposing the assailants to the attacks of the different parties in ambush". Having thus got their attackers where they wanted them:

> A favourable opportunity is taken when the enemy is within a few paces to fire upon them from one side. If the party surprised return the fire on the spot where they see the smoke of discharge, and prepare to rush towards it, they receive a volley in another direction. Stopped by this, and undecided which party to pursue, they are staggered by the discharge of a third volley from the entrance of.the defile.
>
> In the meantime the concealed Maroons, fresh and thoroughly acquainted with their ground, vanish almost unseen before their enemies have reloaded. The troops, after losing more men, are under the necessity of retreating: and return to their posts, frequently without shoes to their feet, lame, and for some time unfit for service [Dallas 7 vol. 1 pp. 41-2].

The survival and success of a Maroon community, constantly harrassed by forces superior in numbers and fire-power, depended primarily upon mastery of the tactics of guerrilla warfare and upon the maintenance of supplies of food. But there were other problems of an administrative nature, which bedevilled the Maroon communities. The solution of one such problem among the leeward Maroons, as recorded in James Knight's manuscript history, emphasises the complex requirements of successful leadership.

Cudjoe, "having experienced that the Divisions and Quarrels which happened among themselves were owing to their different Countries and Customs which created jealousies and uneasiness", is said to have decided to enforce the use of English[5] to replace the several different tribal languages [Knight 18; BM:Ad. MS. 12419, fol. 95].

After hearing the acting governor's message on 7 April, the Assembly approved the extension of martial law for a further three months. Among the reports influencing them to this decision was a letter from a gentleman in St. Ann to the effect that "sixty rebellious negroes (forty of them with fire-arms), had attacked the house of one Spencer, in St. Anns, and that several of the settlers in St. James's were deserting that parish" [*Journals* 3 p. 286].

On 20 June, the Assembly was notified that the acting governor had authorised Colonel Philip "to raise men to assist the parish of St. Elizabeth against the rebels in possession of the inland plantation". They decided that those who served "shall be allowed other and further rewards than such as are prescribed and allowed by the barracking act; which shall be paid by the churchwardens of the several parishes" [*Journals* 3 p. 328].

Early in March of the following year, the new governor having died shortly after assuming office, another president of the Council, John Gregory, was under the necessity of acting as governor.

In his address to the new Assembly in March 1736 Gregory said:

> What now gives us most trouble are the rebels; we have been willing to flatter ourselves with some success, but I fear their numbers have been little lessened by it, they begin to be in motion in several places and in considerable bodies, they have lately done mischief, and the remissness and supiness of the inhabitants, in some places, will but too much encourage them, to further attempts, unless some immediate care be taken to prevent them ... [*Journals* 3 p. 330].

The acting governor then advanced the idea that "the mulattoes and free negroes could be made more serviceable". He considered them "the fittest for the woods" and pointed out that they would be cheaper than the white mercenaries. He felt that:

they might be encouraged to do their duty, if they were put under some proper establishment, formed into companies, and allowed a moderate and regular pay; these being thus made useful, and the barracks completed and garrisoned by soldiers, would... efectually secure us against intestine enemies at an easier expence, and a much more equal and expeditious way than by raising parties.

On 26 March the acting governor sent a further message to the Assembly:

It having been experienced that the methods hitherto taken for the reduction of the negroes in rebellion are ineffectual... and that an entire Confidence is not to be reposed in the most trusty negroes, many of them having gone over to and joined the rebels, and others having proved deceitful and treacherous in other respects, it is therefore proposed, to encourage the bringing over 200 of the Chickesaw or Creek Indians, who inhabit the inland part of North America, on the back of South Carolina and Georgia [*Journals* 3 p. 339].

It was proposed, he said, to pay these Indians "£10 per head for every rebellious negro they kill or take alive".

The Assembly, surprisingly, pursued this proposal, though nothing came of it eventually. Perhaps few of the members remembered that, some 16 years earlier, the hopes the establishment had placed in Amerindian mercenaries imported from the Mosquito coast had proved illusory.

In 1736 the idea of reaching an agreement with the rebels was revived. On 2 April, a report submitted by committees of the Assembly and the Council sitting jointly was approved by the Assembly. It read: "Resolved, it is the opinion of both committees that it will be dangerous to enter into any treaty with the slaves in rebellion, and may be a motive to encourage the slaves in the plantations to join them, in hopes of obtaining their freedom by the same means".

The Committee were, however, of the opinion that:

such of the slaves in rebellion that have been born in the woods, or such as have been runaway before the 2d April 1731, as shall voluntarily surrender themselves, may be entitled to his majesty's pardon, and shall have their freedoms, with lands to settle, and further encouragement, when they shall conform themselves to the laws of this country [*Journals* 3 p. 344].

If by these terms the establishment had hoped to effect a division between those rebels who had been out prior to April 1731 and those who had joined them subsequently, the plan did not succeed. The terms of surrender offered attracted no takers, and the planters had to think again. As the year 1736 drew to a close they had to admit that they were no nearer to a solution of their difficulties.

The Assembly was generous in its rewards to those party leaders who were able to report successes. On 7 May 1736 they accepted the recommendation of their committee that two officers who had led parties be rewarded. Of one, Captain Thomas Dwarris, it was said that he "did take great pains, and act with a great deal of ... tion[6] and good conduct, in discovering and destroying a formidable rebel town in the parish of St. George ..." [*Journals* 3 p. 359]. Of the other, Captain Daniel Doyley, the committee reported that he had "been instrumental as commander of parties, in killing and taking six rebellious negroes, besides two which he avers were killed, but carried away by the height and rapidness of a river wherein they were shot, near Edward's Fort, in the parish of St. George."

The leader of the last mentioned party, Captain Daniel Doyley, was not quite so fortunate on a subsequent outing. In July 1738, while considering a petition from his widow, the Assembly were reminded that he had led an attack on the rebels at "Smiths estate .... this expedition of Mr. Doyley's being so notoriouly known as that he unfortunately lost his life in it". The Assembly voted the widow a pension of £20 per year during widowhood and a further £30 per year for their son until the age of twenty-one [*Journals* 3 p. 450].

In their address "to the King's most Excellent Majesty" on 23 November 1736 the Assembly were as pessimistic as ever: "The slaves in rebellion, which have already cost this island so many lives, and put us to such vast expence, do still continue as insolent, troublesome, and, we have reason to believe, as numerous as ever, although our utmost efforts have not been wanting to reduce them" [*Journals* 3 p. 395].

Early in the New Year, however, the acting governor was able to give the Assembly some encouraging news received by letter.[7] A young woman, "who had some years past been taken by the rebels at Barbados-Valley", had voluntarily given herself up. It appeared that she "had been wife to one Cudjoe, a rebel captain, had deserted the rebels, and had come in and given information of the numbers and settlements, and offered to be a guide to any party to be sent after them" [*Journals* 3 p. 404].

Who was this young Delilah's husband? Had she been wife to Cudjoe, the chief of the leeward Maroons? Or had her husband been some subordinate leader, lower down in the rebel chain of command, who had the same name. The name Kojo was, as we have seen, a common one.[8] But whatever the truth may be, the young woman's defection was obviously of considerable importance to the Assembly who: "Resolved that a clause be inserted in some bill for the making the said negro woman free, and for payment of 40 L. to her proprietors for her freedom" [ibid]: And there, so far as the written record goes, the story ends. But have we heard the last of it? The theme that Hell has no fury like a woman scorned is an attractive one on which some enterprising historical novelist, seeking West Indian material on which to build, may yet construct an interesting tale!

A passage in the acting governor's address to the Assembly, when it reassembled on 21 June 1737, referred to "the return of some of the rebels to windward". This would appear to be a reference to a return journey to the eastern parts of the island made by some of the windward Maroons who, after the loss of Nanny Town in December 1734, had made that remarkable journey across the country with St. Elizabeth as their objective. Afraid that they would "again grow troublesome" the acting governor said: "I know of but two ways of dealing with an enemy, either by force, or treaty; the first we have often unsuccessfully tried" [*Journals* 3 p. 410]. The Assembly, however, did not take up the suggestion.

The writer of the letter to James Knight previously referred to suggested that the reason why these Maroons made this perilous return journey was that Cudjoe had been less than cordial in welcoming them when they had first arrived. Cudjoe is alleged by this unknown writer to have been unwilling to give them more than a temporary refuge in his domains [BM: Ad.MS. 12431]. How reliable this is it is difficult to assess. A possible reason for their decision to return to Portland could have been the news that after 1736 the garrison at the site of the old Nanny Town had not been maintained. Indeed Cudjoe may well have dispatched them with the expectation of reoccupying the area.

Be that as it may, James Knight gave this account of their subsequent movements: "Upon their return to the windward or Eastward part of the island, They made a settlement on the Mountains in St. Georges, where they remained undiscovered and contented Themselves with their Circumstances, rather than give any further umbrage or uneasiness to White People by their Excursions or Depradations" [Knight 18; BM:Ad.MS. 12419, fol. 97].

The minutes of the meeting of the Assembly held on 7 July 1737, contained an interesting item. It was reported:

> that Job Williams, of St. Ann's had refused refreshments to a party from the barracks at Cave River, in Clarendon, on their return from the woods, and when in great distress, declaring that the rebels never hurted him, and that he would not relieve any party sent in pursuit of them, at the same time using opprobious words, and abusing the inhabitants of Clarendon, to the great discouragement of the party and the obstruction of so necessary a work as the reduction of the rebels [*Journals* 3 p. 416].

From this it would appear that not all white settlers were in favour of waging war against the escaped slaves. Job Williams, no doubt a small farmer rather than a plantation owner, had apparently worked out, with the rebels operating in his neck of the woods, a means of peaceful co-existence. Perhaps there are conclusions to be drawn from this.

The conflict between the black slaves and their white masters was at once economic and political — a class struggle and a struggle for self determination. The rebels fought to end their exploitation as labourers on the plantations. They fought also, as persons excluded from civil rights, for the right to govern themselves. Job Williams' experience would seem to suggest that although, to all appearances, this was a struggle between black and white, the blacks were not unwilling, within the society they sought to create, to concede a place to those whites who aspired neither to exploit nor rule them.

There were, however, in 18th century Jamaica few whites who would have been willing to see their privileged position within the community reduced to a status of equality with the blacks. And if and when such a white man was discovered in their midst, the slave owning establishment considered his lack of racial solidarity, with the majority of those of his own colour, unforgivable. Not surprisingly therefore, when the Assembly heard the sentiments expressed by Job Williams, they "Ordered, that, for the same, he be taken into the custody of the messenger; and that Mr. Speaker sign a warrant for that purpose" [*Journals* 3 p. 416].

In 1737 the idea of trying to make peace with the Maroons was once again revived. The Maroons at Accompong have an oral tradition of how their ancestors successfully ambushed a military force, near a place called Peace Cave. When this event occurred it is difficult to say, unless the name of the place suggests some association with a peace initiative, or perhaps a place where a peace initiative subsequently took place.

According to this legend,[9] the Maroons prepared an ambush for a body of soldiers advancing to attack them. In their advance the soldiers had to pass across the mouth of this cave where there was a large flat stone. The Maroons placed a scout within the cave where he could hear the echo of the footsteps as the soldiers trod on the stone. When the echoes ceased the scout knew that the last man had entered the trap and emerged from the cave to sound the signal for the attack on his 'aketty'.[10] Entirely surrounded, all the soldiers were killed.

In or about the middle of 1737 Colonel John Guthrie, in command of the military forces to leeward, had been authorised by the acting governor to explore the possibility of making peace with Maroons. He was to continue the attempt to locate and destroy Cudjoe's principal settlement while at the same time making contact to ascertain the latter's reactions to the idea of a treaty. On 20 August 1737 Guthrie wrote to the acting governor:[11]

> I am confident Your Honour expected to have heard of the Marching of a Considerable Partie in quest of Cudjoe's Town, but when Wee had favourable Weather for that purpose there was Some hopes that Capt. Foster would Succeed in this designed Treaty to the Rebells but as wee are now W'out any hopes from him on that Account, As soon as the Season will addmitt of it, I doubt not but that with Some assistance from Coll. Blake, and good guides, to be able to raise such a Partie As will give a good Account of themselves, if fortune Should favour them Wt a sight of the Rebells.
>
> There is now a Partie out consisting of thirty six Shott Commanded by Lieut. Chambers, It is chiefly intended to make Some useful discovery ...

As if to ensure that there could be no misunderstanding, Guthrie then proceeded to spell out his instructions:

> To those I have allreadie Sent Out I gave Such instructions As I, to the best of my Memorie, receiv'd virabally from your Honour ...
>
> If you come up to the Settlements of any Negroes in Rebellion, you are if possible to take One or More Alive, and when taken to Use them kindly, but in such Manner As they shall be well Secured in Your return.
>
> If you come to have Speech of Any Negroes more especially those under the Command of Cudjoe, offer them in His Honour the President's Name terms of Accommodation, and propose a time, And place to treat of the Said terms the time not to be less than 10 or 12 dayes.
>
> If you come up to Any Town belonging to Cudjoe, On his offering to treat You are not to burn or distroy Such Town, or Suffer the Same to be plundered, that thereby you may give the Rebells, a Testimony of his Honours good intentions touching the Said Treaty ..
>
> yr. Honours most Obedient Servt.
>
> Aug: 20th 1737   John Guthrie
>   [BM: Ad. MS. 12431, Plut. CXIV.H].

Interestingly enough, the acting governor did not mention these instructions given to Colonel Guthrie in his messages to the Assembly at this time, but in view of the rejection of the idea of a treaty by both the Council and the Assembly in the previous year, it is unlikely that John Gregory would have taken this initiative without the knowledge and approval of at least the most influential members of each House. In the period of nearly a year since the matter had last been discussed in the legislature, the suspicion had no doubt grown almost to a certainty that the Maroons could not be defeated. However, nothing appears to have come of Guthrie's attempts to establish a liaison at this time and hostilities continued.

In the following year Edward Trelawny was sent to Jamaica as governor. In some quarters there may have been renewed hopes that under his leadership the armed forces would succeed in crushing the Maroons. Dallas gave this summary of the situation:

> Eight or nine years had now elapsed, since Cudjoe's renown had united all the fugitive Negroes in the island, of whatever origin they were, in a general interest... Force after force had been employed to subdue them in vain... At length the colonists resolved to make every sacrifice, and use every exertion, to put an end to so harrassing a war. All who could carry arms volunteered their services and a large body of persons were assembled under the command of Colonel Guthrie of the Militia and Captain Saddler of the Regulars [7 vol. 1 p. 46].

On 15 June 1738, the new governor told the Assembly in his first address: "I have called you together as soon as it was convenient... not only that I might have the pleasure of meeting you in a body, but because it is necessary to take into your consideration the laws for building barracks, which are now near expiring" [*Journals* 3 p. 438]. These barracks, designed to contain the rebels, had been authorised two years earlier but the building of them had not yet been completed. Why this should have been so was not disclosed, but some reluctance on the part of tradesmen to work in regions frequented by the Maroons would have been understandable.

The new governor also referred to complaints he had received, "from different quarters" since his arrival, "of insults committed by the rebellious negroes". He understood that "They have long infested this country, and still continue to endanger the lives, and damage the fortunes, of many inhabitants". He was aware that "The attempts made to reduce them have been very burthensome to the public", but hoped that the Assembly in its wisdom would "suggest some effectual measures to put a stop, or even an end, to this intestine evil."

Debating the governor's address the Assembly recognised the necessity "that flying parties be sent, and kept out, to pursue and destroy the rebellious negroes". They also expressed their willingness to allow "a number of free negroes, free mulattoes, and free Indians not exceeding one hundred" to be "Raised and detached against the rebellious negroes, under proper encouragement" [*Journals* 3 p. 442].

Before he left England to assume his post Colonel Trelawny had apparently been reading up on Jamaica. From an address in London he had written to the Duke of Newcastle on 30 June 1737: "I am fully persuaded that you will not be of opinion to take a step ... as withdrawing half the forces from thence." In an accompanying memorial he had advised the Secretary of State that "to reduce the number of troops now would be to deliver the island to the blacks. There is nowhere that wants troops more than Jamaica and no place of such importance to this kingdom".

His memorial had warned that:

> The negroes in many of the British plantations have of late been possessed of a dangerous spirit of liberty. They have actually risen in Antigua and have threatened to do it in the rest of the sugar plantations. Should the negroes in subjection in Jamaica fall into the same way of thinking, Jamaica must instantly be lost to the whites if they have not some forces upon whose assistance they can rely ... [CSP 1737 pp. 191-2, no. 379; PRO:CO 137/55, 56].

Perhaps, when he took up office in 1738, Trelawny had hoped that by instilling new vigour into the campaign against the Maroons he could rid the planters of their perennial nightmare. But at the end of that year he was no nearer to achieving a military solution. Indeed, so few had been the successes against the rebels that when Colonel Guthrie reported the killing of one man and the capture of three guns from a party of five in July, the governor ordered that this be reported[12] to the Assembly [*Journals* 3 p. 447].

It appears that at about this time a force of 100 fighting men from the windward Maroons, led by one of their captains, made a second epic journey across the island from east to west to join the ranks of those fighting under Cudjoe's direct command.[13] Whether they made this march on their own initiative or in answer to a call from Cudjoe for reinforcements is unfortunately not recorded.

Meanwhile, according to Dallas:

> There was great apprehension entertained of the uncertainty of the most vigorous measures; the failure of which would not only encourage the enemy and entail a perpetual war upon the island, but might operate on the minds of the slaves, who would be convinced of the power of the Maroons to maintain a successful opposition against the Government. The Governor, Edward Trelawny, was therefore urged by the principal persons of the country to offer them terms of peace [Dallas 7 vol. 1 p. 47].

Trelawny accordingly authorised Guthrie and Saddler along very much the same lines as Guthrie had been instructed in the previous year by the president of the Council. While endeavouring to inflict as much damage as possible upon the rebels, they were to try to contact Cudjoe and, as soon as the opportunity to do so presented itself, offer him a treaty of peace.

Early in the new year Guthrie was able to report that they had made contact with the rebel chief. On 17 February 1739 he wrote to Trelawny:

> It is with some pleasure that I am to Acquaint Your Excellency, that We are now Masters of Cudjoe's Town; We marched Tuesday last from... Montigua Bay, and yesterday morning... We came up to the open Ground where Several Negroes were at work, but being discovered before We could get nigh them there was only a Child killed and a Woman and child taken, this occasioned a General Alarm, on which they retir'd in Considerable Numbers to an Ambush, thro' which We were Unavoidably to pass in our way to this Town:
>
> On our Approach to it the Independents Commanded by Mr Saddler sustained a very great fire, And in Spite of our best Endeavours We were about fifteen minutes before We could gain it, and where one Soldier was killed, and two Wounded. After having passed this first Ambush We came into a Spacious Opening where We halted, and the Town being about a Mile

from us We Resolved to proceed no further that day, but this Morning early We marched to it.

... Resolved to make ourselves Masters of it, We made our way thro' a Strong Ambush, where three more of the Soldiers were wounded, and I am afraid one of them Mortally [Inst. J. Cl. Min/1738].

The Maroons employed their usual guerrilla tactics, abandoning the town to the strong force attacking them, suffering no casualties themselves but from the surrounding bush making the position of their enemies untenable in the open ground. In his journal Captain Saddler wrote:[14] "it being impracticable to maintain the Town on Account of the many Ambushes surrounding it We set it on Fire and March'd back to the Baggage where we halted Yesterday" [ibid].

They stayed about two hours in the town, continued Guthrie: "then burnt it: We are now returned to the Provision Ground where there is great Store of it: tomorrow I propose to destroy what Provisions I can't conveniently guard and next day ... to go about building a Strong House ..."

Anticipating the disappointment of the governor, Council and Assembly at their failure to inflict casualties on the rebels, Guthrie added:

I am Sensible your Excellency will be Surprised, when I mention the Resolution of the ... Gentlemen that composed this party, when We have done so little as to the Affair of taking or killing the Negroes, but if ever your Excellency visits this Town (which now bears your Name) you will not attribute it to any remissness in us.

Emphasising the value of the land which he felt could be permanently wrested from the Maroons if a barracks were established at this place, he continued: "From Montico Bay to this place We judge to be about 18 Miles ... there is land enough to make 70 or 80 large Sugar Works, and the whole exceeding good land" [Cl. Min./1738].

Saddler, however, had reservations on the subject of the proposed 'Strong House'. In his own report to the governor on the same day, after referring to their instructions that if they located the town they should 'garrison' the place and "leave a Party of Soldiers in it", he advised that any barrack would be ineffective "unless it were a Barrack built with Stone and properly Flank'd". He added that: "The Road to the Town from Montico Bay is so... fit for Ambushes... the Baggage will always require an Extraordinary Guard and that subject to be intercepted or cut of with the greatest Ease..." [Cl. Min./1738].

On the most important aspect of their mission, Guthrie appears to have been rather more optimistic than Saddler after their first contact with the Maroon leader. In the same letter to the governor he wrote: "I had a long Conference with Cudjoe this day before We burnt his Town, he seemed inclinable to come to terms, but I cou'd not prevail with him so far as to send one of his people to me, and He and the rest of the Rebells were in places impossible for us to force any Advantage."

Presumably this first exchange took place by the parties shouting to each other from a safe distance. This is how Saddler described the scene: "Cudjoe... was posted in a place not to be attack'd but with the greatest danger... Cudjoe wou'd have no Confidence in the terms propos'd..."

Overnight, however, Cudjoe and his officers appear to have conferred long and earnestly together and to have come to the conclusion, before daybreak, that the possibilities of making peace should be explored. Writing to the governor on 18 February, Guthrie was able to report as follows:

> Since mine to your Excellency of last night We Sustain'd a few Shott from Cudjoe, which brought on a Second Conference with him, now Sir let me Assure you that... it ended in peace. I have had him by the hand, Although by so doing Mr. Saddler and myself run some small risque...
>
> On our First Conference they Offer'd to Assist against any Forreign enemy And to take up for the future, all Runaway Negroes, and I on my part have promised in your Excellency's Name that they shall live Unmolested in this place with all that they now enjoy. It is likewise Stipulated that I shall stay here in a peaceful manner with them for ten days, by which time I hope to receive your Excellency's Commands...
>
> I shall only add that they live in such places as are allmost inaccessible, And to reduce them entirely will certainly cost much Blood and Treasure. I shall with impatience wait your Excellency's pleasure...

Trelawny Town	Your Excellency's Most Dutiful..Servant
Feb: 18th 1738/9	John Guthrie [Cl.Min/1738].

Saddler too wrote to the governor on 18 February, giving more details of the conference:

> We had a second Conference with the Rebells which has produced such an Alteration in regard to our Differences with them as has never before been known in this Island, as we found them Inclinable to Peace ...
>
> One or two of the Rebells ventur'd to show themselves in the Open Ground, and having then Order'd Our Men not to fire Coll. Guthrie and my self met Cap^n Cudjoe Cap^n Coffee and the Cap^n of the Port Antonio Gang (who had not long before joined them with 100 Shott) half way unarmed, where After mutual Civilities passed between us seem'd very well dispos'd to Acknowledge Your Excellency ... to hold a perfect Harmony with the Country and to render themselves as usefull to it as possible by taking up our Runaways and returning them and of their own accord Offer'd to be Assisting ... against the Spaniards or any other Forreign Enemy on Condition that they might have free Possession of this place and be free from Slavery, might not be Disturb'd by Party's and might have a Commerce with us Which we undertook to Answer for, as far as possibly we cou'd presuming it wou'd be agreeable to your Excellency's Pleasure and the good of the Country ... [Cl. Min./1738]. [15]

Replying to Guthrie's letter on 12 February,[16] the governor proposed that freedom be limited to Cudjoe and "those that were born in the woods". Naively he added: "I cannot yet resolve to allow liberty to those that have fled from Masters: all I can as yet think proper to promise them is, that they shall be treated with humanity". Foreseeing that some of the rebels might have "an objection to their returning to their Masters", he thought that those who did "might be employ'd as slaves in the publick service". He thought that the negotiators would "have a difficulty in managing that point" and advised that "it must be handled very tenderly" [Cl. Min./1738].

Meeting on the following day the Council adopted a more realistic attitude. Tactfully including in their instructions a modified version of the governor's suggestion, they nevertheless made it clear, on reading between the lines, that it was not necessary to take it too seriously. They resolved: "that the said John Guthrie and Francis Saddler be instructed to hint to the said Rebels in the most tender manner an

Article in relation to the giving up those Negroes to their Masters who have not been in The Woods above two years..."[17]

But their resolution made it clear that if the negotiators could not "obtain all or any of these points that they make a Treaty with them notwithstanding upon the best Terms they can..." The negotiators were further assured that "if any other matter not mentioned should occur to them which they think advantageous...They may be empowered to negotiate the same" [Cl. Min./1738].

Armed with this authority Guthrie and Saddler concluded their negotiations with Cudjoe on 1 March 1739. The terms were drawn up in writing and signed by the two officers on behalf of the Crown and by Cudjoe, by making his mark, on behalf of the Maroons. Maroon tradition has it that the signatories also took a solemn oath "in the Cromanti fashion", by the mingling of their blood. The full text of the treaty is given in the next chapter.

Writing to John Gregory, president of the Council, on 21 February, Guthrie showed his emotion:[18] "It was y^o Sir that first put a Sword in my hand to fight the Rebells, and also the Scheme in my head to treat with them; I own I have done little as to the former, but as to the latter, I must be so vain to Say, that I have gone a great length..." [BM: Ad. MS. 12431].

Whilst making no direct reference to the mingling of blood in the solemnisation of the treaty, a ritual which would no doubt have been regarded as too barbaric for the king's representative to have indulged in, Guthrie said enough to lend some credence to Maroon oral tradition: "Before I could Bring it to Bear in any Respect I was obliged to tye myself up, by a Solemn Oath, not to fight against them, until he [Cudjoe] should Infringe the same..."

Guthrie's testimonial concerning the Maroon leader suggests a man of impressive personality. He had, he said, found:

Cudjoe... to be a person of much Humanity & I re.....Believe will

> punctually observed on his par[19] those terms of Peace that he Submitts, hiself to, As to his Captains, they pay him the greatest Defference imaginable, they are entirely under his Subjection, and his Word is a Law to them [BM: Ads. MS. 12431].

On 13 March Trelawny reported the ending of hostilities and the conclusion of the treaty to the Assembly, but he was less than frank as to who had taken the initiative in suing for peace. The prestige of the British Raj was no doubt at stake. The governor could not bring himself to an admission in writing that a few hundred blacks, armed with little more than the weapons they could wrest from their oppressors, had for a decade successfully withstood every attempt, by many times their number of well armed troops, to suppress them.

Under Governor Trelawny's facile pen what should have been an admission of failure was elevated into an achievement of victory and a display of magnanimity:

> A party of the militia ... with a detachment of soldiers ... having drove the rebellious negroes, that were situated in the leeward parts of the island, out of their town, and obliged them to sue for terms, I empowered those gentlemen to grant them such as should be reasonable, and for the welfare and tranquility of this island ... [*Journals* 3 p. 457ff].

It has proved difficult to determine the actual numbers of the leeward Maroons. In April 1739 a Committee of the Assembly reported that the number of men in Cudjoe's band was 231, which information they attributed to Cudjoe himself [*Journals* 3 p. 470]. But there may have been a misunderstanding here as Cudjoe's figure may have included only those of Cudjoe's town and may not have included the males at Accompong's town who were also under Cudjoe's command. The full complement of Cudjoe's guerrilla army may have been nearer 500. Certainly the figure given to the Committee excluded the 100 fighting men from the windward Maroons who were with Cudjoe when the Treaty was concluded. No count was made of the women and children but the Committee believed they were "in proportion to the men".

While Guthrie had been pursuing his instructions to

contact and negotiate terms of peace with the Maroons in the west of the island, it would appear that a parallel attempt was being made to reach an accommodation with those in the north-east. Information concerning this is contained in the *Memoirs and Anecdotes of Philip Thicknesse* [32]. Thicknesse was a regular army officer who accompanied the expedition as second in command. He alleged that the expedition was dispatched after the treaty with the leeward Maroons had been concluded. But Thicknesse did not write the introduction to his memoirs until 25 December 1788, nearly 50 years after the event, and his recollection as to the date of this expedition may have been incorrect.

The task of extending peace feelers to the windward Maroons had been given to Lieutenant George Concannen, the officer in command of a detachment of regular soldiers operating against them from "a place called *Hobbie's*, five miles from the sea, in the parish of St. George's". Concannen's regulars had been "reinforced with a Lieutenant and fifty militia men, *black* and *white shot*, as they were termed, and seventy baggage Negroes". Lieutenant Philip Thicknesse was transferred from duty at Port Maria to join him [Thicknesse 32 pp. 56-65].

If indeed the Concannen expedition had occurred after the peace treaty with the leeward Maroons, it seems obvious that the first thing the commanding officer would have been expected to do, on locating a group of the windward Maroons, would have been to inform them of this treaty. Concannen, however, immediately moved to the attack and, finding a number of huts, burned them. This, surely, would have been a serious violation of his instructions and disciplinary action would have been expected to follow. If, however, the expedition had preceded the treaty with Cudjoe, then Concannen's conduct would have been consistent with the instructions under which Guthrie was proceeding in the west — a policy of attempting to locate and destroy the Maroon settlements while at the same time making contact to ascertain their reactions to the idea of a treaty.[20]

For these reasons, and also because of certain difficulties which would follow from an acceptance of the statement that Cudjoe's treaty preceded the Concannen expedition (such as the difficulty of fitting into the period of less than four months between the known dates of the two treaties the events described by Thicknesse, bearing in mind that he stated that three months elapsed between the two expeditions he described), the author is inclined to the view that the first expedition here described preceded the peace treaty with Cudjoe.

Concannen's orders, wrote Thicknesse, were "to march up a certain river-course, till we discovered a wild negroe town, supposed by good information, to be upon its margin, or very near it". After "two or three days march from Hobby's, towards the sun setting", they came to a spot on which "the impression of human feet, *of all ages*, were very thick upon the sands, as well as dogs". Convinced that they were very near their quarry, they decided to "lie quietly all night" and make their attack at dawn.

"Before the sun appeared", wrote Thicknesse, "we perceived the smoak of their little Hamlet, for the Negroes, always have a fire burning in their huts to drive away the *musquitoes*: we therefore flattered ourselves, that we might take even them, napping". Commenting on the customary guerrilla tactics of the Maroons, he added: "if those people, ever stand their ground, it is upon such, as is almost inaccessible by white men, and the first notice of their attack, is a heavy fire, from invisible hands!"

Thicknesse explained that "the little Hamlet" of 74 huts "was not a principal town, but a temporary *fishing* and *hunting villa*, . . . accessible every way, and consequently not tenable". And the soldiers soon realised that their hopes of catching the Maroons unawares had been frustrated. The latter had "discovered our approach" and "were gone off in the night, or perhaps but a few minutes before we entered their town". This they concluded from the fact that in each hut a fire was burning but there was no living creature in any of them.

Their quarry having escaped, Concannen held a parley with his officers. Thicknesse noted:

> Mr Concannen, thought it then became his duty, to communicate to us the orders he had received, in the governor's name, from Captain James Adair ... I do not know what Mr Concannen's *own opinion was*, but he adopted ours... and that was to burn the town, and pursue the enemy; both which, we instantly put into execution.

In withdrawing from the indefensible open site of the hamlet the Maroons, who could easily have outdistanced their pursuers, retreated slowly enough to give the soldiers every hope of catching up with them, moving towards an area where the ground was more suitable for their system of warfare. Unaware that they were being lured into an ambush, the troops followed in hot pursuit. Thicknesse described the chase:

> We followed the very track, which the Negroes had, in some measure made passable, by cutting the bushes before us. At every half mile, we found Cocoes, Yams, Plantains, Ec. left artfully by the Negroes, to induce us to believe, they were in fear of our overtaking them, and at length we found a fire before which they had *left* several grills of wild hog... we continued the pursuit, till near night, and then, hearing their dogs bark, we gave over all hopes of seeing or hearing any more of them.

At this point Concannen decided to abandon the chase: "we had marched with great expedition, the whole day, and were much fatigued, but soon after we got upon, the margin of *Spanish River*, where we intended to enjoy ourselves, and rest that night, and the next morning, to follow the Stream, to the sea side, in order to find our way back to Hobbies":

The soldiers had of necessity been marching in single file, their column being about one mile long. The vanguard consisted of a sergeant with a party of "twelve *black* and *white* shot". Concannen marched immediately behind the vanguard and Thicknesse, as second in command, had up to this point brought up the rear. But now, wrote Thicknesse, "as all idea of service was over, I desired Mr Concannen to permit the militia Lieutenant to bring up the rear, that I might have the pleasure of his company, and conversation, on our way down to the sea side". This was agreed and Thicknesse took his place behind Concannen in the line.

Events then began to move to a dramatic climax, as Thicknesse recorded:

> The Negroes, some of whom, had been in our rear, all the preceding day, and others before us, had placed themselves, from top to bottom, on a very steep mountain, thickly covered with trees and bushes; on the other side of the river, under which, they knew we must pass, as the water was too deep on our side, and as that mountain was not an hundred and fifty yards from the spot, on which we had slept, they had an opportunity of knowing our numbers, and seeing which of us, were the *Grande-men*[21] for as to external dress, we were all very much alike, in course jackets and trowser.

Quite unaware of the presence of the Maroons, the soldiers started their leisurely march along the river course towards the sea: "The Negroes . . . permitted the advanced sergeant, and his party, to pass unnoticed, but the minute us *Grande-men* got under their ambush, a volley shot came down, several of the soldiers . . . were mortally wounded, and the drummer at our elbows, was shot through the wrist".

Thicknesse noted that: "at this instant, the baggage Negroes (seventy) who had just got their loads upon their heads, threw them down, and ran away; and the militia, to a man, their officer excepted, . . . followed them. The wild Negroes at the same time, firing and calling out, *Becara*[22] run away . . ."

As for the officers and the remaining regular soldiers, Thicknesse wrote: "it is probable too, that we should have followed, but fortunately, there were some large masses of the mountain which had caved down, and which lay in the middle of the stream, just under the foot of the ambush, and we took shelter behind them".

But "though we could hear the Negroes and converse with them", Thicknesse noted, "not one was to be seen!" There had been about thirty regulars, he wrote, but now "we were not above sixteen or seventeen behind the rocks". "Nor was it in our power", he added, "to restrain that handful of men we had, from firing at the *smoak only*, of our enemies, till they had not a single cartridge left!" To make matters worse, "the Surgeons instruments, and all the spare ammunition, with the provisions, Ec. was cast down in the river..."

Further describing their perilous situation Thicknesse wrote:

> to say the truth, we durst not run away, for the Negroes, only fired, when they could see a head, or an arm of any of our people, above the rocks, and there we staid, more out of fear, than from any hopes of victory, up to our waists in water for four hours and a half, with a burning sun upon our heads, and in momentary apprehensions, of being all *taken alive*, for I believe *that fear* overcame the fear of immediate death, I own it was so with me.

For a time it seemed that, so long as they remained behind the rocks, the soldiers were sheltered from their adversaries across the river. "At length, however," wrote Thicknesse:

> one of our men, was shot through the knee! it was impossible that he could have been so wounded from the ambush side, and therefore we naturally, and fearfully too, concluded the Negroes had crossed the river, either above or below us, and that they would instantly push in upon us, and take us alive...

Faced with this new threat of encirclement, wrote Thicknesse:

> we... quit our place of shelter and... put the best face we could upon our enemy, on the other side, with *presented but unloaded arms*, for Mr. Concannen, myself and the surgeon only, had a few spare cartridges, we accordingly hastily passed over the river, which was not forty yards, from the thicket, and was as thickly bespattered on our retreat, as by their first salutation.

Some of the men sheltering behind the rocks were so badly wounded that Thicknesse believed that they "perhaps never intended to move from the stones... on which they were reposing for death". But when they saw their colleagues crossing to the other bank they too, "defying their wounds, their agonies, and their miseries, jumped up and followed". One man "who had been shot through the body, at the first fire, received another bullet in at his back, and out at his belly, and yet not only went over, but actually clambered up a steep mountain". There he begged to be put out of his misery.

As they made their escape over the mountain the survivors from the river were joined by the militia lieutenant. When his men ran away, Thicknesse noted, "he had concealed himself behind a tree, for what else could he do?" They climbed, he added:

as fast as crippled, fatigued and for myself, I will add, frightened men could ascend . . . we heard the horrid shouts, drums and rejoicings of our victorious enemies — in the river below; not only rejoicing over our salt beef, bread, hams Ec. Ec. but bearing as we afterwards found, the heads of our dead men in triumph.

The subsequent conclusion of the treaty with the leeward Maroons was of course followed by another attempt to reach an accommodation with the windward Maroons. But on this occasion there could be no question of first trying to get the better of them. The obviously sensible approach was to acquaint them of the treaty signed by Cudjoe and to seek the latter's help in persuading them of the desirability of adopting a similar course. In the event a second treaty was concluded with the windward Maroons, or a substantial part of them under the leadership of Quao, just under four months later.

James Knight, in his manuscript history, gave a brief and uncomplicated account of how the treaty with Quao came to be concluded:

A treaty being thus happily concluded with the leeward Rebells... it was considered what measures were proper to be taken to induce the other Gang in St. Georges who were more Considerable in Number, to accept of the same Conditions or to reduce Them by Force, and Coll. Guthery who had succeeded so well in the last Expedition was thought the properest person to Conduct the same. But it was with some reluctance He accepted of this Commission, because those Rebells were seated in a distant part of the Country, which He was not acquainted with... Lt. Coll. Bennett of St. Katherine was appointed to command under Him [Knight 18 pp. 67-8].

The government's peace mission was made easier, said Knight, by the assistance received from Cudjoe:

Captain Cudjoe being obliged by the Treaty to Engage them to Accept of the Terms and Conditions which were granted to Him and His followers, or to assist in reducing Them, sent one of His Brothers, who is a Captain with fifty men for that purpose. And, some others of Their Chief men were prevailed with to go with Coll Guthery as Guides, and to be Sent with proposals to the Rebells.

Guthrie, however, never reached his destination. The day after he left Spanish Town he was "seized with a gripping pain in His bowells".[23] He continued on his journey, but his illness "bafled all the Endeavours that were used for His Relief". In three or four days he was dead. In the meanwhile he had:

> sent out some of Capt. Cudjoes men, who were acquainted with the Rebells, and where they were settled, to acquaint them with the Terms They had Accepted of, and to invite Them to Submit on the same Conditions. They at the same time assured Them of Strict Justice, and a punctuall Compliance with the Articles.

These assurances from the leeward Maroons appear to have overcome the suspicions of those to windward whom they had contacted because, according to Knight's [18] version of the treaty making, "some of Their Chiefs came down to Lt. Coll. Bennett on whom the Command devolved". On 23 June 1739 the terms of a treaty were negotiated between Quao for the Maroons and Bennett.

Philip Thicknesse, who actually accompanied the peace makers, wrote a somewhat different account of how the treaty with Quao was concluded. This is how he told the story in his memoirs, written nearly 50 years after the event:

> About three months after this unfortunate *run-away* business in Spanish river,[24] Governor Trelawny... honoured me with a *second tryal,* for I was again ordered out with a party of three hundred regular troops, under the command of Captain Adair, we were in possession of a prisoner, one of Captain Quoha's people, and he too was one of their *hornsmen,* and undertook to lead us to their principal town... [Thicknesse 32 pp. 69-74].

Thicknesse was of opinion that there could not at that time have been any direct contact between the leeward and windward Maroons. In this he is unlikely to have been correct. Mention has already been made of the presence with Cudjoe at the time of his negotiations with Guthrie and Saddler of the captain of "the Port Antonio Gang" who, according to Saddler, "had not long before joined them with 100 Shott".[25] If a force of 100 Maroons could make the journey from east to west, there is no reason to suppose that the two groups would have had any difficulty in maintaining communications.

Be this as it may, the purpose of Adair's mission, Thicknesse stated, was to acquaint Quao with the fact "that the western gang had laid down their arms, and were in possession of that for which they contended; LIBERTY". Thicknesse alleged that there had in fact been an earlier emissary, upon whom, possibly in jest, he bestowed the picturesque title of "laird of Leharets". But 'the laird' had been suspected of planning to take their town and had been put to death.

In a conversation subsequently with Quao, Thicknesse enquired about the fate of this man, recording the reply he received:

> Quoha told me, he had put bracelets upon his wrists and determined to have sent him down to Governor Trelawney, with offers of submission upon the same terms, the *laird* had assured him, Cudjoe had accepted; but said Quoha, when I consulted our Obea woman, she opposed the measure, and said, *him bring becara for take* the town, so cut him head off.

The obeah woman referred to may or may not have been the famous Nanny.[26] Thicknesse described Quao's obeah woman as an "old Hagg" wearing "a girdle round her waste, with (I speak within compass) nine or ten different knives hanging in sheaths to it", but he did not give her name. If, indeed, Nanny was a resident of this town at the time, there can be little doubt that the reference was to her.[27]

As the party marched towards its destination the Maroon guide warned that any attempt to take the town by force would fail: "No BODY of men, or scarce an individual could approach that they would not have five or six hours notice, by their ... out centinels". The only accessible approach "was up a very narrow path", over-looking which "holes were cut, from place to place, about four foot deep, all the way up ... with crutch sticks set before them, for the entrenched Negroes, to rest their guns upon ..."

The hornsman-guide explained that two men were allocated to each hole. When the first man had fired his musket his place was taken by his partner whose gun was ready loaded. While he was selecting his target the first man reloaded. As the attacking soldiers could approach only in single file, each man would come under fire as the man before him fell.

"After two or three days fatiguing march", wrote Thicknesse, "the *hornsman*, conducted us to the foot of a very steep and high mountain, where we found in the vale beneath, a plantation of yams, plantanes, Ec." Satisfied "that force of arms would not do", Captain Adair "ordered the *hornsman* to sound his horn, thereby letting the Maroons know that he was with the expedition. Thereupon the Maroons returned the salute "but all this while, not a man of them was to be seen!"

Thicknesse recorded the opening of the negotiations: "we then hailed them with a trumpet, and told them we were come to agree, not to fight; that the governor had given Cudjoes people freedom, and that the same terms were open to them". After a long 'trumpet parle' the Maroons agreed to an exchange of hostages "in order to settle preliminaries". This being agreed wrote Thicknesse, "to our utter astonishment, we saw in an instant an acre of under wood cut down, and that acre covered with Negroes! every man having cut down a bush at one blow in the twinkling of an eye!" Being one of the hostages exchanged, Thicknesse recorded: "I took up my abode at Captain Quoha's habitation". He described his host as one who "had been a plantation slave" and "knew something of the customs, and manners, of the white people". He "spoke tolerable good English, and seemed a reasonable man" [32 pp. 75-6].

When terms had been agreed the soldiers, or possibly only some of them, were allowed to enter the town. Scrambling up the narrow path they "found at proper distances, the holes and crutches exactly as described by the *hornsman*". Nearer to the town the path widened to permit two men to walk abreast.

According to Thicknesse, when the terms had already

"THE MORE HONOURABLE TO THEM"

been settled a 'large party' of the militia arrived on the scene under the command of Colonel Robert Bennett. Being "of senior rank to Adair", Bennett "insisted . . . that the terms of peace should be sent down in his not Captain Adair's name". This dispute "between us regulars, and the militia officers", wrote Thicknesse, "arose to such a height, that Adair had put us all under arms, and if the militia colonel had not submitted, I verily believe we should have come to blows" [32 pp. 74-5].

This story of the clash between the regulars and the militia is unlikely to have been entirely a malicious invention. But on at least one point Thicknesse's memory played him false. The treaty, as it stands in the minutes of the Assembly, purports to have borne Bennett's seal and signature, not Adair's. The conflict between the two parties was so serious however that Thicknesse felt that, but for Quao's knowledge of the ways of the whites, "all had been lost". In the event, the Maroon leader probably viewed the proceedings with considerable amusement!

The treaties signed by Cudjoe on 1 March and Quao on 23 June 1739 brought the First Maroon War to a close. The peace ended a decade of fighting in which the establishment had attempted, on a countrywide scale, to eliminate the communities of escaped slaves, and the latter and their descendants had co-ordinated their resistance and successfully defended their hard won freedom.[28]

The planter-historian Edward Long, despite his strong prejudices, gave a generous assessment of their achievement. He described the event as:

> the tedious and expensive war, carried on for many years, with a contemptible gang of Negroes... who kept possession of these recesses, and held out against forty times their number though unsupported during the time with any fresh supply of arms or ammunition, except what were sold to them by the Jews; and at length were able to put an end to the struggle by a treaty of peace, the more honourable, to them, as it confirmed the full enjoyment of that freedom for which they had so long and obstinately contended [24 vol. 1 p. 124].

FOOTNOTES

[1] This account was given to the author, when he visited Moore Town in 1944, by Maroon captains Crawford and Downer and a senior resident Joseph Ellis.

[2] This is the same Scipio who, according to Sarra (above p. 63), had been placed in over-all command of the warriors who had ambushed the expedition against the windward Maroons in August 1733.

[3] Report of the Committee to enquire into the behaviour of John Tingley, 7 May 1736.

[4] Henry Cunningham to Lords Comm. of Tr. and Plantations.

[5] In this context "English" obviously meant the vernacular spoken by the creole slaves. But Dallas (1803) stated that: "The Coromantee language... superseded the others, and became in time the general one in use" [7 vol. 1 pp. 32-3].

As has been mentioned (above p. 8) there was no Kromanti or Coromantee language in Africa. If, however, a language so called did develop in the Maroon communities in Jamaica, the probability is that it was a synthesis of the Akan languages and other African languages. Such a language, understandable to all members of the community, would not have had the divisive effect of the separate tribal languages that Cudjoe had wished to avoid.

[6] The first syllable is obliterated.

[7] Letter from Colonel Blake to the President of the Council, 29 January 1737, reported to the Assembly 10 February 1737.

[8] See above p. 9-11 where the day names of the Akan languages group are discussed.

[9] This legend was told to the author at Accompong in 1943. The oldest Maroon present, known as Commander Reid, insisted that the 'aketty' or horn on which the signal was given was a deer horn. If so, then this must have been a rare possession. A cow's horn would certainly have been easier to obtain.

[10] The distinction between the 'aketty' and the 'abeng' is obscure. The latter may have been the call sounded on the former. Conceivably 'abeng' could be derived from the imperative 'venga' of the spanish verb 'venir' — to come. Colloquially, in Cuba, this is often pronounced 'benga' or sometimes simply 'beng'. But D. L. Schafer [27] says that the word abeng is Akan.

[11] Colonel John Guthrie to Gregory, 20 August 1737, preserved with miscellaneous papers relating to Jamaica [BM: Ad. MS. 12431].

[12] 5 July 1738.

[13] This is the inference to be drawn from the reference in the letter from Captain Saddler to Governor Trelawny dated 18 February 1739 (see below p. 103) to the presence with Cudjoe on that date of "the Cap^n of the Port Antonio Gang (who had not long before joined them with 100 Shott)".

[14] Captain Francis Saddler to Trelawny, 17 February 1739.

[15] "A Journal of the Expedition to Cudjoe Town by L^{tt} Francis Saddler" is also preserved with these Council Minutes.

[16] Trelawny to Guthrie, 23 February 1739.

[17] Minutes of meeting of the Council, 24 February 1739.

[18] Guthrie to Gregory, 21 February 1738/9.

[19] Words or parts of words torn off the original.

[20] Above p. 100.

[21] Officers.

[22] Bacra — white person.

[23] There was some suspicion, as Knight recorded, that he was poisoned by slaves who feared the consequences of an accommodation between the slave owners and the Maroons. More probably he was suffering from appendicitis.

[24] See above pp. 108-10.

[25] Above p. 100.

[26] Above pp. 44, 80-1.

[27] Nanny may have resided in a different Maroon town which may not have been a party to the treaty signed by Quao. In 1741 a grant of 500 acres of land was made to "Nanny and the people residing with her" [J. Arc: Patents 22: 16-17; Kopytoff 19]. This suggests either that Nanny resided in a different town with which separate arrangements were subsequently made, or that she left Quao's town after a disagreement.

[28] A recent trend, initiated by Orlando Patterson [51 vol. XIX no. 3, 289-325] has been to include all the earlier slave rebellions and sporadic attempts to recapture or suppress escaped slaves prior to the peace treaties as within the First Maroon War. The author prefers to reserve this term for the period commencing about 1729, during which the establishment appears to have pursued its suppression activities on an all-island scale and the escaped slaves responded by some degree of co-ordination of their forces.

CHAPTER FIVE

THE BLACK GENDARMES

Cudjoe's treaty is a document of such interest and significance that it repays publication of the entire text:

JAMAICA SS: At the Camp Trelawny-Town, March 1st, 1738-39[1]

In the name of GOD, Amen. Whereas captain Cudjoe, Captain Quaco, and several other negroes, their dependents, and adherents, have been in a state of war and hostility for several years past against our sovereign lord the king, and the inhabitants of this island;

and whereas peace and friendship among mankind, and the preventing the effusion of blood, is agreeable to God, consonant to reason, and desired by every good man;

and whereas his majesty George the second, king of Great Britain, France, and Ireland, and of Jamaica lord, Ec. has, by his letters patent, dated February 24th, 1738[1] in the twelfth year of his reign, granted full power and authority to John Guthrie and Francis Saddler, esquires, to negotiate and finally conclude a treaty of peace and friendship with the aforesaid captain Cudjoe, the rest of his captains, adherents and others his men;

they mutually, sincerely, and amicably, have agreed to the following articles.

1st. That all hostilities shall cease on both sides for ever.

2d. That the said captain Cudjoe, the rest of his captains, adherents and men shall be for ever hereafter in a perfect state of freedom and liberty, excepting those who have been taken by them, or fled to them, within two years last past, if such are willing to return to their said masters and owners, with full pardon and indemnity from their said masters and owners, for what is past; provided always, that if they are not willing to return, they shall remain in subjection to captain Cudjoe, and in friendship with us, according to the form and tenor of this treaty.

3rd. That they shall enjoy and possess, for themselves and posterity for ever, all the lands situate and lying between Trelawny-Town and the Cockpits, to the amount of fifteen hundred acres, bearing north-west from the said Trelawny-Town.

4th. That they shall have liberty to plant the said lands with coffee, cocoa, ginger, tobacco, and cotton, and to breed cattle, hogs, goats, or any other stock, and dispose of the produce or increase of the said commodities to the inhabitants of this island; provided always, that when they bring the said commodities to market, they shall apply first to the Custos, or any other magistrate of the respective parishes where they expose their goods for sale, for a license to vend the same.

5th. That captain Cudjoe, and all the captains adherents, and people now in subjection to him, shall all live together within the bounds of Trelawny-Town, and that they have liberty to hunt where they shall think fit, except within three miles of any settlement, crawl, or pen; provided always, that in case the hunters of captain Cudjoe and those of other settlements meet, then the hogs to be equally divided between both parties.

6th. That the said captain Cudjoe and his successors, do use their best endeavours to take, kill, suppress, or destroy, either by themselves, or jointly with any other number of men commanded on that service by his excellency the governor or commander in chief for the time being, all rebels wheresoever they be throughout the island, unless they submit to the same terms of accommodation granted to captain Cudjoe, and his successors.

7th. That in case this island is invaded by any foreign enemy, the said captain Cudjoe, and his successors herein after named or to be appointed, shall then, upon notice given, immediately to repair to any place the governor for the time being shall appoint, in order to repel the said invaders with his or their utmost force, and to submit to the orders of the commander in chief on that occasion.

8th. That if any white man shall do any manner of injury to captain Cudjoe, his successors, or any of his or their people they shall apply to any commanding officer or magistrate in the neighbourhood for justice; and in case captain Cudjoe, or any of his people, shall do any injury to any white person, he shall submit himself, or deliver up such offenders to justice.

9th. That if any negroes shall hereafter run away from their masters or owners, and fall into captain Cudjoe's hands, they shall immediately be sent back to the chief magistrate of the next parish where they are taken; and those that bring them are to be satisfied for their trouble as the legislature shall appoint.

10th. That all negroes taken since the raising of this party, by captain Cudjoe's people, shall immediately be returned.

11th. That captain Cudjoe, and his successors, shall wait on his excellency, or the commander in chief for the time being, once every year if thereunto required.

12th. That captain Cudjoe, during his life, and the captains succeeding him, shall have full power to inflict any punishment they think proper for crimes committed by their men among themselves, death only excepted; in which case, if the captain thinks they deserve death, he shall be obliged to bring them before any justice of peace, who shall order proceedings on their trial equal to those of other free negroes.

13th. That captain Cudjoe, with his people, shall cut, clean and keep open, large and convenient roads from Trelawny-Town to Westmoreland and St. James's and if possible to St. Elizabeth's.

14th. That two white men, to be nominated by his excellency or the commander in chief for the time being, shall constantly live and reside with captain Cudjoe and his successors, in order to maintain a friendly correspondence with the inhabitants of this island.

15th. That captain Cudjoe shall, during his life, be chief commander in Trelawny-Town; after his decease, the command to devolve on his brother captain Accompong; and, in case of his decease, on his next brother captain Johnny; and failing him, captain Cuffee shall succeed; who is to be succeeded by Captain Quaco and, after all their demises, the governor, or commander in chief for the time being shall appoint, from time to time, whom he thinks fit for that command.

In testimony of the above presents, we have hereunto set our hands and seals the day and date above written

| John Guthrie | LS | Francis Sadler | LS |
| the mark of | $\frac{1}{W}$ | captain Cudjoe | |

[*Journals* 3 pp. 457ff; PRO:CO 137/23, W.4].

On 19 April 1739 the Assembly passed an Act [2] confirming the terms of the treaty and authorising the payment of rewards to those Maroons who in future should take up, and restore to their owners, runaway slaves [*Journals* 3 p. 476]. On 21 May 1741, on behalf of the king, "Their Excellencies the Lords Justices in Council ... taking the same into Consideration,[3] were pleased with the Advice of His Majestys Privy Council, to Declare their Approbation of the said Act" which they thereupon "Confirmed, finally Enacted, and Ratified accordingly..." [PRO:CO 137/23, W.38]. There was, however, nothing unusual in this time-lag between enactment and ratification. Acts of the Assembly which contained no time limit and to which the governor had given his assent, remained in force unless and until ratification was refused.

It is unlikely that the Maroons had any clear concept of the area of land the ownership of which was guaranteed to them under the treaties. Cudjoe's treaty entitled the leeward Maroons to 1,500 acres, but Guthrie and Saddler may not have appreciated that they resided in two towns – Cudjoe's town (which they named Trelawny Town) and Accompong's Town. When the Assembly finally got around to giving statutory recognition to the land allocation in 1758, nearly 20 years later, they recorded grants of 1,500 acres for the Trelawny Town Maroons and 1,000 acres for those at Accompong [*Journals* 4 pp. 602, 644-45].

Some of the clauses in the treaty signed by Quao on 23 June 1739 were the same as the corresponding clauses in Cudjoe's treaty. But there were also important differences.

The text of the treaty of 23 June originally consisted of the following 14 clauses:

1st. That all hostilities shall cease on both sides for ever, Amen.

2d. That the said captain Quao, and his people, shall have a certain quantity of land given to them, in order to raise provisions, hogs, fowls, goats, or whatever stock they may think proper, sugar canes, excepted, saving for their hogs, and to have liberty to sell the same.

3d. That four white men shall constantly live and reside with them in their town, in order to keep a good correspondence with the inhabitants of this island.

4th. That the said captain Quao, and his people shall be ready on all commands the governor, or the commander in chief for the time being, shall send him, to suppress and destroy all other party or parties of rebellious negroes, that now are or shall from time to time gather together or settle in any part of this island, and shall bring in such other negroes as shall from time to time run away from their respective owners, from the date of these articles.

5th. That the said captain Quao, and his people shall also be ready to assist his excellency the governor for the time being, in case of any invasion, and shall put himself with all his people that are able to bear arms, under the command of the general or commander of such forces, appointed by his excellency to defend the island from the said invasion.

6th. That the said captain Quao, and all his people, shall be in subjection to his excellency the governor for the time being;

and the said captain Quao shall, once every year, or oftener, appear before the governor, if thereunto required.

7th. That in case any of the hunters belonging to the inhabitants of this island, and the hunters belonging to captain Quao, should meet, in order to hinder all disputes, captain Quao, will order his people to let the inhabitants hunters have the hog.

8th. That in case captain Quao, or his people, shall take up any runaway negroes that shall abscond from their respective owners, he or they shall carry them to their respective masters or owners, and shall be paid for so doing as the legislature shall appoint.

9th. That in case captain Quao, and his people, should be disturbed by a greater number of rebels than he is able to fight, that then he shall be assisted by as many white people as the governor for the time being shall think proper.

10th. That in case of any of the negroes belonging to captain Quao shall be guilty of any crime or crimes that may deserve death, he shall deliver them up to the next magistrate, in order to be tried as other negroes are; but small crimes he may punish himself.

11th. That in case any white man, or other the inhabitants of this island shall disturb or annoy any of the people, hogs, stock or whatever goods may belong to the said captain Quao, or any of his people, when they come down to the settlements to vend the same, upon due complaint made to a magistrate, he or they shall have justice done them.

12th. That captain Quao, nor any of his people, shall bring any hogs, fowls, or any other kind of stock or provisions, to sell to the inhabitants, without a ticket from under the hand of one or more of the white men residing with them in their town.

13th. That captain Quao, nor any of his people, shall hunt within three miles of any settlement.

14th. That in case captain Quao should die, that then the command of his people shall descend to captain Thomboy; and at his death to descend to captain Apong; and at his death captain Blackwell shall succeed; and at his death captain Clash shall succeed; and when he dies, the governor or commander in chief for the time being shall appoint whom he thinks proper.

In witness to these articles, the above-named colonel Robert Bennett and captain Quao have set their hands and seals, the day and year above written.

Robert Bennett   LS   The mark of   X   captain Quao

[*Journals* 3 pp. 505ff].

When the terms were submitted for ratification however, the following four additional terms were appended:

That all negroes that have gone to them or have been taken by them, within three years, shall be pardoned their offences and restored to their masters, who shall be obligated to use them well.

That if, hereafter, any of their negroes shall endeavour to entice, or should entice, any negroes from any plantations, the free negroe shall be punished capitally:

That the negroes shall be formed into companies, to be commanded in chief by a white man each, and, when ordered out upon service, they shall receive pay:

That they shall be obliged to cut such roads as the governor shall order and that they immediately cut a road, so as to be rideable, the nearest way possible to a plantation [ibid].

In the copy of the treaty printed in the Journal of the Assembly, these added terms appear, unnumbered, below the signature and seal of Bennett and the mark of Quao. They are also contained in the Act passed by the Assembly in May 1740 embodying the terms of the treaty. By what process or formalities the additional terms are supposed to have been agreed with the windward Maroons is not stated. But they were taken into account in the report of a committee of the Assembly set up to consider, among other things, how Bennett was to be rewarded:

Your committee observe, the terms of this treaty are more advantageous than those made with Captain Cudjoe, as Captain Quao is obliged to return all negroes that have gone to him within three years past, to their respective owners, and Captain Cudjoe is not to return any, unless the negroes have been already restored to the proprietors of them, in pursuance of this treaty [*Journals* 3 p. 514].

No attempt had been made in the treaty with Quao, to quantify the acreage of land to which title of ownership was to be made to the windward Maroons. And indeed, the situation was no less confused in their case than it was with the leeward Maroons.[4] At the time of the treaty the windward Maroons, like the leeward Maroons, had resided in at least two towns. Indeed the unity of command which existed in the west may not have existed in the east.

Bennett may or may not have been aware at the time of the treaty that there were at least two windward Maroon towns. He may or may not have met with the leaders of both towns. But, be that as it may, by the time the Assembly had finalised their land allocations, many of the windward Maroons had moved to new areas. It is possible that the 1,000 acres surveyed at the site of the present Moore Town [*Journals* 7 p. 517] may have been at or near a town already in existence and known as new Nanny Town. Certainly the 206 acres surveyed at the site of the present Charles Town [*Journals* 4 pp. 507, 517] is nearer to the coast than the site of Crawford Town in St. Georges, which may have been the site of the negotiations. Before that survey, however, some of the Maroons from Crawford Town had moved to Scotts Hall, near the boundary between St. Mary and St. Andrew, where the government purchased land for them in 1751 [*Journals* 4 pp. 288, 315]. This may explain the smaller area of the land allocation at Charles Town.[5]

The most significant of the terms added to Quao's treaty was clearly the requirement that the windward Maroons return to their former owners those who had joined their ranks within three years. There was, as we have seen, no such requirement in the treaty with the leeward Maroons. Another noticeable difference between the two treaties is that whereas the windward Maroons were on demand required "to suppress and destroy all other . . . rebellious negroes that now are or shall from time to time gather together or settle in any part of this island",[6] the leeward Maroons were only required to act against rebels who did not "submit to the same terms of accommodation granted to captain Cudjoe and his successors".[7]

Clearly Cudjoe's treaty did not provide for assistance to the establishment in the event of future slave rebellions, though in practice on such occasions the assistance of Maroons from the leeward towns as mercenaries was obtained by the simple expedient of offering financial inducements. The latter may also have been deceived in subsequent years as to the extent of their treaty obligations.

There was also a difference in the wording of the two treaties on the matter of rounding up runaway slaves. The windward Maroons were obliged to "bring in such other negroes as shall from time to time run away from their respective owners".[8] The leeward Maroons, on the other hand, undertook that "if any negroes shall hereafter fall into captain Cudjoe's hands, they shall immediately be sent back to the chief magistrate of the next parish where they are taken".[9] Thus, although they were to be rewarded if they did round up runaways, they were not obliged to do so. But, here again, the practical effect in later years was the same. Many of the Maroons, both to leeward and to windward, began to engage in a regular business of rounding up runaways for reward.

The fact that the terms negotiated by Cudjoe and the leeward Maroons were more favourable than those contained in Quao's treaty, a fact reflected in the circumstance that down to the present day the inhabitants of Accompong pay no taxes while the inhabitants of the other Maroon towns are taxed like ordinary citizens, would seem to cast doubts on the validity of a thesis advanced by a contemporary writer that the windward Maroons were the more militant and courageous and less disposed to make peace. Indeed this writer goes so far as to suggest that Cudjoe was something of an 'Uncle Tom'![10]

That Cudjoe took his obligations under the treaty very seriously indeed is evidenced by his reactions, soon after it had been signed, to the possibility of a Spanish attack. In the event of a foreign invasion the Maroons were obliged to assist the government, placing their forces under the command of the governor as commander in chief of the island's defences. The author of an anonymous manuscript with the Long papers, already referred to,[11] shows that Cudjoe was fully prepared to honour this obligation:

> Cap' Cudjo, the Chief of the Rebellious Negroes, who had lately Submited upon hearing of the Declaration of War against Spain,[12] Sent one of His principall men to the Governor, for Instructions how to Dispose of His People for the Defense of the Island, in Case of an Invasion, and to know in what manner He and They could otherwise be of Service, at that juncture [BM: Ad. Ms. 12431].

The anonymous author thought this a "Remarkable

Instance" which "may Serve as a lesson to some European Princes, who Seem to regard their Engagements no longer than it suits their own Interest or Conveniency".

It appears, however, that not all the Maroons, neither those to windward nor those to leeward, approved of the treaties that had been concluded. In referring to the windward Maroons in his address to the Assembly on 18 March 1740, the governor had reported their agreement to the peace terms, "some few skulkers excepted" [*Journals* 3 p. 504]. He had given no indication as to how many dissenters there were, but the fact that the treaty had envisaged the possibility that Quao might need assistance against "a greater number of rebels than he is able to fight", might indicate that trouble was anticipated.

In Trelawny in 1742 a number of slaves left the plantation belonging to one colonel Forster and the adjoining plantations. They "took with them, when they went away ... a good many arms and a great quantity of gunpowder". The report of a committee set up by the Assembly to investigate the affair,[13] disclosed that "the rebellion ... was concerted between the Coromantee negroes of those plantations, and some of the same country in the woods" [*Journals* 3 p. 594].

According to this report, the conspirators first intended "to cut off all those there that were born in the woods or came from other countries". When that was done, "the rest of the negroes at Forster's were to destroy the white people, and join them, and were to be masters of, and remain in, the woods."

The alliance between the rebellious slaves and disaffected Maroons did not meet with success. According to the report: "colonel Cudjoe, who commands at Trelawny-Town, and Accompong, a negro captain, had notice of their designs and immediately armed a sufficient number of the most faithful of their people, attacked the rebels, killed some, took others, and chased the rest home to their plantations" [*Journals* 3 p. 594]. The prisoners were severely dealt with: "those they took they delivered up to justice, as likewise such of their own people as they found concerned in the said rebellion."

There was also a reference to this conspiracy in the manuscript above referred to: "Capt Cudjo Discovered that some of His Chief men, who were disatisfied with the Treaty ... had Entered into private Caballs with the Negroes in the Neighbouring Plantations, and incited them to Revolt" [BM: Ad. MS. 12431].

According to this anonymous author Cudjoe reacted harshly. Perhaps he saw in these events not only a breach of the recently assumed treaty obligations but also a direct challenge to his own authority:

> he immediately Apprehended four of the Ringleaders and Sent them to the Governour: They were thereupon tried according to the Laws of the Country, two of them were Condemned to Die and the other two ordered to be transported. But the Governor thought proper to Show Linity and mercy, for the first misdemeanour, granted them a Pardon and Sent them back to Cudjo.

But Cudjoe, "who was not satisfied therewith, therefore insisted upon His Own Authority, and to make an Example of them. Accordingly He hanged the Two who were Condemned to Die and Sent the other two to the Governor to be transported, which was accordingly done".

That this conspiracy was on a scale sufficient to cause considerable alarm, the Long manuscript confirms: "Severall of the Plantation Negroes were likewise taken up, and tried. Some were Condemned to Die and others to be transported". The effect was predictable:

> This struck a Terror among the Negroes in generall, who became more tractable than they had been for some Years, Especially since they had met with No Encouragement from the Negroes in the Mountains, who immediately took up all Deserters, and Sent them to Their Masters, according to Agreement [BM: Ad. MS 12431].

The Assembly applauded "the use such an example must be of in preventing other negroes, for the future, from running away in bodies in hopes of being protected by them".[14] Not surprisingly the rewards were generous. Reporting that the Maroons "are very desirious of having a few cattle", the committee recommended that:

two cows should be bought and presented to Colonel Cudjoe,[15] and two for captain Accompong, and one for captain Johnny, one for captain Cuffee, one for Quaco, one for Bumbager, and one for captain Quao with two bulls; one for Trelawny-Town, and one for Accompong's Town; as also a cow for each of the captains in Accompong's Town [*Journals* 3 p. 504].

Forty mercenaries from Crawford Town, recruited by Colonel Bennett, served in the suppression of a rebellion which started in Kingston in 1746 and spread to other areas [*Journals* 4 pp. 11-12; Schafer 26 p. 161]. In 1752 a bounty hunter named George Currie, working with a party of Maroons, earned a reward of £100 for killing a rebel slave named Quaco Venter [*Journals* 4 p. 360; Schafer 27 p. 161].

In their long struggle against the escaped slaves who came to be known as Maroons, the establishment had always been able to rely on the services of free black mercenaries and also slaves loyal to their masters who were prepared to earn their freedom or lesser rewards, as 'black shot' or guides. After the treaties of 1739, and particularly after the events in Trelawny in 1742, the planters and their government found themselves in the happy position of being able to recruit, from the ranks of the Maroons, blacks who would scour the woods for their runaways, fight for them in time of rebellion and serve them generally as gendarmes to intimidate their slaves.

A further departure from the historically revolutionary role of the Maroons occurred in the post treaty period when several of their number acquired slaves. By an "Act for the Better Order and government of the Maroon Towns" the Assembly in 1744 made the sale of slaves to the Maroons illegal. But the practice appears to have continued though on a limited scale. In 1773 the "Superintendent General" of Maroon towns reported: "I find there are about twenty slaves in all the towns, belonging to the maroon officers, which they do not care to acknowledge or give me an account of . . ." [*Journals* 6 p. 466].

FOOTNOTES

[1] According to the Julian calendar, which was still used in Britain until the middle of the 18th century, New Year's day fell on 25 March. In Catholic countries, in compliance with the decision of Pope Gregory XIII to substitute a new calendar, New Year's day had been transferred to 1 January, as from 1582. But in Britain, prior to the *Calendar Act* of 1751, it was the practice when recording a date between 1 January and 25 March to give only the outgoing year or both the outgoing and the incoming years. Unless this is borne in mind one can easily be misled as to dates prior to 1752.

[2] J. Stat. 12 Geo II c.5.

[3] Record of the decisions of the Lords Justices in Council at Whitehall, 21 May 1741.

[4] See above p. 119 and 121.

[5] A study of Maroon land grants is contained in the excellent, as yet unpublished, doctoral dissertation of Barbara Klamon-Kopytoff [19].

[6] Quao's treaty — Article 4.

[7] Cudjoe's treaty — Article 6.

[8] Quao' treaty — Article 4.

[9] Cudjoe's treaty — Article 9.

[10] This thesis is advanced by Orlando Patterson in "Slavery and Slave Revolts in Jamaica, 1655-1740" [50 vol XX, no. 3]. Dr. Patterson purports to discover in Cudjoe an almost cowardly desire to avoid battle and to escape detection. Such criticism suggests a lack of understanding of the tactics of successful guerrilla warfare, tactics which Cudjoe had brilliantly developed centuries before their use by the Chinese and Cuban revolutionaries of modern times!

[11] This manuscript with the Long papers is bound in immediately after a copy of Cudjoe's treaty.

[12] The war, popularly known as the War of Jenkin's Ear, which had started with reprisals against Spain in July, was formally declared on 9 October 1739.

[13] Report of Mr. Fuller, 1 May 1742.

[14] According to D.L. Schafer [27 p. 160], who cites an entry in the Journals of the Assembly in 29 April 1741 [*Journals* 3 p. 556], there had been an earlier occasion when Maroons from Trelawny Town and Crawford's Town were used as gendarmes against "a considerable number of Negroes" who had escaped from plantations in Clarendon and St. Elizabeth.

[15] This report contains the earliest record of the Maroon chief being described as of the rank of colonel.

CHAPTER SIX

TACKY'S WAR

The peace treaties with the Maroons secured for the planters 20 years of relative peace and calm. But this was rudely shattered in 1760 when large numbers of slaves rose in rebellion in two widely separated areas. In yet a third area an uprising which had been planned was discovered and frustrated before it had got properly under way. These rebellions were uncoordinated, though that was not the opinion of Edward Long[1] who believed that there was but one conspiracy to which "almost all the Coromantin slaves throughout the island were privy" [24 vol.2 p.447].

The first uprising occurred in the north central part of the island, in the parish of St. Mary, and commenced on Tuesday 8 April.[2] Bryan Edwards gave this version of how it started:

> Such I well know was the origin of the negro rebellion which happened in Jamaica in 1760. It arose at the instigation of a Koromantyn negro of the name of Tacky, who had been a chief in Guinea; and it broke out on the frontier plantation in St. Mary's parish, belonging to the late Ballard Beckford, and the adjoining estate of Trinity, the property of my deceased relation and benefactor Zachary Bayley, to whose wisdom, activity and courage on this occasion, it was owing, that the revolt was not as general and destructive as that which now rages in St. Domingo" [11 (1st ed.) vol.2 p.268].

Concerning the original participants Edwards wrote:

> On those plantations were upwards of one hundred Gold Coast negroes newly imported, and I do not believe, that an individual amongst them had

received the least shadow of ill treatment from the time of their arrival there. Concerning those on the Trinity estate, I can pronounce of my own knowledge, that they were under the government of an overseer of singular tenderness and humanity. His name was Abraham Fletcher; and let it be remembered, in justice even to the rebels, and as a lesson to other overseers, that his life was spared from respect for his virtues. The insurgents had heard of his character from the other negroes, and suffered him to pass through them unmolested – this fact appeared in the evidence.

Edward Long, also a contemporary of these events, wrote this description of the rebel leader:

He was a young man of good stature, and well made; his countenance handsome, but rather of an effeminate than manly cast... He did not appear to be a man of any extraordinary genius, and probably was chosen general, from his similitude in person to some favourite leader of their nation in Africa [24 vol. 2 p.457n].

In the initial stages the rebels carried all before them. They made a daring raid on Fort Haldane at Port Maria which the suddenness of their attack enabled them to take by surprise. Bryan Edwards' over-simplified account shows little appreciation of the careful planning that must have preceded this attack. This was all he had to say:

Having collected themselves into a body about one o'clock in the morning, they proceeded to the fort of Port Maria; killed the centinel, and provided themselves with as great a quantity of arms and ammunition as they could conveniently dispose of. Being by this time joined by a number of their countrymen from the neighbouring plantations, they marched up the high road that led to the interior parts of the country carrying death and desolation as they went [11 vol.2, pp. 268-9].

At Heywood Hall plantation the rebels set fire to the works and cane pieces. At Esher plantation the resident white staff, warned of their approach, had erected a barricade. The rebels broke through it, killing the overseer and another man. The life of the overseer's mulatto mistress was spared when some of the plantation slaves disclosed that she had in the past interceded to reduce the severity of their punishments. But this information was apparently not disclosed in time to save her from being raped. At Esher, according to Long, "they were joined by fourteen or fifteen of their countrymen" [24 vol.2, pp.448-9].

The rebels then doubled back to Ballards Valley. When

they arrived there, wrote Bryan Edwards, "they surrounded the overseer's house about four in the morning, in which finding all the white servants in bed, they butchered every one of them in the most savage manner" [11 vol. 2pp.268-9].

According to Edwards the rebels drank their victims' blood mixed with rum. Such a ritual would not have been incredible if the persons slain had been noted for their bravery. But as no member of the supervisory staff or indentured servants was reported to have maintained a particularly brave resistance, or credited with any particular virtues which the rebels might have wished to imbibe, the statement must be treated with reserve.

As soon as word of the uprising reached him, the lieutenant governor moved swiftly to cordon off the parish, effectively preventing the rebels from making contact with other parts of the island. By concentrating an overwhelming military force against them with the utmost speed, he succeeded in wresting the initiative from them at the end of the first week.

The planters owed much to their acting commander in chief for the promptness and resolution with which he committed such a large military force to the task of isolating and containing the St. Mary uprising. Fighting in adverse circumstances the rebel slaves needed, above all, time for the news of their initial successes to spread and inspire restless slaves throughout the island. A general disaffection would have compelled the establishment to diffuse its available forces. The rebels also needed time to explore the possibilities of reaching an understanding with the Maroons, as indeed was alleged to have been their intention.

In the event, the rebel slaves were allowed no opportunity for the time factor to operate in their favour. The lieutenant governor was able to use the available military forces to deal with the two major rebellions separately, crushing the one before the other commenced. As for the Maroons, at no time could they have perceived any possibility that the situation would ripen into an island wide slave insurrection which might lead to the destruction of the white establishment. An alliance with the rebel slaves could therefore have offered them no prospect of material gain and the acting governor had no difficulty in obtaining as many Maroon mercenaries as he required.

Reporting to the Lords Commissioners of Trade and Plantations on 19 April 1760 the lieutenant governor[3] omitted all reference to the embarrassingly successful surprise attack on Fort Haldane and the fact that the rebels had obtained their initial supply of arms and ammunition there. He wrote:

> They began by murdering the White People on the Estates and after making themselves Masters of a great quantity of arms and ammunition, they set fire to the Plantations, in order to spread the Terror as much as possible ... The number of White People which they murder'd does not exceed sixteen, & this was done on the first day of the Insurrection [PRO:CO 137/32, fols 4-6].

With this letter he enclosed a copy of the minutes of the meeting of the Council held at Spanish Town, the capital, on 10 April. These minutes record that, on receipt of the first advice of the uprising two days previously, the lieutenant governor as commander in chief had taken immediate steps to commit an overwhelming force of both regulars and militia, supported by Maroon mercenaries, to the task of isolating the affected area. He reported to the Councillors:

> That in Order to give as Speedy a Check as possible to the Desolation which was then Spreading, He had Ordered a Detachment consisting of three Officers and Sixty Private Men from his Majestys 74th Regiment then Quartered in this Town, to ... take their Rout by the Road leading to Saint Mary's over Archers Ridge, and another Detachment of the same force from his Majesty's 49th Regiment had been Ordered from Port Royal to march through Liguania by the road lately cut from thence to that Parish, and that he had sent Expresses to the Commanding Officers of Crawford Town, Nanny Town, and Scotts Hall[4] with Orders to March Immediately a company from each place to their Relief ...

The minutes further recorded that martial law had been declared and that:

> Immediately upon the Proclamation being Issued, he had Ordered the Troop of this Town to March forthwith to Saint Mary's by the Road leading through Bagnalls, and likewise a Detachment from the Kingston Troop to March to the same place and take their Rout through Wag Water, and that two detachments from the 74th Regiment had been sent into the Parish of St. Johns and Ordered to be Stationed at Luidas and Guanaboa till further Orders.

The decision to declare Martial Law was influenced by an apparent reluctance on the part of many members of the militia to appear for duty. Orders had been given:

> to the Officers of the Militia both Horse and Foot to get their respective Corps under Arms, that they might be ready to march in Case any Attempt should be made by the Negroes of other Parishes to join those already in Rebellion. But these last Orders were so farr from being obey'd ... that many of the Private Men had the Insolence to tell their Officers that they would not Appear under Arms, and should be ready to pay the fine of Ten Shillings which the Officers were Impowered to lay on them by Virtue of the Militia Act for their nonappearance [ibid].

At times like these the establishment wanted every able-bodied white man under arms. The reluctance of the militiamen in some areas to appear voluntarily for duty therefore "obliged the Lieutenant Governor to have recourse to the only Means left of Compelling them to do their Duty, which was by Proclaming Martial Law ..."

As the rebels advanced further inland over the next few days they appear to have abandoned their initial policy of discriminating between those who fell into their hands on the basis of how they had treated the slaves. What had occurred to cause this change Bryan Edwards does not disclose. But in such a situation it would have required little more than a rumour of the brutally repressive measures of those who had taken the field against them to erase from their breasts all disposition to be merciful. According to Edwards: "In one morning they murdered between thirty and forty whites and mulattoes, not sparing even infants at the breast..." [11 vol. 2, pp.268-9].

The cleric-historian G. W. Bridges, whose comments on Africans are seldom less than derogatory, was nevertheless generous in his praise of the Saint Mary rebels' valour: "The

Negroes ... fought with desperation. Being allowed no time to conceal themselves amongst the rocks in their usual mode of fighting, they repeatedly charged with fury and were repulsed with loss". Referring to events at the pass at Bagnalls, which a detachment of regulars from the 74th regiment had been sent to seal off, Bridges wrote:

> They ... drew the troops into ambush, and displayed no little military skill in retreating to a narrow pass, where they obtained a decided advantage against a superiority of numbers. With stones and branches of trees, hurled from the rocks above, they committed a dreadful carnage, and the action at Bagnals almost assumed the name of a battle. But it was no victory for either party [5 vol. 2 p.97].

Of another engagement Bridges wrote [5 vol. 2 pp.95-6].

> A fight commenced in the morning, and was maintained till the sun was set, and the night fallen; while the soldiers were astonished at their unusual courage and their formidable numbers. The sincerity of history declares that the glory of Jamaica was sullied by the disobedience of her defenders who were beaten back, and exposed to severe hardships in the centre of a wild and unfrequented country.

The question of whether or not Jamaica's glory was 'sullied' in the fighting that day is of course a matter of opinion. Few Jamaicans today would share that of the reverend historian.

Edward Long recorded a nocturnal attack on a military post: "A party of the 74th regiment lay quartered at a house by the sea side, at a small distance from the woods; in the night the rebels were so bold, that they crept very near the quarters, and, having shot the centinel dead, retired again with the utmost agility from pursuit" [24 vol. 2, p.451].

Bryan Edwards recorded another nocturnal rebel attack:

> ... a detachment of the 74th regiment were stationed at a solitary place surrounded by deep woods, called Down's Cove, they were suddenly attacked in the middle of the night by the rebels. The sentinels were shot and the huts in which the soldiers were lodged were set on fire.
>
> The light of the flames, while it exposed the troops, served to conceal the rebels, who poured in a shower of musketry from all quarters, and many of the soldiers were slain. Major Forsyth who commanded the detachment, formed his men into a square, and by keeping up a brisk fire from all sides, at length compelled the enemy to retire.

There had also been a party of Maroon mercenaries[5] with

the troops at Down's Cove. According to Edwards: "... immediately, on the attack, the whole body of them had thrown themselves flat on the ground, and continued in that position until the rebels retreated..." In the margin of Edwards' personal copy of Long's *History*[6] there is a hand-written note which reads: "At a place called Down's Cove, the rebels set the huts on fire in which the soldiers were quartered and by the light which the fire occasioned were enabled when the soldiers were drawn out to kill several of them".

Of another engagement Long wrote:

> ... the regulars, after a tedious march through the woods, which the steepness of the hills, and the heat of the weather, conspired to render extremely fatiguing, came up with the enemy, and an engagement ensued, in which several of the rebels were killed, and lieut. Bevil of the regulars wounded [24 vol. 2 p. 451].

The lieutenant governor, in his letter of 19 April above referred to, expressed satisfaction with the small number of casualities suffered by the military in that engagement: "Lieut Bevill of His Majesty's 49th Regiment is the only Officer wounded. And the number of Private men kill'd & wounded in the Parties which were sent against the Rebells, extremely inconsiderable" [PRO:CO 137/32, fols 4-6].

The minutes of the next meeting of the Council held on 17 April recorded that:

> Two detachments from his Majesty's 74th Regiment had been Ordered into the Parish of Saint Thomas in the Vale one of which Guarded the Pass which leads into the Parish of Saint Mary's over Archer's Ridge, and the other was quartered at the foot of Guy's Hill in order to Defend the Pass at Bagnalls, and prevent any Communication with the Rebels that Way;

> The Captain of the train from Spanish Town was likewise Ordered to March with two Field Pieces and to do Duty with the first of the above mentioned Detachments, and Dispatches had been sent to the Leeward Negroe Townes[7] to order Companies from each of them to March Immediately; All the Militia Officers ... were Ordered to hold themselves in readiness to March at a Moments Warning and an Embargo was laid on all the Shipping.

The minutes also recorded that the lieutenant governor had requested the admiral of the British naval station at Port Royal to lend assistance and that the latter had:

> Immediately fitted and Manned a Small Vessell which he ... sent ... round to Annotto Bay on the North Side ... and that his Majesty's Ship Lively had since been sent round with a fresh Supply of Provisions and Warlike Stores, and ... that another of his Majesty's Ships should be kept ready to sail at a Moments Warning.

The admiral had given further assurance that he would, if it should prove necessary, "Order all the Troops from Port Royal into the heart of the Country". And in that event "The Marines from on Board his Majesty's Ship Marlborough should be landed at Port Royal and do Duty there".

Bryan Edwards was inclined to depreciate the effectiveness of the Maroons enlisted against the Saint Mary rebels. In the margin of his copy of Long's *History*, beside the latter's account of the rebel attack at Down's Cove, he wrote: "The Maroons behaved most shamefully at this attack lying the whole time on their faces". In his own work Edwards recorded the Maroon contribution to the defeat of the rebels at Heywood Hall in the following passage:

> The whites had already defeated the insurgents in a pitched battle, at Heywood Hall, killed eight or nine of their number, and driven the remainder into the woods. The Maroons were ordered to pursue them and were promised a certain reward for each they might kill or take prisoner.
>
> They accordingly pushed into the woods, and after rambling about for a day or two, returned with a collection of human ears which they pretended to have cut off from the heads of rebels they had slain in battle, the particulars of which they minutely related.
>
> Their report was believed, and they received the money stipulated to be paid to them; yet it was afterwards found that they had not killed a man; that no engagement had taken place, and that the ears which they had produced, had been severed from the dead bodies which had lain unburied at Heywood Hall [11 vol. 2].

Bridges, who referred to both these events [5 vol.2 p.38], attributed the reluctance of the Maroons to engage the St. Mary rebels to cowardice — a taunt which the inheritors of the brave traditions of Cudjoe's warriors seldom deserved. Their conduct nevertheless emphasises their mercenary motivation. In addition to the rewards for every rebel slave killed or captured, Maroons serving the establishment were paid seven pence half-penny per day while their captains received two shillings and sixpence.

On 17 April the lieutenant governor informed the Council that the vigorous measures adopted:

> had been Attended with the greatest Success, as they had cut of the Communication of the Rebells with the other parts of the Country and prevented any Assistance coming to them, by which Means the parties which were Employed against them had Constantly met with Success and that they had killed and taken so many of them, as left no Doubt of their being totally Destroyed in a few days...

He assured the Councillors that "the parties from the Negro Towns were then in Pursuit of the Small Remains of the Rebells, and employed in Scouring the Woods where they had Secreted themselves" [PRO:CO 137/32; Cl. Min. 17/4/1760].

The Council "gave it as their Opinion that the Continuing of the Regulars and parties from the Negro Towns in that part of the Country for some time longer would be ... prudent". But they thought that it would be safe to remove the imposition of martial law as from Monday 21 April "in Case his Honor did not before that time receive Advices of any Tumults or Disorders in order [sic] parts of the Island". No such advices were received by that date, but further "tumults and disorders" were indeed soon to occur.

Writing to the Board of Trade on 9 June 1760 the lieutenant governor reported fresh outbreaks: "The Insurrection in the Parish of Saint Mary's was no sooner happily quell'd, but another broke out at Manchioneal[8] in the Parish of Saint Thomas, in the East" [PRO:CO 137/32, fols 7-8]. The Manchioneal uprising was however of short duration, the conspiracy having been discovered before the plan could be properly put into operation. By reason of "the ready assistance sent to that part of the Country", the letter continued, this outbreak "has likewise been suppress'd with very little loss to the Inhabitants of those parts".

The subsequent uprising at the western end of the island could not be so lightly dismissed. The lieutenant governor went on to say, "I am now to inform Your Lordships that on Whitsun Monday[9] several Estates in Westmoreland rose in

Rebellion, killed about twelve white People and committed great ravages there, and put all that part of the Country into the utmost confusion". Martial law, the lieutenant governor reported, had again been proclaimed on 3 June whereby "the Discipline of the Militia might be enforc'd and their hands Strengthen'd".

Assessing the scale of this uprising the letter went on to say "their numbers were much greater than those concern'd in the two former Insurrections, for most Letters I have had from thence do not mention less than six hundred". Flushed with his quick success against the St. Mary and Manchioneal rebels however, the lieutenant governor appears to have anticipated no delay in suppressing those in Westmoreland: "I immediately upon the first information sent a Vessel down with Arms and Ammunition, and since that, three of His Majesty's Ships have carried down such a number of Forces, as must necessarily, joyn'd to the Militia of those parts, put an end to this Insurrection very shortly".

The acting governor also reported that he had arranged for the fleet, which was to have sailed on 10 June, to postpone its departure for a week, and that he had "been oblig'd to detain the Pacquet[10] a few days, as I apprehend the Credit of the Island would have been greatly hurt by any imperfect account carried home of this Disaster". He appears to have anticipated that, given a few more days, he would be in a position to dispatch the mail boat with letters reporting that tranquility had been restored. Such hopes were soon disappointed by the rebels.

Somewhat inconsistently with his belief that the events of 1760 had been the result of an all island conspiracy among the 'Coromantins', Long reported that the Westmoreland rebels were inspired to rise by news of the St. Mary events, recording that they had been "animated by these reports". He gave the following account of how the revolt started:

> the Coromantins on capt. Forrest's estate, in Westmoreland, broke into rebellion. They surrounded the mansion-house in which Mr. South, attorney to Mr. Forrest, with some friends, was sitting at supper; they soon

dispatched Mr. South and the overseer, and terribly wounded captain Hoare, commander of a merchant ship in the trade, who afterwards recovered [24 vol. 2 pp.452ff].

Once more we encounter the 'loyal' slave:

Three other Negroes belonging to this estate made their escape privately, and alarmed the neighbouring settlements, by which means the white persons upon them provided for their lives, and took measures which prevented the Negroes on three continguous estates from rising.

Long also recorded an interesting incident:

A gentleman, proprietor of one of these estates, remarkable for his humanity and kind treatment of his slaves, upon the first alarm, put arms in the hands of about twenty; of whose faithful attachment to him, he had the utmost confidence: these were all of them Coromantins, who no sooner had got possession of arms, than they convinced their master how little they merited the good opinion he had entertained of them; for having ranged themselves before his house, they assured him they would do him no harm, but that they must go and join their countrymen, and then saluting him with their hats, they every one marched off [ibid].

At the meeting of the Council held on 14 June, the lieutenant governor informed the members that "Immediately upon receiving an Express from Westmoreland, that a Rebellion was broke out there ... A quantity of Arms and Ammunition was dispatch'd for the use of the Militia in those Quarters..."[11] He added that:

The Number of Slaves in Rebellion increasing, Two Detachments of Sixty Men each from His Majesty's 49th Regiment were sent down... and another detachment of Twenty five Men was sent to Saint Elizabeth's, The Inhabitants there being very apprehensive that the Slaves of several Estates in that Parish had an intention of Rising and joyning those in the Neighbouring Parish of Westmoreland.

These Detachments were all sent on board His Majesty's Ships... by Rear Admiral Holmes, who ... not only forwarded them with all dispatch possible, but directed one hundred Marines from on board the Cambridge to be likewise sent down with orders to land and joyn the other Troops there assembled. The Seamen from the Ships were order'd likewise to be landed if their Assistance should be required by the Inhabitants [PRO:CO 137/32].

The lieutenant governor explained to the members of the Council the strategic plan he had devised:

These Troops joyn'd by one Company of the 74th Regiment quarter'd at Savanna la Mar and by the Westmoreland Militia both Horse and Troop and

TACKY'S WAR

Two detachments from the Negro Towns, were employ'd on one side of the Mountains, while the two Companies of the 49th which were quarter'd at Lucea and Montego Bay, joyned with the Militia of Hanover and Saint James's carried on their Operations on the other side.

He claimed that this plan had already achieved gratifying results, and that the troops "by placing the Body of Rebells between their two fires soon dispers'd them and drove them from the place they had pitch'd on for their head Quarters and which they had began to fortify after their manner".

Long wrote of these fortifications with somewhat greater respect:

> Among the rebels were several French Negroes, [12] who had been taken prisoners at Guadeloupe, and, being sent to Jamaica for sale, were purchased by capt. Forrest. These men were the more dangerous, as they had been in arms at Guadeloupe, and seen something of military operations in which they acquired so much skill, that, after the massacre on the estate, when they found their partisans of the adjacent plantations did not appear to join them, they killed several Negroes, set fire to buildings and cane-pieces, did a variety of other mischief, and then withdrew into the woods, where they formed a strong breast-work across a road, flanked by a rocky hill; within this work they erected their huts, and sat down in a sort of encampment [24 vol. 2 pp.452ff].

Long's account of the first attack on the rebels' fortified headquarters is less flattering to the establishment's armed forces than the lieutenant governor's:

> a party of militia, who were sent to attack them, very narrowly escaped being all cut off. The men were badly disciplined, having been hastily collected; and falling into an ambuscade, they were struck with terror at the dismal yells, and the multitude of their assailants. The whole party was thrown into the utmost confusion, and routed, notwithstanding every endeavour of their officers; each strove to shift for himself, and whilst they ran different ways...several were butchered, others broke their limbs over precipices, and the rest with difficulty found their way back again.

Long concluded that:

> This unlucky defeat raised the spirits of the Coromantins in this part of the country, and encouraged so many to join the victorious band, that the whole number very soon amounted to upwards of a thousand, including their women, who were necessary for carrying their baggage, and dressing their victuals.

The lieutenant governor alleged, optimistically, in the same report on 14 July, that:

> The daily advantages gain'd over the Rebells were so considerable, that they were soon reduc'd to great distress and by the last Expresses from Westmoreland it appear'd that out of the formidable numbers which shewed themselves at first in Rebellion no more than Seventy — were supposed to be remaining...

Unrest was reported from two neighbouring parishes and the lieutenant governor made it clear that wherever disaffection appeared it was being mercilessly suppressed without much regard for legal niceties:

> During these transactions an Attempt was made by the Slaves of several Estates in Hanover and Saint James, to rise and joyn those allready in Rebellion. Their Plot was discovered the day before it was to be carried into Execution and the Principal Persons concern'd in it were taken up and Executed.

Nor was the unrest confined to the western parishes, despite the recent suppression of the rebellion in St. Mary and the abortive uprising at Manchioneal:

> His Honor farther informed the Board... that four different Conspiracies among the Slaves had been discovered in the Parishes of Clarendon, Saint Johns, Saint Dorothy's and Saint Thomas in the East, which... were happily frustrated by the vigilance of the Officers in those Quarters, and several Negroes who had attempted to raise seditions there, had been taken up and executed [PRO: CO 137/32].

Writing to the Board of Trade on 20 August, the lieutenant governor referred to:

> repeated Accounts from Westmoreland that many of the Rebellious Negroes are dailey killed, taken and found dead in the Woods, that their number is now so reduced, and those which remain so dispirited for want of Chiefs to animate them to desperate Attempts, that no further danger or distress is apprehended..." [PRO:CO 137/32 B.C. 7].

The time was now right, he said, for martial law to be taken off "to prevent any longer interruption in the Publick Business of this Island".

But the acting governor had to admit, in a subsequent letter dated 7 November 1760, that his assessment had been over optimistic. Referring to a report in his previous letter "that the Leward Rebellion was in great measure suppress'd", he added:

> The plan I had formed would have done it effectually in a very short time,

TACKY'S WAR 143

> but I am ashamed to say that the Obstinancy and Infatuation [sic] of the People in that part of the Country were so great, that... there was no possibility of getting them to do their Duty, and the moment the Power ceased which compell'd them to appear under Arms, they laid them down...

It is possible to form some idea of the extent of the development of the plantations in the various parishes of Jamaica at about this time from the statistics furnished by Edward Long [24 vol. 2] of the numbers of slaves in each parish in 1761. In that year there were 9318 slaves in St. Mary as against 15,158 in Westmoreland. During the next seven years however development of the plantations appears to have continued in St. Mary, the number of slaves rising to 12,159 by 1768 whereas the number of slaves in Westmoreland remained approximately the same at 15,186.

Though the development of the plantations in Westmoreland had been far more extensive than in St. Mary, the former parish was very much larger than the latter and the mountainous woodland areas in the western parishes were extensive. The military were therefore unable to repeat in these leeward parts the rapid success they had achieved against Tacky and his followers in St. Mary. In Westmoreland the fighting continued for many months, inspiring unrest in parts of the adjoining parish to the north. Long recorded that:

> A fresh insurrection happened in St. James's, which threatened to become very formidable, had it not been for the activity of brigadier Witter of the militia and lieut. colonel Spragge of the 49th, who dispersed the insurgents, and took several prisoners; but the rest escaped and, uniting with the stragglers of the other defeated parties, formed a large gang, and infested Carpenters' Mountains for some time [24 vol. 2 p.456].

According to Long [p. 458] "the remains of the Westmoreland and St. James's rebels still kept in arms, and committed some ravages".

When the rebellions of 1760 broke out the Assembly had not been in session. It did not meet until 18 September. In his message read in the Assembly on that date the lieutenant governor explained why he had not called the members together earlier:

> The various scenes of distress, occasioned by the insurrections which have broke out in different parts of the country, would have engaged me to call you sooner together, but I have been obliged to defer it till the usual time of your meeting, as your presence was so necessary in your different districts, to prevent the spreading of an evil of so dangerous a consequence to the whole island [*Journals* 5 p.161].

This was a plausible enough reason, but it is a matter for speculation whether the lieutenant governor, as commander in chief, was not happy to have such an excellent excuse for ensuring that the Assembly was unable to interfere with the conduct of the military operations. The message went on to assure the members that all had gone well: "I have now the satisfaction to inform you, that our expectations have been fully answered, by the vigilance and bravery of the troops..." The dependence of the governor on the Assembly in 1760 had indeed been considerably less than in previous rebellions, due to the presence in the island of the two British regiments which do not appear to have been dependent on the revenues of the country for their maintenance.

The lieutenant governor had to admit that the suppression of the rebellion in the western parts of the island had not been completed. But he assured the Assembly that "the plan now proposed for carrying on their operations, has the fairest prospect of totally suppressing, in a very short time, all the disturbers of the public repose". On 19 September the Assembly viewed the situation as still sufficiently serious for them to request the lieutenant governor to reimpose martial law "in order to suppress the present rebellion in the leeward parts of the island".

The minutes of the House recorded that the lieutenant governor had agreed that this would be necessary. His reply to the Assembly's request stated:

> That it was not until several hours after opening the session that his honor received intelligence from Westmoreland, that the plan laid for reducing the remainder of the rebels... had been rendered ineffectual, by martial law having been taken off; the officers of the militia being, by that means, deprived of the powers necessary to compel the several parties to go out...

The Assembly were informed, in the circumstances:

That his honor . . . agreed . . . in the necessity of laying on martial law again, and continuing it until the rebels are entirely reduced, or until such time as the legislature shall establish some means of vesting the officers of the militia with power sufficient to enforce their orders, without distressing the country by martial law [*Journals* 5, p.164].

On the next day a committee of the Assembly was set up to examine previous legislation relating to the fitting out of parties to suppress rebel slaves. The committee reported that there was no previous legislation which could be "properly adapted for the purpose of suppressing the present rebellion".[13] The Assembly therefore authorised the preparation of a new Bill for this purpose which was hurriedly rushed through all its stages [*Journals* 5 pp.164-5].

On 2 October 1760 a scheme proposed by one William Haynes, that he be allowed to recruit "amongst the free mulattoes and negroes a party of one hundred shot", was considered by the Assembly. The author of the scheme stated that with this party "he will go against the negroes in rebellion, and do his utmost endeavours to suppress them". But he asked that "in case he shall fall short of that number . . . the lieutenant-governor will draft, out of the companies of free negroes and mulattoes,[14] a number to make up the deficiency".

He asked further that each member of his party be given thirty shillings before setting out, to purchase necessaries, and that it be agreed that "for every negro killed, taken or drove in" they be given £20. He also proposed "for the satisfaction of the public, that all negroes . . . which shall be killed by him or his party, shall have their heads cut off, and be brought to the first settlement, and there left" [*Journals* 5 p.165].

Nothing further is recorded of William Haynes and his sanguinary plan. But in a message to the lieutenant governor on 7 October, the Assembly urged that, presumably under powers contained in the new enabling legislation, the commanding officers of the militia regiments in St. Catherine, Clarendon, Vere, St. Elizabeth, St. James, St.

Mary and St. Ann be directed: "to raise, out of each of their regiments, a party of thirty white and black shot, with fifteen baggage-negroes, to be drafted out of the several parishes..." [*Journals* 5 pp.179-80].

The lieutenant governor's letter of 7 November, confirmed the remarkable fact that there were still slaves in the area in which Tacky's rebellion had been so recently crushed, in whom the fire of revolt burned fiercely enough to inspire them to yet another attempt: "A second Insurrection has been attempted in the Parish of Saint Mary's, but by the vigilance of the Officers there, it has been defeated and the Chiefs of it put to Death" [PRO: CO 137/32, B.C.9].

The suppression of these rebellions involved more than the defeat of the combatants and the capture and execution of the organisers. It was also considered desirable to punish, with degrees of severity varying from death or mutilation to flogging, all who had participated. Participation was apparently to be inferred if, during the rebellion, a slave absented himself from the plantation or refused to perform the tasks allotted to him. Those considered likely to show or incite disaffection in future, but insufficiently culpable to deserve execution, were usually 'transported' out of the country.

Concerning the slaves ordered to be transported from the island in 1760 Long wrote:

> Most of them were sent to the Bay of Honduras, which has long been the common receptacle of Negro criminals, banished from this island; the consequence of which may, some time or other, prove very troublesome to the logwood cutters; yet they make no scruple to buy these outcasts, as they cost but little. It is difficult to find a convenient market for such slaves among the neighbouring foreign colonies; but, if possibly it could be avoided, these dangerous spirits should not be sent to renew their outrages in any of our own infant settlements [24 vol. 2, p.462n (a)].

So severe were the reprisals against every slave suspected of complicity in the events of 1760 that many slave owners were disturbed at the possibility of being deprived of more of their slaves than they could afford to lose. In a second letter to the Board of Trade on 20 August,[15] the lieutenant governor had complained that "Many owners and Agents of Plantations with a view of secreting their Negroes from Punishment have made false returns of their Absentees which has made it impossible to obtain a true List of all who were engaged in the Westmoreland Rebellion" [PRO:CO 137/32]. He had added, however, that "no returns to me have made their number less than Nine hundred or more than Ten Hundred and fifty".

Concerning the punishments, the lieutenant governor stated, "Great numbers of Negroes throughout the whole Island have been Executed and Transported ... and Tryals are still held dailey in Saint Thomas in the East, where one of the deepest laid Conspiracies was timely discover'd".

During October 1760 the Assembly considered a number of petitions from slave owners who had suffered losses by reason of the complicity of their slaves in the rebellion. They agreed[16] to pay to the owners the value, not to exceed £40, of each slave executed [*Journals* 5 p.215].

On 11 October an interim payment of £450 was approved for the mercenaries from Trelawny Town and Accompong, and an account of what had been paid to them, and what sum due remained unpaid, was requested [*Journals* 5 p.181]. For services rendered between 6 July and 21 August according to an account date-lined "Charles-Town, 23rd August, 1760" and presented to the Assembly, the Charlestown Maroons were paid as follows:

			£	s	d
1 captain,	46 days, at	2s. 6d.	5	15	0
7 shots-men,	46 days, at	7½d.	10	12	6
7 ditto,	32 days, at	7½d.	7	0	0

[*Journals* 5 pp.226-7]

These payments were exclusive of the special rewards for rebels killed and captured.

There are conflicting versions of how Tacky met his death. Bryan Edwards stated that he was killed "by one of the parties that went in pursuit" [11 vol. 2 pp. 268ff]. He also gave a more detailed account in which he stated that the men who actually killed him were Maroons:

> This unfortunate man, having seen most of his companions slaughtered, was discovered wandering in the woods without arms or clothing, and was immediately pursued by the Maroons in full cry. The chase was of no long duration; he was shot through the head; and . . . his savage pursuers, having decollated the body in order to preserve the head as a trophy of victory, roasted and actually devoured the heart and entrails of the wreched victim!

The statement that Tacky's heart was eaten by those who killed him is not incredible, though Edwards probably added the reference to the entrails to make the ritual that much more distasteful to his readers. The belief that those who ate a portion of the heart of a particularly brave opponent partook of his qualities, was current at one time or another in many different parts of the world. The legendary bravery of Tacky would no doubt have made his heart particularly valuable for such ritualistic purposes. Robert Renny however, whose history is largely plagiarised from Edward Long, alleged that Tacky was wounded by a Maroon and a few days later killed by a party of Whites [Renny 26 p.67]. But Long stated that the fatal bullet was fired by a Maroon [24 vol. 2].

Damon, one of the principal leaders among the Westmoreland rebels, also died in the field of battle. His party scattered, he travelled across country to Mile Gully in the central part of the island. There he was killed [24 vol. 2, p.456]. Another group of the Westmoreland rebels, who had successfully eluded capture, negotiated surrender terms through a Mr. Gordon as their intermediary. They were willing to come in, in return for a promise that they would be transported not executed. According to Long, the lieutenant governor agreed [24 p.457].

The sentences carried out on captured 'ring leaders' were sadistically brutal. The execution of a sentence of burning alive, and the courage with which the victim endured it, was witnessed and reported by Bryan Edwards:

> The wretch that was burnt was made to sit on the ground, and his body being chained to an iron stake, the fire was applied to his feet. He uttered

not·a groan, and saw his legs reduced to ashes with the utmost firmness and composure; after which one of his arms by some means getting loose, be snatched a brand from the fire that was consuming him, and flung it at the face of his executioner [11 vol 2 pp.270-1].

Edwards also gave an eye-witness account of the fortitude with which two other leaders, Kingston and Fortune, went to their death. Their sentence was, he wrote, "To be hung up alive in irons, and left to perish in that dreadful situation" They were, he stated:

> indulged at their own request, with a hearty meal immediately before they were suspended on the gibbet, which was erected on the parade of the town of Kingston. From that time until they expired, they never uttered the least complaint except only of cold in the night, but diverted themselves all day long in discourse with their countrymen, who were permitted; very improperly, to surround the gibbet.
>
> On the seventh day a notion prevailed among the spectators that one of them wished to communicate an important secret to his master, my near relation; who being in St. Mary's parish the commanding officer sent for me. I endeavoured by means of an interpreter to let him know that I was present, but I could not understand what he said in return.
>
> I remember that both he and his fellow-sufferer laughed immoderately at something that occurred, – I know not what. The next morning one of them silently expired, as did the other on the morning of the 9th day [11 vol. 2, p.271].

Long listed a number of other areas in which there were conspiracies and evidence of unrest and disaffection. He told of a man named Kofi in St. Thomas in the East who had been pressed by some Coromantins there to join with them in rebelling. This man, having learned their plans and "professing his zeal to embrace them", betrayed them and caused their arrest. "Conspiracies of a like nature", Long stated, "were likewise detected in Kingston, St. Dorothy, Clarendon, and St. James, and the partizans secured" [24 vol. 2 p.455; *Journals* 5 p. 231].

In Kingston there was a female slave named Cubah whom her fellow conspirators called "queen of Kingston", and who "at their meetings ... sat in state under a canopy". She was "seized, and ordered for transportation" [ibid]. Cubah was transported to Cuba in a sloop belonging to one John Swain. Whether she was sold into slavery there is not known, but somehow she succeeded in securing a passage back to Jamaica in another sloop belonging to the same owner. She landed in Hanover but was eventually recaptured and executed [Long 24 vol. 2 p. 455; *Journals* 5 p. 233].

In all, some 400 slaves were executed and some 600 were transported to slavery in the Bay of Honduras. Long attempted to estimate what these events had cost the planters and their government:

> The suppression of the Coromantins, in 1760 and 1761, cost the island 15,000 £. I have ... estimated the expense of making good losses sustained Ec. at 100,000 £.; and the erecting of parochial barracks, in consequence of that insurrection cost as much more. In the whole the island expended not much less on that account than appears from the earliest accounts to have been disbursed on the reduction of the Maroons; for this was no more than 240,100 £ [24 vol. 2 p.471].

On 17 December 1760 the Council and the Assembly joined with the lieutenant governor in addressing an humble petition to the king. They pleaded that "the Insufficiency of the number of the Regular Troops in this Island hath by fatal experience in the late dangerous Rebellions been fully evinced ..." They pointed out that "your Majesty's forces in this Island, though with the greatest Alacrity assisted by the Seamen and Marines of your Majesty's Ships ... were with great difficulty capable of reducing the Rebellions".

The petitioners therefore prayed that directions be given that a company of regular troops stationed on the Mosquito Shore and four other companies stationed on the coast of Africa, should join their respective regiments in Jamaica. And they asked in addition for "a Reinforcement of another Regiment that this valuable Island may be preserved to your Majesty" [PRO:CO 137/32, B.C.19].

The trials of slaves accused of complicity in slave rebellions were perfunctory affairs, lasting no more than a few minutes. The accused were often condemned to death, mutilation or transportation on nothing more substantial than suspicion. Mere absence from the plantation or refusal to perform allotted tasks was enough at such a time to ensure conviction. Acquittals were rare indeed.[17]

There was, however, one alleged conspirator who succeeded in satisfying his captors of his innocence, and whose subsequent activities cannot but raise the presumption that he may have pulled the wool over their eyes. This man, known as Blackwall, had, according to Gardner, "been tried but acquitted for complicity in the rising of 1760" [Gardner 14 pp.141-2; Long 24 vol. 2 p.467]. Five years later, in the same area in which Tacky's rebellion had been drowned in blood, plans were laid for another uprising. And, according to Long, "Blackwall was the principal instigator" [24 vol. 2 p.468].

Gardner gave this account of the preparations:

> Several of the leaders met in St. Mary's in 1765 when the solemn fetish oath was administered. Into a quantity of rum, with which some gun powder and dirt taken from a grave had been mingled, blood was put, drawn in succession from the arm of each confederate... this cup was drunk by each person, and then came the council. It was agreed that during the ensuing Christmas holidays the rising should take place, and that in the meantime all were to obtain companions [14 pp. 141-1].

Long disclosed the interesting fact that the initiative in the conspiracy for this uprising was taken by slaves who were in positions of some authority on their estates:

> Some time in July 1765, there was a private meeting . . . of several Coromantin headmen, who entered into a conspiracy for a fresh insurrection, to take place immediately after the Christmas holidays; they bound the compact with their fetishe, according to custom, and received assurances from all or most of the Coromantins in the parish, that they would join [24 vol. 2 pp.465-8].

According to Long "the Coromantins on no less than seventeen estates in that parish were engaged in that confederacy".

The plans for the proposed uprising were however discovered, due, in Long's words, to "the impatience of some among them to begin the work". This impatience "hurried them on to rise before the day appointed, and disconcerted their whole plan". On the night of 29 November the works and trash houses at Whitehall plantation were set on fire. The incendiaries' plan was "to decoy the overseer, and other white persons there, from their beds, to extinguish it; and then cut off their retreat to the dwelling-house, secure the arms lodged there, and proceed to murder them, without fear of resistance" [24 vol. 2 pp. 465-8].

Long recorded that "Upon the first alarm of fire, the overseer and white servants repaired to the works, as had been forseen". Meanwhile, "the nine confederates broke through the back door" of the dwelling house where they killed two white men. A white woman in the house was taken out and concealed by some of the house slaves. But the overseer and the other Whites, hearing the cries of one of the white men being killed "and the shouts of his murtherers", realised that there had been an uprising and "fled to Ballards Valley... where they called up the white men to secure themselves, and prepare for their defence".

> The flames, which were seen at a great distance, served as a signal to other conspirators; so that their number was now augmented to fifty or sixty; who, with the most horrid acclamations, (having got possession of all the arms at Whitehall, with powder and ball) began their march... and proceeded on to Ballard Valley [24 vol. 2pp. 465-8].

The events at Ballards Valley marked the end of this premature uprising. Long gave the following description:

> The rebels, being arrived at the valley, laid close siege to the overseer's house, which was garrisoned with about ten white men. This house was erected upon a stone foundation, raised some height from the ground, and furnished with loop-holes below. The rebels were joined by several of their countrymen on this estate; and, surrounding the house, began to use the most insulting language... to provoke the Whites to come forth... but finding this ineffectual, they prepared for burning the house about their ears; for this purpose they collected a parcel of dry trash, which they fastened to the extremity of a long pole, and one of their leaders setting his back to a loop-hole, kindled the trash, and applied it to the wood-work of the roof.

What then followed caused the rebels undoing:

> At that instant he was perceived by one of the centries posted below, who discharged his piece at him; the ball struck against the lock of a gun, which the rebel had in his hand, and recoiling into his body, killed him upon the spot. His fall threw the rest of the conspirators into dismay, for he was one of their chiefs; upon which the garrison, taking advantage of their suspence, sallied out with great spirit, killed two or three, and dispersed the rest, who immediately fled into the woods [24 vol. 2 pp. 465-8].

According to Gardner, "the premature rising at Whitehall

was owing to the impetousity of one Quamin,[18] belonging to their gang, who would not wait the appointed time". Even so he echoed Long's opinion "that it is probable, if they had not met a repulse soon after their first outrage, the insurrection would have been general, from the encouragement their better success would have given to the rest of the conspirators" [Gardner 14 pp.141-2; Long 24 vol. 2 p.467].

As to Blackwall's part in this premature outbreak, Long was not at all clear. He suggested that it was Blackwall himself who started the fire at Whitehall, though this would obviously have been disruptive of his own carefully laid plan. He then told of the elaborate steps taken by Blackwall to deceive the overseer into believing him innocent. When the whites emerged from the dwelling house, "they met with Blackwall (who held a post of some authority on the estate), bemoaning the sad accident, and shewing great alertness in fetching water". Long referred to the overseer as "not having the smallest distrust in him".

After the rebels had been dispersed at Ballards Valley there was, according to Long, yet another attempt by Blackwall to divert suspicion from himself.

> Blackwall, the principal of the gang, finding how matters were likely to end, detached himself from his brethren, and a few hours afterwards presented himself before his overseer in seeming terror, pretending he had narrowly escaped being put to death by his countrymen; to avoid whose fury, he had crawled into a cane-piece, and there hid himself till that instant.

On this occasion, however, Blackwall was less fortunate than he had been in 1760.

> Suspicions arising, that this conspiracy was more extensive than at first appeared, and upon recollection that there had been a merry meeting of the Negroes at Ballard's Valley two nights preceding the insurrection, and that the Coromantins had separated from the rest, a strict enquiry was entered into; and upon examining some Coromantins, who were most suspected, they impeached several of their countrymen; fresh evidence produced further discoveries, and at length the plot was partly unraveled.

Long was apparently aware of Kwamina's unfortunate role:

> Some among them regretted exceedingly the precipitate eagerness of

Quamin, and threw out insinuations that the Maroons were in the secret, and that the insurrection was intended to have opened at once in three different places, at a certain day soon after Christmas; that three days previous notice was to be given of the exact hour of rising; and as they hoped to find the white people off their guard, and to get possession of sufficient arms and powder in the several dwelling-houses, they had full confidence, that, by their precautions, and secrecy, they should carry all before them, and make amends for their former disappointment; they knew, that a large stock of fire arms and ammunition would be absolutely necessary; one of their first attempts therefore was to be, the surprize of the fort at Port Maria . . . [24 voL 2, pp.465-8].

In 1765, as in 1760 the idea of coming to an understanding with the Maroons appears to have been part of the rebels' plan. According to Gardner:

A good deal of alarm was occasioned by the statements of some of the prisoners that the Maroons were to have joined them and divided the country with them. Some thought this was only designed to destroy confidence in these uncertain allies, but the matter was never properly investigated [14 pp.141-2].

Thirteen slaves accused of participation in the uprising and conspiracy of 1765 were executed and 33 were transported.

Not to be outdone by their brothers in St. Mary, a number of slaves in Westmoreland rose in revolt in the following year. Thirty-three Coromantins were involved, wrote Gardner, and within a couple of hours they had killed 19 Whites. Overcome soon afterwards by a military force, those who were not killed in action were executed [14 p.142]. But James Pinnock, the English planter-lawyer, recorded in his diary[19] more modest casualties from this affair. His entry for 5 October 1766 read: "at 4 o'Clock in the Afternoon at Cross Path & Cornwall in Westmoreland 45 Negroes Coromanties rose in Rebellion in one Night killed 4 whites & 11 Negroes" [BM: Ad. MS. 33316].

The leading role played by slaves imported from the Gold Coast in the rebellions and conspiracies of the 1760s was a matter of alarm and grave concern to the planters. A committee set up by the Assembly to enquire into the 1760 rebellions proposed "that a bill should be brought in for laying an additional higher duty upon all Fantin, Akim and Ashantee Negroes, and all others commonly called

Coromantins, that should, after a certain time, be imported, and sold in the island" [Long 24 vol. 2, pp. 470-1].

Long recorded, however, that "No bill . . . was passed, the measure was opposed, and it was dropped". The slave owners valued the capacity for work of slaves from the Gold Coast so highly that their greed overcame their fear. So profitable was the trade in African slaves, and so influential were the traders at this time, that all colonial legislation designed to regulate the trade was disallowed [Williams 35 pp.40-1].

FOOTNOTES

[1] Long believed that there was the common factor of being 'Coromantins' between all those slaves in the different parts of the island who rose in rebellion in 1760. Subsequent historians have accepted this. Monica Schuler, in a study prepared for the University of the West Indies [28], goes further. She describes the 1760 events as an Akan affair. The weakness of this premise becomes apparent when it is appreciated that Tacky, the leader in St. Mary, was not an Akan. His name identifies him as a Ga. The Ga, culturally distinct from the Fanti, Ashanti, Akim and other peoples of the Akan languages group, speak an entirely different language. That Tacky should have been described as a 'Koromantin' or 'Coromantin' emphasises the point that this term signified not a tribe, nation or single ethnic group but simply the port of shipment on the Gold Coast. That much, most of the leaders, but not all of them, had in common (see above pp. 8-10).

[2] Long's statement that the rebellion started on the night preceeding Easter Monday does not accord with the date given in the Council minutes of 10 April 1760.

[3] J. S. [sic] Moore to Lords Comm. of Tr. & Plantations, 19 April 1760. As Moore's first name was Henry these initials are probably a transcription error.

[4] These were the three Maroon towns nearest to the area in which the St. Mary rebellion occurred. The Nanny Town referred to is the new town of that name, now known as Moore Town, in Portland.

[5] According to Long [24, vol. 2, pp.450-1] these Maroons were from Scotts Hall.

[6] Bryan Edwards' personal copy of Long's *The History of Jamaica* was acquired from a London bookseller by Ansell Hart, the author's father.

[7] The Maroon settlements at Trelawny Town (Cudjoe's Town) and Accompong.

[8] Manchioneal appears to have been regarded as part of the parish of St. Thomas in the East until, with the establishment of the parish of Portland, the boundaries were defined.

[9] 2 June 1760.

[10] The 'pacquet' or packet ship was a shipping service conveying mail at regular intervals which also took passengers. Because of the importance of this service the governor was empowered to control the date of its departure.

[11] Minutes of meeting of the Council, 14 July 1760.

[12] It is unlikely that these were Coromantins, i.e. from the Gold Coast.

[13] The committee's report refers to Acts passed in the years 1696, 1706, 1723, 1725, 1730 and 1734 (two).

[14] The companies referred to were apparently separate militia companies of free mulattoes and Blacks which existed in urban areas.

[15] H. Moore to Board of Trade, 20 August 1760. To this document a heading has been added reading "Duplicate of a letter dated 24th July 1760". This heading would appear to have been placed in error on the wrong document.

[16] On 19 November 1760.

[17] The author has been unable to trace any records of the trials of those who were charged in connection with the rebellions and conspiracies of 1760. That this generalisation in relation to the trials of slaves accused of complicity in slave rebellions and conspiracies is valid may however be verified by an examination of the records of the trials arising out of the slave conspiracies in 1823-24 and the rebellion of 1831-32 (see below – Chapters 10 and 15).

[18] Kwamina, a Fanti day name, or Kwame, the Ashanti equivalent see above p. 11.

[19] Diary of James Pinnock – 34 pages of very skimpy entries over the period 1758-1794. Pinnock came to Jamaica in 1763.

CHAPTER SEVEN

THE SECOND MAROON WAR

For over half a century after the conclusion of the peace treaties of 1739, the plantation owners and their government maintained excellent relations with their former enemies the Maroons. Those Maroons who wished to avail themselves of the opportunity could earn the rewards offered for capturing runaway slaves. And whenever any appreciable number of blacks still enslaved rose in rebellion, many Maroons could find employment as mercenaries, with the possibility of earning additional rewards for killing or capturing rebel slaves.

In the three decades following the suppression of the formidable rebellions of the revolutionary 1760s, however, the opportunities for mercenary employment of Maroon companies were few. Their services were not required in Kingston where in 1769, according to Gardner [14], a slave girl betrayed a conspiracy and "a large body of armed men were seized". This indeed may or may not have been the conspiracy alleged to have been discovered in 1771 which the editors of the official *Handbook of Jamaica* [16, 1882 ed. p.49] reported as follows: "A military force surprised an assembly of three hundred armed ruffians prepared to drown the town in blood. A judical sentence consigned many of them to a painful death".

Maroon mercenaries may, however, have been called out in connection with the short-lived uprising in the parishes of Hanover and Westmoreland in 1777: "So great was the consternation that a homeward bound fleet of more than one hundred ships was detained for some days... The ring-leaders of the conspiracy, thirty in number, were executed" [16 p.50].

A Maroon was credited with killing the notorious rebel slave bandit, or alleged bandit, Three-Fingered Jack or Jack Mansong, in 1780.

During the early 1790s it appears that unrest was once more on the increase among the slaves. In the four years from 1792 no less than 93 slaves were considered dangerous enough to warrant transportation from the island, their owners being compensated for their loss.

An advertisement dated 22 May 1795 in the Supplement to the *Royal Gazette* illustrates the day to day dependence of the slave owners on the services of their black gendarmes:

TO THE MAROONS — Five Pounds Reward

RAN AWAY... about nine weeks past, two negro men, named BOB and JACOB, the former a Chamba with the country marks in his face and marked on the right shoulder I R, heart on top... the other a creole... marked W R diamond on top of his right shoulder.

They have ... been seen in Clarendon and Kingston, and higgle between those places... Whoever apprehends and brings them to their owners, or proves to a conviction that they are harboured, by a black or mulatto, shall receive the above reward, and if by a white person, Three Half Joes[1] ... [PRO:CO 137/94-7].

So successful had the planters' accommodation with the Maroons proved, and so great was the confidence they had learned to place in their black allies, that it had become a matter of indifference to them whether or not the ambassadors appointed to reside at the Maroon towns, resided there or elsewhere. Indeed Major John James, the 'superintendent' of Trelawny Town, and his son and assistant Captain John James, both resided at their estate some 25 miles from the town[2] [Dallas 7 vol. 1 p. 141; *Journals* 9 p. 369ff, Ex. 13].

When the Earl of Balcarres, owner of several plantations in the island, arrived as lieutenant governor[3] in 1795, he soon put a stop to this laxity. Dismissing the Jameses, he appointed Thomas Craskell and John Merody to succeed them, insisting that the residence requirements of the treaty be observed. But the scene appears to have been peaceful enough. Writing to the Duke of Portland on 11 May, the new governor said, "I have nothing particularly interesting to lay before your Grace. This Island seems in a State of perfect internal Tranquility & will remain so as long as our Troops are safe in S. Domingo . . ." [PRO:CO 137/94-7].

That this serenity was soon disturbed was due in part to an irresistible itch afflicting the noble commander-in-chief, to win his spurs in battle. The trouble started at the beginning of July when two Trelawny Town Maroons, alleged to have killed some tame hogs, were taken before the magistrates at Montego Bay. The evidence against them was given by two white men and the sentence of "lashes at a cart's tail" was carried out in a common workhouse at the hands of a slave.

That the magistrates should have sentenced these alleged offenders, instead of sending them back to Trelawny Town to be dealt with there, seems extraordinary. Perhaps the nerves of the property owners who constituted the magistrates' bench in Montego Bay were still somewhat frayed. A contemporary letter from the custos to the governor[4] recorded that "A most dreadful fire . . . has laid the most valuable part of this Town in ruins . . . One hundred and ten Houses . . . have been burnt" [PRO:CO 137/94-7].

Be that as it may, the Maroons were furious at this insult, regarding the treatment received by the two men as a breach of their treaty. As a manifestation of their displeasure they drove Captain Craskell out of Trelawny Town. Learning that he had stopped at Vaughansfield, about two miles away, they sent to warn him not to return.

The contemporary historian R. Dallas subsequently took the view, rightly or wrongly, that the Maroons had used the incident at Montego Bay as a convenient excuse, enabling them to air more fundamental grievances:

> It appeared afterwards that these two Maroons were persons of no consideration among them, and that, but for the occasion afforded them by a pretence for complaining, they would themselves have hanged them without ceremony ... The Maroons ... afterwards declared that they wished for permission to hang both of them, having long considered them as runaways and thieves" [Lindsay 23].

This news caused considerable anxiety among the magistrates of St. James. Eight of them signed a letter to Balcarres on July 18 [5] expressing their alarm:

> We are sorry to inform your Lordship that a very serious disturbance is likely to break out immediately with the maroons of Trelawny-Town. They have obliged their superintendent to quit the town; they have threatened the destruction of the two plantations nearest them, and of all the white people on them ... [Journals 9 p. 368, Ex. 1].

The magistrates informed the governor of the precautionary measures they had already taken:

> We have dispatched a letter to general Palmer, to call out the troop; and colonel James has ordered out two companies of militia, for the immediate protection of the plantations in the neighbourhood, and we hope the next intelligence will render unnecessary calling out the rest.
>
> Mr. Vaughan also informs us he has sent an express to colonel Swaby, custos of St. Elizabeth, to have the militia in readiness for action, and to inform the neighbouring parishes on the south side; and has given the same intelligence to the custos of Trelawny [Journals 9 p. 368 Ex.1].

On the same day Colonel Montague, head of the Trelawny Town Maroons, was informed[6] by letter that "the magistrates of St James propose to send four of the oldest justices, to meet four chosen maroons, at Vaughansfield or Hadington, tomorrow, to settle all differences" [Journals 9, 368 Ex.2]. The tone of the Maroons' reply was sharp:

> Gentlemen,
>
> The Maroons wishes nothing else from the country but battle; and they desires not to see Mr Craskell up here at all. So are waiting every moment for the above on Monday.
>
> Colonel Montague, and all the rest [7] [Journals 9 p. 368, Ex.3].

There was, however, a postscript to this reply, added below the signature, which appeared to modify its belligerency: 'Mr David Schaw [8] will see you on Sunday morning for an answer. They will wait till Monday, nine o'clock, and if they don't come up, they will come down themselves". This postscript, which clarifies the meaning of the phrase "waiting every moment for the above on Monday", shows beyond doubt that, despite their sword rattling, the Maroons wanted to parley.

This postscript was omitted from the copy of the letter sent by Balcarres to the Duke of Portland on 19 July. Not until 3 August was a complete copy despatched to the Secretary of State, along with the copies of other correspondence [PRO:CO 137/94-7]. It is pertinent to ask why Balcarres should initially have sent an incomplete copy.

On learning of the trouble Major John James and his son had made their way as quickly as possible to Trelawny Town where, because of their popularity, they were able to exercise a calming influence. They had assisted the Maroons to list their grievances in writing. But John Merody, the suspicious new assistant superintendent, represented their intervention in an entirely different light. Accusing them of using the situation to secure their own reinstatement, he subsequently made the most scurrilous accusations against the Jameses on oath before the governor.

Merody deposed [9] that Major James had held private conferences with the Maroons from which he (Merody) had been excluded, and "took down in writing all their complaints and ... reminded them of many old grievances which they had complained of whilst he was their Superintendent and which they had forgotten" [PRO:CO 137/94-7; *Journals* 9 pp 369ff. Ex.15]. Merody agreed with his noble examiner that this was 'very improper'. He alleged also that he had heard Major James tell the Maroons that if they wished to have him back as their superintendent "they must insist positively upon it with the Governor".

As for Captain James the son, Merody deposed that he had told the Maroons that he would like to see "the business ... accomodated", but that "should it be carried to the length of a Rebellion he would flog the Negroes from his Estate to oblige them to join the Maroons." Even Merody however admitted "that the Maroons [MS. p.177] declared in his hearing ... that Major James was the only Person wearing a red Coat who should be permitted to enter their town".

On 19 July the delegation from the magistrates of St. James kept the appointment with the Maroons. Having listened to their grievances the magistrates reported to a meeting of their fellow planters and property owners. In a letter to the governor on 21 July the custos wrote:[10]

> There has been a meeting held here, to receive the report of the gentlemen who went ... to hear the complaints of the maroons, and to endeavour to settle the differences ... between them and the white people. From their verbal report it appears that three things are necessary to quiet the maroons ..
>
> That the last law should be altered, in respect to the punishment of public whipping:
>
> That their superintendent should be removed, and Mr. James ... or one of his sons, be appointed in his place:
>
> That an addition of three hundred acres be made to their land [*Journals* 9 p. 369ff, Ex. 7].

To this report the custos added:

> The gentlemen assembled on this occasion, both of this parish and Trelawny, are of opinion that such requests should be complied with by your Lordship in part; and by the recommendation of your lordship for that part which depends on the legislature, for the present peace of the country ...

On 20 July a number of prominent property owners and magistrates from the adjoining parish of Trelawny visited Trelawny Town. The circumstances of their visit were reported by chief magistrate James Stewart in a long letter to the governor that same night. Stewart wrote:

> I am directed to inform your honour, that in consequence of several letters received on Saturday last from the custos and magistrates of St. James's, apprizing this parish of a rebellious disposition of the Maroons being discovered, the militia of Trelawny were collected in as numerous a body as the short notice ... would allow of; and that they proceeded from the town of Falmouth yesterday morning to Mr. Atherton's pen, which is distant about

three miles from the Maroon-town, where they arrived about two o'clock in the afternoon.

Shortly after, a Maroon carrying his lance, came down with a letter, which ... required the attendance of the following gentlemen: viz the honourable John Tharp, Jarvis Gallimore, Edward Knowles, James Galloway, esquires, and myself. We accordingly put off the regimentals, and went up to their town, where we found Major John James, their former superintendent, general Reid, and John Mowatt, esquire, who had gone up previously to confer with them.

Stewart gave a graphic description of their reception:

The Maroons, collected in a body of about three hundred men, received us, armed with their usual weapons, and displayed at our entrance into the town evolutions peculiar to their mode of fighting. The gentlemen, first with them, had mitigated much of their rage; but yet their countenances and manners indicated a spirit of violence, which was strongly expressed by the language and gestures employed in the detail of grievances which I have enclosed to you.

Other matters were alleged by them as grievances; which they were induced to relinquish on condition that the gentlemen present would consider themselves pledged to obtain redress for what was specified in the statement; but at the same time shewing a firmness of determination to pursue their object, if their claims were not to be granted.

Reporting on the manner in which he and his collegues had dealt with the situation, magistrate Stewart continued:

Under such circumstances, little time could be afforded for deliberation. We therefore thought it, at the instant, not bad policy to appease them by a promise, that their causes of complaint should be enquired into by the legislature, in order that they might be redressed, with which dependence they appeared satisfied: but would not by any means consent to Mr. Craskell's return to his office, and insisted that major James should remain with them all night, which he agreed to do.

They were acquainted with the intended meeting of the house of assembly early in the next month; when they depend their complaints will be attended to. Seeing an appearance of satisfaction amongst them, we quitted the town about six o'clock in the evening, and returned to the militia ... which was immediately discharged, by order of the colonel ... [*Journals* 9 pp. 369ff. Ex.6].

Bringing his letter to a close James Stewart gave it as his opinion that there was no cause for further alarm, assuming no doubt that some attempt at official conciliation would follow: "We have had no intelligence from the town this morning; therefore I suppose they will continue quiet". With this letter magistrate Stewart forwarded the Maroon's list of grievances:

1. They complain of certain ill treatment suffered by two of their young men, by a whipping inflicted on them at Montego-Bay by the hands of a slave (ordered by magistrates); which they say is an infringement of the treaty.

2. That the lands granted them orginally by the country for their subsistence, being worn out by long and repeated productions, are not sufficient to afford the provisions necessary for their support; they therefore claim from the island an additional quantity of land, and say that the adjoining lands, the properties of messieurs Vaughan and David Schaw, would suit them; and also the lands commonly called and known by the name of Crews, now Robert Kenyon, would be convenient to them.

3. They complain against the conduct of Captain Thomas Craskell the superintendent appointed to regulate the maroon-town; and say that he is not qualified to discharge the necessary duties of the office ... and as they have experienced the disposition and abilities of captain John James, (their late superintendent), they are desirous of his re-appointment.... and are averse to the appointment of any other person.

On 21 July the governor wrote to the Secretary for War:

I am sorry to inform you of an insurrection having taken place among the Maroons in Trelawny Town, who have been for some days in a state of rebellion. If it is merely a dispute with the whites in the neighbourhood, the measures I have taken against them, I trust, may restore quiet. But if the intrigues of the French are at the bottom, it becomes infinitely more alarming...

They have made friendship with the Maroons of the next town of Accompong, who are naturally hostile to them[11] ... they have sent all their women and children into the woods ... the reply to the magistrates who endeavoured to communicate with them was, that they desired nothing but battle, that they were prepared to receive the whites, and, if the whites would not come to them, they should visit the whites [Lindsay 23 pp. 40-1].[12]

There is no mistaking the intentions of Balcarres. By thus misinforming the British government that a state or rebellion existed and by paraphrasing the letter from old colonel Montague in such a way as to invite a misinterpretation of its meaning, omitting its clarifying postscript, the noble earl was undoubtedly paving the way for the campaign he had decided to launch.

Reporting the steps he had already taken, Balcarres wrote:[13]

I immediately marched three troops of dragoons, from the 20th regiment against them. I have sent them only to the neighbourhood, and put them under the orders of the magistrates of Montego Bay, until I have further information.

> If it is a serious and deep-founded plan, I must endeavour to keep the Maroons to the mountains, and separate them from the negroes in the low countries. This I can only do by light cavalry ... [Lindsay 23 pp. 40-1].

James Palmer, the custos of St. James, appears to have regarded the decision to send the dragoons to the area as provocative. In a letter dated 23 July, written after he had received notification that the governor had ordered "three troops of light horse to proceed to St James to reinforce the militia", he advised the governor as follows:

> News having arrived from the interior of the country that the maroons are still in doubts of the peaceable intends of the whites, declaring that we are only delaying the business in order to collect force, we therefore recommend your lordship to reappoint, with as little delay as possible, Major James, or his son, to the station of superintendent ...

The letter ended: "After these reports, we hope your lordship will see the necessity of retaining the light dragoons [14] till these affairs are perfectly settled" [*Journals* 9 p. 369ff. Ex.8].

On 25 July a senior magistrate, about to sail with the fleet from Negril, wrote [15] urging that the Maroons' demands, which he termed 'not unreasonable', be satisfied [*Journals* 9 pp. 369ff. Ex.9].

That Balcarres took a dim view of the conciliatory tactics advocated by the magistrates is apparent from a letter he wrote on 25 July to the titular governor of Jamaica, General Williamson, then commanding the British invasion force in Saint Domingue: "The insurrection among the Maroons has subsided for the moment, the magistrates having conceded everything, notwithstanding I had moved such a force as would have reduced them in a few days ... By such want of exertion, and such timidity among magistrates, are countries lost ..." [Lindsay 23 p. 44]. But the gallant earl made it clear to the general that he personally had no intention of allowing the tension to subside: "I have ordered down the chiefs of Trelawney Town on Friday next, and, if they do not come, I shall treat them as rebels".

Dashing off another letter to the general two days later, before the fleet had sailed for Saint Domingue, Balcarres returned to this theme:

> I have every reason to think the plan of the Maroons deeply founded, that the whole Maroons are in concert,[16] and that an explosion is ready to burst. I have with difficulty opened the eyes of the council. Most of the gentlemen, I see, treat it lightly ... if my hands had not been tied up, I should had extirpated Trelawny Town some days ago [23 p. 44].

The governor's statement, that he had ordered the chiefs of the Maroons to report to him on the following Friday, may have been a reference to a reply he had sent to a message from Trelawny Town that they wished to send their representatives to Spanish Town to see him in person. In reply Balcarres had ordered them to appear before him on 31 July.

News of this appointment did not reach magistrate Samuel Vaughan for notification to the Maroons until 28 July. Assuming that he informed them immediately, it would still have been impossible for their envoys, travelling half the length of the island on foot, to keep it. Vaughan made this point in a letter to Lewis Cuthbert, the government secretary, written that same day: "nor can captain Craskell or the maroons be up by the 31st" [*Journals* 9 pp. 369ff, Ex. 13]. Nevertheless, four of their captains and two other Maroons obtained the necessary passports from the custos at Montego Bay and set out for the capital.

The planters in the parishes adjoining the dissatisfied Maroons had every reason to desire an amicable settlement. They did not doubt the ability of these descendants of Cudjoe's warriors to do their properties extensive damage. In the same letter Vaughan expressed their fears:

> As a further motive for settling this affair without open hostility, I think it proper to inform you, that the negroes of several estates have, within these few days made complaints against management, although belonging to estates that are understood to be managed with great clemency. I was on the bench today, with our custos and another magistrate when a complaint of this kind came from all the negroes at Content estate, in this parish.
>
> Mr. Barrett tells me he goes this evening to Anchovy-Bottom, to quiet a complaint of a similar nature. Tryal negroes have done the same yesterday; and the custos has, within these few days, had four or five similar applications. Whence does this arise, but from the times; and what check have we so effectual as the maroons? [*Journals* 9 pp. 369ff Ex 13].

Advice of this kind was not acceptable to the governor. He demanded of the Maroons a humiliating capitulation, no doubt calculating that their refusal would give him an excuse to destroy them.

Balcarres, the aristocrat, had an obsessive fear of the revolutionary ideas then current in Europe. He did not wish to see them infecting the black population of the British West Indies and felt that this possibility should be firmly forestalled. One of his letters, dated 30 July 1795,[17] is particularly revealing of his state of mind:

> if my hands had not been fettered, I could have put an end to this disturbance last week,—
>
> It may be in my power next week — and a fortnight hence, instead of the action of a soldier, we may hear of the <u>Rights of Man</u>.[18]
>
> We have no force to oppose these doctrines — strike a blow and you will preserve the island until a force arrives; if you do not strike, they will [Lindsay 23 p.46].

But the spread of ideas is one thing. Infiltration by foreign agents is another. Whether Balcarres actually believed that French agents were behind the unrest of the Trelawny Town Maroons is open to doubt. The fact that he played on this theme may have been no more than an additional means of justifying the action he proposed to take.

Though fully aware that it would take the Maroon envoys, who were on their way to see him, several days to reach Spanish Town, he nevertheless declared martial law and convened a council of war on 2 August. Addressing the meeting on that day he said:[19]

> I am of opinion that the minds of the Trelawny Maroons have been corrupted by incendiaries from the enemy . . .
>
> The majority of the magistrates have ascribed the cause of this insurrection to the flogging of the two Maroons; and as they have been alarmed both for their properties and the credit of the island, they have considered it as a wise step to make every possible concession to the insurgents. If peace and quiet could be attained by this most humiliating conduct, perhaps the steps taken by the magistrates might receive the approbation of a part of the proprietors of this country . . . Whether this rebellion has proceeded from internal grievances, or from the machinations of an external foe, it does not alter the fact that they have been in rebellion . . .

> My opinion is, – strike at the Maroons of Trelawny Town. Strike at the source of this rebellion, and its fibres will be cut off... I have rung the alarm – it is long since it existed in my mind [Lindsay 23 pp. 46-8].

The Council of War was concluded on 3 August. Next day Balcarres set out with the main body of troops to take command of the operations in person. Determined to show himself no less zealous than General Williamson in the destruction of rebellious blacks, he could not have chosen more favourable odds. By his own reckoning the Trelawny Maroons should not have had more than 133 fighting men. In his letter to the Duke of Portland on 14 August 1795 he listed the inhabitants as follows: "Colonel – 1 Lieut. Colonel – 1 Captains – 14 Lieutenants – 10 Privates – 109 – 133 Invalids – 5 Women – 201 Boys – 164 Girls – 157 Total 660" [PRO:CO 137/94-7].

The magistrates had estimated the number they had seen in readiness at about 300. Even if they had not exaggerated, the Maroons were heavily out-numbered. Balcarres had under his command the 130th regiment of nearly 400 men [Lindsay 23 vol. 3 pp. 46-8] who, together with the three troops of dragoons and the other soldiers he had detached from the reinforcements due to sail for Saint Domingue, constituted a force of over 1,200 regulars. In addition the militia regiments could be called upon as required.

Bridges [5 vol. 2] thought the gallant earl was disposed to "despise the resistance that two or three hundred uneducated Maroons could oppose to the discipline and valour of from twelve to fifteen hundred regular troops then at his command, supported by several thousands of militia, called into active service by the proclamation of martial law".

Meanwhile the six Maroon envoys on their way to Spanish Town had been arrested at St. Ann's Bay. Balcarres found them there when he arrived in the town on 5 August on his journey westwards. But although he knew their mission and was well aware that they could not possibly have arrived at Spanish Town in time to keep the 31 July appointment, he ordered that they be placed in irons. He then continued his journey to Montego Bay.

On 8 August Balcarres sent the Trelawny Town Maroons this extraordinary communication:

> You have entered into a most unprovoked, ungrateful, and most dangerous Rebellion.
>
> You have driven away your Superintendent ... — you have endeavoured to massacre him.
>
> You have put the Magistrates ... and all the White People, at Defiance. You have challenged and offered them Battle ...
>
> Martial Law has ... been proclaimed. Every pass to your Town has been occupied ... You are surrounded by thousands ...
>
> I have issued a Proclamation offering a Reward for your Heads. That terrible Edict will not be put in Force before Thursday the Thirteenth Day of August.
>
> To avert those terrible Proceedings I ... command every Maroon of Trelawny Town, capable of bearing Arms, to appear before me at Montego-Bay, on ... the Twelfth Day of August ... and there submit themselves to his Majesty's Mercy ... [PRO:CO 137/94-7].

A proclamation issued on the same day offered a reward of £20 for every Maroon capable of bearing arms taken prisoner on or after 13 August, and contained the assurance that "in Case such Maroon Negro should make Resistance and be slain, the like Reward will be given ... upon proof that such Maroon Negro was belonging to Trelawny Town and did not submit himself ..."

Astounded as he no doubt was by the tone of this communication, old Colonel Montague nevertheless counselled compliance with the governor's order. To this end he persuaded "thirty-seven of his best and ablest marksmen" to follow him [Bridges 5 vol. 2 p.228]. They surrendered themselves to Balcarres at Vaughansfield on 11 August. The remaining Maroons, suspicious and chafing at the insulting response to their representations, refused to comply.

The perfidy of Balcarres was immediately apparent. Those who had complied with his order were bound with their hands behind them and marched under guard to Montego Bay, where they were imprisoned in irons aboard a warship.

One proud man was so humiliated that he committed suicide on the way "by ripping out his bowels".

In his letter to the Duke of Portland on 14 August the governor reported that "amongst those who were secured were their Colonel, Lieut. Colonel and eight other Chiefs" [PRO:CO 137/94-7]. An earlier letter dated 11 August, which no doubt went by the same packet ship, explained his field strategy: "I determined to begin my operations even before martial law was declared ... I resolved to blockade their country by seizing on every entrance, — although the manoeuvre was to be performed in a circle of forty square miles of the most rugged and mountainous country in the universe" [Lindsay 23]. This purpose, the letter stated, had been effected by the morning of 9 August, before the Maroons had received his communication.

Deprived of their leaders, the Maroons meanwhile hastily sent for two of their captains, Johnson and Smith, who had left their town some time before and had settled on holdings of their own in the parish of Westmoreland. These two, being men of great courage and ability, were willing to assume command of strong parties and to organise the Maroon resistance.

Two other captains, Palmer and Parkinson, who had been among those taken with Montague, were about the same time released in the expectation that they would persuade the others to surrender. Instead, upon returning to the main body on the evening of the 11th or the morning of the 12th August, they had encouraged them to resist and themselves determined to play a leading part in the war which was about to commence. The brave decision of these two men particularly angered Balcarres. In a proclamation dated 13 August, alleging that they had "behaved in a manner singularly atrocious", he raised the rewards for killing or capturing them to £100 for Palmer and £50 for Parkinson [*Journals* 9 pp. 392-3].

Trelawny Town consisted at this time of two settlements

less than a mile apart and known respectively as "the old town" and "the new town" or "Furry's Town" [20] On 12 August the Maroons set fire to the new town which, because of its more vulnerable position, they regarded as untenable. Thereupon began the Second Maroon War wherein, in the words of Bridges [5 vol. 2 p.229]: "less than three hundred barbarians secure in their native woods and mountains, were the objects and sometimes the assailants of fifteen hundred chosen European troops, assisted by more than twice that number of Colonial militia".

The first to experience the guerrilla tactics of the Maroons were a company of the St. James militia, within a mile of Vaughansfield. A small force suddenly descended on them at day-break, killing two, wounding six and retreating without loss as suddenly as they had come. One of those killed and two of the wounded were blacks, but whether slaves or free blacks serving with the militia is not recorded. On the same day an advanced post of the militia at Chatsworth, about a mile north of Trelawny Town, was fired upon from the heights above them[21] [Lindsay 23; Dallas 7 vol.1].

Balcarres had conceived a plan for a joint attack on the sites of the old and new towns, in pursuit of which he ordered Colonel Sandford to advance on the new town from the Trelawny side. This he did with 45 dragoons and a number of volunteers "supported by a very strong detachment of the Trelawny militia". Sandford's guides were a surveyor, Captain Robertson, and a former Maroon captain named Thomas who had left Trelawny Town. Sandford began his advance at about 5 p.m. on 12 August. R. Dallas, the contemporary historian of the Maroon wars, reported the battle:

> On the approach of the troops, the Maroons retreated within the defile and remained on a position where, unseen themselves, they could observe the motions of the body acting against them ... He [Sandford] instantly advanced with the greatest alacrity and climbed the very difficult acclivities of the mountain, with his dragoons mounted, accompanied by some of the militia and many volunteers and took possession of the site of the New Town.

Encouraged by the absence of resistance, the colonel then decided to push on rapidly through the defile to attack the old town and make his junction with Balcarres there. This led him straight into the trap:

> Taking Captain Robertson for his guide he entered the defile at the head of the dragoons, followed by Colonel Gallimore and his volunteers, and about twenty dismounted volunteer troops. The extent of the column was nearly half the length of the defile, and the Maroons suffered the head of it to reach within a third of the Old Town, without giving the slightest indication that they were ranged behind the bushes.

Having got their attackers under their muzzles the Maroons were ready to deal with them:

> ... an unexpected and tremendous volley of small arms from behind the trees was fired from the left, upon the column from one end to the other; all pressed forward and Colonel Sandford at the head of his men, advanced towards the town where two paths leading to it meet.
>
> Another volley was now poured from behind the trees, and Sandford fell, close by Captain Robertson ... On his death a panic pervaded the whole body; disorder ensued, no one was collected enough to direct or advise, and flight seemed the only recourse for safety.
>
> The troops took the nearest way from the town to head-quarters, some of them keeping up a scattered fire on an imaginary enemy, no Maroon having appeared since the fall of Sandford ... There was no recovering the panic that seized the troops; all contended for the front of the race [Dallas 7 vol. 1 pp. 187-190].

As for the proposed co-ordinating assault from the Vaughansfield side, this never took place. The noble commander in chief, having slipped and blackened an eye in a fall, had decided to postpone the operation. Of Sandford's command, he and his quarter-master, 14 regular troops, Colonel Gallimore and 12 of the militia and eight of the volunteers were killed. Many were wounded. Not a single Maroon had been killed. Thus ended the first day of the war.

On 13 August the Maroons evacuated the site of the old town, leaving a small look-out party in the area while the main body retreated deeper into the woods. Balcarres, expecting the town to be defended, made elaborate preparations for an assualt. He had the bush cleared by slaves working through heavy rain and after two days got a field piece mounted at the site of the new town. Chastened by the first day's results the commander in chief was obviously disposed to show the Maroons a new respect. So slow and cautious was his advance that the site of the old town was not occupied until 23 August [Lindsay 23; Dallas 7 vol. 1].

The report of these events sent by Balcarres to the Duke of Portland on 14 August illustrated his lively imagination. Although there had been no Maroon losses, he nevertheless credited the St. James militia, in their dawn engagement, with having "repulsed the Maroons, with considerable loss". The survivors of Colonel Sandford's routed command he credited with "charging and cutting down eleven of them". Colonel Sandford's defeat, was, he stressed, the result of disobedience of his instructions: "so severe a lesson would", he said, "induce our young soldiers to give in future the most scrupulous obedience to order".

On 24 August, having gained possession of the sites of both the old and new towns, Balcarres wrote confidently of the enemy's impending defeat:[22]

> The Maroons retreated into a country of rocks beyond description wild and barren, into which no white person has ever entered. In this situation they must starve; or if famine drives them out, many parties of militia and armed confidential negroes, equally accustomed with them to range in the woods, are ready, supported by regulars, to fall upon them; and the country is so exasperated against those rebels as to offer very large rewards for their destruction [Lindsay 23].

These rewards were the largest ever offered. For each Trelawny Town Maroon carrying arms the House of Assembly on 27 September 1795, offered 300 dollars [*Journals* 9 p. 387]. The parish of St. James offered a further 300 dollars, the parish of Trelawny 300 and the parish of Westmoreland 20 — a total of 920 dollars [Lindsay 23]. The dollar then in use in Jamaica was the Spanish silver dollar worth 6s. 8d. [Edwards 11 vol. 1 pp.277-80]. If Lindsay is correct this would have made the reward per head equivalent to £326.13s.4d. The reward for killing or capturing a slave who had joined the Maroons was fixed by the Assembly on 27

November at 150 dollars [*Journals* 9 pp. 397-8].

On 25 August Balcarres wrote even more confidently, to the Duke, of his anticipated victory:

> ... they are reduced, by surrender, capture, and deaths upwards of one-third, or nearly one-half of their number capable of bearing arms. Their ground provisions are already in a great measure, and in a few days will be almost entirely destroyed...

> They are driven back among barren and almost inaccessible rocks, and nearly destitute of every species of subsistence... They may escape in small numbers, and give disturbance as a band of robbers, but never are to be considered as an enemy capable of endangering the security of this island. I have accomplished every object that I had in view when I undertook the arduous task... [Lindsay 23].

A council of war was held at Montego Bay on 28 August. On the following day Balcarres again wrote to the Secretary of State, telling him that the council, "attended by the Speaker and many members of the Assembly — in all, thirty-three", had voted unanimously for the continuation of martial law. But the first doubts had apparently begun to form in his mind as to whether the victory of which he was so confident would be achieved quite so easily or so early as he had expected. "The seasons are now against me", he wrote, "and I must secure my posts". But he hastened to add that "Those rains are as much distressing to the enemy, who have consumed all their ground provisions, as to us". And he further consoled the Secretary of State, and no doubt himself, with the argument that, "They must be reduced to despair, — their wives and children will be an insupportable load to them... I think their submission may not be entirely out of the question" [Lindsay 23].

The Maroons soon proved that despite their supposed encirclement they could cause considerable damage in their enemy's rear. On 30 August, a party led by Dunbar slipped through the lines of the military and "burnt the buildings at... Bandon only six miles from the Headquarters on the road to Montego Bay" [Dallas 7 vol.1].

Balcarres did not return to the scene of operations after the council of war at Montego Bay. A little experience in the

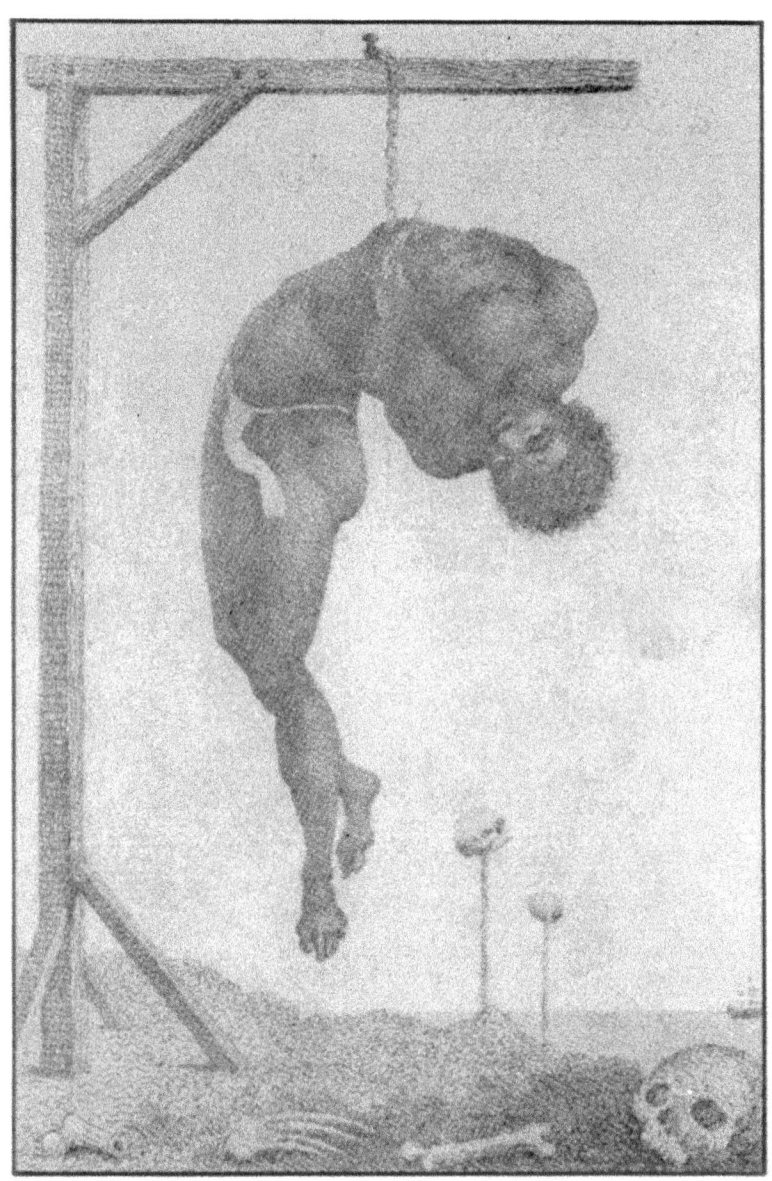

Hung by the ribs to a gallows, Suriname 1773 Engraving by William Blake from a drawing by John Stedman

Jamaican Slave House of Correction

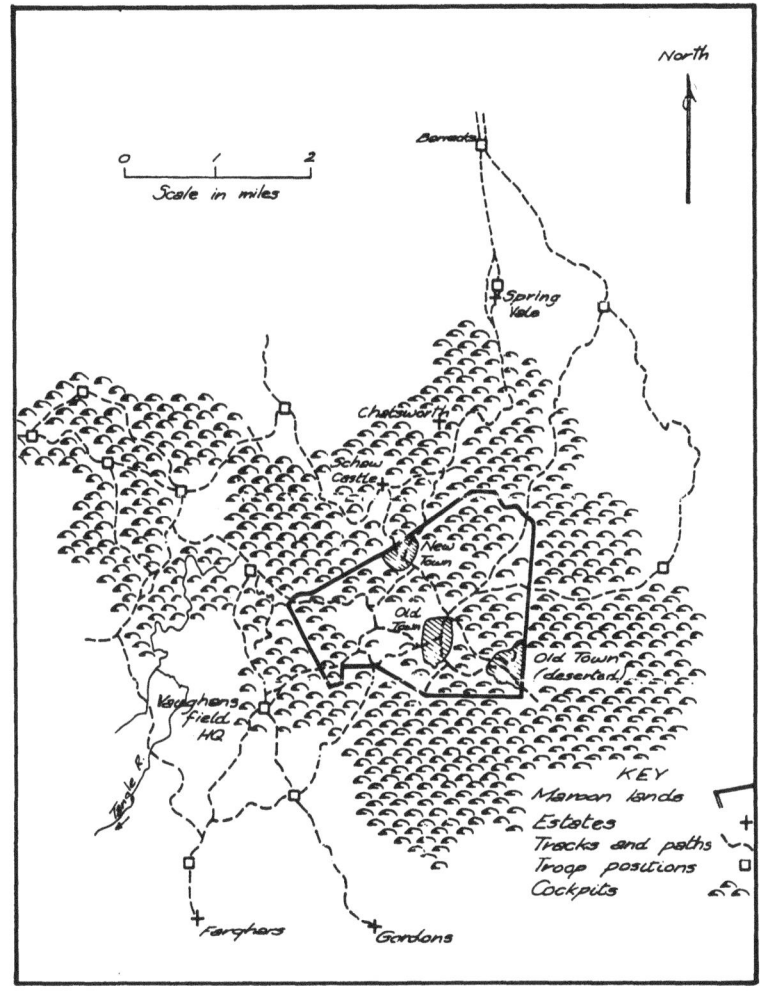

Terrain in Trelawny of the Second Maroon War, 1795. Map by Alan Teulon based on a contemporary plan by William Frazer, Aug. 9, 1795.

*Three-fingered Jack Mansong being attacked by Quashee and Sam
An illustration from* Obi, *published 1800.*

Trelawny Town, chief residence of the Maroons.

Maroons in ambush on Dromilly Estate, Trelawny Painting by J. Bourgoin.

Alexander, Earl of Balcarres, Governor of Jamaica 1795-1801.

Maroon Captain Leonard Parkinson   Engraving by Raimback published Oct. 2, 1796

field had been sufficient to cool his ardour. But he was careful to explain to the Secretary of State that there were good reasons why he should remain at Montego Bay.[23] His slip on the wet plank on 12 August had become by 24 August "a very severe fall, by which I was much wounded in the head" a misfortune which had, he said, "disabled me from visiting the outposts". "I have returned to Montego-Bay", he explained further, "that I may combine Civil Police with Military Operation" [PRO:CO 137/94-7].

Upon Balcarres' withdrawal the command in the field fell upon Colonel Fitch in whom, as he said, he had the greatest confidence. Writing to Balcarres on 2 September, Fitch reported that he had conferred that morning, under a flag of truce, with a party of 11 Maroons led by Parkinson. "They seem desirous of peace", Fitch wrote, "but they will not treat till two or three of their people appear from Montego Bay. They are apprehensive that they have been destroyed..." [Lindsay 23]. In the same letter Fitch reported that the body of Chambers, a captain from Accompong who had been acting as a guide and envoy for the military, had been found with his head "at a considerable distance from the body".

Fitch, conscious of the insecurity of his advanced positions, sounded this warning note:

> Unless a very large body of labourers, properly directed, and well supplied with the necessary tools, are immediately furnished, it will not only be impossible to carry on offensive operations, but it will be equally so to supply provisions, and in consequence the posts of the Maroon towns cannot be maintained.

In order to convince the Maroons that those of their number who had been taken to Montego Bay had not, as they had suspected, been destroyed, and in the hope that if they found them to be still alive they would agree to submit, it was agreed that two Maroons would be allowed to visit the prisoners. Harvey and Dunbar accordingly journeyed to Montego Bay and Colonel Montague was allowed to return with them in the confident expectation that he would advise submission. Having heard what they had to say, however, the Maroons "prepared to fight to the last man rather than surrender" [Dallas 7 vol. 1 p. 216].

Writing on 7 September,[24] Balcarres recorded that there had been a truce for some days to give the Maroons an opportunity to submit. But though he hoped that "from ten to twenty may be induced to surrender" he felt that the truce was "likely to end in hostilities being recommenced". Next day he reported sadly: "None of the Maroons have come in, and they seem determined on inveterate war" [Lindsay 23].

In his letter to the Secretary for War[25] following the resumption of the fighting Balcarres had the sorry duty of reporting the death in action of the new field commander:

> On the 11th inst. Colonel Fitch .... advanced .... a party of the 83rd Regiment to take possession of a very important post near the entrance to the cockpits.[26] He advanced .... to watch the effect of a shell thrown from an howitzer .... Unfortunately he fell into an ambuscade, by which we lost one officer and three rank and file of the 83rd, one volunteer, and two Accompong Maroons, killed – and two officers and six rank and file of the 83rd, and two Accompong Maroons, wounded. I am very sorry to add that the officer killed was Colonel Fitch [Lindsay 23].

He added that "The militia of Westmoreland have sustained a loss of one officer killed, and one officer and five privates wounded, in covering the party charged with the destruction of their provision-grounds".

The victorious Maroons in this engagement had, according to Dallas, been under the command of Captain Charles Schaw. They had been sent "to lie in ambush and surprise these companies, in which they were successful ... they forced them to retreat with the loss of six or seven men killed and some wounded". Dallas added that some of the slaves serving with the soldiers took the opportunity to join the Maroons. Of those who did not do so, ten were killed [Dallas 7 vol. 1 p.217].

Dallas also recorded another attempt to force Guthrie's defile, led by Major John James. James, it will be recalled, had adopted a very understanding attitude towards the demands of the Maroons before hostilities commenced. But he appears to have taken the field against them once the war had started. On this occasion he had led his party through the unfamiliar territory to the mouth of the defile, where their presence was detected by a Maroon look-out and the alarm sounded. A voice from an unseen source was then heard enquiring whether James was with the party and saying: "if he is let him go back, we do not wish to hurt him; but as for the rest of you, come on and try battle if you choose" [Dallas 7 vol.1 p.208]. Wisely the party chose to retire and "exhausted by fatigue and hunger returned by a circuitous route" to their headquarters.

As has been mentioned, some of the Maroons from Accompong served as mercenaries with the military against their brothers. How many did so is not known. But the establishment was grateful enough even for the fact that the Accompong Maroons had not come to the aid of Trelawny Town. The Assembly accordingly voted the Accompong Maroons a sum of £500 for what Dallas described as their 'good conduct'. It does not appear that any Maroons from the other Maroon towns assisted the Trelawny Town Maroons, though they did not provide mercenaries to act against them.

In the first week of September Balcarres ordered the Maroons of the two towns in Portland to attend upon him in Spanish Town, presumably as a test of their loyalty. On 7 September he wrote: "I rejoice to hear from Mr Atkinson that near fifty of the Charlestown Maroons have come in. I look upon this as of the very highest consequence during our present contest [Lindsay 23]. But on 30 September he informed the Secretary of State:

> A report prevails to-day that the Scott's Hall Maroons, a small tribe to windward, have joined the Trelawny Maroons. I could almost wish that it may prove to be true, for it would go far in establishing that the disobedience of the Charles-town and Moore-town Maroons proceeds from their fears only.
>
> The emissaries of the enemy are now working upon these fears, and try to

persuade them that I am sent over to extirpate them all... I hope the steps I took yesterday may remove those terrors, as I appropriated handsome presents for all the Charles-town people... If they do not come in now to receive these ... the rebellion may extend itself to windward ... [Lindsay 23].

On the same day the governor wrote to the superintendent at Moore Town:[27]

> The Moore-town Maroons have deserved and obtained my thanks for their quiet and orderly behaviour. – How is it possible that they can believe that I am their enemy, when I have declared myself their friend? When I speak, they hear the speech of the King. If they are afraid, let them stay where they are, until their fears are past, and then come to me .... [Lindsay 23].

Writing on 1 October to Major General Walpole, the field commander appointed on the death of Fitch, Balcarres said: "The Maroons to windward are all in a state of rebellion, but it seems implied that, if we do nothing against them, they will not for the present act against us ...." There the matter appears to have rested.

Summarising events at the end of September 1795 Dallas [7 vol. 1 pp. 231-2] wrote:

> At this crisis the inhabitants of the island, in looking back, had to view the following meloncholy statement of the war. In the attack upon Captain Hamilton there were two killed and six wounded; in Colonel Sandford's engagement thirty-seven killed and five wounded; the Westmoreland militia, with their working party of slaves, had been ambushed, seven of the soldiers killed and five wounded, and ten of the slaves killed; Captain Oldham, of the 62nd regiment, had perished through fatigue, of Colonel Fitch's party there were eight killed and seven wounded; two express dragoons and a sergeant of the 62nd regiment killed; Brooks house burnt and two men killed; Schaw Castle burnt; Bandon burnt, and twelve negroes carried away; Darliston trash house burnt; Catadupa, Mocha, and Lapland burnt and two negroes carried away; Lewis's burnt.
>
> This was the progress of the losses sustained by the troops and the country; on the other side, not a Maroon was known to have been killed; the rebels had seen the troops abandon in a panic one of their towns, had set fire to both, and retired to their fastnesses.

At the beginning of October Major General Walpole moved cautiously towards Guthrie's defile, systematically clearing the bush as he advanced. But despite this caution, as Dallas reported, part of one of his detachments under a lieutenant Richards was ambushed. "Not one of them lived to return" [7 vol.1 p.242]. Meanwhile a party of Maroons went through their lines and, wrote Dallas [p.245] : "burnt the house and coffee-stores at Nairne and other mountains: and descended upon the sugar plantations, destroyed Amity-Hall works, and forced away some negroes from an adjoining estate".

The largest body of Maroons was under the command of Charles Schaw and contained the women and children. Johnson, according to Dallas, led: "a force inferior in number ... but more active and enterprising. These were the men by whom the greatest ravages were committed ... He had no particular station, but shifted from ground to ground, according to the enterprise he meditated".

Dallas [7 vol. 1 p. 250] paid this tribute to Johnson's effectiveness: "Though known to be at a certain place one day, he would next surprise another place at a distance of twenty miles. He was not encumbered with women or children, and to his own party he had attached about forty slaves whom he had armed".

These slaves had escaped from the plantations during the course of the war to join the Maroons. They were not the last to do so. At the beginning of October Balcarres reported to the Secretary for War[28] that "Forty negroes are missing from one estate; it is possible they may have joined the Trelawny Maroons". Hopefully he added: "If it is true, I think it would weaken instead of strengthening the Maroons" [Lindsay 23 pp.77-8].

Johnson, however, was capable of making disciplined fighters out of raw recruits in a remarkably short time. His methods were so severe that some of the runaway slaves regretted the choice they made. But according to Dallas: "having once joined they could not retract". They were, nevertheless, sustained by the hope "that when the peace took place, they would be included in the terms as Maroons" Such indeed had been the reward of those who had joined

Cudjoe's ranks prior to 1739.

Johnson was completely impartial in the high standard of bravery and discipline he required of those under his command: "Some ... Johnson flogged for not fighting, while he made others captains ... This treatment was general, nor did he scruple to inflict the same punishment on his own sons". He was a man of great personal courage. When wounded in a battle with the Westmoreland militia on 8 November, he cut the bullet out of his flesh with his knife and continued to command his party. He was, wrote Dallas, "a despot over his men, yet under his discipline they fought better than the rest".

One unnamed slave fighting with the Maroons, who was killed in an ambush, was important enough to merit individual mention in the Assembly[29] [*Journals* 9 p. 398]. A slave named Jumbo taken prisoner by Johnson, who was said to have "escaped after having been several weeks his captive", was examined on 30 December. He stated that Johnson had "made a Cromantee negro, named Cudjoe, belonging to Mr Fowler, a captain and ... raised another belonging to the estate of Whittaker, named Casacrui, to the same rank ..." Johnson had great confidence in these two men. According to the witness he had not conferred such an honour on any other plantation slave [Lindsay 23 p. 88].

Walpole did not share the governor's derogatory opinion of the slaves who had joined the Maroons during the course of the war. Testifying to the effectiveness of at least one such slave he was later to write:[30] "There was a runaway of the name of Bowman, who, alone, a great space of time, destroyed plantations, and did infinite mischief" [*Journals* 9 p. 437]. Less than two months after he had made his jibe concerning the runaway slaves Balcarres apparently had cause to make a reassessment. Writing to the Duke of Portland on 29 November he said: "I am somewhat alarmed by accounts I have received this day from the parish of St. Elizabeth, which state that a body of fifty-four negroes have joined the

Maroons in rebellion ..." [Lindsay 23 pp. 92-3].

By mid October Balcarres had undoubtedly been forced to revise also his confident expectation of an easily won victory. On 18 October he addressed a sober memorandum to the President of the Council, the Speaker of the Assembly and the Attorney General.[31] He referred, among other things, to the terrain which "a few men are capable to maintain ... against attack of an army"; to "the intentions of the enemy to raise an insurrection among the slaves"; and to the expectation that during the coming dry season the Maroons would "set fire to cane-pieces, and occasion heavy losses to individuals". He then submitted a number of questions on which he sought their views and those of their colleagues.

Did they, he asked, approve a course of continuing the war by "persevering in our object of starving them by destroying their provisions". Or did the "public consideration ... impose the necessity on the island of making terms with these Maroons?" In the event of "that supposed necessity, what kind of terms could be acceded to, short of restoring to the Maroons their district of country?" [Lindsay 23 pp.82-4].

On 26 October these three gentlemen signed a joint letter to the governor.[32] The consensus they conveyed to him was that the most "judicious" way of continuing the war would indeed be to attempt to starve the Maroons, "any attack upon them [being] very perilous and of doubtful success". Nevertheless, they added:

> We think the species of mischief which the Maroons are likely to do in their despair, when the dry season of the year arrives, is of such important consideration to the public as to make it advisable to accede to any terms which will not endanger a recurrence of the evil we have been combating at a very great expense.

Their view, "after maturely weighing all the present circumstances", was that his lordship might:

> in case of an immediate surrender of their arms, assure them the safety of their lives and those of their wives and children, also either promising to abide the opinion of a Joint Committee of the Council and Assembly in all

other matters respecting them, or requiring them to be confined to a residence in the towns, with the promise of a recommendation to the legislature to make pecuniary provision for them during their lives [Lindsay 23 pp. 82-4].

Fortified by the knowledge that the most influential members of the Assembly would approve his overtures for peace, Balcarres gave the requisite instructions to Major General Walpole, probably at the end of October. Nearly seven weeks were to elapse, however, before a favourable opportunity was found to extend the proposed peace feelers to the Maroons. Meanwhile the war continued.

At the beginning of November the Maroons made a tactical retreat. Reporting this an officer in the field wrote:[33]

> Major-General Walpole entered Guthrie Glade (where they made their last stand). With this went your humble servant, who took special care to scour it well with the howitzer before it was entered. — The Maroons, seeing themselves thus beset, abandoned, without resistance, their boasted cockpits and glade, which, had they defended it, would have cost us many lives in carrying them [Lindsay 23 p.87].

Describing one of these cockpits the officer continued:

> That which Skynner entered was stockaded regularly at the gorges with loop-holes at proper intervals. The inside was level, round, and spacious. It had twenty huts, containing seventy beds, with fires between each. Nothing was found of the parties but a few belts, cartouche-boxes, and helmets, belonging to those whom they had slain, together with Montague James's identical white jacket, which you have seen him wear.

Writing to the Secretary of State on 16 November from Dromilly, Balcarres passed on the latest intelligence on the disposition of the enemy's forces:

> The Maroons seem to have divided into two very strong bodies, one of which has been lurking for ten days past between Fleming's and Wilts, near which Captain Stewart, of the Trelawny militia... had an obstinate engagement with them on the 6th instant.
>
> The other strong party occupies the ground near Mocha, upon the borders of Westmoreland. Near this post, Lieutenant Williams of the militia, had a very smart and extremely successful affair on the 8th instant, having killed seven... and wounded many [Lindsay 23 p. 90].

Interestingly enough, the last mentioned engagement was the one in which Johnson was wounded, but Dallas, who recorded this and stated that the Maroons were forced to retreat, was unaware of the heavy Maroon casualties reported by Balcarres. Indeed, in the same letter Balcarres wrote:

> As it is impossible to get up with these savages without first receiving the fire of their ambush, our loss in every affair is constantly from eight to twelve men killed and wounded; and as the ambuscade is generally formed within a few yards of the track, the return of the killed is often unfortunately, greater than the wounded.

Finally, Balcarres warned the Secretary of State: "It is equally in the power of a few Maroons, as of the whole body of them, to burn down the cane-pieces". But he offered this consolation: "I have a month still to act in, before that dry and dreaded moment arrives".

In his letter to the Duke of Portland dated 20 November, Balcarres reported that, four days earlier, Walpole had discovered "a town of upwards of three hundred huts, which the Maroons had abandoned" [Lindsay 23 pp. 90-2]. On 18 November, Lieutenant Colonel Stevenson, pursuing a party of Maroons with a column of 120 men, caught sight of "their advanced sentinels descending from the tops of the highest trees". Realising that they must be near their quarry, the troops accelerated their advance, but when they reached a camp site they found it abandoned.

Caught at a disadvantage and possibly encumbered with women and children, this band of Maroon warriors had had a narrow escape. In their haste they had been forced to abandon their clothing, provisions, some precious musket balls, some money and even some pots on the boil. Stevenson "pursued their tracks as long as he could find a trace", but the troops never caught up with them. Somehow they had succeeded in melting into the bush [Lindsay 23 pp.90-2].

Not until a month later was Walpole able to report a favourable response from the Maroons to his peace overtures.[34] In a letter to Balcarres dated 20 December, the general wrote: "Hull has agreed... to a sort of truce ... I understand that they will surrender on their lives only, wishing for land to be allotted them to cultivate" [Lindsay 23 pp. 92-3].

Dallas gave an account of this meeting. On 18 December officer Hull had encountered the body of Maroons led by Charles Schaw. Making signals that he wished to parley he had obtained a cease fire. Each side had then advanced one man and, when the nature of the proposed parley had been made known to the Maroons, Schaw and Hull had advanced to meet. When Hull assured him that Walpole himself would come to discuss terms of peace, Schaw had agreed to a truce. Each side then posted two sentries to guard the spring near the meeting place. The Maroons were invited to send some of their captains to meet an equal number of white officers, but they declined, preferring "to reserve their confidence till they saw the General" [7 vol.2 p.137].

Walpole arrived two or three days later. Old Colonel Montague, titular head of the Maroons, was also present. Possibly he had been with Schaw's party, or he may have come specially to lend his authority to the discussions. On 21 December 1795, nearly 57 years after the solemnization of Cudjoe's treaty, another undefeated body of Maroons received an offer of a treaty of peace. On this occasion, however, the tribute to their courage and tenacity implicit in the offer was so much the greater, for the Trelawny Town Maroons had been isolated for attack and none of the other Maroons in the island are known to have come to their assistance.

Under cover of a letter to Balcarres dated 22 December, Walpole forwarded the document, signed by Montague and himself, which read as follows:

Proposals of the Maroons

First:- That they will on their knees, beg his Majesty's pardon.

Second:- That they will go to the Old Town, Montego Bay,

or any other place that may be pointed out, and will settle on whatever lands the governor, council, and Assembly may think proper to allot.

Third:- That they will give up all runaways.

I grant the above

George Walpole, Major-General,

           his
Montague + James
           mark

Done on Guard-Hill, 21st December, 1795 [Lindsay 23 pp. 98-9].

In addition to the written terms there was also an unwritten term. Writing to Balcarres privately on 25 December Walpole made reference to this: "I was obliged to accede on my <u>oath</u>; I promised a secret article, that they should not be sent off the island" [Lindsay 23 p. 99]. In the same letter Walpole gave this further interesting piece of information: "Old Montague is, as far as I can guess, the obstacle to peace, as much as he dares. Some of the Maroons were heard to tell him that they would have peace, whether he would nor not".

This puts a very different complexion on the old man's original decision to comply with the order issued by Balcarres on 8 August. It would appear that Colonel Montague's decision to present himself to the governor on that date had been based not on any lack of courage but on misplaced trust. What Walpole heard and reported in his letter of 25 December shows, however, that in the light of experience Montague was reluctant to trust the gallant and noble earl a second time. How right he was in this assessment events were soon to show.

Dallas asserts that Johnson was in favour of a treaty of peace, but had prepared a contingency plan:

> He had moved to concentre the Maroon force for the purpose of adopting a dreadful alternative, had a negotiation been unsuccessful ... It is a circumstance hardly known, that he meant, on the junction of the whole Maroon force, if he had found no opportunity of treating, or, in

negotiating had failed, to have crossed the island, and on the South of the cockpits, through Cave River, to have made a descent on the estates in the mountains of Clarendon, where he expected to find a more favourable disposition in the negroes than to the Northward and Westward . . .

Assessing the possibilities of such a manoeuvre succeeding, Dallas made the point that in the north and west, presumably because of the Maroons' role as gendarmes over the past half century, the slaves or "the majority of them were actually the determined enemies of the Maroons". On the other hand "in Clarendon, whence the Maroons originally came, a degree of family connexion was still acknowledged among them, and emissaries had been employed to ascertain their inclination" [7 vol.2].

It has been suggested that the readiness of the Maroons to make peace may have been occasioned, or at least increased, by the knowledge that on 14 December the goverment's emissary Colonel Quarrell, who had been sent to Cuba, had returned to the island with a number of Spanish 'chasseurs'.

These chasseurs were professional bounty hunters who, with their savage dogs, were employed to hunt escaped criminals and runaway slaves in Cuba. Quarrell, whose mission to obtain these chasseurs had been a difficult one,[35] was convinced that the news of the arrival of these trained dogs was the decisive factor. But, as Dallas admits, "some persons entertained doubts" respecting the probable result of an encounter between the chasseurs and the Maroons.

At a meeting held by Balcarres at King's House, Spanish Town, on 24 December, with such members of the Council and the Assembly as were able to attend, the arrival of the chasseurs was one of the arguments urged against the wisdom of the proposed treaty of peace, though it does not appear to have impressed the majority present. But there is sufficient reference to the dogs in the subsequent correspondence between Walpole and Balcarres to facilitate an assessment of what their usefulness or otherwise would have been, had it been necessary to make use of them. The correspondence is reviewed in the next chapter.

Another matter which was of the utmost importance to those assembled at King's House was the question of whether the Maroons would be willing to surrender the slaves who had joined them during the course of the war. In a letter to the Attorney General Balcarres recapitulated the main points that had been made during the debate at King's House on 24 December.[36] Some had argued in favour of ratification of the treaty signed by Walpole and Montague and some against. Among the arguments in favour of ratification it was urged "That we had hitherto formed hopes of their being deficient in provisions and ammunition, but these had proved fallacious. It was now clear that they had an ample supply of provisions and as to ammunition, the late conflict had plainly shewn that they were not scanty in that article".

Against ratification it was argued:

> That the effects of not sending the Maroons off the island may in future be severely felt... That, in the event of settling... the Trelawny Maroons in this island, they would... on some future occasion join the Nanny-Town, Charles-Town, and Scott's Hall Maroons; and if this should be the case, we had in fact achieved little or nothing.

It was also argued that "at a time when they were appalled with horror at the idea of being hunted down by dogs of the most terrible description, it would be very unwise ... on our parts to grant them such terms" [Lindsay 23 pp. 100-2].

The discussion concluded, a majority of those present did not consider the contra arguments sufficient to outweigh the dangers involved in a continuation of the war:

> It was resolved, That if the Trelawney Maroons... deliver the runaways that have joined them, and if they... lay down their arms, which arms are to be taken away from them, that then... General Walpole's secret article[37] ought to be ratified, as far as their not being sent off the island; but that they are to remain in Jamaica, subject to such regulations as the governor, council, and Assembly may think proper to enact....

At the foot of the record of this resolution Balcarres added the following endorsement:

> I have received... in Spanish Town, the treaty signed by General Walpole and Colonel Montague James and have ratified the same. I do appoint Friday morning, the first day of January next, at ten o'clock, for the

188   BLACKS IN REBELLION

Trelawny Maroons to come in a body to Castle Wemyss, to perform the treaty.

Dated at Castle Wemyss, this 28th day of December 1795 [Lindsay 23 pp. 100-2].

FOOTNOTES

[1] Because of the chronic shortage of English coins, most of the coins in circulation in Jamaica at this period were Spanish or Portuguese. The "Joe" and "Half Joe" were Portuguese gold coins. In the 1770s the full *Johannes* weighing 18 dwt. 12 gr. was worth £3.12s sterling or £5.10s. Jamaican currency. 3 Half Joes would have been worth locally £7.15s [Long 24 vol. 1; B.M. Ad. MS 12404, 627 addenda].

[2] Exhibit 13 — Magistrate Samuel Vaughan to Government Secretary Lewis Cuthbert, stating that neither of the Jameses would accept the appointment if nine months residence at Trelawny Town were required.

[3] The holder of the office of governor was Major General Sir Adam Williamson. But Williamson was in Saint Domingue in charge of the British invasion force (see vol. 1 Chapter 8). As Balcarres' appointment was that of governor in all but name, there seems little point in calling him anything less.

[4] J. Palmer, Custos of St. James, to Balcarres, undated, enclosed in Balcarres to Portland, 10 June 1795.

[5] Exhibit No. 1 to the governor's message to the Council and Assembly on 22 September 1795 — Wm. Duncan and others to Balcarres, 18 July 1795.

[6] Exhibit No. 2 — Don. Campbell and another to Trelawny Town Maroons, 18 July 1795.

[7] Colonel Montague to St. James magistrates. See also PRO:CO 137/94-7 — document headed "Copy of the Answer of the Maroons in reply to a letter sent to them from the Magistrates of Montego Bay and dated 10th July 1795", enclosed with Balcarres to Duke of Portland, 19 July 1795 (2nd letter).

[8] David Schaw was the owner of a nearby plantation. In a letter dated 19 July from Trelawny Town, John Merody informed his chief Thomas Craskell: "David Schaw ... has taken all the business upon himself; for there will be four magistrates from the bay today at Mr Schaw's property; they do not want any more letters from you" [*Journals* 9 pp. 368ff, Ex.4 n8].

[9] "Examination of John Merody, late assistant to Trelawny Town before the Commander in Chief at Head Quarters Vaughansfield 16th August 1795".

[10] J. Palmer to Balcarres, 21 July 1795.

[11] According to Dallas [7] Trelawny Town and Accompong were in dispute over the custody of the Maroon's copy of the treaty signed by Cudjoe in 1739. What eventually happened to it is not known, but in 1882 Rev. E. Bassett Henry wrote from Siloah on behalf of the Accompong Maroons asking for a copy. The

Colonial Secretary supplied one by letter dated 19 December 1882. This letter and the copy of the treaty, in the possession of the oldest Maroon, Commander Reid, was shown to the author at Accompong in 1943.

[12] Lord Lindsay was a kinsman of Balcarres. He appears to have had access to official correspondence which, for some unexplained reason, is not now to be found in the Public Record Office.

[13] Balcarres to Henry Dundas, 21 July, 1795.

[14] Balcarres had detached these dragoons from the reinforcements about to sail for Saint Domingue. Toussaint Louverture may have been unaware of his debt of gratitude to the few hundred inhabitants of a Maroon town in Jamaica. Dragoons were originally mounted infantry, so called after the gun they carried. Later they became part of the cavalry.

[15] John Tharpe to Balcarres, 25 July 1795.

[16] Balcarres had no justification for this statement. Only one of the five Maroon towns had submitted demands.

[17] Balcarres to Lewis Cuthbert, 30 July 1795.

[18] A reference to Thomas Paine's *The Rights of Man*, published in 1791-2 answering Edmund Burke's reactionary attack on the French Revolution. His book suppressed in England and facing a charge of treason, Paine fled to France where he had been made an honorary citizen.

[19] Balcarres' own summary of his speech to the Council of War, 2 August 1795.

[20] Furry was a Maroon leader who had left the main body with his followers and established a separate 'town'.

[21] Balcarres to Portland, 14 August 1795.

[22] Balcarres to Portland, 24 August, 1795.

[23] Balcarres to Portland, 24 and 25 August 1795.

[24] Balcarres to Major-General Taylor, 7 and 8 September, 1795.

[25] Balcarres to Henry Dundas, September 1795.

[26] The site of this engagement, known as Guthrie's defile, was allegedly the place at which the negotiation of the treaty with Cudjoe had taken place in 1739.

[27] Balcarres to Captain Douglas, 30 September 1795

[28] Balcarres to Dundas, October 1795.

[29] Capt. James Scarlett jnr. to the Speaker, 17 October 1795.

[30] Walpole to Balcarres, 24 December 1795.

[31] Balcarres to President of the Council and others, 18 October 1795

[32] Tho. Tridell and others to Balcarres, 26 October 1795.

[33] Major Dixon to Colonel Atkinson, 6 November 1795.

[34] Walpole to Balcarres, 20 December 1795.

[35] Colonel Quarrell's mission to Cuba is described in detail by Dallas [7 vol.2].

[36] Record of meeting on 24 December 1795 at King's House, Spanish Town.

[37] The meeting at which this resolution was passed was held at King's House, Spanish Town, 24 December. It is therefore apparent that Balcarres had been informed of the 'secret article' before he received Walpole's letter of 25 December. The probabilities are that a private letter accompanied Walpole's official letter of 22 December.

CHAPTER EIGHT
OF PEACE AND PERFIDY

Those present at the meeting of members of the Assembly and the Council at Spanish Town on 24 December 1795 were, as we have seen, divided in their opinions. The majority favoured ratification of the treaty with the Maroons, the minority the continuation of the war. In the summary of the discussion contained in his letter to the Attorney General, Balcarres had reported that those who opposed ratification had taken the view "That the effects of not sending the Maroons off the island may in future be severely felt". Against this those favouring ratification had argued:

> That the residence of the Trelawny Maroons in the island would not appear to be much consequence, when it was considered that their departure would not remove, but only lessen the evil; for that, while the Windward Maroons continued to enjoy their freedom, the island could not be exempt from danger [Lindsay 23 pp.100-2].

Balcarres, however, had been less than frank with the assembled legislators. Although he advocated ratification of the treaty, including the secret article, it is evident that he had no intention of honouring the undertaking that they would not be sent off the island.

In a letter to the Duke of Portland dated 31 December, Balcarres expressed distrust of the intentions of the Maroons, including those of Nanny Town[1] and Accompong, and explained his motives:

> My principal object in ratifying the treaty has been, to prove to the conviction of the country that no pacific intention has ever entered into the minds of the Maroons. If I had refused to ratify it, the whole responsibility for the mischief that may ensue would have been thrown upon my shoulders. Whereas, my having ratified it must unite the country in the opinion that these rebels mean destruction to this island, and that no alternative presents itself but to follow them up, whatever be the difficulties or expense ... [23 pp.102-4].

What Balcarres did not disclose to the Secretary of State was that he had built into his ratification of the treaty a condition which he must have known that the Maroons could not possibly fulfil.

The document signed by Walpole and Montague had left open the question of the date on which the Maroons were to come in and lay down their arms. No right had been reserved to the governor unilaterally to name the day. And even if it be argued that this right was implicit, it could not have been supposed by either of the signatories that he would fix such an early date that the Maroons could not possibly comply with it. But this is precisely what this cunning and perfidious nobleman had done.

In the endorsement Balcarres placed on the document confirming his ratification he had appointed Friday 1 January, 1796 as the date on which the Trelawny Town Maroons were "to come in a body to Castle Wemys to perform the treaty". As the notice of this ratification had been issued on 28 December it is unlikely that any Maroons could have been aware of it prior to 29 or 30 December. Balcarres, who had himself spent several days at the scene of operations at the beginning of the war, was aware of the nature of the terrain. There can therefore be no doubt that the fixing of a date, by which the great majority of the Maroons could not possibly have arrived, was deliberate.

Even those Maroons who were nearest to Balcarres' headquarters at Castle Wemys, near Falmouth, would have had insufficient time to make the necessary preparations for presenting themselves on 1 January. Those deeper in the woods, who comprised the great majority, would not have been aware of the ratification until the date fixed for them to present themselves before the governor had passed. In any event, Balcarres must have been fully aware that it was necessary to allow the Maroon leaders a reasonable time in which to explain the terms of the treaty to their followers and overcome their natural doubts and suspicions.

Not surprisingly, on 1 January, General Walpole was able to report the arrival of only five Maroons. Writing to Balcarres he stated: "only Smith, Dunbar and Williams, and two boys are here. I shall send them to Falmouth to-morrow. I suppose that your lordship will admit them to the terms of the treaty upon which they have surrendered" [23 p.105]. Delighted, Balcarres wasted no time in getting off a letter to the Secretary of State:[2] "The farce has ended as I expected, — only three of them and two boys have come in. I shall be ready to attack them in less than forty-eight hours, preceded by the Spanish dogs . . ." [23 p.105].

Meanwhile, unaware of Balcarres' perfidious intentions, Walpole was engaged in arranging for as many Maroons as were willing to come in to do so. On 4 January he informed Balcarres that he had allowed Smith "to return to the cockpits to bring in his family, which he did in the evening, to the amount of thirteen, — three of them very fine young men". It also appears that between 1 and 3 January Walpole had visited Balcarres at Castle Wemys. In the same letter he referred to the fact that other Maroons had "surrendered, in my absence with your lordship".

Walpole then proceeded to inform the governor that many other Maroons were on their way to his headquarters to comply with the treaty. He had this information, he said, from Smith. And he explained to his lordship why he felt that Smith could be trusted: "He had (which induced me to trust him) given me a strong proof of his fidelity . . . by a material piece of information, that one of those who surrendered ... is a run-away; that this is an experiment on the part of the runaways to try whether they can pass for Maroons". Walpole added that, on Smith's advice, he had allowed this runaway slave to return to the cockpits, doubtless in the hope that he would be able to convince others that they too could pass as Maroons.

Not suspecting that any question would be raised as to whether those Maroons who surrendered had complied with the treaty, Walpole continued:

> A large body are expected in to-day of Maroons, and I hope others, – it will take some days, I suppose, to get in the whole; for they are as mistrustful as possible, and each is desirous that the other should make the experiment before him. All this will naturally and conclusively prove to your lordship the impropriety of holding forth more harsh conditions than those now granted.

He concluded his letter with this sober assessment, alluding to the possibility of aid to the Maroons from revolutionary France: "Should there be any person so dull to common policy and common sense as to think that another turn of the screw would be better, ask him this question, 'Is he prepared to spin out the contest till foreign assistance may arrive?' " [23 pp.105-6].

Now that he was aware that substantial numbers of the Maroons did intend to comply with the treaty, Balcarres authorised Walpole to continue to receive them, thereby making the latter an unwitting accomplice in his nefarious scheme. Writing to Walpole on the following day he said:

> Unless a great number of the Maroons came in last night, or do come in in the course of this day, I hope and trust that nothing will prevent the dogs from going out tomorrow.

> I am perfectly with you, that the pin ought not to receive another screw; but also clear that it ought not to be relaxed [23 p. 106].

Balcarres obviously placed great faith in the effectiveness of the Spanish chasseurs and their dogs. Walpole, however, was doubtful of their value. On 8 January, replying to Balcarres' request that he advance with the dogs against those Maroons who had not come in, he wrote:

> Our misfortune will, I fear, occur as to the dogs — the extreme want of water. There is none, during seven hours' march, between the great cockpit and the spot where Colonel Hull engaged the Maroons. Smith likewise informs me that there is none beyond the last mentioned place, except what may chance to be got from wild pines. If the dogs cannot be got on through want of water, we must leave them behind [23 pp.106-7].

The arrival of the dogs had been given so much publicity and the legislature had placed so much confidence in their effectiveness, that Walpole's letter came as a considerable shock. Much embarrassed, Balcarres replied:[3]

> I sincerely hope and trust that no column shall proceed against the enemy without the dogs until their inefficacy is proved; such a measure, I know, would set the country in an uproar. My own responsibility, as well as my opinion and the report I have made to his Majesty of the intended operations with the dogs, leaves no other alternative than to give immediate and due energy to the enterprise and ideas of the country, in sending, at an enormous expense, for these dogs [23 p.107].

While plans for a fresh advance into the cockpits were under discussion, more and more of the Maroons and their runaway slave allies had continued to come in to General Walpole's headquarters at the site of the Old Town. And the general was, as he disclosed in his letter to the governor of 12 January, in touch with the famous Johnson:

> Johnstone has sent to me to say that he has not been able to prevail on the women, several of whom have been lost, and only one found since the late actions. He desires to know what I have to say in answer to his message; my answer is that I shall move against him unless twenty men come in to-morrow...
>
> I am, however, apprehensive that Johnstone's reply will scarcely arrive in time. They beg till four o'clock; but if I delay till that time, it will be too late for me to move till next day [23 pp. 107-8].

Balcarres was most anxious that Walpole should without delay advance against the Maroons, but the latter wanted to be sure that the consequences which might result from too precipitate action had been fully appreciated. He concluded his letter with this warning: "Your lordship will please to consider what I mentioned this morning..., viz. whether we should be the first to recommence hostilities; certainly we shall not make peace for some time to come, after the first shot is fired".

Later that day, at two-thirty in the afternoon, Walpole again wrote to Balcarres[4] to inform him that he had actually started his advance but that before he had gone two hundred yards he had met a Maroon with a message from Johnson. The latter had assured him "that he would come with his people to-morrow into the cockpit to make their huts", had "begged that I would have provisions for him" and had stated that "he would adjust every point". In consequence of this, said Walpole, he had called a halt, adding: "If Johnstone will build his huts within our posts, I shall permit him to keep his arms till he sees you, then to lay them down. If, on account of the women, he insists on building them in the cockpits, in that case he must lay down his arms to me" [23 p.108].

Balcarres had no alternative but to accept this position in his reply written on the following day: "I think you may give them an opportunity until two o'clock to-morrow afternoon to come in, and then proceed against the remainder. I really am for pushing them hard. We have seen the good effects of it". To this he added a sentence which provides the most damning indictment of all his subsequent shameless duplicity: "Permit me to express the very high sense I have experienced of your punctuality. Although the principle of the order is not discretionary, still I give you free permission to modulate it according to your judgement" [23 pp.108-9].

The surrender of Johnson and his party took place as anticipated. On 14 January Balcarres sent Walpole his orders relating to those Maroons who had not yet come in:[5] "that you do advance against the rebels at the very earliest moment ... Should the Maroons, in a body, offer to surrender, you may receive their arms on the spot ... All the Maroons now in to be sent to Montego Bay as soon you can procure a sufficient escort" [23 p. 109].

On 16 January, in a letter to Spanish Town,[6] the governor joyfully reported the surrenders to date and arranged for suitable publicity:

> I have in my possession, of Trelawney Maroons, upwards of four hundred persons, of whom I count about one hundred and thirty men. Some of the young Maroons are still out; but I think we have a near and happy prospect of extinguishing the embers of this rebellion. You will announce this pleasing event as speedily as possible in the Spanish Town papers [23 p.110].

Acting in good faith Walpole exercised the discretion given to him. On 21 January he informed Balcarres: "I have given assurances to the Maroons of a little longer indulgence for the coming in of their families, some few of whom, from sickness, are still with the remaining Maroons in the woods" [Southey 30 vol. 3, p.101].

Some of the Maroons were indeed in such remote areas deep in the woods that at the end of January they still had not heard about the treaty. Both Walpole and Smith were confident that they would accept its term once these had been explained to them. Writing to Balcarres on 29 January Walpole explained this:

> From the information ... received from Smith, there seems ... little chance of any but a Maroon discovering a Maroon, whenever these people are where they can remain quiet for any time. Dogs cannot scent but on a recent step; I fear that the Maroons are now so deep in the woods that no expedition can be supported against them, without risking failure of food and water for those animals ... [Lindsay 23 pp. 112-3].

Walpole would have preferred that all the Maroons, as they surrendered, should remain at his headquarters until the last of them had been located and offered the terms of the treaty. Balcarres insisted however that they should be sent as quickly as possible to Montego Bay. He wanted these "quick silver rebels", as he described them, "under lock and key" before he met the Assembly. On 20 January he had agreed to let Walpole keep up to ten men and their families with him [Southey 30 vol.3, p.101], but a couple of days later he was again insisting that all should be sent down to the Bay.

Walpole pointed out that Smith was willing to go out with him to locate the remaining Maroons and persuade them to surrender, but the governor obviously had other ideas. Now that the three most formidable leaders had come in with their men, he wanted Walpole to advance with the dogs against the remainder. In a letter dated 23 January Walpole strongly disapproved:[7] "I am not so fortunate as to coincide with your way of thinking and my reason is that a very different line of conduct has produced the success which we have already experienced, and if pursued will probably produce more; the dogs had certainly nothing to do with it" [Southey 30 vol. 3, p. 101].

The last of those who had surrendered to him having been sent to Montego Bay, Walpole wrote again to Balcarres on 29 January regretting that, through failure to take his advice, the opportunity of getting in the remainder of the Maroons might have been lost [30 p.102]. Sensitive to this criticism, Balcarres, on 2 February, gave Walpole permission to keep three Maroons with him, thereby enabling him to keep Smith and Johnson. At the same time Walpole was directed "to get in or destroy the rebels who are still out". The same letter contained this revealing comment: "I do not know your opinion respecting the treaty, nor do I desire to know it; I have formed my own, and must declare it when I am called upon" [30 p.103].

Writing to the Secretary for War on 30 January,[8] Balcarres reported that 30 Maroon men and 100 women and children were still out, but that he did not "compute the effective Maroon warriors now in rebellion to exceed fourteen" [Lindsay 23 pp.114-5]. He estimated that there were runaway slaves still in the woods to the number of nearly 150. Though these were "ill armed and with very little ammunition", he thought "their reduction may take some time".

Balcarres' penchant for deceit and trickery is exemplified in the second letter he wrote to the Secretary for War on the same day:[9]

> I hold the treaty signed by Major General Walpole on the one part, Colonel Montague James, chief of the Maroons, on the other part, and ratified by me — absolutely as nothing. Exclusive of my having been obliged to move against them weeks after it was exchanged, the main article of it, viz. the

surrender of the runaway slaves, is not fulfilled.

I believe Major-General Walpole, and part of the country, think otherwise, – and should any difficulty arise respecting the disposal of the persons of the Maroon prisoners, I shall send you the whole correspondence.

I have purposely kept out of the way of a meeting with the Maroons, consequently the country and myself are unfettered [23 pp. 116-8].

Meanwhile the remaining Maroons, unaware of what Balcarres was planning and taking him to be a man of honour, continued to come in and surrender their arms to General Walpole. On 12 February the latter reported that Johnson had brought in six, adding that he had been told that others had come but, on seeing that those who had previously surrendered had been sent off to Montego Bay, had gone back into the woods [Southey 30 p.103]. In a letter to the Secretary for War dated 15 February Balcarres wrote:

after having ineffectually searched for them from four different points, forty-three more have surrendered themselves, of which six are stout, able Maroon men. The Maroons now out consist of twenty-four men and sixty-three women and children. The body of runaway negroes slaves ... are still out; some, however, have come in ... [Lindsay 23 pp.118-9].

The most remote party of Maroons, led by Palmer and Parkinson, may not even have heard of the treaty until some time in March, when they were finally located by a party guided by Smith. On hearing the terms offered they agreed to come in. According to Dallas, Parkinson brought in 36 Maroons on 21 March, a further 13 arriving next day. Writing to the Duke of Portland on 26 March, Balcarres reported: "Thirty-six Trelawney Maroons and all the runaway negroes who had joined them in rebellion, surrendered their arms on 17th and 21st March" [23 p.122].

Meanwhile, earlier in the month of March, an ugly rumour had reached Walpole's ears. In a private letter to Balcarres dated 11 March he had expressed his grave concern:

For some days past I have been in a state of considerable uneasiness at a report, which seems to gain ground, that the legislature means to infringe the capitulation accepted by me and ratified by your lordship.

My Lord, to be plain with you, it was through my means alone that the Maroons were induced to surrender, from a reliance which they had on my word – from a conviction impressed upon them by me that the white people would never break their faith [23 pp. 120-1].

So distressed was Walpole at the possibility that the Maroons might be made the victims of trickery and dishonesty that he did not hesitate to issue a thinly veiled threat:

> All these things strongly call upon me, as the instrumental agent in this business, to see a due observance of the terms, or, in case of violation, to resign my command; and if that should not be accepted, to declare the facts to the world, and to leave them to judge how far I ought or ought not to be implicated in the guilt and infamy of such a proceeding.
>
> So much the more strong is the call upon me, as there was no occasion to ratify the terms; for your lordship will well recollect that I told you at Castle Wemys that the time appointed... for fulfilling them was expired, and the terms therefore null and void; but your lordship then thought there was so much advantage to the country in those terms, that it would be best not to give them up [23 pp.120-1].

Feigning innocence and concealing from Walpole the fact that he was actively engaged in persuading members of the legislature that they were not obliged to honour the treaty, Balcarres replied: "But the country has a right to every advantage which the treaty affords and I am decidedly of opinion, that if the terms... have been complied with by the Maroons,[10] the country is bound in honour not to send them off the island..." [23 p.122].

Washing his hands of responsibility, he advised Walpole to do likewise:

> I do not enter into what the country, in its wisdom, ought to do. I feel we have done our duty as soldiers... But, in a political consideration of this subject, the country will not be guided either by your politics or mine... for surely, if there is anything upon earth in which a legislature has a right to exercise its judgement, it is internal rebellion[11]... [23 p.123].

Finally, Balcarres expressed regret at Walpole's "determination of quitting the service", of which he had been advised. Replying on 22 March, Walpole explained why. "I was fearful lest it should seem that I had drawn the Maroons into a treaty which I knew was hereafter to be broken; my resignation was meant to declare my entire ignorance of such an intention". Still hopeful that the treaty would be honoured, he added: "perhaps these may now be altered" [Southey 30 vol. 3, p. 106].

Having tricked the Trelawny Maroons into coming out of the bush, surrendering their arms and allowing themselves to be peaceably conducted to Montego Bay, Balcarres then had them removed from their barracks in the town and imprisoned in irons aboard ships in the harbour. In April he met with a joint committee of nine members of the Assembly and three of the Council to decide their fate. Assuring the gentlemen present that the Maroons themselves had broken the treaty, he had little difficulty in obtaining agreement to the proposal that they should be sent off the island.

Perhaps the governor's most persuasive argument with the committee was his disclosure of an extract from a letter he had received from the Secretary of State. The letter had expressed the view that the Maroons should not be restored to their district, and a preference for their removal from the country if this should be possible. The Duke of Portland had written this letter on 8 January, before he had received information relating to the treaty. He was therefore unaware that a pledge had been given not to transport them from the island. But whether Balcarres disclosed this to the committee is doubtful. Writing to the Duke of Portland after the meeting,[12] Balcarres said:

> Among the papers submitted to the committee of the two Houses of the legislature of this island, an extract from your Grace's letter of the⎯⎯⎯, addressed to me, has given most peculiar satisfaction. Your Grace has there anticipated both the wishes and policy of the island, in adopting the measure of sending off the rebel Maroons to another country [Lindsay 23 p.127].

This omission of the date of the Duke of Portland's letter is curious. It is not inconceivable, and would certainly have been in character, that Balcarres had circulated among the members of the committee an undated extract from that letter.

Before finalising their report to the legislature the committee requested further information on a number of points.

Their questions and the governor's answers show the extent to which they relied on his guidance.[13] One of their questions was directed to the issue of whether or not the Maroons had fulfilled their undertaking to surrender the runaway slaves. Balcarres had not expected the runaway slaves to come in and was obviously embarrassed by the fact that they had done so. He did not want to admit that this requirement of the treaty had been fulfilled, so in answering the question he resorted to what can only be described as a quibble: "No runaways have been surrendered by the Maroons; they came in in the character of Maroons" [23 pp.130-1].

The committee were also puzzled by the presence of two men named Harvey and Williams among the prisoners. They asked: "Upon what terms were ... the two brown men received, and did they surrender in the character of negroes?" They were informed that these two had "surrendered as Maroons..."

Reporting on what he had done with the prisoners Balcarres wrote:

> I have embarked about eight hundred of them ... about two hundred of which may be runaway slaves, and some women attending them. The number to be shipped off I should guess to be from four hundred and fifty to five hundred, of which one half nearly may be men and boys. On their arrival at Port Royal harbour, I shall move them ... into two of the transports now lying in that harbour, and they must proceed to sea with the convoy which will sail, I believe, on 1st of June, but possibly on the 21st of May [23 p.127].

The decision to transport the Trelawny Maroons out of the island in breach of the treaty appears to have occasioned surprise and disgust among many white residents. A letter from Balcarres to the Duke of Portland[14] confirmed this:

> I have thought it my duty to submit to your Grace copies of all the correspondence and papers which I laid before the committee on which they have in great measure framed their report. And I feel the necessity of sending these papers, as a violent opposition party in this country have asserted that we have broken faith with the Maroons... [23 pp.125-6].

The joint committee had recommended[15] that all the Maroons should be sent out of the island with the exception of Smith, Dunbar, Williams and their wives and children, and the two boys who had come in on 1 January. To these, they said, should be added "a few who, by their repentance, services and good behaviour since their surrender may have merited protection and favour" [23 pp.127-8; Southey 30 vol.3, pp.106-7]. Among those judged to be deserving of this concession were Johnson and Charles Schaw[16] [Lindsay 23 pp.127-8].

Colonel Quarrell, who had been appointed to accompany the Maroons on their journey into exile, informed these persons that they would be permitted to stay in the island, but they rejected the offer with contempt. Reporting to Balcarres, Quarrell wrote: "From long conversations with Johnson, Smith, Shaw, and other of the chiefs I find that their minds are perfectly made up to leave the country . . ." [23 pp.127-8].

The Trelawny Maroons were, in the first instance, sent to the bleak shores of Nova Scotia. They reached the port of Halifax at the end of the third week of July, and were put to work building fortifications. But, as fate would have it, the winter of 1796-97 was the longest and coldest ever known by the colonists there. An unrecorded number of them perished in the cold. The Duke of Kent, governor of Halifax, reported to the British government that they were malingering and had refused to plant crops, knowing that the government of Jamaica had undertaken to support them until they were self-sufficient.

Eventually, in February 1799, the directors of the Sierra Leone colonisation scheme agreed to accept these unfortunate exiles, receiving as part of the same deal a grant of £7,000 for the colony's fortifications, an annual grant of £4,000 and a promise of a detachment of soldiers. But not until August 1800 was the transport ship *Asia* able to leave for Africa with the 550 survivors, having become ice-bound in the St. Lawrence in the winter of 1799-80. On arrival in Africa the Maroons refused to sign the company's terms, no doubt having had enough of agreements with the whites. They nevertheless settled far more successfully than most of the other immigrants, many of whom had been sent from urban areas in Britain [Fyfe 13 pp.80, 88].

For the Earl of Balcarres the war against the Trelawny Maroons had proved to be a very lucrative adventure. Upon the declaration of martial law he had begun to receive an additional £20 per day, and this had continued throughout the hostilities. In September 1795 the Assembly had voted the sum of 700 guineas sterling to purchase for him a ceremonial sword.

Major General Walpole, to his great credit, would have no part in the shameful betrayal of trust suffered by the Maroons. According to Gardner:

> He regarded as a mere quibble the argument that they did not surrender before the 1st January. They had given themselves up to him, he pledged, in faith that they would not be deported, and without this confidence they would not have come in at all. As for conquest he asserted that treble the number of troops he had could not have brought them in in twelve months.

Nor was this his opinion only. Writing under date of 13 March he said "on this point 'your lordship will permit me to observe that the opinions of field-officers on the spot have never differed'."

When informed that the Assembly had voted the sum of 500 guineas to purchase a sword for him, Walpole indignantly rejected the offer. But in view of the Assembly's power of imprisonment for contempt, he had to choose his words with care. His letter dated 29 April 1796 to the Speaker of the Assembly is a classic of restrained reproach:

> Perhaps, Sir, not any person has ever been placed in a predicament more unpleasant than that in which I am at this moment; but, as the House has thought fit not to accede to the agreement entered into between me and the Trelawney maroons, and as their opinion of that treaty stands on their minutes very different to my conception of it, I am compelled to decline the honour which they have intended for me; but I must beg of you to assure the house that not any person would receive their favours with more gratitude than I should, could I possibly do it with credit to myself [Bridges 5 vol. 2 p. 481].

The shaft struck home. An irate House of Assembly ordered that this letter be stricken from its minutes.

Walpole did not leave the matter there. Resigning from the Army and returning to England he obtained a seat in Parliament. There, recorded Bryan Edwards, he moved: "That the House should resolve itself into a committee, to examine the circumstances of the negociation, and the subsequent departure from the terms of the treaty". He was, Edwards reported: "Indignant at ... having, as he expressed himself, been made an instrument to dupe and entrap the Maroons..." [11 (5th ed.) vol.5, pp.12-4].

But Walpole got little sympathy. The Secretary of State, who should by this time have realised that he too, through his letter written before he was aware of the terms of the treaty, had unwittingly been made a partner in Balcarres' crime, would not agree to support the motion. When the vote was taken there were thirty-three 'noes' against only five 'ayes'. England didn't want to know!

FOOTNOTES

[1] Moore Town in Portland.

[2] Balcarres to Portland, 1 January, 1796.

[3] Balcarres to Walpole, 9 January, 1796.

[4] Walpole to Balcarres – "Jan. 12, half-past two".

[5] Balcarres to Walpole, 14 January, 1796.

[6] Balcarres to Major General Campbell, 16 January, 1796.

[7] Walpole to Balcarres, 23 January, 1796.

[8] Balcarres to Henry Dundas, 30 January, 1796.

[9] Balcarres to Henry Dundas, letter "Number II", 30 January, 1796.

[10] Author's emphasis.

[11] Balcarres' emphasis.

[12] Balcarres to Portland, 20 April 1796.

[13] "Questions proposed to his Honour the Lieut-Governor, and his Honour's answers thereto", annexed to the joint committee's report.

[14] Balcarres to Portland 17 April, 1796.

[15] "Report of the joint committee of the General Assembly", 20 April, 1796 enclosed with Balcarres to Portland, 8 May 1796 [Southey 30 vol.3, pp.106-7].

[16] Quarrell to Balcarres, 8 May 1796.

CHAPTER NINE

THE PERILS OF FREEDOM

Resistance to slavery, needless to say, reached its highest level in armed struggle. But there were other, lesser, ways in which large numbers of slaves were continually demonstrating their desire, and often their determination, to be free. Slaves who, individually and in small groups, had escaped from their owners or the plantations to which they were attached, always formed an appreciable percentage of the total number living in freedom. The estimate of 100,000 escaped slaves living in Jamaica in 1798, given in the 1882 edition of the official *Handbook of Jamaica*, seems exaggerated. On the other hand the estimate given by G.W. Bridges [5 vol.2 p.348] that there were 20,000 escaped slaves at liberty in 1827, may have been too low.

There were different types of runaway slaves. Prior to 1739 escaping slaves could either join one of the existing major Maroon communities or establish small settlements of their own. But this became increasingly difficult and perilous after the whites had concluded their treaties with the Maroons in that year. Thereafter not only was admission to the Maroon settlements impossible, but, as we have seen, roving bands of Maroons began to engage in the business of rounding up runaways for reward. Escaping slaves nevertheless continued to set up small communities in remote parts of the island, some of which eluded detection and dispersal for many years.

Other runaways preferred to take their chance of escaping detection in urban communities. There they maintained a pretence of being either entitled to their freedom or having been authorised by their owners to do jobbing work on their own, making periodic returns of their earnings. For a slave to pass as a free man, even at a place far away from the place of his enslavement, was by no means easy. There was the presumption under the laws of the English colonies that a black man or woman was a slave unless the contrary were proved. The possibility of arrest and identification, or of resale into slavery if no owner claimed him, was ever present.

There was also a fairly numerous class of runaways for whom escape was a temporary expedient. Such runaways would often conceal themselves, or be harboured by other slaves, at no great distance from the residence of their owner or the plantation to which they belonged. They would be prepared to return voluntarily if there was a reasonable expectation that their working or living conditions or their rations would be marginally improved. On occasion they would negotiate their return through the good offices of some acquaintance of their master who was willing to intercede on their behalf. Plantation owners and attornies were sometimes anxious to secure the return of their runaways by this means.

At Amity Hall sugar estate in Vere, where the normal complement of slaves was about 300, there were reported to be 29 runaways in April 1802. A neighbouring planter and former employee on the estate attributed their absence to the overseer's excessive cruelty. In a letter to the mother and guardian of the infant absentee heir, this neighbour wrote:[1]

> During the time of Mr Cragg's concern they were frequently running away & dissatisfied with the Overseer – but the dissatisfaction now is become too general, and the number of runaways increased to an unexampled degree – there being no fewer than from 25 to 30 continually absent –

there is not a day passes but what I see some of them in various parts of the parish — bearing the marks of the greatest severity, several have come to me with whom they are acquainted ... They complain bitterly of the cruelty of Samson [Gbn. P].

In the following month the neighbour again wrote to the absentee owners:

I here inclose a List of all your Slaves now runaways — many of them I very lately have seen, & they are determined to suffer any death rather than return to their duty ... They declare that the moment any other person is appointed to the management of it they will all return ... They want some person to look up to for protection, & to treat them wth. humanity — and when they have such a person ... they will behave as well as any Slave in the Island ...[2]

Two weeks later a further letter conveyed the information that three of the runaways, "worth to you, Madam, £600 currency", had "perished of hunger in woods". It was feared, said the writer, that "several more must share a similar fate if not got home soon ..."[3]

The concerned correspondent, one Alex Moir, explained that though he now managed the neighbouring Carlisle and Knight estates, he had worked on Amity Hall estate from 1789 to 1792, first as a book-keeper and then as overseer. He had, he said, a sentimental attachment to Amity Hall "for there I learnt the first rudiments of my knowledge as a planter". Condemning the inhumanity of the overseer who was then in line for promotion to the vacant post of attorney, he added significantly: "I should be proud to be your Servant again and declare that every one of your Slaves now are, & ever were, well and faithfully attached towards me ..."

The overseer, when informed of Moir's allegations, attributed this neighbourly intervention to jealousy: "It is very common in Jamaica when an Overseer is promoted to be an attorney, that there are allways ... disappointed ... Gentlemen". He admitted that there were "from 12 to 15 Negroes much adicted to running away butt not to say that number daily. This is customary on all Estates, less or more".[4]

But even after the possibility of his obtaining the attorneyship had evaporated Alex Moir pursued the correspondence. He listed the names, with detailed descriptions, of 28 runaways, reported on his conversation with some of them, and assured Mrs. Goulburn that he was motivated by "Two principles, humanity and a sense of what I solemnly consider to be your interest". [5]

The papers of Worthy Park estate, at Lluidas Vale in the former parish of St. John's, disclose a somewhat lower proportion of runaways. Of a total complement of 480 slaves in 1795, nine were at large in the woods. Of a further 13 who were undergoing punishment, some had run away and returned to the estate. Between 1785 and 1790 the average number absent at any one time was seven, but 29 had run away for various periods during those years [Craton 6 pp. 143-4].

Here again was the familiar pattern of a number of slaves who expressed their dissatisfaction by running away but did not regard their departure from the estate as irrevocable. Their eventual willingness to return might be occasioned by several factors. There were those who, having demonstrated their dissatisfaction at specific instances of maltreatment or general cruelty, were hopeful that, though they would suffer punishment for having absented themselves, the maltreatment complained of would not be repeated or the general level of cruelty to the slaves on the estate would decrease. But there were others who, having escaped, had found the hardships of life as a fugitive beyond their capacity for endurance, and yet others who had returned because they had been, or feared they would be, recaptured.

Some who found the problem of survival in the woods beyond their capability nevertheless preferred death to a return to servitude. Such appears to have been the case with the three slaves from Amity Hall who, as mentioned above, starved to death. Listing their names Alex Moir described Richmond as "an excellent Boiler" and March as a "Fine able man". A Worthy Park 'Plantation Book' for 1791 disclosed, under the laconic heading "Decrease of Negroes", that one runaway had "Hanged himself in the woods" [Craton 6 p.144]. For some, the price they were prepared to pay for their freedom was high!

In 1798, partially filling the vacuum created by the deportation of the Trelawny Town Maroons, a community of escaped slaves established themselves in Trelawny under the leadership of another Kofi. By comparison with the Maroon Wars and the rebellions in 1760, their activity was relatively insignificant. But the events in that parish in 1798 are nevertheless important, illustrating as they do the enterprise and daring of a small fugitive band determined to maintain their freedom.

On 6 April magistrate James Stewart wrote to Earl Balcarres to inform him of the appearance of the rebel band [*Journals* 10 p.107]. Stewart enclosed a statement from one Patrick Navin whose house had been raided for arms and ammunition. Navin said that he had been alarmed by "the noise of sundry negroes round about his house" and that "five or six negro men immediately entered ... each of whom carried two guns". He observed that "a negro named Cuffee, belonging to James McGhie ... appeared to be the commander of the party".

The raiders demanded gun powder. When Navin told them he had none, they searched his house and "found about two hundred balls of different sizes, a gun, and one pistol, which they took with them ... and every thing else that suited them".[6] They then raided the neighbouring houses, one of which belonged to a white man named Dickson, the other to a free man of colour named John Shacklock. Navin's life was spared "as they chose to say, in consideration of his not having gone out with the party".[7] But the rebels burned all three houses to the ground.

On 14 April three magistrates and eight vestrymen stated, in a joint letter to the lieutenant governor:[8] "Their numbers are by no means ascertained, but they begin to act with a seeming determination to produce disturbance; we cannot forsee the consequences if they are not speedily suppressed ... [*Journals* 10 p. 107]".

The letter enclosed a deposition made that day by William James Stevenson an attorney of plantations in the parish, who stated:

> on Thursday last the 12th instant, this deponent visited Peru estate, in this parish ... when deponent found that the second driver ... named Boatswain, had, at shell-blow, on the day before, harangued several of his countrymen and others, Mundigoes and Coromantees, and invited them to accompany him into the woods, in order to join the other rebel runaways in that neighbourhood.

Continuing his account, Stevenson said: "the slave named Boatswain, on the same night, returned to the estate, when he was apprehended by the overseer, and immediately confined to the stocks, with three other slaves of that property who had run away in the life-time of Mr Scarlett, but had returned to the property".

Learning of these arrests, on his arrival at the property on 12 April, Stevenson had "left directions that Boatswain should be sent down to the workhouse at Falmouth the next morning, under a sufficient guard". But:

> during the night of the 12th ... Boatswain, and the three other runaways, found means to escape from their confinement at midnight, by the assistance of persons unknown, but supposed to be by one or more of the slaves of Peru ... who, in the most silent manner, cut open the window of the room ... burnt the wood-work of the stocks, and tore away the iron-work.

Stevenson added that: "Boatswain ...threatens to bring Cuffee, the chief of Mr. M'Ghie's runaways, to take off the crop; meaning, as this deponent conjectures, to assist Cuffee in burning the works ..." [*Journals* 10 p. 107].

On 19 April magistrate James Irving and his colleagues sent in another report to Balcarres of rebel activities: "We lament ... to give you the ... information of their attacking, yesterday evening, the house of messieurs Steel and Paulett, which continued ... till sun-rise this morning; and that messieurs Paulett and Biggs are severely wounded, and Mr. Kew killed ..." [*Journals* 10].

A letter from an unknown writer dated 1 May, listed 16 persons in the area who "have left their properties and retired to places of safety" [*Journals* 10]. Another letter laid before the Assembly, dated 15 May,[9] stated: "On Sunday the runaways were at Pantre-Pant, drove all the negroes out of their grounds, and occasioned a most dreadful alarm, they set fire to a house ... the regulars and white people moved quick, and got there in time to extinguish the fire" [*Journals* 10 p. 107].

The rebels, as it appears from this letter, were in a confident mood:

> They told the negroes, 'that they were come down to fight the whites'; and left word 'that if they would go up to a settlement, about a mile aback of Pantre-Pant, called Reid and Brisbane's, they would give them their bellyfull of fighting'.
>
> However, the runaways thought proper not to try it; in half an hour after the alarm we were in good force at Pantre-Pant; but the banditti must have good generals amongst them, the party that were in the low lands had another on the hills in sight, to cover their retreat.

The letter concluded by expressing the fear that "if this business is not soon checked" it might "turn out a second St. Domingo war; their numbers are daily increasing by disaffected negroes joining them".

On 13 June 1798 the Assembly met to consider a message from the governor which read: "... his honour considers the present rebellion to be dangerous in the extreme, unless the legislature, without a moments delay, will adopt the most vigorous measures to crush it..." [*Journals* 10 p. 107ff; PRO:CO 137/100]. What is interesting is the message's assessment of the inadequacy for this purpose of the regular troops and the militia, and its advocacy of a policy of getting blacks to fight blacks.

Informing the Assembly that there were already in the field against the rebels two parties of 'confidential slaves' raised by the parishes of Trelawny and St. James, Balcarres urged that the creation of a larger force of blacks out of public funds be authorised:

> His honour conceives that the militia .. however respectable on other points, are not well calculated to follow, and to reduce, those riotous

runaway slaves, who have entered into a state of rebellion:

That the regular troops are not up to it:

That armed and trusty negroes, under the denomination of black shot, are the description of force the best adapted to effect that service... That he... must earnestly recommend that at least three companies of trusty negroes, under white officers, be forthwith raised, for the purpose of constantly ranging the cockpits, and the woods adjoining:

That these three companies should consist of seventy privates each, with officers and non-commissioned officers in proportion...

These companies, the message continued, ought to be supplemented in a familiar manner: "To the principle of using such a force his honour adds another, namely, employing the Accompong maroons; a body of men who have ever remained faithful to their king and country". The creation of this mercenary black force was seen as all the more necessary because although "the Efforts of these Confidential Slaves", already in the field, "may be Attended with the Happiest Effect, it is evident that the day must arive when these valuable Men must be returned to their masters"[10] [PRO:CO 137/100].

On 17 June Balcarres reported to the Secretary of State:[11]

two parties of Confidential Slaves were raised under the authority of my presence in the parishes of Trelawny and St. James's — The Trelawny party marched into the woods without whites, and did good Service by forming and placing their ambushes with patience and Judgment, by which means some evil disposed negroes fell into their hands who were evidently going with Intelligence to the Rebels —

The other party namely the St. James's marched into the woods with two whites and came up with the Rebel negroe Cuffee and his gang, who had failed in procuring Intelligence from the Cause above mentioned, and also from our having taken up in Falmouth Several very Suspicious negroes [PRO:CO 137/100].

It appears, however, that despite the capture of Kofi's scouts and informants, his attackers were unable to turn it to their advantage. The governor went on to lament that "this very favourable opportunity of putting an End to the Rebellion was entirely lost". The reason for this was, he said, that:

In the Act of surrounding Cuffee's party, five or six of our Slaves fled, others from Panic began to fire upon their own party — the Report gave the alarm to Cuffee, who blew his Shell, beat his Drum, and after giving defiance to our party marched off and was not followed — our two parties still Remain in the woods.

By this date, the report continued, "Upwards of 30 Settlers have been driven from their Habitations, and a few days ago a party of the Rebels Killed two watchmen". Reporting on the probable strength of the rebels the governor added:

> The Force of Cuffee I have every reason to think is 43 and it is Supposed that there is another Party very near him, of 30 Rebels more, under the Command of a Negro who has been out ever since the Maroon Rebellion — whether this is exclusive or Inclusive of the party of Rebels in St. Elizabeths I cannot ascertain.

Referring to his capacity to attack the rebels, Balcarres said: "The only Resource I can propose with any Effect is that the Island shall put into my hands three Companies of a Negro Force who shall be posted in the woods — two or three small Depots of Provisions ought to be formed and some Barracks to be built in the nature of Block Houses". To this he added significantly: "Should the Assembly refuse this I must consider the present Insurrection as a Danger of the first Magnitude, but if they grant it I see no reason for anxious fears...".

A week later Balcarres was able to report that the Assembly had approved his request "of raising three Companies of People of colour for the service of scouring the Woods to Leeward". Though "the expence seems a tremendous one", he commented, [12] "The necessity of such a permanent establishment is obvious". But the Assembly had not given him a blank cheque: "They are granted during the present Rebellion, and no longer, unless any other commotions of danger to the internal peace and tranquility of the country should render a longer continuance of their service necessary" [PRO:CO 137/100].

The pay scales approved by the Assembly for each company were £1. 12s. 6d. per day for a captain, £1 each for two lieutenants and a "Surgeon with Rank ... of lieutenant", fifteen shillings for a quarter-master, ten shilling each for three sergeants, six shillings and eightpence each for three corporals, a "fifer", a drummer and a "hornman" and five shillings each for sixty-one privates. The yearly pay for the three companies amounted to £26,416. 17s. 6d. The bread, beef and rum allowances added a further £6,426, making an annual total of £32,842. 17s. 6d. Jamaica currency. In addition there was to be "Bounty Money" of six months pay to each private on disbandment [PRO: CO 137/100].

On 23 August the Duke of Portland wrote to Balcarres informing him of the royal approval for the raising of the black troops he wanted. The Duke enclosed a letter from one Colonel Brownrigg dealing with the probable date of arrival of the force, from which it is apparent that this "Black Corps" was to be raised outside Jamaica [PRO: CO 137/100]. Meanwhile, in Jamaica, the establishment's efforts to suppress Kofi's band continued.

On 20 July the governor reported to the Duke that although the slaves in his special companies had been "brought into some order" and were doing "excellent service", they "have not ... got hold of Cuffee, nor his Gang, tho' they have often been very near him". But they had "discovered a little town of Huts, capable of holding more than 100 Negroes, with many well-beaten tracts leading to it and from it in various directions". He went on to explain that the officer supervising the operations had ordered both parties to that place and would "subdivide them, so as to follow up the several tracts" [PRO: CO 137/100].

Interrupting the writing of this letter to read a communication that had just arrived from the scene of operations, Balcarres returned to his report with some excitement:

> The Post from the Leeward part ... has this moment brought me a letter from Lt. Colonel Mcmurdo ... dated 17 July ... those tracts led them to several small Towns or Huts: at one of them was five Acres of Provision Grounds, and at others also smaller quantities of provisions. At one of those places they got in with some Rebels, killed two of the Ring-leaders, Hercules and Prince, the former was out in the Maroon Rebellion, and has continued out ever since.

The capture of three of the rebels' women during this operation provided valuable information on the composition and life style of this rebel band. Two of these women, Patty and Juba, were examined before a magistrate at Falmouth on 15 July. The examination of Patty gave an interesting picture of how in practice the rebel community led by Kofi, considerably smaller in numbers than Balcarres had supposed, maintained itself.

Patty said that she had been "the wife of the Head driver at Windsor Penn", whence she had been abducted three months previously by one of the rebels named Harford, whose wife she had then become. She had been taken on a Sunday and they had reached "the largest Town of the Rebels by rapid walking, on Monday night". The community she then joined had consisted of 19 males, nine females including herself and one child. Two of the men were elderly. Among the names she gave was that of Boatswain.

The examination revealed that the band was extremely mobile: "Patty states that Cuffee's party are by no means Stationary — that they move about frequently from place to place, continuing in one Spot but one, two or three days, sometimes two or three weeks, according to the quantity of Provisions at and near the different places they resort to".

Patty explained that, being frequently on the move, "wherever they walk, they build little Huts". She said that "besides their largest and most frequented Town, they have three or four smaller". Her account of the rebels' property relationships was, however, somewhat confusing:

> ... some of them have Grounds, but not in common for all — they are considered as the Grounds of those who first establish them on their taking to the woods — that the Peru People, and Cuffee, with some others have no such Grounds, but that some of Mr McGhie's People, who have been upwards of three years in the Woods have their Grounds. They however diet together, in general — Cuffee and a few others excepted, the provisions, when gathered being in common [PRO: CO 137/100].

The community was obviously unable, in its fugitive existence, to produce all its own food. According to Patty: "they occasionally go to the Settlements for Provisions, particularly to Young's Thicketts (now Scarlett's) and the Flemings — seldom or never to any other". The search for food had its perils: "Pollidore, last month, went to Caledonia to steal Fowls, and was pursued by the Blackshot — that they fired at him, upon which he threw away the Fowls, and ran home to the party. That Cuffee, upon that, raised the whole Party — but in the night was found by the Blackshot . . ."

This attack by the black shot had led to a hurried retreat "into the Interior of the Woods" of the entire party except for Kofi, March and Prince, who had defiantly "declared they would kill any whom they meet, whether White or Black, for that they were helping each other". Soon afterwards they had killed the two watchmen.

Sometimes the entire community went on a raid together. "The week after she joined them", Patty said, "the whole Party went over to Hector's River, killed a brown man, Overseer on a Property . . ." They had on that occasion returned with a recruit — "a new Negro Boy".

Ammunition was a serious problem, but the rebels showed considerable ingenuity:

> . . .all the Party have Guns or pistols — very little Powder: they make Balls by melting Lead in a pot and pouring it down the hollow part of the Stalk of a plantain leaf, forming it first into a solid piece about the Size of a Cartridge, or longer — this they afterwards cut up in smaller pieces with a Knife, and then give each a rounded form by the handle of a Bill or Cutlass.[13]

It would appear that Kofi was well aware that the attacking parties were closing in on them and that he would not be able to keep the whole band together. From the examination of the other woman, Juba, it would seem that he had made plans to split up the band and to move, with the smaller group he would keep with him, to a new area of operations. Juba stated that "Cuffee went away three or four days before the fight in which she was captured, and took with him four men and four women". She said that "he had found means and excuses not long before to change the Guns of those who were left behind, and to give them Guns of an inferior quality" [PRO:CO 137/100].

This was no doubt a difficult decision for Kofi to make, though he appears to have had little choice but to break up the community. He was careful to conceal his plans from these women, whom he must have realised were the least enthusiastic of his followers and the most likely to be talkative on capture. According to Patty he had announced that he and those he had selected to go with him "had gone ... in search of Himba, or Wild Yam". Patty had believed him but Juba was suspicious. Her suspicions had been confirmed when "Pollidore went two days after Cuffe, with the others who were mentioned by Patty to have gone away". But despite her suspicions she had not discovered their destination. She did not know whether "they took the same path".[14]

Of those who remained behind, the three women who were captured appear to have made no attempt to escape. Prince and Hercules, as has been mentioned above, were killed, but seven others made good their escape. Whether Kofi had plans for reuniting his rebel community at some pre-arranged rendezvous or whether each of the three groups into which they were split up was to find a new territory for itself, can only be a matter for speculation. Suffice it to say that at this point the remarkably brave and astute Kofi and his followers disappear from the written record.

FOOTNOTES

[1] Alex Moir to Mrs Mumbee Goulburn, 10 April, 1802.

[2] Moir to Mrs. Goulburn, 1 May 1802.

[3] Moir to Mrs Goulburn, 15 May 1802.

[4] Thomas Samson to Mrs Goulburn, 7 August 1802.

[5] Moir to Mrs Goulburn, 3 September 1802.

[6] Deposition of Patrick Navin, 4 April 1798.

[7] James Stewart to Balcarres, 6 April 1798.

[8] James Irving and others to Balcarres, 14 April 1798.

[9] Extract from letter from William Green at Good Hope, Trelawny, 15 May 1798, addressee unnamed.

[10] Letter to Speaker of Assembly, 13 June 1798.

[11] Balcarres to Portland, 17 June 1798.

[12] Balcarres to Portland, 24 June 1798.

[13] The Examination of Patty 15 July 1798.

[14] The Examination of Juba.

CHAPTER TEN

THE CONSPIRACIES OF 1815 and 1823-24

After their success in securing the prohibition of the slave trade in 1807, Britain's leading abolitionists were, as we have seen[1] unwilling to propose the abolition of slavery. Not until 1823 did they agree to launch a parliamentary campaign with this objective and to organise a society for this purpose. Even then, they were at one with the government of the day in opposing immediate emancipation. Though popularly known as the "Anti Slavery Society," the name of their organisation was in fact "The Society for the Gradual Abolition of Slavery".

The Canning resolution approved by Parliament in 1823, in favour of which Buxton of the Anti Slavery Society had withdrawn his own painfully gradual scheme, had made the coming of emancipation dependent on the nebulous requirement that there should be "a progressive improvement in the character of the slave population, such as may prepare them for participation in those civil rights and privileges which are enjoyed by other classes in his Majesty's subjects". No less important had been the requirement that the "accomplishment" of emancipation should be "compatible ... with a fair and equitable consideration of the interests of private property".

Not until 1830 did the Society propose immediate emancipation. Had the matter been left entirely in the hands of the leaders of the Anti-Slavery Society, one wonders whether they would not have allowed even longer than 22 years, after the prohibition of the trade, to elapse before demanding the abolition of slavery. In the event, the slaves, particularly those in Jamaica, Barbados and British Guiana, prodded them forward by decisive action. The events in Jamaica are described in this chapter. In Barbados there was a major rebellion in 1816. In British Guiana the rebellion led by the slave Jack Gladstone and others in 1823 terrified the establishment and resulted in the arrest of the missionary John Smith and his subsequent death in prison. These events stimulated antislavery sentiment in Britain.

During the last decade of the 18th century, and the first decade of the 19th, events occurring outside the island had had a profound effect on the minds of the slaves in Jamaica. News of the successful slave revolution in Saint Domingue and of the growth of antislavery sentiment in Britain, events heatedly denounced at the dinner tables of the planters, had been relayed to the field and factory workers through the household slaves. These events were avidly discussed and evaluated.

To the slaves the message of the establishment of black power in Saint Domingue was clear. Here was proof positive that the emancipation of the black man and the overthrow of white rule could be achieved by determined armed struggle. The message of the events in Britain, which continued to unfold in the second and third decades of the new century, was more complex. New possibilities had obviously emerged which appeared to suggest to the slaves in the British colonies the viability of more limited objectives than those of their Haitian counterparts.

Prior to the 19th century it is improbable that slaves in revolt had drawn any distinction between the resident whites and those who, as they were no doubt aware, resided in the white people's mother country across the seas. Their struggle for freedom was, in a sense, both a class struggle and a nationalistic one. It was a class war in so far as the slaves were pitted against their masters as owners of the plantations on which they worked. It was nationalistic in that they sought to destroy white rule and achieve black self determination.

Self determination, albeit on a geographically limited scale, was what had been achieved by some of the slaves after a decade of armed struggle in 1739. Self determination was what the Trelawny Maroons had fought to preserve in 1795. It was what Tacky would have established, perhaps on an all-island scale, had the rebellions of 1760 been successful. It was the objective of countless other conspiracies and revolts.

The term 'nationalistic' is used advisedly in this context in relation to the attitude of the slaves. It would however have been inappropriate to apply this term to the parliamentary struggle waged by the plantocracy to preserve their powers of internal self government against the attempts of the British Government to limit the sovereignty of their Assembly.

The white planters were not nationalists. They regarded themselves as Englishmen overseas (notwithstanding the fact that some of them were Welshmen, Scots or Irishmen). As and when they had extracted from the exertions of their black labourers sufficient wealth so to do, they returned to Britain to become absentee proprietors. In this they differed from their counterparts in the Spanish and Portuguese possessions. The slaves on the other hand, despite their involuntary migration from Africa, had no alternative but to make Jamaica their home. They were, of necessity, the Jamaican nation in embryo. The same was true of the slaves in each of the British colonies of the Caribbean area.

By the beginning of the 19th century the situation had changed. Enough news concerning the abolitionists in Britain had filtered through, no doubt becoming exaggerated in the re-telling, to cause the slaves in the British West Indian colonies to perceive a distinction between two kinds of white people. There were those who held them enslaved and those who believed it was wrong that they should be denied their freedom. The justification for drawing this distinction was strengthened with the arrival of the non-conformist missionaries, whose primary concern appeared to be the welfare of those of African descent and who were denounced as enemies of slavery by the planters.

The reasons for the growth of the abolitionist movement in Britain have been analysed in Volume one. Suffice it here to say that, through the angry reactions of the slave owners and their local newspapers on the one hand and information received from the missionaries on the other, the slaves became aware of a series of external events affecting their interests. Among these may be mentioned the abolition of the slave trade by Parliament in 1807, the slave registration controversy after 1812 which culminated in the reluctantly enacted local registration laws, and the pressures exerted by the British government to secure various reforms ameliorating their conditions.

One of the consequences of these developments was a growing belief among the slaves that the people in England and the British government were their friends. By continuing to enslave and oppress them the resident whites were believed to be acting contrary to the wishes of the British people. Reporting to the Secretary of State on the reaction of the Jamaica Assembly to the proposal for registration of the slaves, Governor Manchester, on 26 January 1816, wrote:[2]

> I think it proper to apprize Your Lordship that the agitation of this question by the Assembly and the Strong Resolutions entered into at the several parochial Meetings . . . deprecating the interference of Parliament in the internal concerns of the Colony have certainly created a sensation amongst the Slaves and a suspicion that the Registry Bill contemplates some disposition in their favour which the Assembly here supported by the Inhabitants generally are desirous to withhold [PRO:CO 137/142, no.81].

The belief that Parliament was on their side against the resident whites inevitably encouraged the growth among the slaves of feelings of loyalty to Britain. Nationalistic aspirations towards self determination, based on the assumption that the whites as a whole were their enemies, tended to decline. The struggle for the abolition of slavery became more and more exclusively a local class struggle, quite independent of the colonial relationship with Britain.

From the turn of the century onwards until emancipation the situation in Jamaica was explosive. In December 1799 a conspiracy was discovered among the slaves brought to Jamaica by the fugitive French planters from Saint Domingue. "Upwards of 1000 of the Negroes were transported" [16 (1894 ed.) p.50]. The discovery of a conspiracy in Kingston in 1803 led to the execution of two slaves [Southey 30 vol.3 p.248]. A conspiracy for revolt was discovered in the parish of St. George in 1806 in consequence of which, Gardner recorded [14 pp. 243-4]: "a good deal of alarm was felt . . . One slave was executed, one transported, and of six others acquitted at the same time, the Governor thought it well to order the deportation of four".[3]

In 1808, 50 Africans listed as "Coromantins" and "Chambas", who appear to have been involuntary recruits to the 2nd West India Regiment, mutinied at Fort Augusta, killing two of their officers [Gardner 14 p.245; Bridges 5 vol. 2 p. 289]. In 1809, following the discovery of a conspiracy in Kingston, two were hanged and several transported.

Towards the end of 1815 it was discovered that a number of slaves in the parish of St. Elizabeth had been planning an uprising. The planter 'Monk' Lewis[4] made this entry in his diary:

> The plot was discovered by the overseer at Lyndhurst Penn (a Frenchman from St. Domingo) observing an uncommon concourse of stranger negroes to a child's funeral, on which occasion a hog was roasted by the father. He stole softly down to the feasting hut, and listened behind a hedge to the conversation of the supposed mourners; when he heard the whole conspiracy detailed [22 p.227].

Lewis recorded what he had heard about the conspirators and their plan:

> It appears that about two hundred and fifty had been sworn in regularly, all of them Africans; not a Creole was among them. But there was a 'black' ascertained to have stolen over into the island from St. Domingo, and a 'brown' Anabaptist missionary, both of whom had been very active in promoting the plot.
> They had elected a King of the Eboes,[5] who had two Captains under him: and their intention was to effect a complete massacre of all the whites on

the island; for which laudable design His Majesty thought Christmas the very fittest season in the year, but his Captains were more impatient, and were for striking the blow immediately".

Noting the arrest of the leader and some of his fellow conspirators, the diarist continued:

The next morning information was given against them: One of the Captains escaped to the woods; but the others and the King of the Eboes, were seized and brought to justice. On their trial they were perfectly cool and unconcerned, and did not even profess to deny the facts with which they were charged.

Lewis may or may not have been correct in believing that no Jamaican born slaves were involved in the conspiracy. But the conspirators were certainly well informed on contemporary British parliamentary affairs. In a letter to the Secretary of State the governor wrote:[6]

at a Trial recently held in the Parish of Saint Elizabeth, It appeared in Evidence that Nightly Meetings had been held on the property to which the two Slaves, who were brought to Trial, belonged. That the object of their Meeting was to impress the Slaves generally with a belief that Mr Wilberforce was to be their Deliverer, and that if the White Inhabitants did not make them free, they ought to make themselves free [PRO:CO 137/142, no.92].

The governor's letter confirmed the importance of slaves of Ibo origin in this conspiracy. He quoted one of the leaders on trial as having said "that 'he had all the Eboes in his hand', meaning to insinuate that all the Negroes from that Country were under his controul". The same letter contained some information on the Anabaptist missionary referred to by Lewis:

It further appeared in the Evidence that these two slaves have taught the others to believe that there was no necessity of being Christened by the Clergyman of the Parish, for that they had permission to baptize from a Negro Preacher belonging to Earl Balcarres, and the Negroes so baptized ever after paid a part of what they possessed to the head Preacher whom they call the Bishop...

Lewis recorded the words of a song, very topical indeed, found on the leader of the conspiracy. The leader said he had got the words from the "brown priest":

> Oh me good friend, Mr. Wilberforce, make me free!
> God Almighty thank ye! God Almighty thank ye!
> God Almighty, make me free!
> Buckra in this country no make we free!
> What Negro for to do? What Negro for to do?
> Take force by force! Take force by force! [Lewis 22 p. 227].

The principal leader was sentenced to be hanged, his deputy to be transported. On 26 March 1816 Lewis made this entry in his diary:

> ... the King of the Eboes has been hung at Black River, and died, declaring that he left enough of his countrymen to prosecute the design in hand, and revenge his death upon the whites. Such threats of a rescue were held out, that it was judged advisable to put the militia under arms, till the execution should have taken place; and also to remove the King's Captain to gaol at Savannah la mar, till means could be found for transporting him from the island.

On the following day Lewis wrote:

> The Eboe Captain has effected his escape by burning down the prison door. It is supposed that he has fled towards the fastnesses in the interior of the mountains, where I am assured that many settlements of run-away slaves have been formed, and with which the inhabited part of the island has no communication. However, the chief of the Accompong Maroons, Captain Roe, is gone in pursuit of him, and has promised to bring him in alive or dead [22 pp. 234-5].

According to Lewis, the captain was recaptured. If Lewis is correct it means that he did not succeed in reaching the haven of one of the settlements of runaway slaves. Other writers have referred to the existence of these settlements. Gardner, drawing on the record of a report to the Assembly on 30 November 1819 [*Journals* 13 p. 375] recorded: "2555 runaway slaves were reported to be at large. Some of these managed to pass as free in places distant from those they had lived in as slaves; others were secreted in the woods, and not a few united together and formed dangerous confederacies" [14 p.254].

Gardner referred particularly to an area lying to the south of Spanish Town, between the capital and the south coast:

> A considerable number of these had located themselves in a wild range of mountainous land known as the Healthshire Hills, situated between Kingston Harbour and the Old Harbour Bay. Here they had built villages, whence they now and then descended into the plains to steal cattle and whatever else came handy.

The militia, said Gardner, were sent to clear up the Healthshire Hills area and claimed to have dispersed several bands, but the notorious leader Scipio was never captured.

Not infrequently escaping slaves were assisted by persons who were themselves free. On discovery such persons were severely punished, and sometimes transported from the island. Such was the fate of one Waterman, described as "a free black", who was found guilty of this offence and transported to England early in 1822 [PRO:CO 714/89].[7]

In December 1823 a conspiracy to rebel was discovered in St. Mary due to an unfortunate chain of events. James Sterling, a slave on Frontier Estate who was one of the conspirators, warned his 15 year old son that:

> the Negroes in General were to rise at the fall of Christmas, and desired him to keep out of the way for fear of being hurt, as it was the intention of the Negroes to begin to burn and destroy the Houses, Trash Houses, and Estates, and when such fire took place to murder all the Inhabitants [PRO:CO 137/157].

Even before this warning from his father the lad had realised that something was being planned. He had "twice observed the Negroes assembled in large bodies near a bridge between Frontier Estate and Port Maria, where he heard them speak of an intended rising and at that time they were flourishing their cutlasses declaring that they would destroy all the White People".

The boy then committed the indiscretion, in answering some questions from his suspicious master, of telling the latter that he would "have a bad Christmas and that if he wished to be safe, it would be necessary for him to go on board Ship, as it would be useless for him to go either to the Fort or any other House".

Having heard this the boy's master immediately alerted the authorities. On examination before the magistrates[8] the boy named five other slaves whom he had seen in conference with his father. He also gave the names of two slaves whom he believed had been standing close enough to hear what was being said. Examined on 16 December one of these disclosed that he had "heard a consultation, respecting which way they were to act. That they intended to have risen at Christmas Fall, but in consequence of the appointment of Guards, they changed the day for the day after the full of the Moon Thursday night next, the 18th Instant . . ." This informer further disclosed:

> That the intention was to burn the Trash House, and Works at Frontier Estate, and when the White people came to quench it, they would then destroy them. After which they were to begin at the Top (the East) of the Bay and set fire to the buildings, when a General Massacre was to take place.

Forewarned, the authorities were able to seize the conspirators named and several other suspects, frustrating their plans. The eight men arrested were tried at a Slave Court on 19 December and sentenced to death.[9] The five separate trials were all over in a day. The eight men tried were all from Frontier Estate. Charles Brown, suspected of being the principal organiser, had been the Head Driver but had, said the overseer, been "very severe on the negroes". Because of this "witness removed or broke him and made him a Cooper". The others tried were: Charles Watson, Henry Nibbs, James Sterling, William Montgomery, Richard Cosley, Rodney Wellington and Monice Henry. Nibbs, the alleged owner of two guns, was convicted partly on the evidence of his wife who complained that "he frequently went out after dark and did not tell her where he went".

At one of these trials at which four of the accused were tried together: "It was offered that one should turn King's Evidence but all refused" [PRO:CO 137/157]. On the next day the colonel of the St. Mary militia made his report to the governor's secretary:

> I thought it my duty to insist on the magistrates trying the Negroes that had been taken, immediately, and to send trial and Sentences express, as it will in my opinion, be highly important for the safety of the parish and probably the Island, that they should be executed before the Holidays, as an example to the other Negroes, and to prevent the danger of an escape, or an attempt to release them.

In conclusion the militia colonel mentioned that no hidden arms had been discovered. It had been alleged that one of the conspirators had owned two guns which he had placed at their disposal. The fact that they could not be found led the colonel to conclude that "the Negroes had taken the alarm" and that it would be "to no purpose to continue the search..."

On Christmas Day the colonel reported to the governor [10] that the sentences had been carried out:

> 8 Negroes were executed yesterday, with all due solemnity and decorum... only one of the Wretches confessed to the Revd. Mr. Girod that it was their intention to have burnt Frontier Works & Port Maria & killed the Whites, but none would mention any other negroes concerned with them, or shew any symptom of Religious Repentance. They all declared that they would die like men & met their fate with perfect indifference, & one laughed at the Clergyman... when he attempted to exhort him under the Gallows [PRO: CO 137/157].

The same letter went on to give another interesting bit of information, though what the outcome was and whether there was any direct connection with the events above described is not apparent:

> On the 20th Inst. the Magistrates from information they had received, having thought proper to send a Constable, to take the Head Driver of Oxford Estate, the Negroes became so unruly, that it was with difficulty the Driver was secured, but the Overseer was obliged to quit the Estate; I immediately marched a Company there and restored peace and quietness.

A far more formidable and better organised conspiracy for revolt was meanwhile approaching maturity in the parish of St. George, at about the same time as the St. Mary plot. Originally scheduled to go into operation on the night of Boxing Day, 1823, the planned uprising had been postponed to a date to be named in 1824. But strange activities among the slaves on Balcarres Estate had been brought to the attention of the magistrates who decided to examine some of the participants.

One of the men examined,[11] a slave named Corberand from the neighbouring property Mullett Hall, stated that one night while visiting Balcarres Estate he had seen the slaves 'mustering'. On joining the gathering he had been asked to accept appointment as 'Clerk', but never discovered what his duties were supposed to be. Other office bearers were the 'King' and the 'Governor'. Corberand said he did not "understand what they were talking about". When he returned on the following night with his younger brother, the latter was offered the post of "Second Governor". This, he said, had so offended him that "he did not afterwards return" [PRO: CO 137/157].

Jean Baptiste Corberand was probably, as his name suggests, a native of Haiti. Fugitive French planters from the revolution there had settled in Jamaica with their slaves, but the magistrates may well have suspected that even a Haitian immigrant would have become sufficiently familiar with the Jamaican vernacular to understand it after over 20 years residence!

Another slave, Richard Montagnac, told a story at his examination [12] which made these activities look even more innocent. He said:

> that the Negroes, in the field, made a regulation, that when one negro cursed another, he should be fined 5d worth of rum, that he was the first man fined, and the Negroes in the evening met at his house, to drink the rum, it was proposed that all fines should be drank at his house, which was in consequence called the Court House; ... James Thompson, came to drink ... and said he would be King. Dennis Kerr said he would be Governor, but all was meant in fun.

Continuing his story Montagnac said. "the negroes so assembled some times made play, with their sticks, and paraded to James Thompson's house, and that some of them had wooden swords...". Other slaves, on examination, told much the same story. Obviously they had gone to considerable trouble to create this pretence as a cover for their conspiratorial activities. And indeed so well did they carry off their elaborate deception that they very nearly got away with it. That they did not succeed was due to the treachery of a runaway they had been harbouring in their midst.

Early in January 1824 a slave named Mack, a runaway from Cambridge Estate in the neighbouring parish of Portland who had been sheltered by the slaves on Balcarres Estate, voluntarily returned to Cambridge. He was placed in the stocks where he remained until the thought struck him that he had something to bargain with. In return for his release he offered to disclose what he had learned of the plans of the disaffected slaves in the neighbouring parish. On 7 January he was taken before the magistrates, and the story he had to tell put a very different complexion on the goings on at Balcarres.

The informer Mack gave evidence of an elaborate conspiracy. He named Thompson, Kerr, Corberand and a number of others as participants, and disclosed the name of their leader Henry Oliver. All the conspirators named were rounded up as fast as they could be found and on 8 January Corberand was again brought before the magistrates.[13] To save his own life he agreed to turn king's evidence against his fellow conspirators.

Corberand confirmed that Henry Oliver was the leader of the conspiracy and disclosed their plan. On the night before Christmas Day:

> the negroes of Balcarres were to prepare themselves at the Cow Pen, and then proceed to the works, break in on the Overseer, Kill him, and the Book Keeper, after which a Torch ... was to be lighted ... as a signal to the Negroes of the neighbourhood to come and join them, after which they were to proceed up the River, kill all the Buckras, and fire their houses, and then to ... proceed down River, Murdering and burning as they went.

It had not been possible, however, to adhere to the original time table. Shortly before the Christmas holidays, the witness told the examining magistrates, a company of the militia had unexpectedly turned up to guard the estates in the area. "When the Guards were sent", Corberand continued, "H. Oliver expressed surprise and concern ... a meeting of the Conspirators was in consequence held, when they resolved to defer the execution of their Plan, till after quiet had been restored to the Country".

Corberand also disclosed that the rebels had obtained guns which had been brought from Kingston by a slave named Manhertz and delivered to Oliver. The guns and ammunition had, he alleged, been purchased for them by Lecesne, whom he identified as "the person lately shipped off" the island.[14] He added that "since Lecesne's being sent off, H. Oliver has appeared much dejected".

Initially Corberand attributed his knowledge of the alleged fire-arms, and of Lecesne's assistance to the conspirators, to what he had heard from Oliver. He said that the latter "had told him he had given the guns and ammunition to John Braeme to conceal least [sic] they should be discovered on Balcarres, as Braeme's residence, was not so liable to suspicion". Braeme, a slave belonging to a Mrs. Mure, was alleged by Corberand to have "made the balls".

But, despite these disclosures, one of the magistrates, before whom Corberand told his story, suspected that he was holding something back. In a letter forwarding the examination to the custos, this magistrate wrote: "[Coberand] evidently knows more than he has told, and we are anxious to obtain from him where the Arms of the Balcarres Rebels, are secreted" [PRO: CO 137/157]. It is probable that considerable pressure was applied to Corberand, and, by the time he came to give evidence at the trial of his fellow conspirators, he had considerably improved his story. There seems little doubt that, being personally at risk, Corberand was anxious to please the authorities. Whether he did so by disclosing things he had at first tried to conceal, or drew on his imagination to tell them what he thought they would like to hear, can only be a matter for speculation.

Giving evidence at the trials, Corberand said that he himself had made the trip to Kingston with the courier, James Manhertz, to meet with Lecesne and his associate Baptiste and collect the guns. Baptiste he described as "a fine looking tall young man, black colour", who "wore a small crucifix" and "came from St. Domingo on purpose to stir up the negroes". It was this man, he said, who had "introduced Oliver to Lecesne" [PRO: CO 137/157].[15]

Although he had got them the arms they required, "Lecesne did not sell guns", said Corberand. But the conspirators had had to find the money for their purchase, and the witness gave an interesting account of how this had been done: "the prisoners were in the habit for the last three years of going to the different properties to get money to give the minister in Kingston, as they said a mackaroni[16] each month, this money they sent to buy Guns and powder..." Naming the several estates where the money was collected "under religious pretences at meetings made for praying", the witness added that those who paid the money "did not know what it was for". Corberand said further that Lecesne had promised that when they were ready to start the uprising he would send men with Baptiste to help them. He also mentioned an occasion when "a man who came from Kingston to H. Oliver, for orders, said that the negroes there were ready to revolt".

How much of the evidence relating to the guns and the involvement in the conspiracy of Lecesne was true and how much was invention, it is difficult to say. No one answering the description of Baptiste was ever arrested. Nor were any guns discovered. The overseer of Mullett Hall, who gave character evidence for the accused Samuel Haughton, volunteered the information that "he had sent a negro with a mule down to Kingston to get a stand of arms for him". This suggests that perhaps the arms alleged to have been transported for the rebels might in fact have been a perfectly lawful delivery to Mullett Hall.

Confirmation of the fact that the conspirators had received some guns was, however, provided by one of the last of their number to be arrested. This man answered to the name of Jack and Corberand described him as "a Guinea negro" who "understood how to do everything and knew every sort of bush". He was accused, in addition to the charge of conspiracy, of practising obeah and using his pretended supernatural powers to bolster the courage of his fellow conspirators. He did this, it was alleged: "by rubbing the said Negroes and other Slaves with certain Bushes at the Same time saying that such rubbing... would give them Strength and cause them to be invulnerable..."

From the skimpy record of what this accused is supposed to have said at his trial on 19 February 1824, it appeared that Jack was a runaway who was being harboured on Balcarres estate. He said that two mules had been brought there one night "which carried Six Guns each... in flannel bags". When the mules arrived, Manhertz had awakened Oliver who had taken delivery of the guns. These guns had come, said this accused, "a month before Xmas", and it was "a little before Xmas when they heard that Buckra were going to search the Houses". Corberand, Oliver and Braeme, he continued, then "hid the Guns and would not allow any one else to do it". Only Corberand, he concluded, "can shew these Guns, and if he does not... Buckra will never see them again".

Corberand's evidence concerning the preparations for the uprising showed Henry Oliver to have been a tireless organiser with a capacity for considerable cunning. It was Oliver's practice, he said, "to walk round the Country and tell the negroes to join the plot". In his examination before the magistrates he had said Oliver, "who never was at work, had walked everywhere arranging with different persons how they were to act".

That it should have been possible for Oliver to do this becomes credible in the light of the evidence of Thomas Learmond, the overseer at Balcarres, that he (the overseer) also had duties on other estates. The overseer stated that he personally "never missed him [Oliver] from his work more than one day — but had himself..., often been off the property when he could not tell whether Oliver was about or not". Even so, other slaves on Balcarres estate must have been very clever at covering up for Oliver when he was absent.

The play acting at Thompson's house had apparently been organised to provide an opportunity for drumming up support among those not fully initiated into the conspiracy. It appears to have been a substituted plan. Oliver had originally asked him, said Corberand, to organise a dance which was expected to have drawn a "great company", and "Oliver was to come and ask the negroes to join his party". But the dance did not come off, the witness said, and they had had to meet at Thompson's house instead.

Corberand said further that "the rulers at Balcarres", by whom he appears to have meant the leading conspirators, "had been practising more than a year in the use of arms". If this was true then they must be presumed to have had at least one gun prior to the alleged arrival of the guns from Kingston in November 1823.

The conspirators took a solemn oath. How this was administered was described by the informer Mack:

> they had a large Basin standing in the middle. Henry Oliver Cut his finger and put the Blood into the Basin. The Obeah Man then threw a quart of Rum into it, and something else but could not tell whether grave dirt or Gun powder, he saw the prisoners there drink of it and swear to one another, they then proceeded to the low pen to learn Exercise, they had all there different Stations . . .

The arrest of the leading conspirators and the frustration of their carefully laid plans was followed by several trials at the Buff Bay Court House. Henry Oliver, Richard Montagnac, Dennis Kerr, Leon, George and Jack were sentenced to be hanged. One hundred pounds, their assessed value, was paid to the owners of each of them, except Montagnac and the African born Jack whose owners received £70 and £84 respectively. Jack was, in fact, tried twice. His trial and conviction on 19 February was found to have been illegal due to a technicality and he was again tried and convicted on 7 April.

James Thompson, James Manhertz and six others were sentenced to transportation for life, their owners receiving compensation in sums from £100 to £70 each, with the owner of the accused Prince getting only £54, presumably because of his poor health or tender age.

Many of the slaves, particularly in the western parishes, had by the 1820s come to believe that the abolition of slavery was imminent. A letter to W. Bullock, the government secretary, from Samuel Vaughan, a magistrate in St. James, written on 9 October 1823, shows how widespread this belief was: "It appears there is a general Expectation among the negroes of freedom being given shortly by Government at home.[17] The negroes are everywhere behaving well & perform their work as usual, but still entertain this belief" [PRO:CO 137/157]. Magistrate Vaughan recounted a number of incidents reported to him from different parts of the parish which had led him to reach this conclusion.

Towards the end of the year an atmosphere of tension and excitement began to prevail and many of the planters became convinced that an uprising was being planned. On 19 December Magistrate Sharpe presided at a "Special Session of the Peace" at the Montego Bay Court House, at which several witnesses were examined. The magistrates then ordered the arrest of 17 slaves on Unity Estate. Four days later further statements were taken.

In a second letter to Bullock dated 23 December Vaughan reported: "The Examinations have been referred to a committee of Gentlemen . . . but so far . . . there does not appear to have been any fixed or general place or any great preparation if any for a Rebellion" [PRO: CO 137/157]. He added that the overseer at Unity "gives a bad character of the two young men" who had been the chief informers, but commented that "this bad character amounts only to the very general one of Idleness".

On 29 December the committee of St. James magistrates, convened to investigate the current rumours and examine witnesses, reported their findings:

> That they have Evidence before them which confirms their opinion that some mischief has been intended and that there has been a great deal of communication among the negroes in the neighbourhood of Unity Hall on the subject.
>
> They have strong evidence against a negro sufficient ... to put him on his Trial altho they do not at present recommend it ... they ... believe that the Unity Hall and other negroes at present in Confinement have agreed not to betray each other and they therefore recommend that each Prisoner be confined separately and that further Examinations ... be taken [PRO: CO 137/157].

The fears of the planters that an insurrection was being planned continued to mount and when the magistrates met again on 5 February 1824 they decided that eight of the slaves arrested should be placed on trial and four others kept in custody. There would appear to have been further arrests because, at the end of January, 15 slaves were placed on trial in Montego Bay [PRO: CO 137/157].

The evidence established the fact that the current rumours of impending emancipation were being avidly discussed among the slaves and had created an atmosphere of excitement and expectancy. But there was absolutely nothing before the court on which anyone could properly have been convicted. Nevertheless, such was the state of hysteria among the slave owners that a majority of the five magistrates found thirteen of the prisoners guilty. Four were found guilty on all counts of the charge of rebellious conspiracy.[18]

The ridiculous nature of this trial was readily apparent from Magistrate Vaughan's letter reporting to the government secretary on the verdict and sentences:

> The Court were divided. The minority ... were of opinion, there was no conspiracy ... Nothing but common amusement.[19] The majority viz. Messrs Gray Boyd & myself, conceived there was legally, conspiracy, & that there was great criminality.

> As, however, there was no specific plan proved, nor the possession of arms, nor preparation by exercising, nor any overt act of rebellion or threat of murder of any white ... the Majority of the Court did not think the Punishment should be capital, & stated their intention to the Jury ...

The Jury, while accepting the view of the majority, came up with an idea of their own:

> It was proposed to the bench, only to single out one criminal for Transportation, altho' there were 4 found guilty nearly in an equal degree ... hoping this might be sufficient for an example & the preservation of the peace of the country, & they proposed various degrees of Punishment.

With this compromise solution in mind, reported Vaughan, the jury had valued for compensation purposes only the one slave they had recommended for transportation. But their crowning achievement was that they had selected, as the man to have the honour of serving as an example, the only one of the four who was weak and sickly and of the smallest monetary value which they fixed at £55.

By the next morning however the magistrates, having reconsidered the matter, came to the conclusion that they could not lawfully impose a lesser sentence than transportation on the other three accused who had been adjudged equally culpable. They no doubt reached this conclusion with great reluctance since, with the abolition of the slave trade, the transportation of healthy male slaves had its disadvantages. But they had no alternative and so, as Vaughan reported, the jury were required to return and value the other three. These they valued at £92, £84 and £82.

The other nine prisoners had meanwhile been sentenced to periods of imprisonment ranging from twelve months to one month with flogging, except in the cases of one elderly man and one of the women. Summing up his report, Vaughan offered his own conclusions:[20] "The present disposition, is entirely owing to the reports of what is going on in England & had it not been for the Arrest it cannot be doubted, there would have been Overt acts of Rebellion, but luckily for the Country, & the Negroes, it was nipped in the bud."

Confronted with the record of these ridiculous proceedings, and conscious of the scrutiny the Colonial Office was giving to all matters relating to the slaves at this time, the governor found himself in an embarrassing position. The letter written at his bidding to the magistrates of St. James can only be described as a masterpiece of tact.[21] It also revealed the reluctance with which the sentences of the court were reversed:

> Were Saint James the only Parish in which instances of insubordination amongst the Slaves had occurred His Grace might for the sake of example have possibly been induced to visit the offences of the Persons tried at Montego Bay with heavier punishment. But as unhappily in the Parishes of Saint Mary and Saint George Crimes of a more marked and decided Character have placed His Grace under the painful necessity of inflicting the punishment of Death on Many And on others that of banishing them the Island for Life — His Grace feels that were the Slaves now in imprisonment at Montego Bay to undergo the same punishment which the Conspirators in Saint Geroge have suffered — it might carry the appearance of Undistinguishing Severity . . .
>
> It has afforded His Grace particular satisfaction that . . . he has not been able to discover any concert or Combination amongst them for any Criminal purpose — There seems to have been a very active Spirit of Enquiry which may be naturally accounted for without attributing to them any Criminal Intentions . . .
>
> Under these circumstances His Grace the Governor fortunately finds himself in a Situation which enables him to make a discrimination between the Conspirators in St. Mary and St. George and the Slaves who have been convicted of different offences in St. James and he can with propriety give effect to the humane disposition of the Magistrates . . . by mitigating the Sentences which it seems the provisions of the Consolidated Slave Law had compelled the Court to pronounce [PRO: CO 137/157].

So much then for the excuse found by the governor for commuting the sentences on the three able bodied men sentenced so reluctantly to transportation. But what of the sickly young man they had been willing to make an example of? The governor's formula for reversing his sentence, without too much of an adverse reflection on the Court, was ingenious:

> In regard to Trelawny although he certainly made use of very unjustifiable Language Still when it is considered how incompetent he must be from his

infirmities and unlikely ... to exercise any sort of influence over the minds of the slaves ... His Grace is induced to commute his Sentence to three Months confinement to such labour as he is able to undergo.

But as the magistrates had wished to punish Trelawny more severely than the other three, said His Grace, he would honour their wishes in this respect. He would therefore fix the sentences of these three at one month's imprisonment.

Finally, with respect to the other nine slaves, the government secretary concluded: "it is rather to be regretted that so many were brought to Trial, and His Grace does not see any useful purpose in detaining them longer in Confinement".

Ludicrous as the proceedings before the St. James magistrates may have been, there is no mistaking the fact that, even in areas where no leaders had as yet emerged capable of laying plans for rebellion, there was an explosive atmosphere of excitement and expectancy among the slaves which was capable of turning in a revolutionary direction. Throughout 1824 this widespread state of unrest, particularly evident in the western parishes, continued unabated.

In or about the middle of the year, according to Gardner [14 pp. 260-1]: "Hanover was thrown into a state of excitement, though treachery once more baffled the designs of the conspirators, whatever they may have been ... Six slaves were hung at Argyle, five at Golden Grove, and a number of others transported or flogged".

Of the leaders of this conspiracy the governor, in a confidential dispatch,[22] stated that they were "fully impressed with the belief that they were entitled to their freedom and that the cause they had embraced was just and in vindication of their rights". He added that one of the leaders had said that "the war had only begun" [PRO:CO 137/156].

Gardner [14 pp.260-1] also reported that "a small band about the same time created alarm between Kingston and Yallahs". Of these, he said, "four were hung, and others punished in different ways".

It is interesting to note in passing that deportation from the island did not necessarily mean that the rebel slaves or conspirators deported were lost to the anti-slavery struggle. "In March 1820", writes H. Aptheker in his *American Negro Slaves Revolts* [2 p. 266] "slaves newly brought into Florida from Jamaica rebelled and were quickly subdued by a detachment of United States troops . . . one Negro was killed, but what other casualties occurred, and what punishments were inflicted are not known".

FOOTNOTES

[1] Volume I, Chapter 10.

[2] Duke of Manchester to Earl Bathurst, 26 January 1816.

[3] See also Bridges [5 vol. 2 pp.284-5] who states that this was a Cromantee conspiracy. Alan Burns, *History of the British West Indies* (George Allen & Unwin 1954, p.599) mentions a revolt in 1807 which he says was "easily overcome", but he cites no reference.

[4] Mathew Gregory Lewis, Member of Parliament, author of *The Monk*, a popular work of fiction.

[5] Ibos

[6] Manchester to Bathurst, 13 April 1816.

[7] Jamaica Alphabetical Index (No. 18553) of Official correspondence 1815-70, fols. 111-12-March 1822.

[8] "Examination of Two slaves taken at the Court House, St. Mary on 16th December 1823".

[9] Bundle with back sheet marked "19 Decem. 1823. Trial and Sentences of Sundry Slaves in Saint Mary", enclosed in Henry Cox to W. Bullock, 20 December 1823.

[10] H. Cox to W. Bullock, 25 December 1823.

[11] Examination of Jean Baptiste Corberand at Buff Bay Court House, 26 December 1823.

[12] Examination of Richard Montagnac, 26 December 1823.

[13] Examination of J.B. Corberand, 8 January 1824, enclosed in R.G. Kirkland to W.A. Orgill, 9 January 1824.

CONSPIRACIES

[14] Louis Celeste Lecesne, a free coloured man of Haitian descent. With John Escoffery he had been deported to Haiti by the governor in 1823, because of their activities on a committee formed to agitate for civil rights for free persons of African descent. Making their way to England, Lecesne and Escoffery were maintained there at government expense until, their deportation declared illegal, they were returned to Jamaica with compensation. Lecesne was not subsequently called upon however, despite Corberand's evidence, to answer a charge for obtaining guns for the rebels.

[15] "Jean Baptiste Corberand, alias Dimancha, belonging to Mullett Hall plantation, Crown Evidence" at the trial of Henry Oliver and others at Buff Bay, 19 January 1824.

[16] 'Macaronis' were coins minted for Jamaica worth 5d, 10d and 20d sterling. According to Alan Burns (note 3 above) these coins were introduced in the 1820s.

[17] The white residents invariably referred to Britain as 'home', though many of them had been born in Jamaica. They regarded themselves as Englishmen overseas.

[18] Report of Trial at a Slave Court at Montego Bay commencing 28 January 1824.

[19] The alleged conspiracy was supposed to have been hatched at a dance.

[20] Vaughan to Bullock, 2 February 1824.

[21] Bullock to Vaughan, 9 February 1824.

[22] Manchester to Bathurst, 31 July 1824.

CHAPTER ELEVEN

SAM SHARPE — ORGANISER OF THE EMANCIPATION REBELLION

The atmosphere in Jamaica at the end of the third decade of the 19th century was electric. Everywhere there was an air of excitement and expectancy. Parliament had decided in 1823 that the abolition of slavery, though ultimately to be desired, was not to be contemplated in the near future. But the British government had increased its pressure upon the colonial Assemblies to enact legislation modifying some of the most obvious cruelties and inhumanities of the system, and the resident planters had reacted angrily and defiantly.

In Jamaica there was open talk of secession and advocacy of union with the United States of America as a means of preserving slavery. In November 1831 the Assembly went so far as to refuse to discuss the British government's proposal for legislation prohibiting the flogging of slave women, a reform introduced in the Crown colonies in 1823-24. Not only did they resist British pressures for reform, but provocatively approved legislation in February 1831 to reduce the number of free days the slaves were entitled to enjoy immediately after Christmas. Writing to the governor, the Earl of Belmore, on 16 June 1831, Secretary of State Goderich commented: "Thus the three annual holidays are reduced to two and the slave is deprived of the security formerly given him . . ."

Referring back to this comment, in a subsequent memorandum to the governor dated 1 March 1832, Viscount Goderich wrote:

> When writing this passage, I was strongly impressed with the importance and danger of such an innovation knowing that the value of a holiday could not be correctly estimated, except by endeavouring to enter into the feelings of those who were to enjoy or lose it, and believing that the slaves would attach to this very ancient privilege an importance which, to persons in a very different condition of life, might easily appear exaggerated...
> [*The Watchman*, 16 May, 1832].

Another factor adding to the atmosphere of expectancy was the news of the anti slavery campaign in Britain. This had been intensified following the resolution of the Anti Slavery Society in May 1830 to propose immediate emancipation. Thanks to educational work among the slaves, conducted for the most part by the non-conformist missions, increasing numbers had learned to read English and could follow reports of British and local events in the newspapers. Indirect oral reports of angry denunciations of the British government and leading abolitionists at the planters' dinner tables were now supplemented by the printed word.

Despite repeated denials, rumours to the effect that freedom was about to be granted, which began to regain currency in the 1820s, had gathered momentum. Many of the slaves, uninhibited by any understanding of the subtleties of the constitutional monarchy, believed that "the king had made them free, or was resolved upon doing it" and that freedom was being delayed by the local slave owners [Bleby 4 pp. 110-2].

A slave named William Binham reported [1] that this belief was particularly strong among slaves who were members of the Baptist churches in the western parishes: "The Baptists all believe that they are to be freed; they say, the Lord and the King have given them free, but the white gentlemen in Jamaica keep it back..." [PP, Vol. XLVII p. 212].

In an attempt to scotch these persistent rumours, also current in the other West Indian colonies and in British

Guiana, a proclamation in the name of King William IV was issued on 3 June 1831:

> Whereas it has been represented to us that the slaves in some of our West-India colonies and of our possessions on the continent of South America, have been erroneously led to believe that orders have been sent out by us for their emancipation:
>
> And whereas such belief has produced acts of insubordination, which have excited our highest displeasure...
>
> We do hereby declare and make known that the slave population in our said colonies and possessions will forfeit all claim on our protection, if they shall fail to render entire submission to the laws, as well as dutiful obedience to their masters... [PP, Vol. XLVII pp.276-7; *Votes* 1831 pp. 111-2].

Curiously enough this proclamation, when it was first received, was not publicised as widely in Jamaica as it was in the other colonies. The governor appears to have taken the view that it would only stimulate discussion of the subject among the slaves and give the rumours wider credibility. He may have been right. At all events, the leading conspirators in the western parishes, who cannot have been unaware of the proclamation, were not deterred by it.

When eventually the governor did decide to give the proclamation wide publicity on 22 December 1831, posters containing it were put up in many public places and it was read out to the slaves on all plantations. A circular to all Custodes, dated 22 December 1831 and issued from King's House, enclosed printed copies of the proclamation and directed that it "be read to the slaves by the persons in charge of the several plantations in your parish" [PP, Vol.XLVII p.276, no.1]. But the slaves do not appear to have been impressed, if indeed they believed that the proclamation was genuine. The lieutenant colonel in command of the militia in St. Thomas in the East, a parish to which the organisation for the rebellion had not been extended, stated: "I ordered the Manchioneal company out on the first day of January, and did so in consequence of the excited feeling which appeared amongst the slaves, and the evident contempt with which they treated the King's proclamation when it was read to them in chapel on that day" [*Votes* 1831 p. 307].

In the months of August and September 1831, the plantation owners "in many, if not all the parishes throughout the island" held public protest meetings. In violent and intemperate language they denounced the resolution of the British parliament approving in principle the abolition of slavery and the action of the British government in endeavouring to force the colonial legislatures to enact legislation ameliorating the conditions of the slaves. These meetings passed angry resolutions. Those approved at St. Anns Bay and in Trelawny will serve as illustrations.

The St. Ann resolution asserted that "perfidy and determined oppression, as far as regards the colonies, are the ruling principles of the British Cabinet". It concluded with the strident declaration that "when we see ourselves scorned, betrayed, devoted to ruin and slaughter, delivered over to the enemies of our country, we consider that we are bound by every principle, human and divine, TO RESIST".

The Trelawny resolution warned that "the means devised by a faction in the House of Commons to deprive us of our property, if carried into effect cannot fail to create a servile war of too horrible a nature to contemplate". It stated that "thrown", as they were about to be, "as a prey before misguided savages", they would "have no other alternative than to resist". They would then, continued the resolution, pray the King "that we may be absolved from our allegiance, and allowed to seek that protection from another nation which is so unjustly and cruelly withheld from us by our own" [*Facts and Documents* 12].[2]

These meetings were conducted in the full view and hearing of large numbers of slaves. Apart from adding to the increasing tension, their proceedings lent confirmation to the growing belief that the British government was about to abolish slavery and that the local slave owners were determined to resist it, if necessary by force.

Towards the end of the year tension was particularly high in the western parishes. An advertisement appearing in a contemporary newspaper disclosed an increasingly common occurrence, though the rewards offered may have been more than usually generous:

> Office of Police, Montego Bay, Dec. 19, 1831, 250 Dollars Reward! *Whereas* certain Negroes belonging to Salt-Spring Estate in this Parish, namely David Bowen, James Allen, William Johnson, James Fraser, and Thomas R. Bernard, have, after turbulent and disorderly conduct, absented themselves from the property, *Notice is hereby given* that the Magistrates offer a Reward of Thirty Dollars, and the proprietor of the Estate, a further reward of Twenty Dollars each, for the apprehension, and bringing the above slaves to the Police Office [*Royal Gazette* 24-31 December 1831 No. 53, postscript].

Most of the white non-conformist missionaries of whom there were about two dozen in the island at this time, and some of the Presbyterians, were opposed to slavery. This was particularly true of the Baptists who formed the largest group. But the missionaries were at pains to persuade their converts that the issue would be settled for them in England, and to dissuade them from taking matters into their own hands.

The Presbyterian missionary, H.M. Waddell, recorded the advice he gave on the eve of the rebellion to the slaves in his Trelawny congregation:

> Before any blow had been struck, I admonished my congregation on the subject. One with them, I said, in desiring their freedom, and not doubting they would yet receive it, I assured them it could come to them only in a peaceable and lawful way, — by the efforts of their friends in Britain, — while violence on their part would surely retard its progress, and perhaps insure their own destruction [Waddell 34 p.51].

After the Christmas holidays Waddell went with his patron Samuel Barrett, the Scottish proprietor of Barrett Hall and other plantations, on a tour of the latter's properties in Trelawny. Their object was to persuade the slaves to return to work. In this task they enjoyed some success. But when they got to Spot Valley estate, belonging to an absentee proprietor, "the case was different", as Waddell recorded:

> they listened to Mr Barrett reading the proclamation issued by Sir Willoughby Cotton, till it spoke of their returning to work, when they all

lifted up their voices and overwhelmed him with clamour. 'We have worked enough already, and will work no more. The life we live is too bad; it is the life of a dog. We won't be slaves no more; we won't lift hoe no more; we won't take flog no more. We free now... no more slaves again' [34 pp. 59-60].

Some of "the head men of Spot Valley" subsequently assured Barrett and Waddell that they would "try to bring round all the people" to a resumption of work, but whether they succeeded in doing so Waddell did not say.

Despite the opposition of many of the missionaries to slavery, they, without exception, advised "that even slaves were required patiently to submit to their lot, till the Lord in His providence is pleased to change it" [Bleby 4 p. 117]. Many slaves, however, including several of the church class leaders and lay preachers, were unable to accept the idea that "the Lord in His providence" exercised His powers of inspiration only in England. Surely, they reasoned, if slavery was contrary to God's will, he would expect them to take steps to terminate it.

Far from diminishing after the execution and transportation of the leading conspirators of 1823-24, the belief, reported to be then current, that they were "entitled to their freedom" and that to fight for it was "just and in vindication of their rights"[3] had gained greater currency. As William Binham explained: "they said, if they did not fight for freedom they would never get it. I heard them all [the Baptist slaves] say this" [PP, Vol.XLVII p.212].

This growing determination to win their freedom was to be found not only among the field slaves, whose toil was the most exacting, but among all the servile occupations. Even drivers, including a number of influential head drivers, whose task it was to ensure that the field labourers did not relax at their work, had become convinced of the necessity for action. In the late 1830s the time was ripe for rebellion. What was needed was an organisation and a plan.

This is how a slave named Linton, one of those condemned to death for his part in the events of 1831-32, subsequently described the situation: "Every year back at Christmas or October we were to begin, but were afraid to jump off until this year; we were very near beginning it either in last March or last October. There are a great many people concerned in this business..." [PP, Vol. XLVII pp. 209-20].

Linton's statement was recorded by Rev. Thomas Stewart, the Anglican rector of Westmoreland. Stewart took a series of 'confessions' from prisoners during the rebellion, some of whom, like Linton, had already been condemned to death and some of whom were awaiting trial. He saw them for this purpose despite the fact that most of them were non-conformists, and appears to have been acting as a sort of police agent.

Linton himself was an illustration of how widespread was the conviction of the necessity for rebellion. He was the head slave on Hermitage estate. A fellow conspirator, William Binham, described him as "a brown man... a kind of busha[4] there" [p.212]. He was, in other words, a person of a relatively high status which in normal times would have ensured his loyalty to the establishement.

The number of slaves involved in the rebellion who had occupied supervisory positions[5] or whose treatment, by comparison with the sufferings of the majority, had been relatively mild, surprised the plantocracy. According to Bleby:

> Sharpe acknowledged to me that he had, as an individual, no reason to find fault with the treatment he had received as a slave. His master, Samuel Sharpe, Esq., and the family, were always very kind to him, and he had never been flogged beyond the occasional and slight correction which he had received when a boy. But he thought, and he learnt from his Bible, that the whites had no more right to hold black people in slavery, than the black people had to make the white people slaves and, for his own part, he would rather die than live in slavery [4 p.116].

A plantation owner giving evidence before a committee set up after the event to establish its causes,[6] had this to say about two other principal rebel leaders

> Gardner and Dove both admitted being treated with great kindness by their attorneys and overseers; that much confidence had been placed in them;

that they never before had had a charge made against them, nor ever had been punished, as by examining their skins would be proved [PP, Vol. XLVII p.193].

Similar comments were made concerning a number of other prominent rebels. At the end of their enquiry the Assembly approved, on 5 April 1832, this curiously philosophic resolution.

> Resolved, that it has been a remarkable and unprecedented feature in this rebellion, that many of the chief conspirators and ringleaders were to be found amongst those slaves who, from their situations as head-people or confidential servants were the least worked, were the best clothed, and received the most indulgence [*Votes* 1832 p. 110].

The plan for a rebellion to commence after Christmas, 1831, was conceived and worked out by Samuel Sharpe, a 31 year old creole field slave on Croydon estate in St. James[7] [PRO:CO 137/185]. The rebel Robert Gardner, who was given the rank of colonel, acknowledged Sharpe as leader of the rebels. He referred to him as "General Sharp", saying that he was "the head planner and mentioned how everything was to be done" and had "sworn all the people under him" [PP. Vol. XLVII pp.216-7, no.8]. The rebel captain Thomas Dove also confirmed Sharpe's leading role. Dove's 'confessor' recorded him as saying: "Samuel Sharpe was leader of the whole of the negroes at the commencement of the rebellion, and the only instigator, as far as he knows" [ibid p.214].

Questioned further during his imprisonment in the gaol at Savanna la mar, Gardner said: [8] "Samuel Sharp swore every man all round, from the parish of St. James, part of Trelawny, part of St. Elizabeth, Hanover, and the upper part of Westmoreland". Asked what they were sworn to do, he said, "The oath was, that every man should fight, and do his utmost to drive the white and free people out of Jamaica; if they succeeded, a governor was to be appointed to each parish".

In answer to the question: "Was Samuel Sharp the only ruler; if so, how did he get that appointment?", Gardner naively replied: "At first, Samuel Sharp was the only ruler.

He was in the habit of going two or three times a week to Montego Bay, and must have got his appointment there". Gardner said further about Sharpe: "He can read, and used to read the newspapers, and hear the people talk at the Bay; he would then bring up all the news, and spread it among the negroes; sometimes he would bring the newspapers from the Bay, and read them to the negroes" [ibid pp.217-8, no.10].

The Methodist missionary Henry Bleby, who saw Sharpe in the gaol at Montego Bay, was deeply impressed by his sincerity and intelligence and the power of his personality. Bleby wrote:

> The insurrection... was planned by one person, and that individual himself a slave. Samuel Sharpe was the man whose active brain devised the project and he had sufficient authority with those around him to carry it into effect, having acquired an extraordinary degree of influence amongst his fellow-slaves. I had much conversation with him whilst he was in confinement; and found him certainly the most intelligent and remarkable slave I ever met with.

Describing Sharpe's physical features Bleby wrote:

> He was of the middle size; his fine sinewy frame was handsomely moulded, and his skin as perfect a jet as can well be imagined. His forehead was high and broad, while his nose and lips exhibited the usual characteristics of the negro race. He had teeth whose regularity and pearly whiteness a court-beauty might have envied, and an eye whose brilliancy was almost dazzling.

As regards Sharpe's powers of persuasion Bleby was ecstatic:

> I had an opportunity of observing that he possessed intellectual and oratorical powers above the common order; and this was the secret of the extensive influence which he exercised. I heard him two or three times deliver a brief extemporaneous address to his fellow-prisoners on religious topics, many of them being confined together in the same cell; and I was amazed both at the power and freedom with which he spoke, and at the effect which was produced upon his auditory.
>
> He appeared to have the feelings and passions of his hearers completely at his command: and when I listened to him once, I ceased to be surprised at what Gardner had told me, 'that when Sharpe spoke to him and others on the subject of slavery', he, Gardner, was 'wrought up almost to a state of madness' [4 p.115].

Sharpe, a Baptist lay preacher, was often referred to by his co-religionists as 'Daddy' or 'Ruler', in recognition of his position of authority in the church. This added to the prestige which he enjoyed by virtue of his own magnetic personality. According to Dove:

> The negroes believed all that Samuel Sharpe said to them, because he being born and brought up on the Bay,[9] was intelligent and could read, and besides was head leader at the Baptist church, and always attended there; and the negroes considered that what Sharpe told them when he came to the mountains must be true, as it came from the church [PP, Vol. XLVII pp. 214-5].

Sharpe's owner appears to have approved of his religious work and to have allowed him considerable latitude for his nocturnal proselytising. Of this he took full advantage, using his religious services as a cover for his organisational meetings. An account of one of these meetings was given to Bleby by Edward Hylton, one of his fellow conspirators:

> During the year 1831 (he could not tell the month) he received a message at Mountain Spring from Sam Sharpe, desiring him to meet him on the following Saturday night at the house of Johnson, at Retrieve estate in St. James. This was the Col. Johnson who led the attack, and was killed, at Montpelier ...
>
> At the time appointed Hylton went to Retrieve, where he met with Sharpe, Johnson, and others whom he named. After they had held a prayer-meeting, most of the people went away, Sharpe, Johnson, Hylton and a few more, remaining behind: and the party was afterwards enlarged by several others, who stealthily and with extreme caution made their way into the house, and who were evidently expected by those already assembled.

Hylton gave a dramatic account of the proceedings which followed:

> After the lapse of some time, Sharpe rose to address the meeting, speaking in a low, soft tone, that his voice might not be heard beyond the walls of the building ... He then proceeded with his address to those around him, speaking for a long time on various topics relating to the great subject he had at heart, and with an eloquence which, from Hylton's account, kept all his hearers fascinated and spell-bound from the beginning to the end of his speech.
>
> He referred to the manifold evils and injustice of slavery; asserted the natural equality of man with regard to freedom; and referring to the holy Scriptures as his authority, denied that the white man had any more right to hold the blacks in bondage than the blacks had to enslave the whites ...
>
> He concluded by observing, that because the king had made them free, or was resolved upon doing it, the 'whites and Grignon'[10] were holding secret

meetings, with the doors shut close, at the house of Mr. Watt of Montego Bay, and had determined... to kill all the black men, and save all the women and children, and keep them in slavery; and if the black men did not stand up for themselves, and take their freedom, the whites would put them out at the muzzles of their guns, and shoot them like pigeons.

Hylton confirmed Bleby's assessment of the power and persuasiveness of Sharpe's speech: "This address, delivered with great fluency, and with all the pathos and earnestness of which Sharpe was eminently capable, told with powerful effect upon his auditors".

Bleby concluded his account of the interview with Hylton with the latter's statement of what can best be described as the resolution of the meeting:

Further discussion ensued, and their deliberations were carried on far into the night; when, all scruples being set at rest, and the plan of operations more fully detailed by Sharpe, the whole party bound themselves by oath not to work after Christmas as slaves, but to assert their claim to freedom, and to be faithful to each other. If 'Buckra' would pay them, they would work as before; but if any attempt was made to force them to work as slaves, then they would fight for their freedom [4 pp. 110-2].

All present then took the oath and kissed the Bible.

The strike was obviously the most important organisational factor in Sam Sharpe's revolutionary plan. Given the atmosphere of expectancy that had been steadily developing over the past seven to eight years, the call for a general refusal to work again as slaves after the Christmas holidays was attractive and electrifying. It was a proposal capable of gaining the widest support among the slave population, support which it would not have been possible to achieve on anything approaching the same scale had the proposal been a simple call to rise in arms against their oppressors.

It has been suggested that the strike was not merely the core but the whole of Sharpe's plan; that he neither intended the destruction of property nor desired that the people should fight for their freedom. Assuming that Bleby recorded accurately what Sharpe said to him in the gaol at Montego Bay, this was certainly the impression he sought to leave with the minister. According to Bleby, Sharpe "expressed deep regret that such an extensive destruction of property and life had resulted from the conspiracy which he had promoted; but declared that this formed no part of his plan" [4 pp.116-7].

This is how Bleby recorded his understanding of Sharpe's sentiments:

> He did not wish to destroy the estates, nor did he desire that any person should be injured: his only object was to obtain freedom. But to his great disappointment he found that the spirit of revolt, once evoked, was not susceptible of control. He had not sufficiently taken into account the excitable character of the negroes whom he sought to benefit, and their probable want of self-government when they should be suddenly emancipated from the yoke to which they were subject; and he too hastily concluded that he should find them the same patient and submissive beings as he had ever known them ... [ibid].

No doubt this is how the non-conformist missionaries would have liked to think of Sharpe. And perhaps, when out of the goodness of his heart Bleby came to see him in gaol, Sharpe realised that this was what Bleby hoped to hear from him. But it is from Bleby himself that we learn of Sharpe's capacity to deceive his listeners. Discussing the belief, widely held among the slaves in the western parishes, that freedom had actually been granted to them but was being withheld by the local whites, a rumour which Sharpe deliberately disseminated, Bleby wrote:

> Sharpe was not deceived himself concerning the slavery question; he was, I believe, too intelligent not to be aware of the true state of the case. Living in the town of Montego Bay, where he had frequent opportunities of reading the newspapers, containing reports of the movements of the Anti-Slavery party in England ... he knew very well how matters stood both in England and in the colony. But being favoured by the absence of his minister, Mr. Burchell, from the island ... he formed the daring design of imposing upon the slaves, in that part of the island, the belief that they had actually been made free by the king, and of putting himself at their head, to commence a struggle for freedom [4 pp.115-6].

Though Sharpe had stressed the point, at the meeting at Johnson's house reported above, that they should be ready to fight for their freedom if the planters did not yield to their demands, he does not appear to have made this point at all his meetings. There were occasions when, no doubt having shrewdly assessed both the level of militancy of those present and the security situation, he confined himself to plans for the general strike. This was the case at another meeting at Retrieve held during the week before Christmas at the house of a slave named Tucker. One of the men present, giving evidence subsequently at Sharpe's trial, said [11] "there were a great many people there. Prisoner swore me amongst the rest — he said we were to be free & after Xmas we were not to go to Work — he said nothing else" [PRO:CO 137/185, fols 310-14].

Another conspirator present at the same meeting said, [12] "He said we must all agree to set [13] down after Xmas. I said Yes — and so did everybody in the House . . . he said we must set down. We must not trouble any body and raise no Rebellion. We must set quite peaceable . . . We did not swear to burn any where or to fight".

Both witnesses however testified that after the start of the rebellion they joined a company of rebels personally commanded by Sharpe. And when Sharpe addressed the members of his company on the day after their successful engagement with the militia at Struie, he left them in no doubt as to his resolution to fight. James Clarke, a slave who gave evidence at Sharpe's subsequent trial, stated: "The next morning the party eat Breakfast at George Reid's at Cambridge, and after Breakfast Sharpe called all his Men and said Freedom was due to them a long time & they must now seek and fight for it, and the one that fell back when they went to battle, the others must shoot him".

The overseer at Ginger Hill estate in St. Elizabeth held prisoner there by the rebels, reported that Sharpe visited that estate on the third day of the rebellion. He recorded the rebel leader as saying: [14] "he did not wish to take away the life of any person who did not stand between him and his rights; . . . that freedom was their right and freedom they would have".

He said "a great deal more" stated the overseer, "all tending to show, that, from the religious notions he had imbibed, he conceived that the slaves had a right to be free" [PP,Vol. XLVII p.286, no. 18].

If indeed Sharpe had, initially, been naive enough to expect the plantocracy to yield to the strikers demand without first making an attempt to coerce them to return to work as slaves, he would have been unlikely to adhere to this view when the disposition of the militia over the Christmas holidays became known to him. But is it at all conceivable that a man of Sharpe's intelligence would not have anticipated that the slave owners would fight to preserve their property and privileges? The evidence speaks overwhemingly to the contrary. Nor is there any doubt that Sharpe was prepared to sacrifice his own life in pursuit of the cause he had embraced. Bleby recorded Sharpe's firm statement to him while awaiting execution: "I would rather die upon yonder gallows than live in slavery". As he spoke these words, wrote Bleby, "his frame expanded, and his eagle-eye seemed to shoot forth rays of light" [4 p. 116].

The rebellion had the enthusiastic support of the great majority of the slaves in the parishes of St. James and Hanover and in upper Westmoreland, and of considerable numbers in Trelawny and western St. Elizabeth. But confidence was not equally high in all areas, nor were Sharpe's recruiting agents all blessed with the capacity for patient explanation. Sometimes, when recruiting timid souls, they gave them a bit of encouragement, of one sort or another, to take the oath. A slave who claimed to have been a reluctant recruit, made this deposition concerning the manner of his enrollment:[15]

> When we were sworn in at Haughton Grove Gate Pasture, Richard Trail was there from Shuttlewood, he had a gun, and said if we did not take the oath he would shoot us. Thomas Haughton belonging to Shuttlewood, was there, and had a large Bible, both acted as headmen. Andrew Llewellyn, from Silver Grove, was there, and John Martin also, both had guns. Thomas Haughton said this is not time to make fun with; 'if they come back here they will destroy us all', meaning the white people [PP, Vol. XLVII p.208].

That the slaves were discussing the idea of the strike appears to have been known to many of the white people on the plantations in the western parishes. But they appear to have dismissed it as idle chatter. Major General Sir Willoughby Cotton, commander of the British troops, referred to this knowledge of the local whites in one of his early dispatches [16] after the commencement of the rebellion:

> That the overseers, or attornies, or magistrates, should not have acquainted the Executive Government the extent to which the determination of the negroes had gone all around this district, 'not to work after New-Year's Day, without being made free', is most astonishing, as it would appear to have been known on almost all the estates that these were the sentiments of the negroes [PP, Vol. XLVII p. 295, no. 30].

Preparations for the calling of the strike would seem then to have been well laid. What may not have been so well and widely understood was what was to be done after the planters had refused to yield to the demand for the payment of wages. Indeed, doubts were subsequently expressed by the commander of the troops as to whether, beyond their general determination to fight for freedom if an attempt was made to force them to work, and to destroy the plantations by fire, the rebels had any plan at all. When he was asked the question: "What do you consider was the plan of the rebellion preconcerted or adopted by the slaves?", the General replied: "The only plan I can perceive was a simultaneous rising to resist working if they were not declared free at Christmas, and the determination to burn the different properties; as to any organised plan of resistance in the field, I have never either met or heard of it" [ibid p.208].

Sharpe did have a plan for a rebel military formation of sorts, but this was so rudimentary and inadequate for the task of dislodging an establishment with strong armed forces at its disposal, that it is not surprising that a military man should have dismissed it as non-existent. Sharpe's military plan envisaged the formation of a large mobile body of fighters organised in three or four companies, and of local units based on a plantation or a group of adjoining plantations. Participants in the rebellion described these divisions of the main body by a confusing variety of familiar military terms – "regiment", "company" or simply "force" or "party".

Gardner, as we have seen, described Sharpe as their "general". There were also two rebel "colonels" — Johnson (or Johnstone) and Gardner — and a number of "captains". Sharpe and the colonels commanded the companies of the main force and for the most part the captains appear to have led the local units. But some captains may have led forces of company size or acted as deputies to the colonels.

The main problem was that there was little or no possibility of training the proposed mobile army prior to the commencement of the rebellion or, at the earliest, the beginning of the Christmas holidays. The bringing together of slave conspirators from widely separated plantations would have been both difficult to achieve and easy to detect. Had such a training programme been organised for groups of recruits it would probably have led to exposure of the plans for the rebellion and the premature identification of the rebel cadres. Faced with these difficulties it is possible that Sharpe considered it unwise to do more than appoint a number of officers in advance, perhaps instructing them that when the time came they would have to do most of their own recruiting.

Though it is probably safe to assume, from the speed with which they took up their appointments, that a number of the officers had been appointed in advance, there appears to have been confusion at the last moment as to whether these divisions of the main army would operate separately or together and who was to command. The rebel colonel, Robert Gardner, provided some interesting information. But some of his evidence, given while he was in captivity and was endeavouring to discount his own role in the planning of the rebellion in the hope of saving his life, is suspect. Subject to this limitation, what Gardner had to say is nevertheless of some assistance towards understanding the rebels' military formation.

According to Gardner:[17] "on Tuesday night after Christmas-day, Sharp sent a great number of men for me to command, and to urge the others in the neighbourhood [of Greenwich and Belvidere estates] to join". These men "said

Sharp had sent them to me to command that I was to take them, and all the people in the district, as a 'force' to go against Westmoreland and Hanover" [PP, Vol XLVII p. 216, no. 8].

When we look at the information concerning the local units supplied by the rebel William Binham, we learn that Greenwich and Belvidere had a "gang" under Gardner and Dove. It would appear therefore that Sharpe wanted Gardner to put together a company consisting of the men he had sent him and the men of Gardner's own district. The company was then to move out of that area for offensive action.

Gardner said further that the men sent to him had reported "that Sharp desired them to tell me that he had a multitude of people under his command; that they consisted of all the people in St. James's and part of Trelawny, extending up to Chesterfield, Ginger Hill, Ec.; that he would command in person".

Gardner was required to rendezvous with Sharpe at Hazelymph estate before setting off on his Westmoreland and Hanover assignment, and he went there on the evening of 27 December. "While I was at supper with Fred Zuicke, at Hazelymph", said Gardner, "I heard General Sharp's army coming. They were wild, furious, blowing shells, and making a great shouting". Within this 'army', however, there appears to have been at least one company ("regiment") capable of being hived off for any particular operation. According to Gardner, "a regiment of Sharp's, under the command of Captain Johnstone" was soon despatched to burn the trash-houses at Belvidere estate as a beacon.

That night the rebels held a parley at Hazelymph. Perhaps it was there that the decision was taken to delay Gardner's departure for Westmoreland and Hanover, so that he and his men could participate with Johnson's company in the attack on the St. James militia. If Gardner was right in giving Johnson's rank as 'captain' on the evening of 27 December, then the latter was soon to be promoted — perhaps on that very night. When the militia were attacked at Montpelier on 29 December, Johnson was in command with the rank of colonel. Charles Campbell of York was his deputy. Gardner and Dove, according to Bleby [4 p.11], were "acting in subordination to them".

In his own account of the Montpelier battle, given later to the Baptist missionary William Knibb,[18] Gardner however referred to Campbell as being in command of one "company" and to Johnson (Johnstone) as leading another. [*Facts and Documents* 12 pp. 11-2].

Some evidence is available, from the record of the rebel leader's subsequent trial, as to Sharpe's activities in direct command of one of the companies of the ragged rebel army. The witness Joseph Martin said: "Saw Prisoner with a party on Thursday after Xmas — about 20 men. More than half of them had Guns — some had Macheats and some lances & swords. Prisoner had a little Macheat — the party always followed him, & he gave Orders to them ..." [PRO:CO 137/185, fols 310-14].

But the members of Sharpe's company, and this was probably true of the other companies also, did not stay permanently together. Probably they dispersed to their respective homes after each operation and reassembled for the next one. The same witness spoke of Sharpe coming to Cambridge by himself on one occasion, whence "6 or 7 men walked with him" and "a large party met at Cow Park".

Sharpe's and Gardner's companies then carried out a combined operation against the militia at Struie (near the Westmoreland-St. James boundary) in which "Sharpe commanded the party he went with" and "Gardner commanded his own party". Thereafter "Sharpe returned to Cambridge the same day with his party where they separated" [ibid]. At some stage Sharpe appears to have exchanged his machete for fire-arms. Martin says "Sharpe had a fowling piece at Cambridge". Two other witnesses at Sharpe's trial saw him with a "gun" and one with a "small pistol" [ibid].

Information concerning the local units and their 'captains' is to be found in the 'confession' of William Binham, extracted from him by the Westmoreland rector while he was under sentence of death in the gaol at Savanna-la-Mar. Binham said:

> There are several gangs of rebels; Hazelymph has a gang under the command of John Tharp (not Daddy Ruler Tharp), a doctor-man to the property ... Chester Castle, another, under a full-faced man who carries a gun. Copse has one too, but I do not know the name of the captain [PP, Vol. XLVII p.212].

Gardner, when in captivity, denied previous knowledge of Sharpe's military plans. If he received his rank of 'colonel' prior to 27 December, he would in all probability have been aware of Sharpe's intention to create an 'army'. But unfortunately there is no record of when he was given that appointment.

Gardner considered Captain John Tharp to be a man of some importance. To the Anglican rector he spoke [19] of Tharp as "a great ruler" and "a very dangerous man to this country, if the white gentlemen want to keep the peace" [PP. Vol. XLVII pp. 217-8, no. 10]. To the Baptist missionary Knibb he said that "John Thorp Lawrence, *alias* Daddy Tharp ... is not praying at all". Referring to Tharp's achievements he said that he "was a great horseman" and had "attacked the white people at Long Hill". Gardner said further of Tharp that a "white man at Lethe gave him his gun and pistol, and told him how to make cartridges, and that he did right to fight for freedom" [*Facts and Documents* 12 p. 11].

Other important rebel cadres were John Morris from Ducketts and Thomas Horton (Haughton) from Shuttlewood Cave. Binham described Morris as "a yellow man" and "a captain and leader" [PP, Vol. XLVII p.212]. According to Knibb: "Gardner stated, that John Morris, from Ducketts ... said that he had one pistol, and that he had given three guns to his people; that he had taken three more guns, and four pistols from Mr. G. Hale's mountain..."

Knibb quoted Gardner as saying further: "One night John

Morris, and Thomas Horton . . . met more than 100 men armed . . . I came down in the morning, when I found them drawn up like soldiers, and they make me go with them to Argyle ... John Morris and Thomas Horton were in command" [*Facts and Documents* 12 p. 11].

Other rebel cadres mentioned by Binham were "Father Roberts" and M'Lacklan who, he said, were both "captains", and Robert Morris of Struey (Struie) who was "second in command under M'Cail" [PP, Vol. XLVII p.212]. Dove told Knibb of "Bailey, a yellow skin negro belonging to Miss Williams" who "read the paper about freedom to the people in the country, and told them that it came from England". Bailey, Dove said, "was a captain" and he "saw him and heard him tell the people to fight" [*Facts and Documents* 12 p. 11].

Some slaves, who had absconded from their place of enslavement long before the rebellion commenced, joined the ranks of the rebels. Dove told Knibb about one such person, James Heulier from Belvidere, who "was a chief man among . . . the rebels" and "had been a runaway for five years" [ibid].

The weak link in the rebel conspiracy was undoubtedly the mobile army. Not only was it recruited hurriedly in a matter of days, but, given the conditions under which Sharpe laid his plans, it is difficult to see how it could have been otherwise. Had Sharpe been able to find a suitable military leader for the task, he would perhaps have been better advised to encourage a number of slaves to abscond from their work places and withdraw into the mountains, there to form the nucleus of a guerrilla army. But the Jamaica of 1831 was a very different place from the Jamaica of a century earlier. Not only was there less undeveloped land, there was also the black gendarmerie, the Maroons, to contend with. It would have been a difficult, if not impossible, task for a mobile guerrilla force of runaway slaves to have been armed, trained and maintained in the mountains in preparation for the Emancipation Rebellion.

"Sharpe's army", as Gardner described it, was an untrained, inexperienced, ill-disciplined and poorly armed multitude. In its initial stages its members no doubt possessed abundant enthusiasm and the determination to be free. But it was totally inadequate for the task of carrying out successful military operations against well-equipped and disciplined soldiers. Indeed, many of the rebel slaves believed that the British troops in the island would not take the field against them, and that they would only have to face the guns of militia.

The small local units, on the other hand, were tremendously successful. They appear to have been multipurpose groups, combining the tasks of ensuring that no work was done on the plantations after the commencement of the rebellion and of destroying the sugar works and other buildings when the time for that came. What they lacked in conventional fire-power was more than compensated for by their use of the power of fire. They effectively destroyed, over a wide area, the material basis of their enslavement. When the rebellion was three weeks old a local newspaper commented:[20] "The negro fights but badly with the musket: but his conquests with the torch have been fearfully satisfied".

The subsequent tally of property destruction shows that the rebels were eminently successful in destroying many of the sugar factories and estate buildings. But it is interesting to note that their initial tactics involved the firing of only the trash houses. These were the sheds in which the bagasse or trash, remaining after the juice had been expressed from the cane, was stored for fuel. That this tactic caused some speculation after the event appears in the examinations of several of the witnesses who gave evidence before the committee set up by the Assembly to enquire into the causes of the rebellion.

A magistrate who owned property in Westmoreland told the committee:[21]

> They commenced by burning the trash-houses alone. Belvidere works were not burnt, nor any others, I believe, till subsequent to Colonel Grignon's

retreat from New Montpelier. At Chester Castle on the night of the 28th, they burnt the trash-houses; the mill-houses took fire, and I believe there is sufficient proof that the slaves on that property endeavoured to extinguish it [PP, Vol. XLVII p. 197].

Another witness, an estate manager and overseer in St. James, was asked [22] "What motive, as far as you have been able to learn, induced the rebels to burn only the trash-houses at first, and not to burn the works and other buildings until the return of the militia?" He replied: "I should suppose that burning the trash-houses was merely a signal for a general rising, as all the trash-houses in that neighbourhood were burnt in one night I mean on all the properties above where the militia was stationed".

His questioner then asked: "What do you consider was the object of the rebels in delaying to burn the works and other buildings?" His only response to this was: "I cannot say". [ibid p.195].

A possible explanation of the rebels' delay in implementing a policy of total destruction of plantation buildings lay in their hope that the refusal of a majority of the slaves in the western parishes to work as slaves after Christmas would prove sufficient to bring the system to an end. The rebels may have reasoned that it was necessary to keep the possibility of a return to work for wages open, in the event that their general strike achieved the desired result. The burning of the trash-houses may have been designed to serve both as a signal to their comrades and as a warning to the planters of what might befall them if the strikers' demands were not met.

But whatever may have been the explanation of the hiatus between the firing of the trash-houses and the wholesale devastation which followed, the Assembly and some of the witnesses believed that the firing of the works and other buildings had been planned by the rebels from the beginning. Asked "whether the burning of properties was not part of the plan of the rebellion laid by the conspirators from the moment when they determined to attempt the rebellion?", the magistrate from Westmoreland said that though he "never was so informed by a slave", he had "heard that it was so" [ibid p. 197].

Not all the rebels were agreed on the advisability of destroying the plantations. On some properties the slaves, whilst participating fully in the strike, protected the works and buildings against attempts by others to destroy them. This, according to the Presbyterian minister Waddell, was what happened at Carlton estate in Trelawny, where "The head driver... said that he would never lift a hoe again as a slave, though he would neither burn nor kill". When Waddell tried to persuade the slaves to resume work, on the ground that they were not yet free, he was accused of having been hired by the planter-magistrates to deceive them [Waddell 34 pp.56-7].

At Cornwall on the night of 29 December a lone agitator was unable to persuade the slaves to start a fire. Waddell recorded that he was awakened by "the voice of a man" calling: "No watchman now, no watchman now, nigger man ... burn the house — burn buckra house! Brimstone come!... bring fire, and burn massa house!" For Waddell and the proprietor these were "anxious moments; for the incendiary continued his cries up and down among the negro houses". But "none seemed to answer, nor did the danger increase". Significantly, however, no slave came out of his house to apprehend or remonstrate with the intruder, whose voice eventually "ceased to be heard".

Another source of weakness for the rebel leaders was the difficulty of communicating their intentions to the slaves in the central and eastern parishes of the island without giving away their plans for the uprising. Realising the dangers of saying too much, Sharpe appears to have adopted the strategy of spreading rumours designed to create an inflammable situation. Even so, a slave courier could not travel great distances from his place of work, unless he was prepared to live the insecure life of an absconded fugitive.

According to Bleby "Sharpe sent a man named Edward Ramsay round to all the properties to tell the people that free paper had come" [Bleby 4 p.114]. But one wonders how much ground this courier was able to cover. That he was a slave is apparent from a statement subsequently made by Dove to the Baptist missionary William Knibb: "Edward Ramsey told us and the people, that he had often heard his master say, that the negro was to be free after Christmas" [*Facts and Documents* 12 p. 11].

There was some support for the rebellion among free black and brown members of the Baptist church. Bleby mentioned some of these men:

> The powerful influence which Sharpe exercised over the people around him will appear from the fact, that he succeeded in enlisting several free men in the struggle. Two persons called Mackintosh, father and son, another named Largie, and a person named Campbell, all men of colour, were implicated, and, with the exception of Largie, were executed for being actively concerned in the insurrection.

But Bleby could have been more generous in his appreciation of the considerable idealism with which these men must have been inspired. Instead, he attributed their participation, as free men in a slave rebellion, to ignorance and gullibility:

> With these persons, whom I found to be very ignorant, I held repeated conversations; and on making inquiry concerning their motives for engaging in the slave revolt when they themselves were already in the enjoyment of freedom, I ascertained that they had been accustomed to attend religious meetings with Samuel Sharpe, under whose influence and advice they had taken part in the rebellion ... they had never seen a white Baptist minister, until they saw Messrs Burchell and Gardner in the gaol at Montego Bay; the only instruction they had received being that which they obtained from Sharpe [Bleby 4 pp.119-20].

In a "Return of every Freeman tried and convicted during the late Rebellion ... or in consequence thereof ...", a document preserved in the Public Record Office, all four are described as brown creoles. Alexander Campbell's occupation is listed as a killer of hogs. James McIntosh is listed as a planter, his son Donald as a carpenter. John Largie was also a carpenter. The total number of free persons convicted of offences connected with the rebellion was 14. Eight were convicted on charges of rebellion or incitement to rebellion, one on a charge of murder, and one of attempted murder.

Two were convicted of concealing and aiding rebellious slaves and two of sedition. Three were described as 'black', two as 'sambo',[23] five as brown, one as white (a sailor), and three, if the record is to be taken literally, had no complexion at all [PRO:CO 137/185].

The rebels may also have had some encouragement from a white book-keeper, as appears from the following intriguing item which appeared under a Montego Bay date line of 21 January 1832 in the *Royal Gazette:*[24]

> Alfred Smith, the Bookkeeper on Lethe estate, who we mentioned in our last as having remained with the negroes on that property, was yesterday committed by order of the General Court Martial to await his trial for being it is alleged connected in the rebellion & rebellious conspiracy.

That Smith showed the rebels, of the band led by Tharp of Hazelymph, how to make bullets seems to have been established. Whether he did so voluntarily is another matter. Thomas Stewart, the rector of the parish of Westmoreland, who acted as a sort of police agent, in taking 'confessions' from rebel prisoners at the Savanna-la-Mar gaol, appended this footnote to the second statement he took from Robert Gardner:

> Upon questioning Gardner again respecting Smith, the impression on my mind was that Tharp had forcibly detained him, and compelled him to make cartridges, Ec. Gardner's words were, 'Tharp told me he had taken up a white man at Lethe'. I said, 'Tharp, if you have, you have done a very bad thing' [PP, Vol. XLVII p.218].

Smith himself alleged that he had been a prisoner of the rebels and his story seems to have been believed. But in his subsequent statement to Knibb, Gardner painted a decidedly more positive picture of what Tharp had told him about Smith "John Thorp Lawrence, alias Daddy Tharp . . . told me (Gardner) that white man at Lethe gave him his gun and pistol, and told him how to make cartridges, and that he did right to fight for freedom" [*Facts and Documents* 12 p. 11].

As has been mentioned, large numbers of those who participated in the uprising believed, in the early stages, that the British troops would not take the field against them. The rebel headman Linton said: "we all thought the King was upon our side: Gardner constantly kept telling us that he and other head people had been told that the King had given orders for his soldiers here not to fight against us ..." [PP, Vol. XLVII pp.209-10]. Likewise, Thomas Dove stated: "The negroes were always led to believe that the King would give no assistance to the white people if they, the negroes, fought for their freedom" [ibid p.214-5].

It is difficult to believe that Sharpe was sufficiently naïve to have thought that the British troops would remain neutral. That he allowed this belief to spread and encouraged it is, however, a probability. He may indeed have seen the dissemination of this rumour as a means of encouraging the timid and hesitant.

That Sharpe was a person of foresight is illustrated by the fact that he took the Maroons into account as a possible danger and made the attempt, for what it was worth, to neutralise the nearest Maroon settlement. At the commencement of the rebellion he sent his emissary Peter Douglas, with a guide to show him the way, to see the colonel of the Accompong Maroons. Douglas was to inform Colonel White that the rebel chief wished to make him a handsome present. He was to endeavour to persuade him that the Maroons should not oppose the rebelling slaves.

Douglas subsequently gave an account of his appointment and his mission. This is contained in the rough transcript of his trial by court martial:[25]

> That he was at Home at Mountain Spring Thursday morning. Ten men came to Mountain Spring, 5 with guns, 5 with muschett & Lance ... They said ... 'you are all to come away to Greenwich'. I ran back to my House took my Muschett & followed with the rest. At Greenwich Gardner told me that I was to go to Belvidere, but to his House, where Col Sharp was ...
>
> After some time Dove Gardner & Sharp came to him & said he was to go to Maroon Town. That he got a Horse for him gave him Pistol & Powder Horn, & told him that Sharp would give him a person to show the way to Maroon Town to Col White and to tell him he wanted to see him. Particularly he wished to know whether he would arrange about fighting the White People & that he did not wish him to fight but had a Present for him [PRO:CO 137/85].

Douglas said that he went to Catadupa with another rebel named Tharp. There Tharp "called John Williams & told him to take him [Douglas] to Col. White but not to blow shell or make any noise". Williams, he said, took him by the short cut, "crawling on their hands". In the event, the stealth of their approach was probably unwise. When they arrived at their destination, said Douglas, a group of Maroons seized him and "hauled him to the town". Having ascertained the purpose of their mission, said Maroon Major Rowe at the trial, the Maroons handed the two men over to the St. Elizabeth regiment.

Tried on a charge of "being engaged in and going abt. to entice Maroons of Accompong Town to engage in a Conspiracy, Traitorous Rebn. & hostile acts agst. His Majesty's authority or Govt .. between 25th Dec 1831 and 2nd Jan 1832", Douglas made no attempt to deny his embassy [ibid]. John Williams, on the other hand, pleaded that he had only guided Douglas to Accompong because the latter had threatened him with a pistol. But the Maroons, who knew Williams, made no distinction between the guide and ambassador. Giving evidence against Williams Major Rowe told the presiding officers: "he said he came from his general to the Maroons to get them to join the Negroes against the White People". Asked whether Williams had told him that the blacks had killed any whites, Rowe said: "He told me they had killed 5 Whites and one Brown man" [ibid]. Both men were sentenced to be shot and promptly executed.

On 19 December Colonel Grignon visited Salt Spring estate in St. James for which he was attorney. Some of the slaves on the estate "behaved with great insolence" towards him. When two constables were sent there "to convey the ringleaders to Montego-Bay", they were assaulted and "deprived of pistols with which they were armed, as well as their mules". They reported that "the Negroes has expressed their determination not to work after New Year's-day"[26] [PP, Vol. XLVII p.289, no. 9].

Later that day 12 magistrates, attending special sessions at the Montego Bay court house, addressed a joint letter to the officer commanding the 22nd regiment at Falmouth.[27] They reported disorderly behaviour on the part of the Negroes at

Salt Spring estate. They urged the need for a military force to be stationed in the Montego Bay barracks to contain the slaves during the approaching holidays [ibid p.279, no.6].

The governor's decision on 22 December to widely publicise the royal proclamation [28] was taken in the light of his "having received intelligence that a disposition of insubordination had manifested itself amongst certain slaves on a plantation in St. James". But this last minute posting up of copies of the proclamation does not appear to have had the desired intimidatory effect.

The missionaries, when they began to suspect that the slaves were about to take action themselves, made an attempt to discredit the organisers of the rebellion. Opening a new Baptist chapel at Salters Hill, St. James, on 27 December, William Knibb issued this stern warning:

> I learn that some wicked persons have persuaded you that the King has made you free ... What you have been told is false – false as Hell can make it. I entreat you not to believe it, but to go to your work as usual. If you have any love to Jesus Christ, to religion, to your ministers, to those kind friends in England who have given money to help you build this chapel, be not led away by wicked men [Reckord 40].

Waddell stayed at Knibbs' house in Falmouth on the night of 28 December. Knibb had just returned from Salters Hill where his attempt to discourage the people from going on strike had not been well received:

> His assurances that no 'free law' had come for them, were discredited by the assembled thousands, – his exhortations to be quiet and return to their estate duties enraged them . . . They accused their ministers of deserting them; and the immediate destruction of all the properties in the surrounding districts was their fierce reply to his admonitions [Waddell 34 pp.55-6].

In his own account of how he and other Baptist missionaries had tried in vain to dissuade their audience at Salters Hill from supporting the impending rebellion, Knibb wrote: [29] "After much more earnest entreaty, both private and public, we left them with a promise that they would attend our instructions; but I have since had too much reason to fear, that the idea of freedom had so introxicated their minds as to nullify all I said" [Hinton 17 p.118].

FOOTNOTES

[1] "Confession of William Binham, a Prisoner sentenced to Death".

[2] This collection of documents, etc. is believed to have been assembled by William Knibb, possibly assisted by other Baptist missionaries.

[3] See above pp. 226-227, 241.

[4] A 'busha' was a plantation overseer.

[5] For statistics illustrating the numbers of slaves enjoying supervisory status among the convicted rebels, see below, p. 238.

[6] Examination of Thomas M'Neel, "Proprietor of Caledonian Pen and Newton and Retirement settlements, and Overseer of Petersfield estate" in Westmoreland.

[7] Sharpe's age and occupation as a field slave appear on the Return of slaves in St. James tried and convicted before the civil courts. A copy of the Indictment against him and a record of his trial, is preserved in the Public Record Office under reference CO 137/185 (copies on microfilm of the collection of documents contained under this reference have been obtained for the libraries of the Institute of Jamaica and the University of the W.I.). From the evidence assembled in *Parliamentary Papers*, vol. XLVII it is known that Sharpe's place of work was Croydon Estate, but William Annand (ibid) wrongly names his owner as T.G. Grey. Samuel Sharpe, Esq. (his owner from whom, in accordance with a servile custom, he had no doubt taken his name) may have had a town house. According to the rebel Captain Dove, Sharpe was born and brought up at Montego Bay.

[8] Robert Gardner's answers to questions of Rev. Thomas Stewart.

[9] Montego Bay.

[10] A reference to W.S. Grignon, planter and plantation attorney, magistrate and colonel of the Western Interior militia regiment. His slaves nick-named him "little breeches".

[11] The King against Samuel Sharpe, 19 April 1832 — evidence of Joseph Martin.

[12] Evidence of Robert Rose.

[13] 'Set', a word which in the vernacular context would be equivalent to 'sit'.

[14] Deposition of William Annand, 2 January 1832.

[15] Deposition of Donald Malcolm of Ramble.

[16] Sir Willoughby Cotton, M.G., to Belmore, 5 January 1832, 10 a.m. from "Head Quarters, Montego Bay".

[17] "Confession of Robert Gardner, alias Colonel Gardner", taken in the Savanna-la-Mar gaol, 11 February, 1832 by Rev. Thomas Stewart, Anglican rector of Westmoreland.

[18] Confession of Gardner and Dove to Rev. William Knibb.

[19] Robert Gardner's second statement to Rev. Thomas Stewart, 11 February 1832.

[20] *The Cornwall Chronicle* 14 January 1832 reprinted in *The Watchman,* 21 January 1832.

[21] Examination of Anthony Whitelock, proprietor of Bulstrode Park in Westmoreland.

[22] Examination of Henry G. Groves, "Manager and Overseer of Hazelymph Estate".

[23] The term 'sambo', originally used to describe the child of a Black and a mulatto, later came to be used to indicate a dark brown complexion.

[24] "Postcript" to the *Royal Gazette* for the week 21 to 28 January, 1832, reprinting item from the *Jamaica Courant* newspaper.

[25] "Courts Martial held for the trials of divers Slaves for Rebellion in Jamaica", proceedings of a general court martial at Y.S. Estate on 9 January 1832, trial of Peter Douglas.

[26] Jas. Macdonald to Governor, 28 December 1831.

[27] L. Hislop and others to Major Pennefather, 19 December 1831.

[28] See above p. 246.

[29] Knibb to Rev. Dyer, 14 February 1832

CHAPTER TWELVE

"KENSINGTON ON FIRE"

Although the rudimentary organisation for leading the rebellion did not extend beyond the five western parishes, the spirit of unrest was nevertheless apparent in other parts of the island. On 23 December the governor received an application from certain magistrates and property owners in the parish of Portland "desiring that a vessel of war might be ordered to Port Antonio, on account of ... discontent among the slaves in that quarter". The governor "applied ... for a ship of war to proceed to ... Port Antonio; and ... also recommended that ships of war should be dispatched to Montego Bay and Black River, which Commodore Farquhar ... immediately complied with" [1] [PP, Vol. XLVII p.272, no.7].

From his headquarters at Shettlewood Colonel W.S. Grignon of the militia informed the governor on Monday 26 December:[2]

> That insubordination had appeared on Salt Spring estate in St. James; that he had ordered out the western interior regiment; that the negroes were determined to strike work at Christmas, but no slaughter to be committed unless any of the rebels were killed in taking arms from white people [PP, Vol. XLVII p.279, no.7].

That day he moved his headquarters to Belvidere in order, as he explained,[3] "to concentrate the regiment as much as possible" [p.286, no.23].

On 27 December Colonel Tyler of the Trelawny militia reported on "The alarming situation of the district about York estate, where the rebels had burnt the trash-house". Unable to send the whole of his regiment to the area, "he was obliged to withdraw the detachment he had stationed at York" [p. 272, no. 7].

That same day Colonel Grignon informed the governor "that he received information that 500 men had assembled near Lapland, who had bound themselves by a solemn oath to obtain their freedom or die in the attempt" [ibid]. He asked for a detachment of regular troops. Afraid that his Belvidere division would be unable to contain the trouble he expected, he explained that he had that day retreated with them "to form a junction with the main body at Great River" [p. 286, no. 23].

Several property owners appear to have been aware of plans for the commencement of the rebellion, though because the air was so thick with rumours they may not have known how much credit to give to the information they had received. J.H. Morris, owner of Kensington estate six miles from Maroon Town in St. James,[4] subsequently stated that on Tuesday 27 December he had received a letter from another property owner "apprising me that my house was to be burnt, and my family destroyed as of that evening".

Morris took the warning seriously, but when he applied to the commander of the Maroon Town garrison for protection, the latter called him an alarmist and said that "he was satisfied nothing would take place". Though disappointed that the garrison commander felt unable to give his property military protection, Morris had not then been aware of the importance of the proposed firing of his house in the plan for the launching of the rebellion. "I did not tell him" he subsequently stated, "that my house was to be a beacon, because I did not know it myself at the time". He nevertheless decided to leave and he and his family departed in his carriage for Montego Bay. "I had not left my house 10 minutes", he recorded, "before it was attacked and plundered by the rebels; it was set on fire about seven o'clock on the evening of the 27th".

In leaving when he did, Morris was more fortunate, or more prudent, than his uncle George who stayed on to protect his property and was killed by the rebels. Morris stated further:[5]

> I afterwards learned from Captain Lawrence, one of the rebels, that the properties were ...[6] by them. This property being an elevated situation, was numbered one, and they intended proceeding with their fires from the opposite hill. Blue Hole estate was numbered two. The overseer remained on the property with a small party, which prevented it being burnt. Lugan estate, the next property, was immediately set on fire as an answer to the beacon [PP, vol. XLVII, pp.199-200].

Rev. H. M. Waddell gave this account of what he found when he returned to his station at Cornwall[7] on the evening of 27 December:

> The congregation which had assembled was dispersing in affright, and would not return to my call. The only answer ... that could be got was, – *'Palmyra on fire'*. It was not an ordinary estate fire they spoke of ... It was the preconcerted signal for our part of the country that the struggle for freedom had begun ... It was the response to *'Kensington on fire'*, another sugar estate high up the mountains towards the interior. Both were visible to each other, and over a great stretch of intermediate country ... The one hoisted the flaming flag of liberty, and the other saluted it, calling on all between and around to follow their example. And it was followed. These were grand beacon-fires ... Scarcely had night closed in, when the sky towards the interior was illuminated by unwonted glares ... as fires rose here and there in rapid succession ... [Waddell 34 pp. 53-4].

Viewing the commencement of the rebellion at 9 p.m. that same evening from the Montego Bay post office, the Collector of Customs wrote[8] "there is at this moment a serious fire raging in a south-easterly direction from this town, apparently about eight or ten miles distant, and it is supposed to be at Hampton estate, but from the glare I fear it extends to other estates in its vicinity lying more to the northward".

Half an hour later he added a postscript: "I have just been informed that Kensington Pen and Mr. Tulloch's settlement have been burnt. We have one company of the 22nd regiment in this town" [PP, Vol. XLVII p.281].

At 10 p.m. the colonel of the St. James regiment of the militia also sat down in Montego Bay to write a letter:[9] "since sun-set six fires, apparently of estates, have been seen from the court-house, in the neighbourhood of Kensington, extending northerly to Content, and they seem gradually to be extending to the northward". In a postscript he commented "I fear the whole of the east part of the parish will be destroyed before day-light".

At five o'clock in the morning the colonel added yet another postscript, but he was so upset that he noted the time incorrectly: "Five P.M. A trooper has just arrived from Palmyra, with a despatch ... stating that the negroes on that estate set fire to the trash-house, when his men were searching the negro houses for arms, agreeably to my orders". The incendiaries, a man and a woman, had, he said, been captured, and the head driver had been arrested on suspicion of being an accomplice. But "Hampton estate is threatened to be destroyed to-night" [ibid].

According to Morris, the owner of Kensington, he had learned that the rebels had arranged for similar beacon signals in the neighbouring parish: "Shaw Castle settlement was to have been set on fire, and Georgia estate in Trelawny, in answer to the beacon, as both of them were on elevated situations" There, however, the plan appears to have gone wrong as neither property was fired. This led Morris to express the view, no doubt by way of a censure on the Maroon Town garrison commander, that "if Kensington had been saved the whole of St. James would have been saved" [PP, Vol. XLVII pp.199-200].

Seated in his Falmouth, Trelawny, office on the evening of 27 December the editor of the *Cornwall Courier*, was able to see the drama beginning to unfold from a different angle. He published this up-to-the-minute account of developments:

> For the last few days the parishes of Westmoreland and St. James, and this parish, have been in a state of considerable excitement, in consequence of reports and official information to the Magistracy, of intended insurrections among the slave population. Not willing to create any unnecessary alarm, we shall defer entering into detail until we receive the fullest information, which is hourly expected. Should it not arrive before our usual hour of going to press, we shall publish whatever *authentic* information we may receive in a second edition.
>
> We understand that the Westmoreland Regiment and Troop of Horse have been on duty since Saturday. The Western Interior, St. James's and Trelawny Regiments have been under arms since Monday morning.
>
> The work of destruction has commenced — we now see two fires evidently in the direction of St. James's.
>
> Ten O'clock.
>
> We have just received intelligence that the fire at Palmyra estate was extinguished, after burning one trash house. The head driver and three negroes belonging to the property have been secured. A company of the St. James's Militia, under the command of Capt. Cleghorn, moved from Adelphi on the first notice of the fire, and remained there. We understand that the drivers on the neighbouring estates, instead of going to their Overseers for orders, as usual, this being the last day of the holidays, have taken their mascheats and gone off, as they say, to their grounds.
>
> Eleven O'clock at night.
>
> The work of destruction is going on. The whole sky in the South West is illuminated — From our office we at this moment perceive five distinct fires — one apparently in this parish, the others in St. James's, and at no great distance from us.
>
> Midnight.
>
> One fire is still raging with unabated fury — we apprehend it to be the whole of the works and buildings on York estate, in this parish .[10]

On 28 December Colonel Grignon withdrew with his Western Interior regiment from the Great River station, retreating to Montpelier where he joined forces with the company from the St. James regiment. He explained this manoeuvre as having been necessary because "the barracks at Great River were quite insufficient for the accommodation of the regiment" [PP, Vol. XLVII p.286, no. 23], an excuse which did not favourably impress the Assembly when they subsequently came to review the course of the rebellion.

That same day Colonel Lawson of the St. James regiment again wrote to the government secretary from Montego Bay:

> so many fires have taken place that I have deemed it proper to withdraw the out-posts, as I do not wish to expose them to a contest which I do not consider them equal to, and to concentrate them here, with the exception of one company, which I have directed to move in support of Colonel Grignon, whose situation, with that of his regiment, I fear is extremely critical. I have also directed the Hanover company, stationed at Round-hill, to move on for the same purpose.

Clearly the gallant colonel had little faith in the ability of the militia to hold the rural areas against the rebels. He closed his letter with the dramatic conclusion: "I am now convinced the contest must be decided in the streets of Montego Bay" [ibid].

The decision to attack at Montpelier was a bold one. The militia were there in strength, the Western Interior Regiment having been supplemented by a company of the St. James regiment. According to Bleby, between four and five hundred rebel slaves participated in the attack, divided into two "parties". But the great majority were without firearms. Bleby [4 p.11] suggests further that the attacking force was recruited locally:

> When the attack was resolved upon, Johnson went round to the several estates in the neighbourhood to collect a sufficient force. At the time appointed they met at the sheep-pens and mustered altogether from 400 to 500 men. Dove was armed with a pistol, and about fifty of the rebels had guns. They were divided into two parties; one under the command of Johnson, the other under Campbell, Dove and Gardner acting in subordination to them.

What Gardner and Dove had to say about the fighting at Montpelier, when they subsequently made their 'confession' to William Knibb, is not entirely to be relied upon. Following Knibb's acquittal on a charge of complicity in the rebellion, he had been "requested by the Hon. The Chief Justice and W. Miller, Esq. late Custos of Trelawney, to use his exertions to discover the mode in which the insurrection was planned". Knibb agreed, and: "To facilitate the enquiry, a promise was made to two of the principal prisoners, styled Colonel Gardner and Captain Dove, that their lives should be spared if they made a full confession" [*Facts and Documents* 12 p.9].

It is evident, both in what he said to Knibb and his 'confessions' to the Anglican rector Stewart, that Gardner was endeavouring to discount the part he had played in both the planning of the rebellion and the military activities. He may also have been trying to exonerate his friend Dove. His evidence is nevertheless helpful to the extent that it confirms the presence of his party at Montpelier and the employment there of companies of the rebels' embryonic mobile army mentioned above. The recruitment of men for the attack may not have been as spontaneous as Bleby imagined. This is what Gardner said:

> Both of us were present at the attack made upon Mr. Grignon, and the soldiers at the Montpeliers. Dove had a pistol, it was loaded, but he did not fire it; he was frightened at the bullets, and went under the wall. Charles Campbell was commander, and told those who had not any guns to keep back.
>
> Campbell led his company along the king's road, and Johnstone led his company by the negro houses as ambush. Johnstone was killed on the spot, and so near the white people that they could not carry him away [12 pp.10-1].

Knibb was obviously not very competent at taking a statement. At this point his narrative lapses into the third person and it is by no means clear whether he was recording the words of Gardner or Dove or his own impression of what had happened after the battle:

> Campbell was shot through the body. They took him to Gardner's house, at Greenwich, and sent for Gardner, who had gone into a grass piece. We both went to see him, but he could not speak. He died in the morning — we made a rough coffin, and buried him. Gardner read the burial service over him. Dove declares that he never left the property to fight after this battle [ibid].

The loss of these two military leaders was a severe blow to the rebels. Thereafter it would appear that the leadership of their companies fell into the far from decisive hands of Gardner. But the rebel attack at Montpelier had been sufficient to cause the militia to beat a hasty retreat.

Colonel Grignon subsequently sent his own account, dated 2 January 1832, of the events at Montpelier to the governor:

> At about seven o'clock the rebels advanced upon us in four columns. The first body moved upon the trash-houses, to one of which they set fire, and became engaged with Captain Ewart's company, and the piquet-guard of the Western Interior under Ensign Gibbes. The officers and men behaved in the most gallant manner, and shortly dispersed the enemy. This division ... consisted of about 40 men.
>
> The three other divisions attacked the main body of the W.I. regiment, who had been formed into solid square, and kept up considerable firing of musketry upon them. The regiment reserved their fire until the rebels had advanced within 30 or 40 yards, when they commenced a very rapid fire, which continued for about 20 minutes, when the enemy dispersed in all directions.
>
> One body of the enemy, who attacked by the main road, could not have consisted of less than 200 men; the numbers in the other divisions I cannot judge of, as they were covered by a stone-wall fence and the Hill-house; but both divisions appeared to have many fire-arms. Where all behaved with so much gallantry, it would be invidious to name any individual ... I regret to add, that in this encounter we had one man killed and four wounded ... I could not learn the exact number of the rebels killed and wounded, but I understood afterwards that they admitted they had lost 10 men killed and 25 wounded ... [PP, Vol. XLVII pp.288-9, no.23].

On the following day the militia withdrew, surrendering the Montpelier area and the country behind it to the rebels. Grignon gave this explanation for the withdrawal:

> On the 30th, I ordered one of the companies of the Westmoreland regiment to move up to Montpelier but as I could place no dependence on their doing so ... and as the company of the St. James's regiment most positively refused to remain at the post, and being in want of both ammunition and provisions, I called a meeting of the officers, and they were unanimously of the opinion that I could not maintain the post, and I therefore retreated with the whole body to Montego Bay. The information received by the company from Saint James's was, that an overwhelming body of negroes was collecting in every quarter around us, and I also received similar information [ibid].

Writing to the governor on 28 December, James Macdonald, the Custos of Trelawny, stated that "many of the estates in this parish are at this moment in an actual state of rebellion and I believe nine-tenth of the slave population have this morning refused to turn out to work" [PP, Vol. XLVII p.289, no.9].

An interesting account of how the rebel cadres on Ginger-Hill estate in St. Elizabeth carried out their assignment to seize control of and destroy the works and buildings was given by the overseer William Annand. Annand lived to tell the tale because he offered no resistance. He remained unharmed as a prisoner of the rebels for four days. In a deposition given subsequently, he stated that he had been warned by the overseer on Y.S. estate that "the slaves from Ginger-Hill to Belvidere estate, in St. James's, intended to disarm the white people during the Christmas holidays", and advised to come down to Y.S. However, as he had "seen nothing in the conduct of the slaves" to induce him "to suspect anything of this kind", he had disregarded the warning and stayed on. On the morning of Wednesday 28 December, he said:

> when they were ordered to turn out to work, seeing several of the slaves about the house, I asked what they wanted; a slave belonging to Ginger-hill, named William Buchannan, said they had come to beg Busha for today, as Sunday was Christmas-day. I said I had already given orders to the driver to that effect; all that I wanted was to see them turn out, and see they were all there, and they should have the remainder of the day [pp. 285-6, no. 18].

It was at this point that he was, to use his own word, 'undeceived':

> I went into the house, and was followed immediately by ... Buchannan who laid hold of me, saying, 'Busha, you now my prisoner', and called for his accomplices ... William Arnold, Charles Longmore, George Barrett, Alexander, Thomas Hedley, and Johnny, all slaves belonging to Ginger-hill. On enquiring what was the matter, they said they had worked long enough as slaves, and intended now to fight for their freedom ...

The rebels made their captive's position quite clear: "all they wanted of me was to deliver up my arms, and whatever powder I had, then I might remain undisturbed on the property as long as I chose, provided I did not interfere against them".

Annand said that he had "endeavoured to reason with them on the impropriety of such conduct", but without effect: "they said that I knew as well as themselves that Jamaica was now free and half the estates from there to Montego-bay were burnt down the night before". His captors, he said, were convinced of the righteousness of their cause. They told him "that they were obliged to assist their brethren in this work of the Lord; that this was not the work of man alone, but they had assistance from God".

Appreciating that "a refusal of their demand was useless", Annand delivered up his arms and what powder he had in the house. His captors then departed, advising him not to leave the house. They told me, he said, that "if I attempted it, I should certainly be shot by some of their guards who were posted on all sides of the property". Wisely, the overseer remained where he was.

Annand said that he "observed them through the day bringing in arms from the settlers around". On the next day, Thursday 29 December, he "saw a great many strange negroes" whom he understood belonged to the neighbouring estates of Chesterfield, Retrieve, Richmond-hill and Belvidere. Some of them had fire-arms, others had "lances, cutlasses, Ec". They had scouts "posted on all the hills around, from the Y.S. Estate, extending towards St. James's, to give them notice of the approach of the militia".

The rebels, said Annand, on learning that a company of the St. Elizabeth regiment was approaching, "had suspected from the notice they had received from their scouts, that the said company was moving towards Ginger-hill". They had prepared an ambush to meet them "and collected all together in a narrow defile, called John's River, to await their approach". But the company had gone instead to Ipswich and the rebels had thereupon returned to Ginger-hill [ibid].

What the captive overseer did not then know was that the rebels there had sent for help. In response to a message that "the white people were coming", Sam Sharpe had taken his company to Ginger Hill on 29 December. This was subsequently disclosed at Sharpe's trial.[11] Only by the chance decision to go to Ipswich instead of Ginger Hill, had the militia escaped falling into a well prepared ambush. The witness Robert Rose, a member of Sharpe's company, said: "They wanted us to go to a neighbouring Estate Ipswich", but apparently this was considered unwise. Rose added: "We did not go but returned to Content that Evening and slept there". Another witness, Joseph Martin, told a different story. Sharpe had told him and some others to go on to Ipswich. "We were going on and when we got part of the way it began to Rain and we turned back" [PRO: CO 137/185, fols 310-4].

Learning of the rebels' intention to burn the Ginger Hill estate buildings Annand sent for the head driver, who confirmed his information and conducted him to the house of a free black living nearby. Soon afterwards the incendiary party, on coming to the estate house and enquiring for the overseer, "expressed themselves happy" that he had gone away. Half an hour later they returned "taking away every moveable thing out of the house and stores, which they accomplished by dusk, and afterwards set fire to all the buildings".

That evening the rebel leader, accompanied by a number of others, paid the overseer a visit. They took the arms of the owner of the house away from him, and Sharpe made his guest swear that he "would never stand between them and their rights". Annand does not appear to have realised that the person he was talking to was the organiser and leader of the whole rebellion. He said: "The active person in this scene, and who seemed to have command of them, was a slave named Samuel Sharp, belonging, I was told, to T.G. Grey Esq. of Croydon,[12] in St. James's, and who, I understand, is a ruler (so called) of the sect of the Baptists".

Annand gave this account of his conversation with Sharpe:

> He said he did not wish to take away the life of any person who did not stand between him and his rights; that it was but lately that he had begun to know much of religion but that now he knew, and I knew as well, that

freedom was their right, and freedom they would have ... He said a great deal more, all tending to show, that, from the religious notions he had imbibed, he conceived that the slaves had a right to be free.

Sharpe also stated, said Annand "that letters had long ago been sent out from England to that effect, but that the people of Jamaica kept them as slaves, without any authority for doing so" [PP, Vol. XLVII pp.285-6, no.18].

"By day-light on the morning of Friday the 30th", stated the captive overseer William Annand, "the buildings of Ginger-hill were in ashes". Prudently he remained in the house where he had taken refuge, having been warned by the rebels that if he attempted to escape he "would be killed by the guards". He learned that "A large part of them ... went this day to Ipswich, but seeing a company of militia there, returned, leaving a few hands to burn the buildings of that estate, should an opportunity offer during the night" [PP, Vol. XLVII pp.285-6, no.18].

On the following morning a revealing incident occurred. This is how the captive overseer recorded it:

> three of the party ... William Buchanan, S. Barett,[13] belonging to Ginger-hill, and G. Little, belonging to Mistress Milne, gone off the country, came to me, two of them with fire-arms, and the other with a sword; I asked William Buchanan what he wanted; he said, here is the captain, pointing to G. Little. I then asked the latter what he wanted; he said, pointing his sword to my breast, that they would give me my choice, whether I would give up my life or my authority on Ginger-hill, which latter they demanded in writing.

The captain informed Annand that when they had obtained this document from him "they intended presenting it at Black River [capital town of the parish] with others". From this it would appear that at least some, if not all, of the rebel leaders naively believed that, confronted with documentary evidence of capitulation by the property owners and their managerial personnel, the authorities would officially recognise that the control of the estates had passed into the hands of the slaves.

"I gave them", Annand deposed, "an acknowledgement

under my hand that I had given up the charge of the place". But the captain, being unable to read, thought it just as well to advise him of the consequences of trying to deceive them:

> they then warned me to take care what I had written, as they had a man below who would read it to them, and if they found anything wrong in it they would pay me another kind of visit. The said George Little said that they had lost one of their profession; and now intended showing less mercy than they had done.

The captain told his prisoner that he and two others "had burnt down the buildings of Ipswich the night previous, driving the whole guard before them". He also said "that they intended entering Saint Elizabeth's on New-year's-day with 200 men".

Annand's release from captivity came that same afternoon when a slave "who had been forced against his will to join the rebels", brought him the news "that the white guard had come to Ginger-hill, taken the negroes by surprize, dispersed them all, and set fire to the negro-houses". Shortly afterwards this was confirmed by the appearance of the grenadier company of the St. Elizabeth's regiment who, said the overseer: "rescued me from my perilous situation" [ibid].

A Council of War held on 30 December decided on an immediate declaration of martial law. The proclamation required every member of the militia who had not already done so "to repair forthwith to their several and respective regiments and stations" [PP, Vol. XLVII p.282, no.13]. An order issued on the same day [14] required regiments in certain parishes not affected by the uprising to march to the areas in which hostilities had broken out. The Clarendon regiment, for example, was required to march to Trelawny. Militiamen in the parishes farthest from the scene of the rebellion were temporarily excused from duty, but their officers were to be "prepared to assemble them at the shortest notice" [PP, Vol. XLVII pp.282-3, no.14].

On the night of 31 December the governor received a despatch from Major General Robertson of the Hanover militia, written a day or two earlier, "by which it appeared, that the depredations committed by the negroes in ... St. James had extended along the great river towards the parish of St. Elizabeth". The initiative remained with the rebels, but the officer commanding the Westmoreland militia regiment had, the despatch reported, posted troops at Haddo estate and the St. Elizabeth regiment had been placed in a state of readiness.

In a subsequent despatch, written on the same day, Robertson reported that "the rebels were proceeding in the direction of Ipswich and New Savanna, and that he had moved a large body of men to oppose them". But on the following day, on a more sombre note, he wrote: "I am of opinion that all the force in my district is unequal to suppress the incendiarism and destruction, without the cooperation of the regular troops" [PP, Vol. XLVII p.272ff, no.7].[15]

A subsequent despatch from Robertson to the governor, however, reflected a change of fortunes in St. Elizabeth on 31 December. Writing from Y.S. estate[16] he was able to report that at least one militia force had taken the initiative from the rebel slaves:

> two companies of St. Elizabeth's regiment, viz. the grenadiers ... and the 5th battalion company .. were ordered up last evening to Ipswich estate and Ginger-hill plantation ... (the works of which properties had been burned down) where they found the rebels in great force, and attacked them. As far as can yet be ascertained, 20 of them were killed and many prisoners made; they retreated leaving many stands of arms, and a great quantity of ammunition was found in their houses.

According to Robertson, these rebels had been counting their chickens before they were hatched. When attacked "they were preparing to come down here to attack this post at Y.S. estate; and so confident were they of success, that they had provided a great quantity of meat, liquor, Ec. for a feast on their return to Ipswich" [PP, Vol. XLVII pp.283-4, no.16].

On the following day Robertson again reported to the

governor. He stated that "Since the defeat of the rebels in this quarter on Saturday evening, a company was advanced to occupy the district they had quitted" By examining the prisoners, he said: "I have discovered the names of some of the rebel commanders, viz. Colonel Gardiner, belonging to Greenwich estate, Captain Dove, belonging to Belvidere, Captain Johnson, belonging to Retrieve, and General Ruler Sharp, alias Daddy Ruler Sharp, director of the whole, and preacher to the rebels".

In the light of this information, said Robertson, he had "deemed it advisable to offer a reward of three hundred dollars to any free person or maroon, and freedom, with an annuity for life, to any slave who will bring in, dead or alive, either of these ringleaders of the rebels".

He expressed the hope that the offer of these rewards would be speedily confirmed [p.284, no.17].

Despite the outcome of the engagement on 31 December, however, Robertson was "sorry to say discontent is spreading generally in this parish, as the slaves on many properties, as well as those under my control, have refused to return to their labour this day". But "the maroons who came to head quarters last night", he added, "have gone home for their arms, and I expect them to join us during the day". Meanwhile, he was "most anxiously looking for a detachment of regular troops in this quarter".

On 31 December "Sharpe went with his party to Struie" said Joseph Martin, a rebel slave who gave evidence at Sharpe's subsequent trial. "When we got there they said a party of the Militia were coming to burn down the Negro Houses". Gardner's party, said the witness "had gone on to Struie the night before". There, according to the evidence of Edward Hilton, "they laid an Ambush" for the militia company approaching from Westmoreland. From the evidence of three of the witnesses at Sharpe's subsequent trial, it appears that the rebel operation was successful. According to Martin, "Sharpe's party and the others fired at the Militia. Saw one

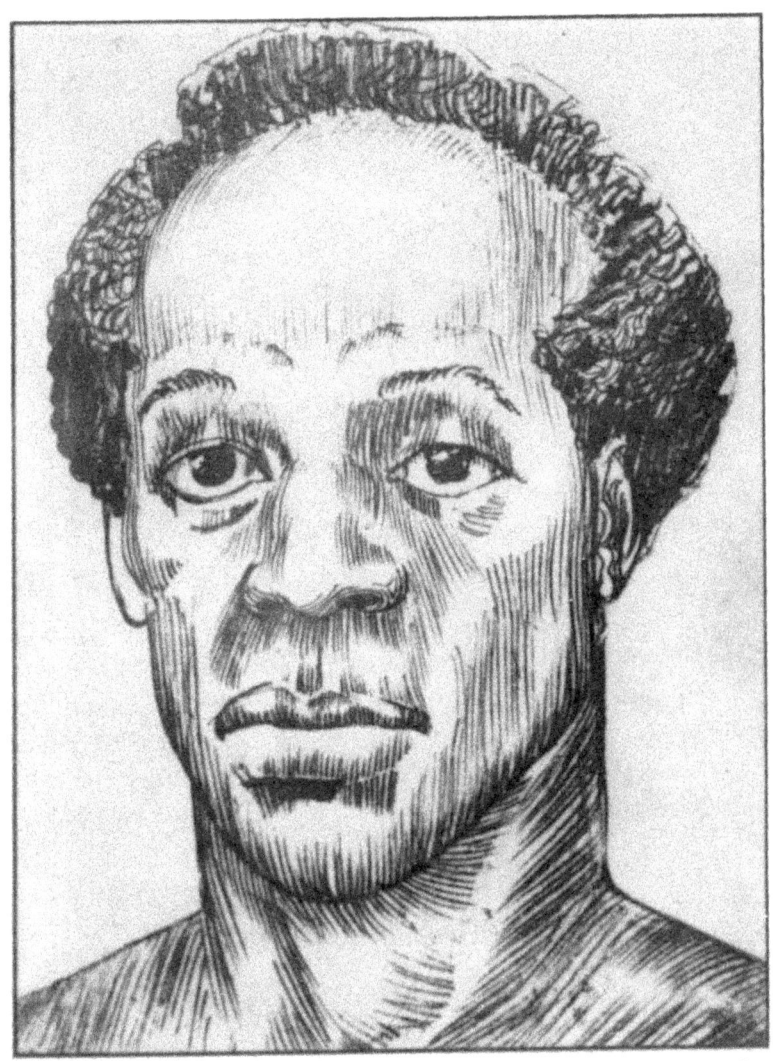

Artist's impression of Sam Sharpe, the leader of the 1831-32 "Emancipation Rebellion."

*Rebels destroying a road during the 1831-32 rebellion, while in the background, Reading Wharf, Montego Bay, goes up in flames.
Lithographed by A. Duperly, 1833*

Artist's impression of the surrender of rebel Colonel Robert Gardner to Lieut. McNeal on Feb. 8, 1832.

The destruction of Roehampton Estate by rebel slaves, January, 1832   Lithographed by A. Duperly, 1833.

The gentry welcome troops in Kingston, returning from action against rebel slaves in Clarendon, 1832.

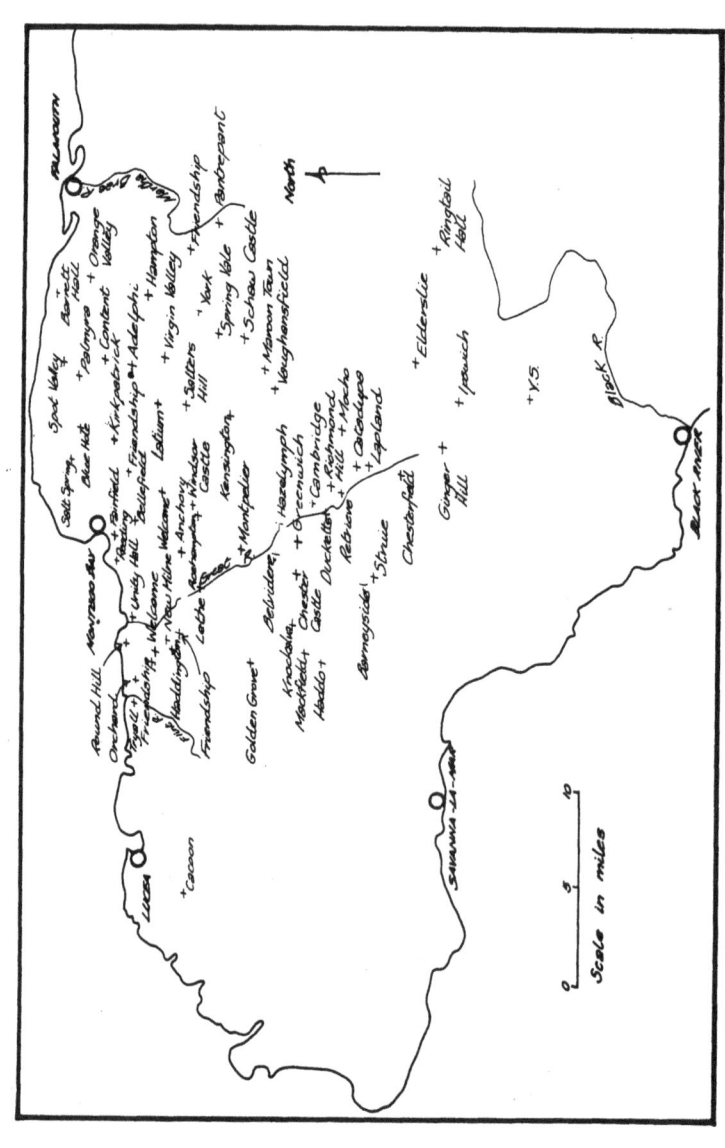

Western Jamaica showing the places affected by Sam Sharpe's "Emancipation Rebellion," 1831-32.
Map by Alan Teulon

The Governor of Jamaica reviews a procession to the Baptist Church, Spanish Town, under the Rev. J.M. Phillippo on the 1st August, 1838, celebrating the Abolition of Slavery and the end of Apprenticeship.

Symbolic slave family in exhultation over the end of slavery, 1st August, 1834
Published by Joseph Thomas, London, 1835

of the men chop a white man and kill him & I heard another was shot. Sharpe commanded the party he went with to Struie. Gardner commanded his own party".

But according to the witness John Davis, at Struie Sharpe "was head man". Martin said that Sharpe "had only the macheat". Another witness, James Sterling, said he had a gun "but did not see him fire it" [PRO: CO 137/185, fols 310-4].

The conspiracy for the rebellion had not extended to the central and eastern parishes of the island. Sharpe had, however, endeavoured to circulate as widely as possible the belief that it had been decided in England that the slaves were to be free after the Christmas holidays. There is no means of knowing how far his couriers had been able to travel, but certainly, though matters never reached the level of participation in the planning of the rebellion, there were expectations of freedom in parts of the two most easterly parishes. And the destruction of property that subsequently took place in Manchester during the course of the rebellion, would seem to indicate unrest, albeit unorganised and unchannelled, in parts of central Jamaica.

There had been uneasiness, as has been mentioned, among certain magistrates and planters in the eastern parishes. But the custos of Portland had informed the governor that he regarded as "ill-founded apprehension of the hostile disposition of the negroes in that quarter". Never had he considered "the negroes in that neighbourhood to be more peaceable and contented". It was therefore with some surprise that on 31 December the governor received a letter from this same custos[16] "stating that the negroes on three estates had refused to work, and had betaken themselves to the woods" [PP, Vol. XLVII pp.272ff, no.7].

FOOTNOTES

[1] Belmore to Goderich, 6 January 1832.

[2] "Heads of Information received at the King's House, relative to the Disturbances on the North Side of the Island".

[3] W. S. Grignon to Governor, 2 January 1832.

[4] This refers to the former residence of the Trelawny Maroons, who had been transported from the island after the Second Maroon War in 1795. A detachment of regular troops under the command of a major, was garrisoned there at this time.

[5] "Examination on oath of John Henry Morris . . . proprietor of Kensington before the Committee appointed to inquire into the cause of, and injury sustained by, the recent Rebellion among the Slaves of this Island".

[6] There is a blank space here in the transcript.

[7] This is a reference not to the county of Cornwall but to an estate on the north coast in Trelawny, where the Scottish proprietor Barrett had allowed the Presbyterians to establish a church.

[8] John Roby to W. Bullock, 27 December 1831.

[9] E. M. Lawson to Bullock, 27 December 1831.

[10] These quotations from the *Cornwall Courier*, are quoted here from reprints in Postscript to the *Royal Gazette* 24 to 31 December 1831 – No. 53.

[11] The King against Samuel Sharpe, 19 April 1832 – evidence of Robert Rose, Joseph Martin and others.

[12] The name of Sharpe's owner is given in the indictment against him as "Samuel Sharpe Esquire".

[13] Annand may have been referring to George Barrett, unless there were two Barretts among the rebel leaders at Ginger Hill.

[14] M.G.O., 30 December 1831.

[15] Quoted in Belmore to Goderich, 6 January 1832.

[16] Major General D. Robertson to Belmore, 1 January 1832.

CHAPTER THIRTEEN
20,000 SLAVES IN REBELLION

On 1 January 1832, General Sir Willoughby Cotton, the officer commanding the British troops stationed in Jamaica, arrived at Montego Bay aboard H. M. S. *Sparrowhawk.* He had been preceded by H. M. S. *Racehorse* which had landed marines on 29 December. Next day he was followed by the commodore of the fleet stationed at Port Royal who transported, aboard H.M.S. *Blanche,* 300 soldiers of the 33rd and 84th regiments and 16 artillerymen with "two 8 field pieces, rockets Ec". [PP, Vol. XLVII pp. 287-8, no. 20], Already in the area affected by the rebellion were the regular troops garrisoned at Maroon Town and Falmouth. With the proclamation of martial law, the militia regiments in the western parishes also came under the general's command.

Reporting to the governor [1] on what he had observed on arrival in Montego Bay, General Cotton stated that he had: "found the town in the greatest confusion and panic, from the apprehensions they have been under of its being the intention of the negroes to fire it every night, and from the immense destruction of property that has taken place all round this place" He had, he said, "relieved apprehension, and quieted the feeling of alarm" in the town, "but the eastern part of Hanover, and the whole of the northern portion of St. James's, are in open revolt, and almost the whole of the estates destroyed, and the negroes gone boldly away" [ibid].

Cotton announced his intention to "send a force of King's troops to accompany some companies of Colonel Grignon's regiment to Montpelier barracks". At the same time he had ordered Lieutenant Colonel Williams to move up on the Westmoreland side to Haddo and Crown Tavern. "This will effect, I hope", he explained, "the . . . object of opening the road to Savanna-la-Mar".

Immediately on arrival Cotton had authorized "the assembling of a general court martial to try some villainous ringleaders, who have been proved to have been the most active incendiaries". The court, he said, had "sentenced two men to be shot, and two women". He had confirmed the sentences on the men so that their execution might serve as an immediate example, but the women's sentences would be subject to his lordship's 'pleasure'.

Cotton's object was "to employ the troops in such manner as to prevent, as far as practicable, the horrid incendiary system from spreading, and the spirit of rebellion from contaminating the districts now tranquil". "I have sent regulars", he reported, "to Irwin and Latium, as they are well disposed there, and this will protect these points and others in the neighbourhood which are not as yet fired". But it would be an "utter impossibility", he pointed out, to provide "parties of military to every estate". That would only "fritter away the troops, and render them liable to be beat in detail, nor would 10,000 men be sufficient to do it".

To meet this problem the general had worked out tactics which he explained to the governor: "Whenever I can ascertain where they are collected, I shall endeavour to strike a blow by simultaneous movement that will have decided effect". But it was not going to be easy, the general said, to find a large body of rebels to attack: "from the accounts I have received, that are to be depended upon, they are moving every hour from one place to another". The rebels, he had discovered, were for the most part operating in numerous small parties and there, he admitted, "the difficulty rests" [ibid].

On 2 January, the general issued this printed warning:

To the Rebellious Slaves

Negroes,

> You have taken up arms against your masters, and have burnt and plundered their houses and buildings. Some wicked persons have told you that the King has made you free, and that your masters with-hold your freedom from you. In the name of the King I come amongst you to tell you that you are misled.
>
> I bring with me numerous forces to punish the guilty, and all who are found with the rebels will be put to death without mercy. You cannot resist the King's troops; surrender yourselves and beg that your crime may be pardoned.
>
> All who yield themselves up at any military post *immediately,* provided they are not principals and chiefs in the burnings that have been committed, will receive His Majesty's gracious pardon, all who hold out will meet certain deaths.
>
> Willoughby Cotton
> Major-General Commanding
> God Save the King [PP, Vol. XLVII p. 288, no 21; *The Watchman*, 4 January 1832].

That same day, according to a letter to the governor from the Custos of St. James at Montego Bay:[2]

> Bellefield estate was destroyed, being within three miles of the town; an officer and twelve men were stationed there, but were driven off by numbers. A detachment of the 22nd on the next estate (Fairfield) marched upon the rebels, but too late to save the buildings; however, they killed twelve of them, and must have wounded many. The Ramble (the great house of Bellefield, and on the hill above it) was burned at the same time.
>
> It is supposed that 100 plantations and settlements are already in ashes. If the rebellion spreads, our force is quite insufficient to put it down; all depends on the moral [sic] effects of the employment of the King's troops [PP, Vol. XLVII p. 292, no. 26].

Referring to Cotton's proclamation, the Custos wrote, "I have some hopes that, backed by an imposing force, and the many losses the rebels have already suffered, this measure will cause amongst them differences and suspicions of each other, if it answers no other purpose".

On 3 January, the governor, accepting Major General Robertson's recommendation,[3] issued a proclamation offering rewards for the capture of the principal rebel leaders:

> Whereas it has been ascertained that certain incendiaries have been employed to poison the minds of the slaves in some parts of the island, and to induce them to be guilty of acts of outrage and insubordination; and whereas it is necessary that the ringleaders of this disturbance should be brought to condign punishment, I do hereby in His Majesty's name, offer a reward of 300 dollars to any person or persons who shall apprehend either of the following slaves.

This was followed by the names and descriptions of the four leaders supplied to the governor by Robertson, and a promise that any slave assisting in apprehending them, except those who had been guilty of incendiarism or of attempting to kill a peaceable inhabitant, would receive "His Majesty's most gracious pardon". From the wording of the offer it would appear that His Excellency assumed that any slave who could give the required assistance must of necessity have been in rebellion [ibid p.287, no.19].

On the same day 50 regulars of the 77th regiment, with a supply of arms and ammunition and under the command of a major, were sent by sea aboard H.M.S. *Rose* to Black River in St. Elizabeth[4] [ibid p.272ff, no.7].

On 3 January, Cotton made a further report to the governor. Dealing specifically with the incendiarism he said:

> The burnings are executed from signals on the heights by moveable parties of negroes, not belonging to the properties they set on fire; but the negroes on those properties must be in the conspiracy, and co-operators when these men arrive, otherwise they have the means of preventing their effecting their purpose...

> The incendiaries set on fire Belvidere, as Captain Smith's 22nd was moving up. He immediately moved upon them, routed them in every direction, and killed about fifteen men; but the fire could not be extinguished... Combustibles were found in a house here [Montego Bay] belonging to the wife of one of the men shot yesterday, and no doubt exists she intended to fire it. She, with the incendiaries caught in the face, are now trying [ibid p. 292, no. 25].

Cotton wasted no time in instituting a local reign of terror. As most of the slaves in the western parishes were believed to be in rebellion — his own, very rough, estimate[5] was 20,000 [ibid p.208] — there were obviously very large numbers who qualified for inclusion under his threat that all "found with the rebels will be put to death without mercy". It is apparent, from Cotton's report to the governor on 3 January, of what he had learned of the conception of the rebellion, that numbers of captured slaves had already been executed:

> The whole of the men shot yesterday stated they had been told by white people for a long time past, they were to be free at Christmas, and that their freedom order had actually come out from England, but was withheld; that they had only to strike work *en masse* and they would gain their object that the whole of the estates in Trelawny and St. James had agreed so to do; that if they were attempted to be forced to turn out to work, they were then to fire the properties, but not the canes, or the provision grounds, or their own huts; that this would make the proprietors come to terms [ibid p.291, no.25].

In the same letter, Cotton reported that he was receiving the fullest co-operation and assistance from the Commodore of the fleet, who had: "permitted nearly 150 sailors and marines to land every evening, and be placed as picquets on the roads leading from the town [Montego Bay]". The fort, he added, "is under their charge" and they "by row-boats protected the bay and shores". Over on the south coast, at Savanna la Mar, H.M.S. *Blossom* had "afforded assistance by marines and others".

Cotton asked the governor to "order Colonel MacLeod to send 100 men from Kingston and its neighbourhood, if you are all quiet there". But he also urged that it was "absolutely requisite to have a large force disposable" in Kingston and Spanish Town "should symptoms show themselves there".

Finally, Cotton reported that he had written "to call upon the maroons [of Accompong] to send a force to Belfont, and to cut off the insurgents from passing the Great River, and to offer 300 dollars for their bringing in any of the chiefs of the insurrection ...". If the Maroons, he explained, "will cover the Great River from Chesterfield to Dacket Spring, we prevent them [Gardner's company?] effectually from entering Westmoreland" [ibid].

Meanwhile, over at the north-eastern end of the island, the strike was gaining momentum. In a letter to the governor from Manchioneal dated 3 January, a prominent plantation owner and magistrate wrote:[6]

> I feel it my duty to make known to your Lordship the state of insubordination, amounting, I may almost say, to rebellion, under which the slave population at present labour.
>
> I yesterday morning heard that my own people, as well as those of four adjacent estates, had refused to go to their work. I used every persuasion, but with no effect. Every hour since informs us of similar delinquency on the part of other estates; and from the manner in which the insubordination first shows itself, there can be no doubt but that it is organized upon a system.

The writer of this letter had no confidence in the ability of the local planters to defend their property:

> To protect this district, fourteen miles in length, and containing a population of 3,000 slaves, we have only one company of militia ... whose utmost force I may estimate at forty. We have sent to Port Antonio for military assistance, but I fear the similar insubordination existing there will prevent the possibility of any assistance coming from that quarter.

In view of this alarming situation, at the opposite end of the island to the area in which the rebellion was raging, the worried letter writer ventured to suggest: "that a man-of-war of a small class, with a detachment of troops on board, if speedily sent round, may possibly restore tranquility" [PP, Vol. XLVII pp. 290-1, no.24].

In his despatch to the Secretary of State on 6 January [ibid pp. 240-4 No. 7] the governor reported that having "anticipated the necessity of checking any insubordination which might appear in that quarter", he had assembled the three eastern militia regiments. "Forty men also of the 77th [regiment] had been conveyed .. from Port Antonio to Manchioneal". And "30 men of the 33rd regiment, embarked on board of His Majesty's ship Hyacinth, to proceed to Morant Bay". These had orders "from thence to march through a populous and as yet tranquil district, where however the St. Thomas-in-the-East regiment were assembled, to Manchioneal".

"The appearance of this force will, I trust", commented the governor, "be sufficient to check any disposition to revolt in that quarter". He noted, hopefully, that in St. Thomas, "although the negroes on some estates had refused to work, no act of destruction had been committed in that quarter..." [ibid p.242ff].

On 4 January, Cotton reported to the governor:

> It appears beyond doubt that the burnings are conducted by regular parties; they are dressed many in blue jackets and black cross belts; some thus accoutred (four or five) were distinctly seen yesterday by Captain Burnett, who advanced, by his report this morning, higher up the hills than I at first understood [ibid pp. 292-3, no.27; *The Watchman* 7 January].

This information about uniformed rebels is interesting. When were the uniforms made? Were they prepared in advance, to be supplied as far as they would go to members of the rudimentary mobile army referred to in the previous chapter? Or were these uniforms made by the women in the course of the struggle, representing perhaps an initiative of the organiser of one or other of the companies or "regiments"? The latter possibility is suggested by the fact that, a week later the St. James militia regiment encountered a rebel force wearing a different style of uniform.[7]

How many uniformed rebels there were is not known, but certainly Gardner wore a uniform and an officer's sword. The artist's impression of Gardner's surrender, contained in the book about the rebellion written by the "retired military officer" Bernard Martin Senior, shows Gardner in full officers regalia [Senior 29]. How faithfully the actual uniform was reproduced by the artist is not known, and it is doubtful whether Gardner was wearing it when he surrendered.

Cotton reported to the governor on 4 January, on the first results of his "severe measures", with some satisfaction:

> The measures adopted, together with the proclamation issued, has had the most extraordinary effect; I have this afternoon received accounts from Pitfour and Latium, stating the negroes were coming in fast, and the road to Maroon Town is open. The attacks made yesterday, and the number of

men they have lost in the various affairs... has spread a panic amongst them that has cleared them from this neighbourhood; and I think the movement tomorrow will stop any further depredations hereabouts.

I have closed Colonel Hilton upon Falmouth and begged General Cox to send three companies of the militia to Rio Bueno; Colonel Hilton will occupy, till further orders, Duncans, Cambridge and Mountain Spring; my great object will be to get them between my columns.

I have begged the Commodore (who has acceeded directly) to let a sloop of war move immediately to the mouth of the Great River, and land a party of marines and sailors to occupy the post of Round-hill, from which Colonel Campbell will move at four to-morrow morning. The road is perfectly open but it is requisite to ensure its continuance... [PP, Vol. XLVII pp. 292-3, no.27].

Cotton also referred to a report from Captain Burnett that he had sighted about 300 to 400 persons of whom "not more than 20 were armed" and had hailed to them. In reply "they hallooed, War, war", but had quickly disappeared "upon the sailors and marines firing" — a sad commentary on the inability of poorly armed rebels to withstand their well equipped adversaries in open country.

Writing to the government secretary on the same day [8] the Custos of Trelawny suggested that the strikers in his parish had been "induced" by "the acts of vigour which have been pursued... to return to their work". He admitted however that: "Orange Valley, and one or two estates in that neighbourhood, are still holding out". But it had been reported to him "that the noise of artillery has been heard in that direction" and he was "in great hopes that Major Neilson, with his strong detachment, has fallen in with them" [PP, Vol. XLVII pp. 293-4, no. 28; *Votes* 1831-2 p. 172].

Reporting the presence in Falmouth of "about 150 prisoners", the custos insinuated that he regarded the taking of rebels alive as an undeserved leniency. Callously he recorded: "My advice to Colonel Cadien was, to take as few prisoners as possible". Nevertheless, he thought the courts martial about to be convened to try the prisoners could, depending on how they were conducted, be used advantageously. "I hope they will be able to bring acts of rebellion home to them", he added cynically, "to enable us to make such an example as will intimidate the others".

The custos then criticised a somewhat more liberal-minded planter who, he alleged, had escorted out of the parish "one of the incendiary preachers", thus frustrating an intention to imprison him in Falmouth. He expressed the hope that when this man reached Kingston, the governor would have him arrested there.

Before the custos could finish his letter, he received word that "many of the Orange Valley negroes have turned out to work", but that those at Kent estate "still continue refractory". Adding this information to the letter, he reported gleefully that the personal belongings of the Orange Valley slaves, which they had removed from their huts and hidden, had been "discovered and burnt".

The alleged incendiary preacher was the Weslyan missionary Box. By letter dated 6 January the government secretary advised the custos that "although your letter does not state the charge preferred against him, his Excellency considers it quite sufficient to cause him to be detained until he may hear further from you". However, as the custos failed to inform the governor of any "substantial charge" against the missionary, the latter, as he reported to the secretary of state on 16 January, caused Mr. Box to be "immediately liberated" [pp. 308-309, no.9].

A Westmoreland planter and magistrate, Anthony Whitelock, gave an account[9] of a clash with the rebels at Knockalva:

> On the morning subsequent to the burning of the trash-houses at Dry Works in Westmoreland, (I believe the 4th January), Colonel Williams marched upon Mackfield with his regiment, and part of the Westmoreland troop ... On reaching the place [the blowing of] shells were heard in all directions, and in a few minutes the rebels appeared in considerable force on the neighbouring hills [ibid p. 198].

From Whitelock's account it would appear that Augustus Beaumont, the maverick American born editor of the

Jamaica Courant newspaper suspected of sympathising with the rebels, had distinguished himself as a volunteer against them. Whitelock stated that a party under a captain, "consisting of 10 men, and 10 mounted grenadiers", was ordered "to advance for the purpose of reconnoitreing" and, stated Whitelock, "we came close to the rebels, who made a stand on the other side of an opposite wall". The captain "ordered me to obey his command, and go round about for the purpose ... of surrounding them. But "The rebels seeing us ... lengthening our distance from them came down upon us, and took a station about 100 yards from the gap on the right". Whitelock thought the situation critical: "there were about 40 with guns, and within shot".

At this moment, Whitelock continued, Beaumont who was bringing up the rear of the retreating troops, turned his horse and called out "Charge". "The rear then became the front the captain faced about, and also followed; the rebels fired upon us, and then fled in all directions; several were shot and sabred". This sudden turning of the tables Whitelock attributed to Beaumont's bravery and initiative.

Whitelock's purpose in giving this account to the Assembly's committee of enquiry was to exonerate Beaumont who, perhaps because he could not conceal his contempt for the militia, had been accused of inciting the slaves. A female slave owner from Clarendon had reported, to the committee set up by the Assembly to enquire into the cause of the rebellion, that her slaves had told her that Beaumont had encouraged them to abscond and had suggested a place where they could hide. One of her slaves confirmed the story. In view of Beaumont's military activities during the rebellion such reports must be viewed with skepticism.

A report dated 7 January and published in *The Watchman* on 11 January stated:

> Colonel Grignon's detachment, with the 33rd regiment, had an affair on the 5th instant with the rebels, the details of which had not reached the Major General [Cotton], owing to the road on Redding-Hill having been

cut off after the troops had passed. Two troopers, with dispatches to Colonel Grignon, from the Major General, had returned being unable to deliver them.

On 5 January, in a letter to the governor from Montego Bay, Cotton reported a decline of the rebellious spirit among the blacks: "tranquility is returning fast to all this neighbourhood; the negroes, availing themselves of the proclamation I issued, are coming in from all directions". The road to Lucea in Hanover and the area all around Montego Bay were clear, he said. And the three columns put in motion to open the road to Savanna la Mar would, he was sure, "reach their points without any opposition". Many proprietors and attornies "are now proceeding to visit their estates" [PP,Vol. XLVII p.295, no.30].

But despite the general's belief that the tide of rebellion had started to ebb, there were still very large numbers of rebels in the field who were pursuing with determination their task of destroying the material bases of their enslavement. A postscript to the same letter contained this, perhaps unintended, tribute to the courage and conviction of an unnamed rebel incendiary: "Colonel Campbell has taken a ruler, who came with torches, in the act of setting fire to a property, and when questioned, fully avowed the purpose he came for".

Cotton's response was predictable: "I have ordered them to try him instantly", he wrote, "and if found guilty, to approve the court-martial and shoot him". Attempting to justify this pre-trial prescription of the sentence he said: "It is the fear of punishment that alone acts upon them to come in; for depend upon it there is a bad spirit amongst them".

A newspaper report published in *The Watchman* on 7 January, reprinted from the *Kingston Chronicle*, stated: "The rebels appear to have taken to the interior and other commanding heights, and have communication with the negroes by means of signals".

A letter, written four days earlier by a correspondent in Savanna-la-Mar in Westmoreland, appeared in the same issue: "A conspiracy has broken out... The island (at least the county of Cornwall) will be ruined. The slaves are well armed, and are firing sugar estates, pens, and settlements. They say they are fighting for their freedom..." But *The Watchman*, despite the known position of its publishers as advocates of the abolition of slavery, railed editorially against the rebels, disclosing the editor's overriding concern for the preservation of property:

> Do they suppose they would be allowed to burn down the properties of their owners and go unpunished? We warn those who entertain such diabolical notions at once to abandon them... What have they gained by their improper conduct? Have they gained freedom? No. The bullet or the bayonet will terminate their existence... Let them rather return peaceably to the duties of their several stations, and await the issue of time – Let them bow with submission to their masters, and by every effort... strenuously endeavour to attone for the crimes which they have perpetrated ... [7 January].

A party of soldiers was surprised in the interior of St. James on 9 January. A crudely chiselled inscription still visible on a large stone by the side of the road, about two miles from Barneyside near Leamington, records that Obed Bell Chambers, a "private of the Light Infantry Company... on the 9th January, 1832 fell into an Ambush of Rebellious Slaves". He did, the inscription states, "die at this spot" being "cruelly Butchered".[10]

A report from St. James, date-lined 1.30 p.m. on Tuesday, 10 January and published in *The Watchman,* on 11 January, stated:

> The Insurgents had taken up a position with all they can collect, at a place called Catadupa. Captain Hilton, with the Maroons, intended to have attacked them, but he found them too strong.
>
> Colonel Williams of the Westmoreland Regiment, was to join Sir W. Cotton on the 8th from Mackfield, and on the morning of the 9th, the whole were to advance and attack Catadupa and push on to Vaughan's field.

From the same report it would appear that the headquarters of the rebel command had been established somewhere between Catadupa and Vaughansfield: "The rebel high priest and sundry colonels are at these two places; after their reduction the rebels will be driven to the woody recesses of the mountains".

The same issue of *The Watchman* commented editorially: "This rebellion is one of the most serious and the most extensive, that ever has occurred in this island — From the best accounts received from the scene of action, it has been but too well organised..."

A subsequent issue of the same newspaper [14 January] published a bulletin dated 11 January containing the following: "... The insurgents had doubled back after their dispersion at Hazelymph and burnt several properties on the coast road on the 9th inst. and had cut trenches across the road..."

This bulletin also told of fighting near Anchovy, to the west of Montego Bay, some three miles inland from the coast:

> A party of the St. James's regiment were attacked at Anchovy Bottom on the 9th inst. by a body of armed and other negroes; they were driven away, and their Chief, (dressed in a red uniform, with black sleeves, with red stripes up the seams, and blue pantaloons) and eight men were killed in a cane piece.

Rebel parties were also still active in the area of the St. James-Hanover border, near the sea: "On the 8th instant, Tryall estate, adjoining Flint River, was completely destroyed; on the 9th, the Orchard estate" [ibid].

An attempt to estimate the number of slaves in rebellion in the parish most affected, in the same bulletin read: "It is supposed about 12000 of the slaves, including women and children, are out from the parish of St. James, alone".

If this was correct, then General Cotton's guesstimate that the total number in rebellion in the western parishes was 20,000] PP, Vol. XLVII P. 208], may have been too low.

On 10 January, stated a report in *The Watchman,* as a result of a meeting of the captains of vessels in the port of Montego Bay, a force was organised from their crews to defend the town. This was in response to a request from the commodore on the frigate H.M.S. *Blanche.* The commodore had stressed that: "The Rebellion now existing amongst the negroes . . . requires (and calls forth) every possible exertion on the part of every loyal British subject" [*The Watchman*, 18 January].

The *Cornwall Courier* recorded a set-back for the rebels on Friday 13 January at a place from which one of the first beacon signals for the rebellion to commence had been given on the evening of 27 December[11] ". . . a party went off to Kensington, a stronghold of the rebels. They succeeded in dislodging them with the loss of one man . . . killed . . ." [*The Watchman*, 21 January].

Recording the fact that: "On Saturday and Sunday January 14th and 15th, several estates negroes to windward had returned to their duty", the same newspaper commented that this was "not to be depended upon". They sounded this note of caution: "The negro fights but badly with the musket: but his conquests with the torch have been fearfully satisfied".

The rebel slaves in 1831-32 were, on the whole, far less competent in the use of fire-arms than the Maroons and the troops. But that was not their greatest problem. The fact was that all but a small minority of them lacked any fire-arms at all, let alone training in their use. But despite this severe handicap, rebels armed with nothing better than a cutlass, a sharpened stick or a wooden club, on numerous occasions bravely attacked armed militiamen and regular soldiers.

The rebels were, however, far more successful in destroying by fire the property of their oppressors than the lives of their attackers. The most celebrated of the rebel incendiaries was William Hall. The *Cornwall Courier* [9 June 1832] paid him a posthumous tribute as: "the celebrated rider on the white horse possessing such a power of ubiquity as rendered it almost incredible how he was seen at distant places nearly at the same time . . ."

In a despatch on 15 January, from his "bivouac" near Mackfield, Cotton announced the formation of the Cornwall

Rangers — a force of fifty volunteer troopers and privates under a lieutenant colonel with a complement of officers and sub-officers. "Two men from each company of the different regiments in Cornwall are permitted to volunteer" [PP. Vol. XLVII p. 232, no.1, Encl.1].

The general referred to his visits, apparently on 14 or 15 January, to several estates near the military post at Mackfield "on which the negroes have returned, or are fast coming in". They had, he said, "listened attentively" when he addressed them. But at one property, Golden Grove, where "the people appeared to be under the influence of one or two ill-disposed head people", he had observed that "there appeared to be still some dissatisfaction".

Calling a halt to the indiscriminate firing of black people's houses which had been taking place, the general stated that "positive directions" had been issued "that no more negro huts were to be destroyed without authority from headquarters".

The official bulletin issued from King's House on 17 January, in which the above despatch was referred to,[12] also contained extracts from Major Pennefather's despatch from the garrison at Maroon Town dated 14 January. The major reported that:

> as he and Lieutenant Butler, of the 22nd regiment, were returning from duty at Latium Estate to Maroon Town, about half a mile from Kensington, they came to where a tree had been felled, and lay across the road; and on dismounting to try to open a passage, three shots were fired at them from some thick bush quite close to the road ... one hitting Lieutenant Butler in the arm, and the other in the head.

The two officers beat a hasty retreat to the post at Kensington, returning later with "some of the party stationed there to cut away the impediment". This done, "they proceeded on to Maroon Town, Lieutenant Butler requiring medical advice, being very weak from loss of blood".

On the same morning, Pennefather reported, the ensign in command at Kensington, with a party of the 22nd regiment, attacked "a horde of insurgent negroes". Three rebels were shot, and the major: "two of them notorious leaders and burners, named Quim-quam and Prince". The people's huts were also destroyed, the soldiers having found therein "an immense quantity of plunder, with 500 musket balls and a great quantity of powder". According to the major: "Many dangerous people are still abroad, and it is considered very difficult to get at them, except by cunning" [PP, Vol. XLVII pp. 232-3].

According to a despatch from Colonel Cadien, the Trelawny militia regiment, with the assistance of "six confidential black shots", had "scoured the woods in the direction of Virgin Valley and Friendship negro grounds, and proceeded to Adelphi Mountains where a number of runaways had collected". The rebels, said the colonel, "had fled", "Eleven huts were destroyed" in which were found quantities of plundered clothing, beef, Ec".

In Trelawny, continued the official bulletin, a detachment of troops had discovered (presumably on 14 January) "a number of huts in the fastnesses". These had been occupied by the rebels led by Captain Dehany, and appeared "to have been the resting-place the night previous, as there were fires and victuals in them". Had these rebels "not been disturbed by firing in the neighbourhood", the bulletin speculated, "it is supposed Captain Dehany and his gangs would have been secured". Concluding, the bulletin of 17 January reported: "It is supposed most of the determined rebels had retired far into the interior of the woods. Most of the negroes in this parish [Trelawny] have returned to their respective estates..."

That same afternoon, at four o'clock, a second bulletin was issued from King's House. It reported the return to work on the previous day of the slaves on Golden Grove estate, and plans for the movement of two columns of troops into the area around Maroon Town. A lieutenant of the regulars "with his rocket men and some of the Hanover [militia] regiment" were said to have been ordered "to scour the neighbourhood of Round Hill, where some rebels were reported to be still harbouring" [ibid p.233].

On 17 January, General Cotton reported from Montego Bay that on the night of Sunday, 15 January a party of the Trelawny regiment had "surprised Dehany's gang, killed two, and made five prisoners". Cotton added that two of these prisoners had been "tried and condemned", that two others were "on their trials" and that the fifth "having offered to conduct a party to the different haunts of the rebels, was sent back to Spring Vale, to proceed with the detachments sent out" [ibid p. 234].

The official bulletin containing this information [13] also reported the capture of "the notorious villain Bacchus, who had been ordered to be tried". But from Georgia, said the bulletin, the officer commanding the troops "reports that a disposition to violence and insubordination is still predominant among the negroes on that estate". At Sportsman Hall estate also there had been "some symptoms of commotion among the negroes" and the instigator, a negro from Vale Royal, had been "secured, and ordered to Falmouth for trial".

On 16 January the trial took place at Falmouth of Joseph Rodriques, "a free brown man" who held the rank of "Sergeant of the black company" of the St. James's regiment. The evidence against the accused implicated other members of the Rodriques family. The rebel leader Dehany was said to have had his headquarters at the home of the accused's eldest daughter, Leah, on a hill between Vaughansfield and Elderslie. His eldest son Moses Rodriques was shot, while trying to make his escape, when surprised by a military party.

Joseph Rodriques, stated a contemporary newspaper report, was condemned to be shot, on a charge of "making his house a depot for plunder, and furnishing the rebels with gunpowder and bullets". He admitted at his trial that his deceased son Moses "had taken the part of the rebels", but his own defence, that he had acted under threats from the rebel leader, was not believed. Another son, Elias Rodriques, was convicted "for the same offence" and sentenced "to receive 300 lashes in the military manner, and to be transported for life to the Hulks in England" [*Cornwall Courier; The Watchman*], 17 January 1832].

The trial and conviction of another free man who had sided with the rebels was mentioned in the same newspaper report: "Thomas Chambers Bayley, a free black man, was found guilty of acts of rebellion, and sentenced to receive 300 lashes in the military manner in front of the Court-House this morning January 16 at 7 o'clock, and to be transported for life to the Hulks in England".

On 17 January a detachment of regulars drawn from the 84th regiment "proceeded . . . to scour the country behind Round Hill, towards Haddington . . ." Reporting on this operation next day, General Cotton regretted that "such is the agility of the negroes, it is quite impossible for the troops to come up with them" [PP, Vol. XLVII p. 234, no. 1, Encl. 1].

Also on 17 January, a party consisting of 25 regulars of the 84th and 30 militiamen of the Western Interior Regiment reoccupied the abandoned post at Bandon. "On the march they fell in with several impediments, the rebels having felled down trees as barricades, and intercepted the roads by cutting deep trenches". Arriving at Plumb, the party found that "the negroes had deserted their houses, and entirely removed their property". The soldiers set fire to the empty huts [ibid].

The same official bulletin issued from King's House on 20 January, in which these events in St. James were reported, also referred to a report from Major Pennefather in Trelawny that "there are still a great many of the leaders out". He trusted, however, that "on the arrival of the Maroons" he would be able "with their assistance and the militia . . . to break up their association". The major also reported that a military post was "about being established at Summer-hill, half way between Vaughansfield and Kensington, which will be the means of dislodging the insurgents who infest the roads in that direction" [ibid p.235].

The bulletin also recorded the death of the rebel captain H. Campbell "who had separated from his men, and was shot by the Maroons". But the report of the gun warned the members of Campbell's party who were able "to retire unseen ... without being observed". A party of twenty Maroon mercenaries had also captured "two other ringleaders" at Ring-tail Hall. It was planned to send thirty-four Maroons, accompanied by an army captain, to search the cockpits south of Vaughansfield next day.

A despatch from St. Elizabeth dated 20 January reported the advance of: "strong detachments ... of the St. Elizabeth's regiment, and ... of the Westmoreland, to the property of the Rev. Mr. Reid, in consequence of information received from some prisoners, that a strong party of the rebels had assembled in the negro houses of that property". Reporting the outcome, the despatch continued: "In advancing to this post, the rebels fired on the troops and Captain Finlayson was dangerously wounded. Captain Locke and several men were also wounded, one only dangerously; two privates killed".

The despatch writer, Major-General Robertson, commented: "This unfortunate affair, it is feared, will give the rebels confidence". The detachment was, however, "pursuing the insurgents". Meanwhile, "a strong force had been sent towards Chesterfield, as the rebels from St. James had retreated into the back woods in that direction". In conclusion the militia general reported that "The whole of the properties on which the negroes had struck, had been visited, and examples made of the principals" [ibid p.236].

The King's House bulletin on 21 January reporting this despatch also reported the execution to date of three of the five members of rebel Captain Dehany's band who had been captured on 15 January, and that "on 20th instant, Petersgill, a notorious rebel", was hanged at Spring Vale estate. The arrival by sea at Falmouth of "The Maroons, from Port Antonio, 107 in number, under the command of Captain

Fyfe" was also announced. They were said to be "a very effective body, and anxious to be employed".

In a letter to the Secretary of State on 10 February 1832, Governor Belmore stated: "Having received an offer from the Maroons belonging to Moore Town, in the parish of Portland, and Charlestown in the parish of St. George, to serve in this district, I ordered a detachment of 107 men, under the command of Captain Fyffe, superintendent at Charlestown, to embark at Port Antonio and proceed to Falmouth, there to act under orders from Sir Willoughby Cotton, who speaks highly of their services ... I considered it important to avail myself of their offer, not only on this account, but also that by employing them, I thereby secured their fidelity, a consideration to which I attached much importance in the critical position of affairs at that time" [ibid p.229].

Reporting the arrival of these Maroons the *Royal Gazette* stated: "They were marched during the night to Maroon-Town, whither Sir Willoughby Cotton had gone to arrange for their immediate operations in dislodging or killing the Rebels, who had taken refuge in the fastnesses of the mountainous parts of the country, aback of Vaughansfield" [*Royal Gazette* 21-8 January Suppl.].

From Maroon Town on 21 January, Sir Willoughby Cotton reported that "many of the fugitive negroes had, within the last few hours, returned to their respective estates". Of those in Trelawny who still refused to surrender he said: "those who remain out are so harrassed and straitened by the repeated excursions of the parties, who constantly make prisoners, that their strong holds in that part of the country cannot much longer be tenable" [PP, Vol. XLVII pp.236-7].

That same day, according to a contemporary newspaper report, the governor told his Council of War at Spanish Town that: "At present, the rebels had been completely driven from the plains, and had been compelled to retire into the fastnesses of the country [and that] their forces were greatly diminished". The Governor was reported to have added that:

"In the situations in which they were at present, they could not be encountered with facility, and the measures to be adopted for overpowering them, would take some time to operate before the rebels could be effectually vanquished" [*The Watchman* 28 January]. The Council of War thereupon "unanimously resolved that Martial Law should be continued for thirty days longer".[14] [*Royal Gazette*, 21-8, January, postscript].

FOOTNOTES

[11] Major General Sir Willoughby Cotton to Belmore, 2 January 1832.

[2] Richard Barrett, Custos of St. James to Wm. Bullock, 2 January 1832.

[3] Above, p. 288.

[4] Belmore to Goderich, 6 January 1832.

[5] "Questions to Sir Willoughby Cotton" (undated).

[6] Edward Panton to Belmore, 3 January 1832.

[7] Below, p. 303.

[8] Macdonald to Bullock, 4 January 1832 *Votes* (1831-32) p. 172 – 11 April 1832.

[9] Examination of Anthony Whitelock before a committee appointed by the Assembly to enquire into the cause of and losses sustained by the rebellion.

[10] The Bell Chambers stone, seen by the author in 1949, bears an inscription that it "was erected to his memory by the Officers and Men of the 6th Battalion Company".

[11] See Above, p. 276.

[12] Official Bulletins from King's House – Bulletin of 17 January 1832.

[13] Bulletin issued from King's House at one o'clock, 18 January 1832.

[14] Reprinted item from the *Jamaica Courant* a newspaper published in Kingston.

CHAPTER FOURTEEN

THE COST OF THE REBELLION

On 23 January "a strong detachment of the St. Elizabeth's regiment and a company of the Westmoreland regiment" moved up to Struie. They had "received information that the rebels were in great force about two miles distant, and apparently inviting (by frequently showing themselves) an attack". This, as it transpired, was what remained of the rebels' main force "commanded by the rebel chiefs, Colonel Gardiner and Captain M'Cail". They were better armed than other rebel bands and would appear to have decided to make a stand against this militia force.

At 1 a.m. on the morning of the 25th "a strong detachment, under the ... command of Lieutenant-colonel Farquharson" moved out for an attack on the heights occupied by the rebels. "They reached the place ... at 3 a.m." Though "one of the sentinels of the rebels discovered the advance of the troops, and fired," it would appear that the rebel force was not in readiness for this nocturnal assault. They were caught entirely unprepared.

According to a despatch sent by Major-general Robertson on the afternoon of 25 January, based on information sent back to Struie by Farquharson:

> the whole detachment advanced in a rush up the hill. The rebels fled in every direction, leaving 15 stand of excellent arms, chiefly rifles, two

pistols, 35 cutlasses, some lances, and two bugles; also a quantity of ammunition of every description; many were wounded, and two female prisoners taken [PP, Vol. XLVII p. 239].

Farquharson was confident that he had Gardner, and the remainder of his men, trapped. He reported to Robertson "that he had driven them into a large cave, where he had left his men surrounding and digging them out".

The cave was well defended and it took the soldiers a long time, possibly a couple of days, to force the entrance. When eventually the soldiers forced their way in, they discovered that all but four of those who had retreated into the cave, had escaped through another, undetected, outlet. The retreat had been well covered. *The Watchman* newspaper cited a despatch from Robertson dated 28 January as stating: "The sentinel placed by them within the Cave defended his post bravely, but was shot with three others" [*Watchman* 1 February 1832].

This defeat was a serious blow to the rebels. It meant that Gardner's company was no longer a real threat to the militia. In their retreat they "only saved seven stand of arms" [ibid]. Gardner himself stated later:[1] "From that time we never rallied. The men were scattered, and are now wandering about in small parties" [PP, Vol. XLVII p. 216].

General Cotton's despatch from Montego Bay dated 25 January reported plans for a concerted movement both from Barrack Bridge in Westmoreland and "from the Hanover side". This movement, he said, "will have the effect of scouring the whole line of the Great River from Unity Hall to Eldersley, into which country, the greater part of the fugitives had been driven" [ibid p.238; *Watchman*, 25 January].

The King's House bulletin referring to this despatch[2] also recorded a despatch from Hanover to the effect that a party of Accompong Maroons had "secured 19 insurgents". Thereafter these Maroons had "proceeded to the neighbourhood of Bandon and returned the same evening, bringing in the ears of eight negroes killed and 27 prisoners".

Meanwhile, the mercenaries from the Maroon settlements at Moore Town and Charlestown were reported to have shot a man named John Waite and to have captured rebel captain Gillespie and one Quamina. "Those two insurgents", reported the bulletin, "are notorious ringleaders in this part of the country". They had been armed with "a double-barrel gun, two pistols, a sword, and four pounds of powder and some ball".

The rebels were said still "to be in force about Mocho" and it was proposed to send some of the Accompong Maroons, and 30 men of Captain Fyffe's party [of Maroons from Moore Town and Charlestown] supported by ... [a] company of the Trelawny regiment "to scour the woods in that direction" [ibid].

The *Royal Gazette* carried the following item in its supplement [21-28 January]:

Falmouth, Jan 25

We regret to find that the continued disturbed state of the island requires that Martial Law be continued for 30 days longer.

We had hoped that by the early arrival of the Commander of the Forces in St. James's, with the overwhelming disposable force of Regulars and Militia under his command, the Rebels would, long ere this have been captured or killed. Such we lament to say is not the case ...

The Rebels have had breathing time allowed them; of this they have availed themselves most amply, and they are now much better organised than they could possibly have been at the commencement of the insurrection.

A news item in the same issue of this newspaper, about some prisoners, discloses how some of the rebels overcame the problem of a shortage of bullets: "We learn that fourteen Rebels from Unity Hall Estate, St. James's were on Monday sent up from Round-Hill, by water, to take their trial at Montego Bay. They were all armed and had a quantity of gunpowder – in lieu of bullets, each man was provided with a bag of cooper's rivets".

General Cotton's despatch from Montego Bay on the morning of 26 January referred to an incident at Virgin Valley. When the troops had made their approach on the previous day, the slaves of the estate had concealed themselves among the growing canes in a large cane piece. Their hiding place discovered, it "was surrounded and set on fire, but would not burn. The field-piece ... was then brought up" and the officer in command adopted the course "of proclaiming an amnesty if they would come out and surrender themselves: only one woman took advantage of it". Five were captured, apparently trying to make a get-away. Then "several rounds of cannister shot was fired into the cane-piece, by which it appears one man was wounded, who crawled out in the morning and was taken". Somehow, under cover of darkness, the others had made their escape [PP, Vol. XLVII p.238].

The bulletin from King's House on 27 January referring to Cotton's despatch, also cited a despatch from a lieutenant of the Royal Artillery accounting for the movements of his unit.[3] Operating with a company of the St. James militia, they "fell in with a small party of rebels" on 24 January, half a mile to the north of Roehampton.

They wounded and captured one man. Next day they "fell in with nine new huts in the woods, and a cave of 70 feet long, in which was a great quantity of plunder and provisions, all of which was burnt. 13 new huts in the provision grounds of Windsor Castle Penn had also been destroyed" [ibid p.239].

The lieutenant then rounded off his account of the destruction of the people's homes with the news that "at the latter place Captain Bowen had a rebel hung by the name of Baby". Just like that! No mention of the convening of a court martial. One wonders how many rebels, whose deaths went unrecorded in the official statistics, were despatched in this summary fashion during the course of the rebellion.

The rebel leader Captain Dehany was captured on or about 30 January [*Royal Gazette* Postscript]. He had shown himself merciless to the upholders of slavery, as was illustrated in the evidence given to the Assembly's committee of inquiry by a proprietor and magistrate from Westmoreland:[4]

> I found the overseer of Moco in a cave, shot in the neck; he told me he had been there for several days and that Dehany, a slave belonging to Mr. Grizzle, had shot him, and chopped off his brother's head in his presence. The overseer . . . died subsequently of his wounds [PP, Vol. XLVII pp.197-8].

Dehany was also a man of great courage and determination, who remained defiant in captivity and at his trial, and went to the scaffold unrepentant. Thomas M'Neel, another witness before the same committee, spoke of a conversation with Dehany after his capture:

> I was informed by a rebel chief, styling himself Captain Dehany, in the court-house at Montego Bay, on the day he was tried and executed, that it was the intention of the negroes to burn the properties from the interior towards the sea-side, and then the towns; and those white or free persons who had the good luck to get on board the ships, it was their good luck [ibid p.194].

M'Neel, a Westmoreland property owner who was an officer in the militia, having learned that there was a prospect of a parley with the rebel colonel Robert Gardner, set out on 31 January to explore the possibilities. "I went to meet him", M'Neel stated, and "at some distance from, and out of sight of, the station, I took off the arms, sword and pistols, and placed them on a stone wall". No rebels emerged to meet him, however, and he returned to the post. Only subsequently did M'Neel learn, as he put it, that "several guns were pointed at me", and that but for Gardner's intervention "I should never have returned alive to my company" [ibid p.192].

A meeting between M'Neel and the rebel leader did however take place approximately one week later. M'Neel subsequently told the Assembly's committee of enquiry what had happened:

> On the morning of the 8th of February last, about 9 o'oclock [sic], I was informed, by a slave belonging to Greenwich Estate, that a rebel chief, styling himself Colonel Gardner, wished to meet me if I would make my appearance unarmed some distance from the military station. I complied immediately, and at a distance of about half a mile from Greenwich, in the old road leading to York Estate, Gardner made his appearance; instantly another negro made his appearance, who was subsequently introduced to

me by Gardner as Captain Dove [ibid].

Exactly what Gardner had hoped to achieve by this meeting is not recorded. M'Neel said: "I do not think he had fully made up his mind to deliver himself up at our first meeting". But the rebel leaders were in no position to bargain from strength and M'Neel appears to have convinced them that further resistance would be hopeless: "after a conversation of some length I prevailed on them both to surrender, and promised to accompany them to Colonel Williams. I made no promise of forgiveness, nor in any way induced them to believe that their lives would be spared". But M'Neel qualified this by saying: "I offered to be of use to them should it be in my power".

The rebel colonel's conduct, after his surrender, was not consistent. Bernard Martin Senior, the army officer who subsequently wrote a book about the rebellion he had been engaged in suppressing, wrote of Gardner:

> His conversation was apparently undisguised, and, with the utmost promptitude, he frankly answered every question put to him. He spoke even magnanimously of some encounters he had sustained with the whites, lauding in the highest terms the valour of his own troops on those particular occasions and boasting of the havoc they had committed among the military in two or three instances [29 p.260].

When Gardner and M'Neel reached the common pasture at Belvidere, on their way to Colonel Williams' Headquarters, Gardner recounted an incident which had taken place there:

> Gardner said that the negroes were determined to fight the regiment under Colonel Grignon, and as he could not advise them against it, he pointed out the position he had posted his men in, and said that a challenge had been sent twice to Colonel Grignon who was at Belvidere, or at the barracks close by, to come out and meet him in fair fight the following morning.

Grignon, he complained, had not accepted his challenge but had retired with his regiment from Belvidere.

But this mood of confidence and pride in the courage and spirit of his ill-trained revolutionary force soon gave way to an attitude more in keeping with what he knew was expected of him as a slave. He expressed regret and repentance and claimed that he had been misled by others. He even expressed the hope that a slave of Grignon's named George Guthrie, a leading member of the Montego Bay Baptist church at whose house Sharpe's plans for the rebellion had first been explained to him, "should be taken up" [PP, Vol. XLVII p.192].

Questioned about the conspiratorial supper held at Guthrie's house, Dove said that Guthrie had proposed a toast to the downfall of his owner in these terms: "I hope we shall overcome Little-breeches for he has said, that before Jamaica shall be free he (Colonel Grignon) will lose every drop of his blood" [ibid p.214]. Gardner's version of this toast by Guthrie was more explicit: "May Little-breeches and the other gentlemen who oppose us lay at our feet" [ibid p.215].

By the time Gardner made his statement to Rev. Thomas Stewart in the gaol at Savanna-la-Mar, he was saying that he had been a reluctant participant in the rebellion and that his military command had been forced upon him. Here is how he sought to explain the circumstances in which he became a rebel commander:

> On Tuesday night after Christmas day Sharp sent a great number of men for me to command ... I heard the multitude coming, and, although at supper, I got up and slipped out at my back door, because I knew what they were coming for, and wished to have nothing to do with it.
>
> I waited concealed a long time, but being hungry and finding that the men would not go away without seeing me, I returned to my house; they then all surrounded me and said that Sharp had sent them to me to command that I was to take them, and all the people in the district, as 'a force' to go against Westmoreland and Hanover ... I was overruled, and went to Hazelymph immediately, that being the rendezvous.

Gardner said further that when "General Sharp's army" had arrived at the rendezvous at Hazelymph "The business was talked over" and he had "entreated them to burn no place". He had, he said, advised:

> that ... on Wednesday, the day the negroes were expected to turn out for work, they should every one go peaceably into the high road near Montpelier (Gravel Hill), and wait there till they should see some respectable gentleman passing by; they should then ask him if it was really true that they were freed from Christmas? If the gentleman should say, no, they were to return to their work ...

Gardner ended this implausible story with this lament to his 'confessor': "Oh, Sir, if I had had any good friend to tell me the real truth, as I now find it to be, I never would have been brought to this" [ibid p.216].

In view of Gardner's obviously disingenuous attempt to represent himself as a man who had tried unsuccessfully to dissuade his fellow slaves from rebelling, and had had his position of leadership unwillingly thrust upon him, it is difficult to distinguish in his evidence the true from the false. Though he told Rev. Stewart that he had "fled" and was not with his men when, during the course of the battle which commenced near Struie on 25 January, they retreated into the cave, it is probable that he was lying. If indeed he had shown any bravery and resourcefulness in leading his rebel company, he was obviously most anxious that this should not be known to his captors.

The sorry performance of Robert Gardner during the period he was in custody in the Savanna-la-Mar gaol is of course to be explained by his hopes and expectations of thereby obtaining an official pardon. A promise had been made by the Chief Justice and the Custos of Trelawny to Gardner and Dove that their lives would be spared if they assisted the Baptist missionary William Knibb "to discover the mode in which the insurrection was planned" by making a "full confession" [*Facts and Documents* 12 pp. 11-2].

Gardner did disclose much of what he knew about the origins of the conspiracy and the organisation and conduct of the rebellion, attempting at the same time to reduce his own role from that of a principal conspirator and military leader to that of a misinformed and reluctant participant. In the event he did himself a great disservice and profited nothing by it. Bleby records that while others were pardoned "in consequence of information thus communicated", such good fortune did not attend Gardner, "whom it was intended also to spare". Gardner lost his life because:

> the local authorities, taking advantage of the absence of the major general, and indignant that one who had taken such a leading part in the revolt

should be allowed to escape with comparative impunity, brought the un fortunate man to trial, and hurried him to the gallows, before any measures could be employed to save him, and in direct violation of the governor's instructions to submit to him for confirmation all capital sentences that might be passed on criminals [4 p. 110].

But let us return to the chronological narrative. On 11 February *The Watchman* newspaper, reprinted this item from the *Cornwall Chronicle:* "The Military movements of the week are few in number, and there is nothing in the way of novelty to relate regarding the insurgents. They are now driven into close recesses, and have comparatively little scope for any extraordinary depredation".

Even the legalised slaughter of rebel prisoners was by this time being somewhat reduced in intensity: "The executions during the week have been considerably diminished being in number only 14".

The report added the interesting fact that one of those executed "was the first and only female that has suffered the ultimate penalty of the law in this town [Falmouth]. Her name was Ann Bernard, belonging to Kirk Patrick Hall, a part of which property she set on fire..."

On Monday 6 February, the rebel Patrick Ellis had been killed. His death was reported in the *Cornwall Chronicle* of 11 February [*The Watchman* 18 February]. Bleby recorded how bravely he had died. Surprised and surrounded, Ellis refused to surrender. Stepping forward he uncovered his breast and cried out: "I am ready; give me your volley. Fire, for I will never again be a slave" [4 p.32].

By the middle of February 1832 only small parties of rebels remained in the field. A majority of the slaves had returned to their work as slaves on the plantations. But though the rebellion had been suppressed the spirit of unrest had not subsided. *The Watchman* of 18 February reprinted an item from the *Cornwall Chronicle* reporting the arrest of "nearly seventy prisoners ... from New Miln, Friendship, Welcome and Haddington estates, and Cacoon Pen all of whom had been accessories either to the firing of properties, or had been using fire arms in rebellion". But their arrest had not been uneventful and the newspaper, reporting this, drew the necessary inference:

> The slaves on New Miln evinced a riotous and rebellious disposition when the prisoners were removed from among them ... We are convinced from this that the rebellion is not quite so effectually crushed as the heads of departments imagine, none of the fire-arms of those lawless people having been discovered, or given up by themselves after their capture. That these arms are among them we have now evidence to prove ...

Two months later, when all effective resistance had ceased, the atmosphere was still tense in the western parishes. Beneath the outward calm there was a deep-seated resentment and discontent. In this atmosphere, events which would otherwise have been regarded as normal assumed a deeper significance. Uneasiness was widespread and the air was thick with reports and rumours of further threatening unrest. On 21 April *The Watchman* reported nervously:

> Information has reached us that several of the slaves in St. James have again fled into the woods, in consequence of their having been deprived of their 'shell blow' or dinner time. We should hope, for the sake of their masters and those in authority over them, that this report is unfounded.

The mood of the slaves was one of sullen dissatisfaction and resentment. They believed that they had been cheated of the freedom that was justly theirs and betrayed by those who had been expected, if not to support them, at least to refrain from assisting the planters to keep them enslaved. Their determination to be free was undiminished and it was evident that they would never again accept their enslavement as part of the natural order of things.

On the basis of his experience at Deans Valley and his conversations with the prisoners in the Savanna-la-Mar gaol, the Westmoreland rector Thomas Stewart was convinced that there was every possibility of a fresh outbreak. Giving evidence before the Assembly's committee of enquiry he stated:

> This and the assurance of the prisoners under sentence of death that they had all been sworn to do their best to drive the white people off the island, convince me that the feeling of insurrection was general, at least on that side of the country. *I think, moreover, that the rebellion will break out again*[5] not only from the same causes which I have stated to have occa-

sioned the late one, but from the confession of the two prisoners, Linton and M'Kinlay, that in about three or four years the negroes will break out again, for they cannot help believing that the King had given them freedom ... [PP, Vol. XLVII p. 204].

A St. James merchant named Robert Watt, giving evidence before the same committee of the Assembly, was asked: "Do you think the slaves are now tranquil, or that another rebellion is to be apprehended?" He replied:

There is a very great deal of agitation among them still, I think. With regard to my negroes upon my own plantation in St. Elizabeth's, they were only kept quiet by the military force that was in the neighbourhood. Early in January, when I went over the water to them, they were doing little or nothing.

Since the Friendship negroes were punished, those at Lacovia have been quiet enough and doing their work nearly as well as before. There is a property in Westmoreland called Prospect, which I am concerned for, from which a number of negroes, I believe 12 or 14 are still out, and cannot be found [ibid p.205].

Nor was the feeling of unrest confined to the western parishes in which the rebellion had occurred. Asked by the Assembly's committee of enquiry whether he considered "that it was the intention of the slaves generally throughout the island to have rebelled if the rebels had not been so speedily checked?" General Cotton replied: "As far as I am able to form an opinion, I do; and that they merely waited to see the course events took on the north side" [ibid p.208].

Writing to the governor on 23 May,[6] the day of Sam Sharpe's execution, a realistic white resident made this assessment of the situation:

The question will not be left to the arbitrament of a long angry discussion between the Government and the planter. The slave himself has been taught that there is a third party, and that party himself. He knows his strength and will assert his claim to freedom. Even at this moment, unawed by the late failure, he discusses the question with a fixed determination [PRO:CO 137/191].

At the beginning of the rebellion the rebels had burned only the 'trash houses' on the plantations as signal beacons.[7] But once it had become obvious that the planters were not going to yield to the demand that their slaves be up-graded to wage-labourers, a policy of putting the works and other plantation buildings to the torch was widely applied. When the rebellion had been crushed and the cost had been counted a sombre picture of destruction emerged.

In St. James the works and buildings on 101 plantations had been wholly or partially destroyed, in Hanover on 65, in Westmoreland on 37, in St. Elizabeth on 23 and in Trelawny on 10. In a report to the Assembly the value of the losses sustained in these five parishes was estimated as follows:

St. James	£606,250. 0.0
Hanover	425,818.15.0
Westmoreland	47,092. 0.0
St. Elizabeth	22,146. 9.7
Trelawny	4,960. 7.6

Total for the 5 western parishes: £1,106,267.12.1

There had also been extensive damage in Manchester (£46,270) and a small amount of destruction in St. Thomas in the East (£1,280) and Portland (£772.10.0). The total loss was estimated, with nice precision, at £1,154,590.12.1 [PP, Vol.XLVII pp.219-25.

To arrive at an assessment of the total cost of the rebellion, continued the Assembly report, it would be necessary to take into account also the expense incurred, £161,569.19.9, in suppressing it. There was also:

> a further expense, not yet ascertained, which has accrued since martial law ceased, being the pay and rations of a portion of the Maroons, as well as detachments of the Island Militia employed in pursuit of such rebellious Slaves who have not surrendered themselves but remain out and are sheltered amongst the almost inaccessible forests and fastnesses in the interior districts of the island [ibid].

Taking this tally of loss and destruction into account and making allowance for the relative value of money in 1832, it would appear that the rebels, though defeated, had destroyed an appreciable part of the material basis of their enslavement. They had succeeded in making slavery an insupportably expensive system to maintain.

FOOTNOTES

[1] Gardner surrendered on 8 February. His 'confession' to the Westmoreland rector in the Savanna-la-Mar gaol was probably made about a week later.

[2] King's House Bulletin of 26 January 1832; *The Watchman*, 25 January 1832.

[3] Despatch of Lieutenant St. John of the Royal Artillery.

[4] Examination of Anthony Whitelock.

[5] Author's emphasis.

[6] J.B. Zuicke to Belmore, 23 May 1832.

[7] Above pp. 264-266.

CHAPTER FIFTEEN

THE REBELS RE-SET THE TIME TABLE

Whilst they still had the initiative in the early stages of the rebellion the rebel slaves, despite the deep resentment that they must have felt towards those who had for so long profited from their degradation, had been surprisingly merciful to those whites who fell into their hands. With few exceptions the lives of proprietors, attorneys and overseers, taken by surprise, had been spared and their families had been allowed to go free. Instances of ill-treatment of prisoners, though not unknown, had been rare.

This was as Sam Sharpe had wished it to be. As he explained to the captive overseer at Ginger Hill, he wanted to avoid unnecessary destruction of life, not wishing anyone to be harmed who did not oppose the rebels by force. This explains why only 14 whites and three of their brown allies were killed and only 12 whites and two browns were wounded.[1] In St. Elizabeth the three whites killed and wounded were soldiers. The returns from the other parishes do not specify whether the killed and wounded were soldiers or civilians. No blacks, not even the ubiquitous "Uncle Toms", were harmed [PRO:CO 137/185].

The whites behaved very differently towards the blacks. The number of rebels killed during the fighting may not have been excessive, having regard to the scope of the rebellion and the fact that both the regular soldiers and the militia were well armed. One hundred and twenty-four rebels were reported killed in St. James, 58 in Hanover, six in Westmoreland, four in Trelawny and nine in Manchester — a total of 201 reported killed in action. It is significant, however, that only 23 were returned as wounded [PRO:CO 137/185 pp.53-8]. This relationship between the number killed and the number wounded is not what would normally be expected. The figures would seem to suggest that the policy of taking no prisoners, so strongly recommended by the custos of Trelawny,[2] may have been applied in other areas. The small number reported wounded also suggests the possibility that severely injured rebels, who had breath enough to escape into the bush, regarded the possibility of bleeding to death as a preferable alternative to being shot or cut to death upon capture.

But it was through the instrument of their military and civil courts that the whites wreaked their most fearful vengeance upon the blacks and their handful of brown allies. As a ruling class whose position and privileges had been threatened, they no doubt felt that their survival and that of their system, depended upon how effectively they could teach the blacks a lesson.

Most of the so-called trials of rebel slaves were so perfunctory that they gave not even an appearance of justice. The record of the trial at Montego Bay "on Sir W. Cotton's Warrant" of two men charged "For Act of Open Rebellion"[3] deserves to be quoted in full as an illustration:

Wm. Mitchell Kerr, Master of Slaves, sworn.

Q. Are not the Negroes on S.G. Estate in a State of open Rebellion?

A. I consider the whole of them are.

Q. Have they not burnt down your works & shewn other acts of violence?

A. They have not left a smallest building on the Estate standing. What other acts of violence they have done I do not know.

Q. Can you identify the Pris. at the Bar?

A. I can

Q. Name them

A. John McLaren & Thos. Mitchell

Q. Do you consider the whole of the Negroes on your Estate in a State of Rebellion?

A. Yes

The Slaves asked if they had not always been good Servants; wch the Master allowed.

Both denied the Charge. Mitchell sd. he wished to save ye Trash House when fired but was knocked down. The other told a long story, amounting to this that he tried to save some things. In one point (not material to his guilt) he was contradicted by his Master. There was no other evidence.

They were found guilty & sentenced to be <u>shot</u> – <u>Executed</u> [ibid].

Trials like this by courts martial were held almost daily from 3 January to 7 February. Thereafter, trials began also in the 'Slave Courts'. Trial in the civil courts, however, involved no appreciable improvement in the standard of justice available to the accused.

Approximately 750 slaves and 14 free persons were convicted for alleged participation in the rebellion. The official returns of convictions, in both military and civil slave courts, are preserved in the Public Record Office [CO 137/185]. The returns for convictions by court martial are complete as regards totals for each parish and show an aggregate of 376. Those of convictions in the civil slave courts are incomplete (239), there being no returns for Trelawny and St. Elizabeth, two of the five western parishes most affected by the rebellion. The author has arrived at his estimate of total numbers by assuming that the ratio of military to civil convictions in Trelawny and St. Elizabeth would have been approximately the same as the ratio between civil and military convictions in the other three western parishes. Calculated in this way the grand total arrived at is 772, justifying a conservative estimate of approximately 750.

The following table shows the number of slaves convicted by parish and occupation. It provides an illustration of how widely based the rebellion was. The field slaves were of course in the majority, but it is interesting to note the high percentage of those possessing mechanical and other skills who participated. Most significant of all is the involvement of

328   BLACKS IN REBELLION

CONVICTIONS OF REBEL SLAVES

OCCUPATION STATUS	BY MILITARY COURTS							TOTALS	BY CIVIL COURTS							TOTALS	GRAND TOTALS	%
	St. James	Hanover	Westmoreland	Trelawny	St. Elizabeth	Manchester	St. Thomas ye Vale	St. Thomas in the E	Portland		St. James	Hanover	Westmoreland	Trelawny (St. Elizabeth)	Manchester	St. Thomas ye Vale	St. Thomas in the E	Portland			
FIELD WORKERS	85	30	20	27	54*	5	6	6*	11	244*	43	22	44	82*	5	–	3	–	199*	443*	57.4
LIVESTOCK AND CART MEN	2	3	–	3	2*	2	–	–	–	12*	1	10	–	9*	1	–	–	–	21*	33*	4.2
WATCHMEN	–	1	–	–	1*	–	–	–	–	2*	–	3	–	2*	–	–	–	3	8*	10*	1.3
SKILLED TRADESMEN	6	13	4	15	9*	3	3	4*	8	65*	23	26	5	41*	4	–	1	2	102*	167*	21.7
DRIVERS	2	9	1	5	5*	4	–	1*	3	30*	12	7	–	13*	5	–	1	–	38*	68*	8.8
HOUSE SLAVES	3	1	–	1	1*	–	–	–	1	7	–	1	–	–	–	–	–	–	1*	8*	1.0
MISCELLANEOUS AND UNSPECIFIED	1	1	1	11	1*	1	–	–	–	16	2	11	3	10*	1	–	–	–	27*	43*	5.6
TOTALS	99	58	26	62	73	15	9	11	23	376	81	80	52	157	16	–	5	5	396	772	100.0

*These are the author's estimates. An explanation of the grand totals for Trelawny and St. Elizabeth civil convictions (157) is given on p. 327. The breakdown into occupational groups for these two parishes was assumed to be in the same ratio as obtained in the civil courts of the other three western parishes. The occupational breakdown for those convicted in the St. Elizabeth courts martial (73) was assumed to be in the same ratio as obtained in the military courts in St. James, Hanover and Westmoreland (Trelawny figures left occupation largely unspecified and were not used). The occupations of those convicted in the St. Thomas in the East courts martial (11) were assumed to be in the same ratio as obtained in the Portland and St. Thomas ye Vale military courts.

such relatively large numbers of drivers, often the head drivers, whose position in servile society was the equivalent of the modern foreman.

By far the greater number of those slaves who were placed on trial were sentenced to death. Other sentences were often so severe that only the hardy could have survived their infliction. Of 106 slaves tried by courts martial in St. James, 99 were convicted, six were acquitted, one was pardoned and two had their cases adjourned — results unrecorded. Of the 99 convicted no less than 84 were sentenced to death. In the civil slave courts in the same parish there were no acquittals. Of the 81 convicted 54 were sentenced to death.

Other punishments in St. James included one sentence of 500 lashes, one sentence of 300 lashes with hard labour for life, six sentences of 300 lashes simpliciter, one sentence of 200 lashes with six months' hard labour, three sentences of 200 lashes with three months's hard labour, five sentences of 200 lashes simpliciter and other sentences to lesser numbers of lashes of the whip with or without imprisonment.

In Hanover 96 of the 138 slaves convicted were sentenced to death, though 11 of the death sentences were subsequently commuted. Other sentences in this parish included: one of three months' imprisonment with 300 lashes at the beginning and 200 lashes at the end of the term; four of 300 lashes simpliciter; one of 6 months' imprisonment with 200 lashes on incarceration and 50 on release; two of 200 lashes with imprisonment and five of 200 lashes simpliciter.

In Westmoreland 33 of the 64 slaves convicted were sentenced to death. In St. Elizabeth the courts martial imposed 16 death sentences, one sentence of 500 lashes, four of 350 lashes, six of 300 lashes, and three of 250 lashes. Six rebels from St. Elizabeth, six from Westmoreland, seven from St. James and one each from Portland and St. Thomas in the East were sentenced to transportation for life — a sentence meaning that they would be sold abroad as slaves regardless of their family ties in Jamaica.

But it was in Portland, one of the two parishes farthest from the scene of the fighting, that the most macabre vengeance was exacted upon the bodies of the slaves there convicted of acts of rebellion. One rebel's fate was recorded thus: "Death by being Hung & his head cut off and placed in a conspicuous part of Fairy Hill Est". Two others were similarly sentenced, their heads to be conspicuously exhibited respectively at Fairfield and Sion Hill estates [ibid].

Rev. Henry Bleby wrote this contemporary account of the execution of the death sentences [4 pp.25-7]:

> At first shooting was the favourite mode of execution and many were thus disposed of. But when the novelty of this had ceased the gallows was put in requisition ... The gibbet erected in the public square in the centre of the town [Montego Bay] was seldom without occupants, during the day, for many weeks. Generally four, seldom less than three, were hung at once. The bodies remained stiffening in the breeze ...
>
> Other victims would then be brought out and suspended in their place, and cut down in their turn to make room for more; the whole heap of bodies remaining just as they fell until the workhouse negroes came in the evening with carts and took them away, to cast them into a pit dug for the purpose, a little distance out of the town.

Bleby [pp. 29-30] also commented upon the manner in which many of the rebel slaves faced execution:

> The undaunted bravery and fortitude with which many of the insurgents met their fate formed a very remarkable feature of the transactions of the period; and strikingly indicated the difficulty attendant upon the maintenance of slavery, now that the spirit of freedom had gone abroad, and many of the Negroes had learned to prefer death to bondage.
>
> I have seen many led out to die, who were as calm and undismayed in walking to the scaffold as if they had been proceeding to their daily toil. There was nothing that had the appearance of bravado; nor was there aught like effort to get up a scene, or make a display of heroism; yet the eye was undimmed; not a lip trembled; no muscle of the face could be seen to quiver, but, with the dignified bearing of men untroubled with misgivings as to the justice of their cause, they yielded themselves to their doom.

Particularly moving is Bleby's account of the trial and execution of the rebel leader Dehany. An attempt was made at his court martial to induce him to incriminate the Baptist missionary Burchell, but he steadfastly refused to do so. He marched bravely to the scaffold where he was to be hanged simultaneously with three other condemned rebels. But whereas his three companions died almost instantly, the rope by which Dehany was suspended could not bear his powerful frame. The rope broke and he fell half strangled and unconscious. When he had been revived he stood without uttering a sound until another rope had been procured and he had, once more, been strung up to die. This time the attempt to extinguish his life was successful.

There is no record of how Sharpe fell into the hands of his captors. He was held in custody in the gaol at Montego Bay where Bleby was able to converse with him. And it is thanks to Bleby alone that we know that Sharpe, unlike Robert Gardner, retained his spirit and convictions to the end.

Sharpe's conduct in captivity reflected his deep religious beliefs and his revolutionary firmness. His assertion to Bleby that he "would rather die upon yonder gallows than live in slavery" has already been mentioned.[4] Bleby recorded his last impressions of the great architect of the Emancipation Rebellion [p.117]:

> Sharpe was the last victim that was put to death for taking part in the insurrection.[5] He was executed at Montego Bay on the 23rd of May, 1832. For several weeks before his execution, the magistrates ... had prohibited our visits ... but, the last time I conversed with Sharpe, he repeated his expressions of sorrow that he had been the cause of so much mischief. He was not, however, to be convinced that he had done wrong in endeavouring to assert his claim to freedom.

This is particularly interesting, because the non-conformist missionaries, in an effort to save their souls, were bent on trying to convince the rebel leaders that they had been guilty of a sin in organising the rebellion. This was perhaps the greatest disservice rendered by the missionaries to these courageous men.

One cannot avoid the feeling that when Bleby chose to remind Sharpe, not of how Jesus violently expelled the money-changers from the temple, but of the far less authoritative proposition "that the Scriptures teach men to be content with the station allotted to them by Providence", he was being unfairly selective. Bleby claimed that on hearing this

Sharpe "was a little staggered". But he seems to have recovered his composure quickly enough, for he gave to Bleby's argument an irrefutable religious answer: "If I have done wrong in that, I trust I shall be forgiven for I cast myself upon the atonement" [ibid]. That Sharpe should have been able to stand firmly by his convictions at such a time, in the face of moral pressure from persons he respected and trusted, is an indication of his strength of character.

Sharpe was tried at Montego Bay on 19 April.[6] The evidence adduced at his trial related both to his organisational meetings and his military activities in direct command of one of the rebel companies. The account of the trial [PRO:CO 137/185, 310-4] does not suggest that the facts alleged by the prosecution were disputed, either by Sharpe himself or on his behalf.

The record shows that questions were asked of some of the witnesses called by the prosecution by a 'Mr. Grignon'. Whoever Mr. Grignon may have been, and one assumes that he was a lawyer for the defence appointed by the court or by Sharpe's owner, he is not recorded as saying anything favourable or at all on behalf of his client. His questions to some of the witnesses neither challenged the facts as stated by them nor suggested that his client had had a justifiable motive for organising the rebellion.

But the fact that there was a lawyer purporting to act for the defence probably explains why there is no record of Sharpe having been afforded an opportunity to speak for himself. The appointment of a lawyer to represent Sharpe at his trial could conceivably have been a shrewd establishment move. It may well have been the means whereby the accused, who was eminently capable of delivering an eloquent and devastating condemnation of the whole servile system, could be required to remain silent.

The fact that Sharpe did not himself give evidence is of no particular significance, since he did not deny the allegations against him. An address to the court would, however, have been most appropriate. But one searches the record in vain for the sort of ringing declaration of his convictions before the court, such as he had made to Bleby when in custody awaiting trial.

Bleby gave this moving account of how the organiser of the Emancipation Rebellion met his death:

> His execution excited a good deal of interest; and a considerable number of spectators assembled to witness it. He marched to the spot where so many had been sacrificed to the demon of slavery, with a firm and even dignified step, clothed in a suit of new white clothes, made for him by some female members of the family of his owner, with all of whom he was a favourite, and who deeply regretted his untimely end.
>
> He seemed to be entirely unmoved by the near approach of death; addressed the assembled multitude at some length in a clear unfaltering voice, acknowledging that he had transgressed against God and against the laws of his country: and said, 'I depend for salvation upon the Redeemer, who shed his blood upon Calvary for sinners'.

Sharpe's reference to the crucifixion of Jesus by the Roman power was well chosen. The significance of relating that event to his own execution could not have escaped his audience. "He then proceeded to vindicate the accused missionaries, and declared that they had nothing whatever to do with the insurrection", thereby taking full responsibility upon his own shoulders. "In a few moments", wrote Bleby "the executioner had done his work, and the noble-minded originator of this unhappy revolt had ceased to exist" [4 pp.117-8].

Bleby was obviously deeply impressed by Sharpe's dignified departure: "I witnessed the execution; for, having had so much intercourse with him, I was anxious to see how he would demean himself when actually confronted with the stern and solemn realities of death and eternity".

The Methodist minister accepted with resignation the official justification, recording also his own reactions:

> I could not dispute the justice of the sentence; nor could I challenge the wisdom of the government in carrying it into effect, so far as the preservation of slavery was concerned. He had certainly been a daring violator of he existing laws; and had unquestionably occasioned a fearful destruction of life and property ... But I could not help feeling deep sorrow and indignation, — as I turned from his death-scene, and brushed away the tears

which the contemplation of his tragical fate called forth, — that such a man as Samuel Sharpe, who possessed a mind ... capable of noble things, should be thus immolated at the polluted shrine of slavery.

And without meaning it as a compliment, for he added these words by way of explanation of the governor's failure to pardon him, Bleby paid Sam Sharpe the highest tribute that any freedom fighter could desire [p.118]: "He was such a man, too, as was likely, nay, certain, had he been set free, to commence another struggle for freedom: for he felt acutely the degradation and monstrous injustice of the system, and was bent upon its overthrow".

In 1832, then, the great rebellion whereby the slaves had endeavoured to emancipate themselves was crushed. But that is not to say that it had all been in vain. This is how Bleby assessed its significance:

The revolt failed of accomplishing the immediate purpose of its author, yet by it a further wound was dealt to slavery, which accelerated its destruction for it demonstrated to the imperial legislature that among the Negroes themselves the spirit of freedom had been so widely diffused, as to render it most perilous to postpone the settlement of the most important question of emancipation to a later period.

The evidence taken before the Committee of the two Houses of Parliament made it manifest, that if the abolition of slavery were not speedily effected by the peaceable method of legislative enactment, the slaves would assuredly take the matter into their own hands, and bring their bondage to a violent and bloody termination [4, p.118].

Though he saw things from a different point of view, much the same conclusion was drawn by Bernard Martin Senior, a military officer who had participated in suppressing the rebellion [29 p.293].

It will not be surprising that so propitious a circumstance as the late rebellion should be seized with avidity for their furtherance and immediate accomplishment. A bill was brought into Parliament ... by which it was enacted that 'all slavery should cease throughout the British dominions on the first of August 1834'.

The Emancipation Rebellion in Jamaica was the last and greatest of a succession of 19th century rebellions and rebellious conspiracies in the British sugar colonies[7] which made it impossible for the British government, as had been its wont, to delay indefinitely the emancipation of the slaves. The abolition of slavery was carried out from above by legislative enactment. But barring the minor details, it was the rebellious slaves who re-set the time table for emancipation.

Not surprisingly, the form in which the legislation abolishing slavery was enacted by Parliament in 1833 sought to make the slaves pay the slave owners for the loss of their services. This was to be achieved by a device, referred to as 'apprenticeship', whereunder the former slaves were required to work for their former owners for 40½ hours per week without pay for six years in the case of 'praedial' (agricultural) labourers and for four years in the case of 'non-praedials'.

The attitude of many of the planters in the Leeward Islands to the proposed apprenticeship system makes an interesting comparison with that of the planters in the larger territories with available unused land. Knowing that their slaves would have nowhere else to go for employment, even if they were legally free to leave the plantations, the slave owners of Antigua rejected apprenticeship. The Antigua Assembly passed its own legislation providing for total emancipation in 1834. A similar proposal in the Montserrat Assembly was lost, but only on the casting vote of the speaker.

Slaves who were converted into 'apprentices' in August 1834 took not at all kindly to this strategy for delaying the advent of their freedom. Here again it was their intervention that effected revision of the imperial time table. In all the sugar colonies the planters found it impossible, despite the most drastic punishments, to make apprenticeship work.[8] The most resolute struggles occurred in the eastern Caribbean island of St. Kitts where the ex-slaves, refusing to work as apprentices, rose in rebellion.[9]

Four years after the act replacing slavery by apprenticeship, the attempt to make the slaves pay for their freedom had to be abandoned. On 1 August 1838 complete emancipation became a reality in all the British colonies.

By their revolutionary activity the slaves had succeeded in setting the time table for the abolition of slavery. But their triumph was only partial. Because of the suppression of their rebellions, the slaves did not preside over the process of abolition. The exercise was carried out by the establishment by parliamentary means. The consequence of this was that only the system of exploiting labour was altered. Property relationships were not disturbed. The planters continued to own the plantations and, in addition, these former slave owners (or their creditiors) received from the British government twenty million pounds sterling in compensation.[10] But those who had been slaves, and therefore propertyless, before the transition remained propertyless and uncompensated after it.

For the majority, their acquisition of human status also marked their transformation into propertyless wage earners or seekers of employment. They entered the historical stage as free men, but so divorced from the ownership of property capable of producing wealth that for 150 years the great majority of their descendants have known only persistent poverty.

The abolition of slavery, like the abolition of other social and economic systems, has often been described as a social revolution. If this term is to be applied with any degree of accuracy to the events of the fourth decade of the 19th century in the British sugar colonies, then it must also be recognised that the revolution did not then complete, and has not yet completed, its full cycle.

FOOTNOTES

[1] Returns of the numbers of whites and free persons of colour killed and wounded in the rebellion, and Returns of slaves convicted.

[2] Above p. 298.

[3] Record of the trial by court martial at Montego Bay on 3 January 1832 of John McLaren, aged 50, and Thos. Mitchell, aged 26, before seven officers of the rank of captain and upwards under the presidency of Colonel Lawson, the officer commanding the St. James Militia Regiment.

[4] CO 137/185, fols: 94-7, 237-41, 419-20, 457-64, 573-83, 625-30, 716-8, 765, 793-7, 894-5.

[5] In fact Sharpe was not the last to die. Robert Gardner was hanged at Lucea on 26 May and William Hall, the famous equestrian incendiary, on 28 May. Nor were these the last executions. On 31 October, 1832 three men, and a boy named Robert who had been a member of Dehany's party, were tried and all four were later executed. [PRO: CO 137/188, fols 30-43].

[6] "The King against Samuel Sharpe — a Slave to Samuel Sharpe Esquire".

[7] The most important of these, in order of date, were: the so called Ibo conspiracy in St. Elizabeth, Jamaica in 1815; the Barbados rebellion of 1816; the rebellion of 1823 in Demerara; and the wide-spread conspiracies in Jamaica in 1823 and 1824.

[8] For an account of the operation of the apprenticeship system see: Madden, *Twelve Months' Residence in the West Indies during the transition from Slavery to Apprenticeship*, (2 vols. London, 1835); W. L. Burn, *Emancipation and Apprenticeship in the British West Indies*, London 1937).

[9] For information on the events in St. Kitts the author is indebted to Richard Frucht for sending him, in advance of publication, a copy of his manuscript "Emancipation and Revolt in the West Indies: St. Kitts 1834".

[10] Of this sum, the slave owners in Jamaica received approximately £6 million for 311,000 slaves.

REFERENCES

BOOKS

[1] ANON., *Interesting trades relating to the Island of Jamaica*, Lewis, Luman & Jones, St. Jago de la Vega, 1800.

[2] APTHEKER, H., *American Negro Slave Revolts*, Columbia Univ. Press, New York, 1943.

[3] BARHAM, H., *The Most Correct and Particular Account of the Island of Jamaica*, unpublished, 1722 BM: Sloane MS 3918.

[4] BLEBY, Henry, *Death Struggles of Slavery*, (3rd. edit), London, 1868.

[5] BRIDGES, G.W., *The Annals of Jamaica*, John Murray, London, 1827.

[6] CRATON, M. and WALVIN, J., *A Jamaican Plantation, the History of Worthy Park 1670 to 1970*, W.H. Allen, London & New York, 1970.

[7] DALLAS, R., *History of the Maroons* (2 vols.) London, 1803.

[8] DAMPIER, William, *Two Voyages to Campeachy*, 1699.

[9] DAVIES, D.B., *The Problem of Slavery in Western Culture*, Pelican Books, London, 1970.

[10] EDWARDS, Bryan, *The Proceedings of the Governor and Assembly of Jamaica in regard to the Maroon Negroes*, John Stockdale, London, 1796.

[11] _____, *History, Civil and Commercial, of the British Colonies in the West Indies*, London: 1st edit (2 vols) 1793; 4th edit (3 vols) 1801; 5th edit (5 vols) 1819.

[12] KNIBB, W. and others (eds.) *Facts and Documents connected with the late Insurrection in Jamaica*, Teape & Son, printers, Tower Hill, London. n.d.

[13] FYFE, Christopher, *A History of Sierra Leone*, Oxford Univ. Press, London, 1962.

[14] GARDNER, W.J., *The History of Jamaica from its Discovery... to the Year 1872* (1st edit 1873) new edit., T. Fisher Unwin, London, 1909.

[15] HAKLUYT, Richard (ed.), *The Principal Navigations Voiages Traffiques & Discoveries of the English Nation* (First pub. 1589) J.M. Dent & Sons, London & Toronto, 1927.

[16] (various eds.), *Handbooks of Jamaica*, Kingston Jamaica.

[17] HINTON, John, *Memoir of William Knibb*, Houlston & Stoneman, London, 1847.

[18] KNIGHT, James, *The Natural Moral and Political History of Jamaica... to the year 1742.* (unpublished) BM: Ad. MS 12419.

[19] KOPYTOFF, Barbara Klamon—, *The Maroons of Jamaica*, (unpublished) Univ. of Pennsylvania, U.S.A., 1973.

[20] LAS CASAS, Bartholeme de, *Historia de las Indias*, (6 vols.) Seville, 1552-3.

[21] LESLIE, Charles, *New & Exact Account of Jamaica*, Edinburgh, 1739.

[22] LEWIS, M.G., *Journal of a West India Proprietor*, Murray, London, 1834.

[23] LINDSAY, Lord, *Lives of the Lindsays or a Memoir of the Houses of Crawford and Balcarres*, (2nd. edit — 3 vols.) John Murray, London, 1858.

[24] LONG, Edward, *The History of Jamaica*, (2 vols) London, 1774.

[25] MORALES PADRON, Francisco, *Jamaica Español*, Escuela de Estudios Hispano Americanos de Sevilla, Seville, 1952.

[26] RENNY, Robert, *An History of Jamaica*, London, 1807.

[27] SCHAFER, D.L.,*The Maroons of Jamaica*, (unpublished) Univ. of Minnesota, U.S.A., 1973.

[28] SCHULER, Monica, *Slave Resistance and Rebellion in the Caribbean During the Eighteenth Century*, (unpublished) Univ. of the W.I., Mona, Jamaica, 1966.

[29] SENIOR, BERNARD MARTIN (published anonymously) *Jamaica as it was, as it is and as it may be comprising ... an authentic narrative of the Negro Insurrection in 1831 ... by a Retired Military Officer*, London, 1835.

[30] SOUTHEY, Thomas, *Chronological History of the West Indies*, London, 1827.

[31] TAYLOR, John, *History of His Life and Travels in Jamaica*, Vol. 2, London, 1688 — cited in Schafer [27/34].

[32] THICKNESSE, Philip, *Memoirs and Anecdotes of Philip Thicknesse*, William Jones, Dublin, 1790.

[33] THURLOE, John, *A Collection of State Papers of John Thurloe, Esq.* (7 vols.) London, 1742.

[34] WADDELL, H.M., *Twenty-nine Years in the West Indies and Central Africa*, London, 1863.

[35] WILLIAMS, Eric, *Capitalism and Slavery*, Chapel Hill, U.S.A., 1944.

[36] ——— , *From Columbus to Castro 1492–1969*, Andre Deutsch, London, 1970.

[37] WILLIAMS, J.J., *The Maroons of Jamaica*, Boston College Press, Boston, 1938.

ARTICLES

[38] FRANCO, Jose Luciano, "The Palenques: Runaway Slave Settlements," *Granma*, 15 November 1969.

[39] PITMAN, F.W., "Slavery on British West Indies Plantations in the 18th century", *Journal of Negro History*, Vol. XI, 509.

[40] RECKORD, Mary, "The Jamaica Slave Rebellion of 1831", *Past and Present*, No. 40, July 1968.

[41] VANDERWAL, R.L., "Problems of Jamaican Pre-History", *Jamaica Journal*, Vol. 2. No. 3, September 1968.

PERIODICALS AND NEWSPAPERS

[42] *Cornwall Chronicle,* Montego Bay, Jamaica.

[43] *Cornwall Courier,* Falmouth, Jamaica.

[44] *Granma* (English weekly Edit.), Havana, Cuba.

[45] *Jamaica Historical Review,* Kingston, Jamaica.

[46] *Jamaica Historical Society Bulletin,* Kingston, Jamaica.

[47] *Jamaica Journal,* Kingston, Jamaica.

[48] *Journal of Negro History,* Washington, U.S.A.

[49] *Past and Present,* Oxford, England.

[50] *Royal Gazette,* Kingston, Jamaica.

[51] *Social and Economic Studies,* Institute of Social and Economic Research, U.W.I., Mona, Jamaica.

[52] *Watchman* (Later *Watchman and Jamaica Free Press*), Kingston, Jamaica.

OFFICIAL DOCUMENTARY SERIES

Abbreviation	Title of Series
Acts (1681–1737),	*Acts of the Assembly Passed in the Island of Jamaica from 1681 to 1737 inclusive,* London, 1743.
Acts (1738),	*Acts of Jamaica,* London, 1738.
Acts (1769),	*Acts of Assembly,* Jamaica, 1769.
CSP,	*Calendar of State Papers (Colonial Series – America & the West Indies)*
Hsd.,	*Hansard*
J. Stat.,	Statues enacted in Jamaica identified by reference to year of reigning monarch
Journals,	*Journals* of the Jamaica Assembly
Votes,	*Votes* of the Jamaica Assembly

Cl. Min.,	Minutes of the Council (Jamaica)
PP.,	*Parliamentary Accounts & Papers*
P. Deb.,	*Parliamentary Debates*
HCJ	*House of Commons Journal*
SP,	*Las Siete Partidas,* del Rey Alfonso el Sabio

UNPUBLISHED MANUSCRIPTS LETTERS AND PAPERS
(Abbreviations used in text shown in brackets)

WHERE PRESERVED	DESCRIPTION OR SERIES	REFERENCE
BRITISH MUSEUM (BM)	THE LONG PAPERS	Ad. MS
	THE JAMES KNIGHT MS "The Natural Moral and Political History of Jamaica ... to the year 1742"	Ad. MS 12419
	THE JAMES PINNOCK DIARY	
	THE BARHAM MS "The Most Correct and Particular Account of the Island of Jamaica"	Sloane MS 3918
PUBLIC RECORD OFFICE, London (PRO)	COLONIAL OFFICE (CO)	137;
	TREASURY (T)	
INSTITUTE OF JAMAICA (Inst. Ja.) Kingston, Jamaica	MINUTES OF THE COUNCIL JOURNAL OF CHRISTOPHER ALLEN JOURNAL OF THOMAS PETERS	W.I. Reference Library MSS file 1731/32
JAMAICA GOVERNMENT ARCHIVES (J. Arc.) Spanish Town, Jamaica	RECORDED INVENTORIES (Inv.) RECORDED DEEDS	
SURREY RECORD OFFICE, County Hall, Kingston on Thames, England	GOULBURN PAPERS (Gbn. P) Family papers of the Goulburns, owners of Amity Hall, Vere, Ja.	

INDEX TO PERSONS 345

Adair, Capt. James, 107, 112-4
Adubal, 86
Albuquerque, Duke of, 4
Allen, Lt. Christopher, 49-53, 55, 58 (11), 80, 81 (1)
Allen, James, 251
Altamirano, Bishop J. de laC., 3
Annand, William, 256-7, 272 (7) 282-6, 325
Ashworth, Major (Lt. Col.) 54, 55, 56, 65, 68
Assado, 68

Baptiste, 233-4
Barrett, Richard, 166, 293
Barrett, Samuel, 248-9, 290 (7)
Bayley, Thomas C., 308
Bayley, Zachary, 130
Beaumont, August, 299-300
Beckford, Ballard, 130
Bennett, Col. Robert, 111-2, 114, 122-3
Bevill, Lt., 136
Bleby, Rev. Henry, 250-255, 257, 266-7, 279, 319-320, 330-34
Bob (the runaway), 158
Booth, Simon, 35
Box, Rev., 299
Bridges, Rev. G.W., 134-6, 171, 208, 242 (3)
Brooks, Col. George, 74-9, 84
Bullock, William, 237-41
Burchell, Rev. Thomas, 255, 267, 330
Burke, Edmund, 189 (18)
Burnett, Capt., 297-8
Buxton, Thomas F., 221

Cadien, Col., 298, 306
Campbell, Alexander, 267
Campbell, Col., 298, 301
Canning, George, 221
Castilla, Julian de, 4, 28 (4)
Chambers, Obed Bell, 302
Chambers, (M), Capt., 175
Concannen, Lt. George, 106-10
Cornwallis, Lt. Col., 48

Cotton, Sir Willoughby, 248, 258, 291-4, 297-8, 300-305, 307-8, 310, 313-5, 322, 326
Craskell, Thomas, 159, 160, 163-4, 166
Crawford, (M) Capt., 115 (1)
Cromwell, Oliver, 4
Cudjoe, (M) Capt./Col., 25, 42, 43, 44, 58 (8, 9), 85-6, 87-8, 89-90, 94-5, 96-105, 107, 110, 111, 114, 116 (5, 13), 118-21, 123-7, 137, 166, 179, 184, 189 (26)
Cudjoe (Kojo), 65
Cuffee (Kofi), Col. Needham's, 63
Cuffee (Kofi), William, 80
Cupid, 81, 83 (15), 86-8

Dallas, R.C. 30 (36), 42, 43, 44, 49, 77, 89-90, 98, 99, 116 (5), 159, 171-2, 176-80, 182-3, 185-6, 199
deBolas (Lubolo), Juan, 5, 6
de Lemelier, Capt., 47
Downer, (M) Capt., 82 (13), 115 (1)
Doyley, Capt. Daniel, 93
Dudley, Robert, 37
Dun, Jno., 63
Dwarris, Capt. T., 93

Edwards, Bryan, 37, 43, 60, 130-2, 134-5, 137, 147-9, 205
Ellis, Joseph (M), 115 (1)
Escoffery, John 243 (14)

Farquharson, Capt., 312-3
Finlayson, Capt., 309
Fitch, Col., 175-6, 181
Fletcher, Abraham, 130
Forrest, Capt., 139, 141
Forster, Col., 126
Fraser, James, 248
Fyffe, Capt., 309-10, 314

Gallimore, Col. Jarvis, 163, 175
Gardner, Rev. Francis, 267
Gardner, Rev. W.J. 14, 150-4, 157 204, 227-8, 241

Goderich, Viscount, 244-5
Gordon, Mr., 148
Goulburn family, 211-3
Governors & Lt. Governors
    Balcarres, Earl of, 159-87, 188 (3), 189 (37), 191-204, 211, 213-6, 217, 226
    Beckford, Peter, 21, 22
    Beeston, William, 6, 29 (24)
    Belmore, Earl of, 244-6, 274, 294, 296-7, 299, 310-11
    D'Oyley, Edward, 5
    Hamilton, Lord, 23
    Handasyd, Thomas, 22
    Hunter, Genl. R.O., 32, 33, 34, 38, 42, 44-5, 47, 48, 49, 54, 56-7, 58 (11), 67, 68, 70, 71, 82 (10), 85
    Inchquin, Earl of, 29 (21)
    Lawes, Newton, 26-7
    Lynch, Thomas 13
    Littleton, 6
    Manchester, Duke of, 224, 240-41
    Molesworth, Charles, 29 (17, 20)
    Morgan, Henry, 14
    Moore, H., 132-4, 137-44, 148, 150, 155 (3)
    Portland, Duke of, 27
    Trelawny, Edward, 98-105, 112, 116 (13), 127
    Williamson, Maj. Gen. Adam, 165, 168, 188 (3)
Governors, Acting
    Ayscough, John, 73, 77, 82 (10), 84-6, 88
    Gregory, John, 91-2, 96-7, 100, 104
Goviner, (Gummor), 85-6
Granvill, Lt. Bevil, 85-6
Gregory XIII, Pope, 129 (1)
Grey, T.G., 285
Grignon (the lawyer), 332-3
Grignon, W.S., 253, 264, 270, 272 (10), 274-81, 292, 300-301, 317-8
Guthrie, Col. John, 96-105, 106, 111-2, 117 (23), 118, 120

Hakluyt, Richard, 37
Harris, Badja, 82 (13)

Haughton, Samuel, 234
Hayes, Col., 45-6
Haynes, William, 145
Hercules (the guide), 53
Herring, Capt., 18
Hilton, Capt., 302
Hilton, Col., 297
Hull, Col., 183-4

Irving, James, 215

Jacob (the runaway), 161
Jacob (the Jew), 63, 65
James, Capt. John, 158-64
James, Maj. John, 158-65, 176-7
Jeremy, King, 27, 31(40)
Jesus, 332, 333
Juba, 217-9
Jumbo, 180
Johnson, William 248

Kent, Duke of, 203
Kerr, William M., 326-7
Knibb, Rev. William, 262-3, 267, 268, 271, 272 (2), 279-10, 319
Knight, James, 8, 13, 25, 28 (9), 42, 58 (9), 90, 94-5, 111, 117 (23)
Kopytoff, Barbara K. 81, 117 (27), 129 (5)

Lambe, Ebenezer, 54
Largie, John, 267
Las Casas, Bartholeme de, 28 (1)
Lawrence, Capt., 276
Lecesne, Louis Celeste, 233-4, 243 (14)
Lee, Capt., 53
Leharets, Laird of, 112-3
Leslie, Charles, 78-9
Lewis, M.G. (Monk), 225-7, 242 (4)
Lindsay, Lord, 188 (12)
Long, C.E., 13
Long, Edward, 5, 8, 13, 19, 29 (23), 79, 115, 130-1, 135-7, 139-43, 146, 148, 149-54, 155 (1, 2, 5)
Louverture, Toussaint, 192 (14)

MacDonald, Jas., 282, 298
Mackintosh, Donald 267

INDEX TO PERSONS 347

Mackintosh, James, 267
Mansong, Jack, (Three-Fingered), 158
Maroon leaders
   Accompong, Capt., 29 (12), 42, 89, 120, 126, 128
   Adou, Capt., 10, 83 (15), 86
   Apong, 122
   Bumbager, Capt., 128
   Clash, Capt., 10, 29(16)
   Cudjoe, Capt./Col., 25, 42, 43, 44, 58 (8, 9), 85-6, 87-8, 89-90, 94-5, 96-105, 107, 110, 111, 114, 116 (5), 118-21, 123-7, 129 (10), 137, 166, 179, 184, 189 (26)
   Dunbar, Capt., 174-5, 193, 203
   Guy (Gay), 64
   Harvey, 175, 202
   Johnny, Capt., 42, 120
   Johnson, Capt., 170, 179-80, 182, 185, 195-6, 198-9, 203
   Kishee, Capt., 10, 55, 81 (1)
   Kofi (Cuffee) of the Leewards, 42, 102, 120, 128
   Kofi (Cuffee) of Nanny Town, 64, 65, 86,
   Kofi (Cuffee), John, 87-7
   Kojo (Cudjo), 93-5
   Kwaku (Quaco), 42, 118, 120, 128
   Lubolo (de Bolas), Juan, 5, 6, 28 (6)
   Montague (James). Col., 160, 164, 169, 170, 175, 182, 184-7, 192, 198
   Nanny, 10, 44, 58 (13), 64, 80-1, 82 (13), 83 (15-17), 86, 113, 117 (27)
   Palmer, Capt., 170, 198
   Parkinson, Capt. Leonard, 170, 175, 199
   Pompey, 62, 68
   Quao, 111-5, 117 (27), 121-6, 128
   Quarentine, 86
   Rowe, 270
   Rowe, Henry A., 80, 82 (12)
   Schaw, Capt. Charles, 176, 179, 183-4, 203
   Scipio, 63, 86, 115 (2)
   Serres, Juan de, 6
   Smith, 170, 193-5, 197, 199, 203
   Tomboy (Thomboy), 86, 122
   White, Col., 269
McGhie, James, 211-2, 217
McLaren, John, 326-7
McMurdo, Lt. Col., 216
M'Neel, Thomas, 272 (6), 316-7
Merody, John, 159, 161-2
Mitchell, Thomas, 326-7
Moir, Alex, 208-10
Moore, Henry, 132-4, 137-44, 148, 150, 155 (3)
Morris, George, 276
Morris, J.H., 275-7, 290(5)
Mowatt, John, 163
Mumbee, Maj. 74, 76

Nanny, 10, 44, 58 (13), 64, 80-1, 82 (13), 83 (15-17), 86, 113, 117 (27)
Navin, Patrick, 210
Needham, Col., 62, 65
Neilson, Maj. 298
Newcastle, Duke of, 36, 72, 99

Ogle, Chalenor, 73

Paine, Thomas, 189 (18)
Palmer, Genl. James, 165
Patty, 217-10
Pennefather, Maj., 305-6, 308
Peters, Capt. Thomas, 49, 51-53, 58 (11), 80, 81 (1)
Phillip, Varney, 35, 91
Pinnock, James, 154
Plysham, Capt. Nicholas, 39, 58 (6)
Portland, Duke of, 159, 161, 168, 170, 173-4, 180, 182-3, 191-2, 199, 201-2, 216
Price, Charles, 59 (16)

Quao (Quayhoo), 65
Quarrell, Capt. Wm., 57 (4)
Quarrell, Col. William D., 186, 203
Quashee (Kwasi), 63

Reid, (M) Commander, 116 (9), 188 (11)
Richmond, 210
Robertson, Capt., 171-2
Robertson, Maj. Genl. 286-8, 294, 309, 312-3
Roby, John, 276-7
Rodriques, Elias, 307-8
Rodriques, Joseph, 307
Rodriques, Leah, 307
Rodriques, Moses, 307

Saddler, Capt. Francis, 98, 100-3, 112, 116 (13, 15), 118, 120
Sambo, Capt., 49, 50, 55-6
Samson, Thomas, 208-9
Sandford, Col., 171-3, 178
Sarra (Syrus), 51, 58 (13), 81, 115 (2)
Sedgewicke, Maj. R., 4
Senior, Bernard Martin, 297, 317, 335
Sharpe, Sam (Daddy), 250-64, 266-7, 269-70, 272 (7), 284-5, 288-9, 290 (11, 12), 318, 322, 325, 331-4
Sharpe, Samuel (Esq.), 250, 272 (7), 290 (12), 333
Shelton, Leopold, 78, 82(11)
Slave Rebels and Conspirators
  Alexander, 282
  Arnold, William, 282
  Baby, 315
  Bacchus, 307
  Bailey, 263
  Barrett, George, 282, 290 (13)
  Bernard, Ann, 320
  Binham, William, 245, 249, 260, 262-3
  Blackwall, 150-3
  Boatswain, 212, 217
  Bowman, 180
  Braeme, John, 233, 235
  Brown, Charles, 229

Buchanan, William, 282, 285
Campbell, Charles, 279-281
Cambpell, H., 309
Casacrui, 181
Cosley, Richard, 229
Cuba (Cubah), 149
Cudjoe (Kojo) (Fowlers), 180
Damon, 148
Dehany, 306-7, 309, 315-6, 330-1, 337 (5)
Douglas, Peter, 269-70, 273 (25)
Dove, Thomas, 250-3, 260-1, 263, 267, 269, 279-81, 288, 316, 319
Ellis, Patrick 320
Fortune, 148-9
Gardner, Robert, 250-2, 259-64, 268, 269, 279-81, 288-9, 295, 312-3, 316-20, 324 (1), 331, 337 (5)
George, 236
Gillespie, 314
Gladstone, Jack, 222
Guthrie, George, 317-8
Hall, William, 304, 337 (5)
Harford, 220
Haughton (Horton), Thomas, 257, 262-3
Hedley, Thomas, 282
Henry, Monice, 229
Hercules, 216, 219
Heulier, James, 263
Hylton (Hilton), Edward, 253-4, 289
Jack, 234-6
Johnny, 282
Johnson (Johnstone) rebel Col., 253, 255, 259-61, 279-80, 288
Kerr, Dennis, 231-2, 236
Kingston, 148-9
Kofi (Cuffee) (1686), 15, 16
Kofi (Cuffee((1798), 211-9
Kwamina (Quamina), 314
Leon, 239
Linton, 249-50, 268, 322
Little, George, 285-6
Llewellyn, Andrew, 257
Longmore, Charles, 282
Manhertz, James, 233, 235, 237

INDEX TO PERSONS 349

Mansong, Jack (Three-Fingered), 159
March, 218
Martin, John, 257
Martin, Joseph, 256, 284, 288-9
M'Cail, 263, 312
M'Kinley, 322
M'Lacklan, 263, 312
Montagnac, Richard, 231, 236
Montgomery, William, 229
Morris, John, 262-3
Morris, Robert, 263
Nibbs, Henry, 229
Oliver, Henry, 232-6
Peter, 14
Petersgill, 309
Pollidore, 218-9
Prince (1798), 216, 218-9
Prince (1823), 237
Prince (1831-2), 306
Quamin, 153-4
Quarentine, 86
Quim-quam, 306
Ramsey, Edward, 266-7
Roberts, Father, 263
Rose, Robert, 256, 283
Scandenburg, 14
Scipio, 228
Sharpe, Sam, (Daddy), 250-64, 266-7, 269-70, 272 (7), 284-5, 288-9, 290 (11, 12), 318, 322, 325, 331-4
Sterling, James, 228-9
Tacky, 10, 130, 143, 147-8, 150, 155 (1), 223
Tharp (Thorp), John, 262, 268, 269
Thompson, James, 231-2, 236-7
Trail, Richard, 257
Trelawny, 239-41
Tucker, 256
Watson, Charles, 229
Wellington, Rodney, 229
Williams, John, 269-70
Slave Informers
   Corberand, Jean Baptiste, 230-36, 244(15)
   Mack, 232, 236

Smith, Alfred, 268
Smith, John, 66, 68-9
Smith, Rev. John, 222
Soper (Soaper), Capt., 39, 40, 52
Southey, Thomas, 22
Sterling, James, 289
Stevenson, Lt. Col., 183
Stevenson, William James, 212
Stewart, James, 162-4, 211
Stewart, Rev. Thomas, 250, 262, 268, 280, 318-9, 321-2
Stoddard, Capt., 75, 78-9
Swanton, Thomas, 66-8, 73

Tacky, 10, 130, 143, 147-8, 150, 155 (1), 223
Tello, John, 34, 57 (3)
Teulon, Alan, 82 (11)
Thicknesse, Lt. Philip, 83 (16), 105-15
Thurloe, 5, 28 (5)

Vaughn, Samuel, 160, 164, 166, 237-70
Veragua, Duke of, 32

Waddell, Rev. H.M., 248-9, 266, 271, 279
Walpole, Maj. Genl. 82 (12), 178, 180, 181-7, 191 (37), 192-200
Waterman, 228
Watt, Robert, 254, 322
Whitelock, Anthony, 264-6, 299-300
Wilberforce, William, 226-7
William (M), 193, 202, 203
Williams, Lt. Col., 292, 299, 302, 317
Williams, Job, 95-6

Ysassi, Cristoval, 4

Zuicke, Fred, 260
Zuicke, J.B., 322

GENERAL INDEX

Abeng, 116 (10)
Abolitionists, 221-2, 224, 245, 305
Absentee owners, 42, 47, 211-3, 226
Accompong Town, 44, 80, 82 (12), 89, 96, 105, 116 (9), 121, 125, 128, 147 (7), 164, 175-7, 188 (11), 269-70, 295, 313
Adelphi, 278, 306
Africa, 3, 9, 13, 116, 131, 150, 203, 223, 225
African names, 9-13
Akans, 9-11, 13, 28 (10), 29 (12, 14), 58 (8), 116 (5, 8, 10), 155 (1)
Aketty, 96, 116 (10)
Akims, 8-12, 155 (1)
America
  Central, 27
  North, 69, 72
  South, 1, 3, 246
Amerindians, 1-3, 4, 15, 27, 28 (1, 2, 3), 31 (40), 37, 47, 59 (16), 70, 92, 98
Amity Hall (Vere), 30 (39), 208-10
Anabaptists, 225-6
Anchovy, 169-303
Antigua, 335
Anti-Slavery Society, 221-2, 245, 255
Anglicans (Church of England), 262, 280
Apprenticeship, 335-6, 337 (8)
Arawaks, 1-3, 4
Archers Ridge, 133, 136
Argyle, 241, 263
Ashantis, 8-9, 11, 154
Asia, The, 203
Assembly, The Jamaica, 3, 7, 9, 16, 17, 20, 22, 23, 26, 27, 28 (2, 6), 33, 35, 38, 41, 42, 45, 46, 47, 48, 54, 55, 56, 60, 61, 62, 65, 70, 71, 73, 74, 79, 82 (12), 88, 91, 92, 93, 94, 95-6, 97, 98, 99, 104, 105, 120, 121, 123, 126, 127, 128, 129 (14), 143-5, 147, 150, 154, 173, 174, 177, 180-1, 184, 186-7, 191, 195, 197, 200-1, 204-5, 213, 215-6, 223-4, 230, 254, 264, 265, 278, 300, 315, 316, 321-3

Assemblies, West Indian, 244, 335
Attornies, 208-10, 212, 253, 260, 301, 325

Bagnalls, 133, 134-5
Balcarres Estate, 230, 232, 233, 235-6
Ballards Valley, 151-3
Bandon, 174, 178, 308, 313
Baptists, 245, 248, 249, 252, 261, 262, 267, 271, 285, 318, 319, 331
Barbados, 222
Barbados Valley, 69-70, 93
Barneyside, 302
Bell-Chambers stone, 302, 311 (10)
Belvidere, 258, 259-60, 263, 264, 269, 274-5, 282-3, 294, 317
Black companies (militia), 7, 307
Black River, 274, 286, 294
Black shot, 8, 49-56, 76, 106, 108, 128, 145, 171, 173, 213-6, 218, 306
Blackwall's Rebellion, 150-4
Blue Mountains, 1, 44, 49, 52, 55, 74, 78, 79, 81
Board/Lords of Trade, 20, 21, 23, 24, 32, 40, 44, 46, 61, 72, 82(8), 85, 133, 138, 142, 146
Britain, 33, 41, 45, 69, 70, 71, 72, 118, 129 (1), 204, 221-5, 245, 248
British Empire, 32, 222, 223, 307, 335-6
British Government, 6, 7, 36, 71, 73, 164, 203, 223-4, 240, 244-5, 247, 335-6
British Guiana, 222, 246
British Navy, 6, 7, 61, 62, 70, 71, 73-4, 136, 139-40, 150, 169, 291, 294, 295, 296, 298, 306
British Parliament, 205, 221, 224, 226, 244, 247, 334, 335
British/Regular troops, 5, 6, 7, 21, 23, 32, 42, 43, 45-7, 48, 58 (10-11), 61-2, 65-7, 71-2, 73, 74-9, 84, 90, 91, 96, 98, 99,101, 105-15, 133, 136, 138, 140, 143, 144, 150, 164, 165, 168, 171, 173, 178, 199, 203, 213-4. 258, 264, 268-9, 275, 277, 288, 291-5, 296, 302, 304, 306, 308, 314, 315, 325-6

British West Indies, 167, 223, 244-6
Buff Bay, 71, 236

Calendar Act (1751), 129 (1)
Cambridge, 256, 261, 298
Canning Resolution, The, 221
Cape Coast, 9
Caracas, 57 (4)
Caribbean, 2, 3, 6, 9, 32, 223, 336
Carpenters Mountains, 143
Carrion Crow Hill, 62
Cartagena, 2
Castle Wemys, 187, 192-3, 200
Catadupa, 178, 269, 302
Cave River, 95, 185
Cave Valley, 6
Caymanas, 14
Chambas, 158
Charlestown, 124, 147, 177, 187, 310, 314
Chester Castle, 262, 265
Chesterfield, 260, 283, 295, 309
Chickesaws, 92
Church of England, 262, 280
Church Wardens, 70, 91
Clarendon, 6, 14, 16, 17, 20, 28 (8, 22, 35), 58 (9), 60, 69, 82 (7), 88, 89, 95, 129 (14), 142, 145, 150, 169, 186, 287, 300
Cockpits, 89, 118, 182, 194, 195-6, 214, 309
Coins circulating, 159, 174, 188 (1), 234, 243 (16)
Colonial Office, 240
Conspiracies of
    1675, 14
    1742, 126-7, 128
    1760 (St. Mary), 145-6
    1760 (Kingston), 149
    1760 (Manchioneal), 138-9
    1765, 150-4
    1769, 160
    1799 (St. Domingue), 225
    1803, 225
    1806, 225
    1809, 225
    1815, 225-7, 337 (7)
    1823-24, 228-43, 249, 337 (7)

Content, 166, 280, 287
Cornwall (county), 290 (7), 302, 305
Cornwall Chronicle, 320-1
Cornwall Courier, 280-1, 290 (10), 304
Cornwall estate, 154, 266, 279, 290 (7)
Cornwall Rangers, 304-5
Coromantis (Kromantis), 8, 9, 25, 28 (10), 70, 116, 126, 130, 139-40, 141, 149, 151, 153-4, 155 (1, 12), 180, 212, 225
Cotter-wood, 55
Council, The, 6, 15, 16, 20, 21, 23, 24, 27, 39, 40, 60, 61, 62, 73, 91, 92, 97, 133, 136, 137, 138, 140, 150, 155 (2), 180-1, 186-9, 191, 201
Council of War, 167-8, 174, 286, 310-11
Courant newspaper, 302, 314 (14)
Courts Martial, 62, 268, 269-10, 272 (25), 292, 298, 301, 315, 326-30
Crawford Town, 124, 128, 129 (14), 133
Croydon estate, 251, 272 (7), 287
Cuba, 2, 19, 37, 68, 116, 149, 186
Cudjoe's Town, 96-7, 100-2, 105, 116 (15), 121, 155 (7)

Danes, 9
Deans Valley, 25, 321
Deficiency Laws, 20, 23, 24, 26, 30 (39)
Dinah's Town, 50, 81 (1)
Distance Mountain, 49
Dogs, 186-7, 194-5, 197
Down's Cove, 135-7
Dragoons, 164-5, 168, 171-2, 178, 188 (14)
Drax Crawl, 69-70
Dromilly, 182

Edwards Fort, 71, 93
Elderslie, 307, 313

GENERAL INDEX 353

England, 42, 46, 50, 99, 205, 224, 228, 246 (14), 248, 249, 255, 263, 271, 285, 289, 295, 308
English, 3, 4, 5, 6, 8, 9, 13, 28 (4), 32, 37, 208, 223, 243 (17)
Espanola (Hispaniola), 2
Europeans, 2, 5, 6, 20, 28 (3), 32, 82 (7), 171
Ewes, 9

Fairfield, 293, 330
Fairy Hill, 330
Falmouth, 162, 192, 193, 212, 270, 271, 277, 291, 298-9, 307, 309, 310, 320
Fantis, 8, 9, 10, 11, 12, 154
First Maroon War, 32-115, 117 (28), 211
Forsters plantation, 126
Fort Haldane, 131, 133
France, 14, 30 (31), 118, 189 (18), 193
Free Blacks, 7, 70, 91, 98, 119, 128, 145, 155 (14), 158, 171, 267-8, 308
Free Coloured (Brown), 7, 70, 91, 98, 145, 155 (14), 158, 211, 215, 218, 267-8, 270, 307-8, 325
Free rebels, 267-8, 310-11
French, 37, 164, 166, 225, 231
French Revolution, 190 (18)
Friendship, 306, 320, 322
Frontier estate, 228-30
Furry's Town, 170

Ga, 9, 10, 13, 29 (12, 13, 14), 155 (1)
Ga-Adagme, 9
Gay's (Guy's) Town, 64-5
Georgia Estate, 280, 307
Ghana, 10, 29 (11)
Gibraltar regiments, 42, 45-6, 48, 73-4
Ginger Hill, 256, 260, 282-7, 325
Gold Coast, 8, 9, 130, 154, 155 (1)
Golden Grove, 241, 305-6
Goulburn Papers, 30 (39)
Great Pedro Point, 5
Great River, 69-70, 278, 295, 298, 313

Greenwich, 258, 259-60, 269, 283, 291, 316
Guadeloupe, 141
Guanaboa, 15, 133
Guinea, 8, 13, 43, 130, 234
Guthrie's Defile (Glade), 176, 178, 183, 189 (26)

Haitians, Haiti, 222, 231, 243 (14)
Hadington, 160, 308, 321
Hampton, 279-80
Hanover, 60, 69, 70, 82 (7), 89, 140, 141, 149, 158, 241, 251, 256, 260, 281, 289, 291, 301, 303, 306, 313, 318, 323, 326, 328
Hazelymph, 260, 262, 268, 303, 318
Healthshire Hills, 228
Heywood Hall, 131, 137
Hispaniola (Espanola), 2
Hobbys, 52, 61, 62-3, 86, 106-8
Honduras, Bay of, 146, 149

Ibos (Eboes) 86, 225-7
Indentured servants, 7, 23, 24, 26, 29 (19), 32, 33, 54, 131
Ipswich, 284, 288-90

Jamaica Courant, 300, 311 (14)
Jamaica currency, 209
Jews, 41, 63, 65, 115
Juan de Bolas, 28 (6)
Julian Calendar, 129 (1)

Kensington, 274-7, 304, 305, 308
Kingston, 20, 28 (8), 62, 65, 128, 149, 157, 158, 225, 228, 233-4, 236, 241, 295, 299
Kingston Chronicle, 301
Kromantine (Kormantine), 9, 28-9 (11)
Kromanti (Cromantee, etc.), 8, 9, 25, 28 (10), 70, 116, 126, 130, 139-40, 141, 149, 151, 153-4, 155 (1, 12), 180, 212, 225

Latium, 292, 297, 305
Leeward Islands, 335

Legislation, 8, 20, 22, 23, 24, 26, 35, 38, 44, 57, 62, 70, 120, 145, 154, 155 (13), 244, 334-6
Lethe, 262, 268
Liguanea, 15, 16, 49, 130
Logwood cutters, 146
London, 23, 34, 40, 70, 72, 99
Long Papers, 13-14, 28 (9), 125-7, 129 (11)
Lucea, 140, 301
Luidas Vale, 5-6, 28 (6), 133, 210
Lyndhurst Penn, 225

Macaronis, 234, 243 (16)
Mackfield, 299, 302, 304-5
Madagascars, 25, 30 (36)
Magistrates, 159-60, 162-5, 166, 167, 168, 169, 210, 231, 233, 235, 236, 238, 240-44, 251, 258, 267, 268, 269, 273, 277, 279, 281, 296, 299, 331
Malagasie, 30 (36)
Manchester, 289, 323, 326
Manchioneal, 138-9, 142, 155(8), 249, 296
Manumissions, 4, 19
Maroon (the word), 36-7
Maroon Town, 275, 280, 293 (4), 294, 297, 305-6, 310
Maroon War, First, 32-115, 117 (28), 214
Maroon War, Second, 82 (12), 157-87, 191, 211, 216, 290 (4)
Maroons
   Accompong, 44, 80, 82 (12), 89, 96, 105, 116 (9), 121, 125, 128, 147, 155 (7), 164, 176-8, 189 (11), 191, 214, 269-70, 295, 313,
      Charles Town, 124, 147, 177, 187
      Crawford Town, 124, 128, 129 (14), 133
      Cudjoe's Town, 96-7, 100-2, 105, 116 (15), 121, 155 (7)
      Deportation of, 191, 202-5
      East-west contacts of, 44, 86-9, 94-5, 99, 112, 116 (13)

fighting tactics of, 43, 44, 45-6, 53, 75-7, 84, 87-8, 89-90, 96, 107-10, 113-4, 137, 171-2, 174, 176-7, 179, 182
government of, 63-5, 118-20, 121-3, 127
independent bands of (post 1730), 85-6
land allocations to, 83 (17), 117 (27), 118, 120-1, 123-4, 129 (5)
Leeward, 25, 29 (12), 42, 43, 44, 47, 60, 86-91, 94, 96-105, 106, 110, 111, 115, 118-21, 123, 124-5, 126-8
Moore Town, 80, 82 (13), 84, 115 (1), 124, 187-8
Nanny Town, 44, 51, 60, 63-5, 74-81, 84, 86, 94, 124, 133, 155 (4), 187, 191
oral history of, 44, 80, 84, 96, 104
payments to, 119, 122, 125, 127-8, 137, 147, 157, 323
peace feelers to, 85, 92, 96-7, 100, 106, 181-4
policing role of, 103, 119, 121-8, 129 (14), 132, 133, 135-8, 140, 147-8, 157-8, 166, 185, 207, 263, 269, 288, 302, 308-10, 313-4, 323
pre-1730 bands of, 4-6, 15-16, 17, 18, 21, 22, 24, 25-6, 27, 34, 35, 36, 38-40
slave rebel liaisons with, 126-7, 153-4, 269-70
Scotts Hall, 124, 133, 155 (5), 177, 187
settlements of, 34, 35, 36, 39, 41, 43, 44, 47, 49, 52, 53, 55, 60, 62-5, 68, 73, 75-7, 79-81, 86-7, 95, 96-7, 100-2, 106, 115, 115 (1), 118-24, 125, 136-8, 140, 147, 155(4), 158, 159-64, 165-6, 168-73, 175-7, 195, 207
slaves owned by, 128
Spanish period, 4, 5, 6, 37
spies for, 51, 58 (13), 62-5, 81

GENERAL INDEX 355

Treaties with, 87, 101-5, 106, 110-2, 115, 118-29, 130, 157, 159, 164, 184-7, 188 (11), 189 (37), 191-205
Trelawny Town, 102, 118-21, 126, 129(14), 147, 155(7), 158, 159-73, 175-87, 204, 210, 222, 289(4), 291
Windward, 10, 37-40, 44, 49-53, 60-81, 84, 86, 94, 99, 105-15, 121-5, 126, 128, 178, 191

Martial Law, 14, 17, 88, 90, 133, 138, 142, 167-8, 286, 291, 311, 314
Mercenaries, 7, 8, 16, 26, 34, 35, 37-42, 44, 45, 48, 49-53, 54, 55, 56, 58 (11), 66-9, 70, 71, 73, 87-8, 91, 92, 93, 98, 106, 108, 131, 133, 135, 137-8, 157-8, 177, 213-4, 215-6, 309-11
Mestizos, 4, 28 (3)
Methodists/Weslyans, 255, 299, 334
Militia, The, 7, 15, 18, 20, 21, 30 (39), 32, 33, 47, 54, 55, 62-3, 71, 74-9, 98, 105, 108-9, 110, 133-4, 136, 138, 140, 141, 144, 145, 155(14), 162, 165, 168, 171-3, 176, 178, 180, 182, 213-4, 228, 229-10, 246, 256, 260-1, 264, 265, 270, 274-5, 279-81, 283, 285-7, 289, 291, 296, 298, 300, 302, 304, 306, 308, 309, 312-5, 316, 323, 326
Missionaries, 224, 225-6, 245, 248-9, 262, 267, 271, 302, 331-3
Mocha (Mocho), 178, 182, 314, 316
Molly's Town, 50, 81 (1)
Monarchy/Monarch (British), 21, 23, 33, 42, 46, 61, 70, 71, 72-3, 118, 120, 150, 178, 246-7, 255, 268-9, 271, 293, 294, 322
Montego Bay, 54, 101, 140, 159-60, 164, 166, 168, 169, 174-5, 184, 196, 197, 199, 201, 237, 238, 252-8, 267-8, 270-71, 274, 276-7, 279, 281, 283, 291, 293, 294, 295, 301, 303, 307, 313, 314, 316, 318, 326, 330, 331, 332
Montpelier, 253, 261, 265, 279-81
Montserrat, 335
Moore Town, 80, 82(13), 84, 115(1), 124, 177-8, 310-314
Morant Bay, 296
Mosquito Indians, 27, 31 (40), 47, 92
Mosquito Shore, 31 (40), 92, 150
Mountain Spring, 54, 253, 269, 298
Mulattoes/Browns, 4, 7, 28 (3), 35, 70, 91, 98, 131, 134, 145, 155 (14), 158, 267-8, 270, 307-8
Mullett Hall, 230, 234
Mundingoes (Mandingoes), 211, 212

Nanny Town, 44, 51, 60, 63-5, 74-81, 84, 86, 94, 124, 133, 155 (4), 187, 191
Negro River, 50
Newspapers, 158, 197, 247-8, 255, 264, 268, 272 (20), 280-81, 290(10), 300, 301-4, 310, 313, 314, 320-21
Non-Conformists, 224, 245, 248, 319, 331-3
Nova Scotia, 203

Obeah, 80-1, 82 (16), 113, 235-6
Orange Valley, 298-9
Overseers (Bushas), 17, 21, 26, 131, 139, 151, 208-9, 212, 218, 230, 234-5, 237, 250, 258, 265, 278, 282-6, 316, 325

Pacquet (Packet), 139, 155 (10)
Palenques, 4, 5, 6, 13, 28 (6)
Palmyra, 276-7, 281
Pantre-pant, 213
Paretty, 5
Peace Cave, 96
Peru estate, 212, 217
Petty River Bottom, 89
Piracy, Pirates, Privateers, 20, 21, 30 (26)

Planters, 7, 13, 24, 42, 66, 68-9, 71, 72, 95, 99, 131, 154, 157-8, 160, 162, 166, 208, 224, 225, 231, 238, 244-5, 250, 255, 256, 265, 266, 274-5, 296, 299, 301, 323, 335
Port Antonio, 32, 36, 37, 38, 40, 41, 45, 46, 50, 60, 61, 66, 68, 70, 72, 73, 102, 112, 274, 296, 309, 310
Portland, 28 (8), 69, 80, 94, 155 (4, 8), 232, 274, 289, 323, 328-30
Port Maria, 106, 131, 153, 228, 230
Port Royal, 20, 28(8), 37, 45, 46, 48, 50, 61, 133, 136-7, 202, 291
Porto Bello, 34
Portuguese, 223
Presbyterians, 258, 266
Privy Council, 16, 17, 18, 20, 120

Quamboos, 8

Reading (Redding), 300
Rebellion
  of 1673 (Lobby's), 13, 17
  1676 (St. Mary), 14
  1676 (Caymanas), 14
  1683 (Lucy's), 15
  1685 (Guanaboa), 15
  1690 (Suttons), 17, 18, 20, 29 (22, 23), 35, 58 (9)
  1704, 22
  1733 (Hanover), 70
  1742 (Forsters), 126-7
  1746 (Kingston), 128
  1760 (Tacky's), 10, 130-9, 142, 143, 145-9, 150, 157, 211
  1760 (Manchioneal), 138, 139, 142, 157
  1760 (St. James), 143, 157
  1760 (Westmoreland), 138-44, 146, 148, 157, 211, 223
  1765 (Blackwall's), 150-4, 157
  1777 (Hanover & Westmoreland), 158
  1798 (Kofi's), 211-19
  1807, 242 (3)
  1808 (W.I. Regiment), 225
  1816 (Barbados), 222, 337 (7)
  1823 (Demerara), 222, 337 (7)
  1831-2 (Sharpe's "Emancipation), 244-337
  1834 (St. Kitts), 335, 337 (9)
Retrieve estate, 253, 256, 283, 291
Rewards to slaves, 15, 47, 57, 128, 288
Rewards to Maroons, 119, 122, 124-5, 127-8, 137, 147, 157, 158, 177, 288, 295
Rewards to others, 16, 34, 35, 41, 45, 48, 79, 88, 92-3, 128, 145, 169, 170, 173, 288, 294
Rights of Man, 167, 193 (18)
Rio Grande, 51, 52, 53, 58 (14), 84
Rio Juana, 4, 5
Roehampton, 315
Roman Catholics, 129 (1)
Round Hill, 281, 298, 306, 308, 314
Royal Gazette, 158, 268, 290(10), 310, 314

St. Andrew, 20, 82 (7), 124
St. Ann, 6, 13, 14, 17, 54, 60, 69, 91, 95, 145, 250
St. Ann's Bay, 2, 168, 247
St. Catherine, 14, 15, 16, 20, 28 (6, 8), 111, 145
St. David, 20, 28 (8)
St. Domingue/Domingo, 130, 159, 165, 168, 188 (3, 14), 213, 222, 225, 233
St. Dorothy, 142, 149
St. Elizabeth, 5, 14, 18, 20, 60, 69, 82 (7), 86, 87, 89, 91, 129 (14), 140, 145, 160, 180, 225-6, 251, 256, 270, 282-3, 286, 287, 294, 309, 312, 322, 323, 325, 327-30
St. George, 16, 17, 28(8), 38, 66, 71, 74, 93, 95, 106, 111, 225, 230, 231, 310
St. Jago de la Vega, 14, 15
St. James, 60, 69, 82 (7), 89, 91, 140, 141, 145, 149, 160, 162, 165, 171, 173, 213, 214, 237-8, 243-4,

GENERAL INDEX

251, 253, 256, 260, 265, 270-71, 272-5, 277-83, 291, 293, 295, 296. 297, 302, 303, 307, 308, 309, 314, 321, 323, 326, 328-30
St. John, 133. 142, 210
St. Kitts, 336, 337(9)
St. Mary, 10, 14, 16, 17, 28 (8), 38, 82 (7), 124, 130-9, 142, 143, 145, 149, 150-4, 228, 229-30, 240
St. Thomas in the east, 28(8), 70, 138, 142, 146-7, 149, 155(8), 246, 296-7, 321, 328-30
St. Thomas in the Vale, 15, 16, 17, 20, 28 (8), 82 (7), 136, 329,
Salt Spring, 251, 270-71, 274
Salters Hill, 271
Sambo, 273 (23)
Savanna la Mar, 140, 251, 262, 268, 292, 295, 301-2, 318, 319, 321
Scots, 47-8, 223, 248
Scott's Hall, 124, 133, 155(5), 177, 187
Seamen, 66-8, 71, 140, 150
Secession, 244
Second Maroon War, 82 (12), 157-87, 191, 211, 216, 290 (4)
Sevilla Nueva, 2
Shaw/Schaw Castle, 178, 280
Shuttlewood (Shettlewood), 257 262, 274
Sierra Leone, 203
Sion Hill, 330
Slave Courts, 327-30, 332-3
Slavery, Abolition of, 221-2, 224, 244, 247, 302, 334-7
Slaves
    Abduction of, 24, 25, 26, 38-9, 43
    African born, 3, 8, 20, 225
    African names of, 9, 10, 11, 13
    Amerindians as, 28 (2)
    Arson by. 131. 151-2, 228, 229. 258, 264-6, 284-5, 291, 292, 293, 301, 302, 304, 306, 316, 320, 321, 323
    Baggage, 8, 37, 49, 51, 52, 54, 66, 109, 145
    Black-shot, 8, 49, 50, 51-3, 54, 55-6, 76, 213-6, 218, 309
    Branding of, 158
    Compensation paid for, 147, 158, 237, 242, 235-6, 337 (10)
    Creole, 225-6
    Death sentences/executions, 22, 142, 145-6, 147, 148-9, 150, 154, 157, 158, 227, 229-30, 240, 241, 270, 292, 295, 301, 316, 320, 322, 327-30, 333-4, 337 (5)
    Drivers/headmen, 151, 217, 230, 249-50, 266, 268-9, 278, 284, 328, 329
    Field, 252, 327-8, 329
    French, 141
    Household, 151, 222, 329
    Holidays of, 244-5, 254, 256, 259, 271
    Imprisonment of, 242-4, 328-30
    Informers, 14-5, 58(13), 62-5, 81, 93-4, 139, 149, 157, 214-6, 237
    Legislation affecting, 22, 26, 44, 55, 57, 69-70, 120, 123, 128, 144-5, 224, 244, 334-6
    Manumission of, 4, 19
    Maroon allies of, 179-80, 193-5, 198-9, 202
    Oath taking by, 150-1, 236, 251, 254, 256, 257
    Owners of, 4, 19, 79, 128, 146-7, 158, 214, 257, 293, 295, 325
    Praedial, 335
    Price/Value of, 147, 237, 239
    Rebels in uniform, 297, 303
    Registration of, 227
    Rewards to, 15, 47, 57, 128, 288
    Runaway, 4, 5, 6, 7, 8, 16, 17, 19, 21, 22, 25, 27, 35, 36, 47, 70, 72, 102-3, 118-9, 121-2, 124-5, 128, 146, 157, 179, 180, 186, 187, 193-5, 198-9, 202, 208-12, 212, 227, 231-2, 235
    Settlements of runaways (see Maroons), 5, 8, 13, 16, 17, 18, 22, 25, 26, 34, 36, 39, 41, 43, 44, 47, 49, 52, 53, 55, 60, 62-5, 68, 73, 75-7, 79-81, 86-7, 95, 96-7, 100-2, 106, 115, 207, 216-8
    Skilled, 328, 329

Spies for Maroons, 51, 58 (3)
Trials of, 146-7, 150, 156(17), 157, 226, 229, 233-5, 236, 237-41 270, 284-5, 289, 290(11), 292, 298-9, 307, 316, 326-30, 332-3, 337(3, 5)
Torture and maiming of, 146, 148-9, 328-30
Transportation/deportation of, 47, 128, 146, 148, 154, 158, 239-40, 241, 242
Trusted, 33, 92, 213-6
Whipping of, 146, 239, 241, 244, 250, 328
Slave Trading, 8, 9, 13, 28 (2), 139, 154, 221, 224
Spain, 30 (31), 32, 46, 125, 129 (12)
Spaniards, 1, 2, 3, 4, 5, 19, 32, 34, 37, 57 (4), 68, 103, 186
Spanish
  Aid to rebels, 34
  Chasseurs, 187-8, 194-5
  monarchy, 1, 3, 4, 19, 30(26), 32, 34, 37
  officials, 4, 19
Spanish River, 108, 112
Spanish Town, 14, 48, 68, 111, 133, 136, 166-9, 177, 187, 191, 196, 197, 227, 295, 310
Spot Valley, 248-9
Spring Vale, 307, 309
Struie, 256, 261, 263, 289, 312-3, 319
Sugar, 1, 8, 19, 32, 64, 335

Tabon people, 13
Tacky's War, 10, 130-9, 142, 143, 145-9, 150, 157, 211
Taxation, 7, 17, 41
Titchfield, 68, 82 (6)
Trade & Plantations, Council /Lords of, 20, 21, 23, 24, 32, 40, 44, 46, 61, 72, 82 (8), 85, 86, 133, 138, 142, 146
Treaty of Madrid, 30 (26)
Trelawny, 82 (7), 89, 128, 160, 162, 173, 213, 247, 248, 256, 260, 266, 275, 277, 278, 279, 282, 289, 295, 298, 306, 301, 308, 310, 314, 319, 323, 326, 327
Trelawny Town, 102, 118-21, 126, 129 (14), 147, 155 (7), 158, 159-73, 177, 195
Trials of free people, 307-8
Tryal estate, 166, 303

Unity Hall, 237-8, 313, 314

Vaughansfield, 159-60, 169, 171-2, 302, 307, 308, 309, 310
Vere, 15, 20, 35, 82 (7), 145, 208
Vermahollis, 6
Vestries, 7, 70, 211
Virgin Valley, 306, 314
Voluntary Parties, 8, 26, 37-42, 44, 45, 49-53, 70, 71, 73, 87-8, 93, 98, 145, 171-2, 307-8

Wag-Water, 87, 133
Watchman, The, 300, 301-4, 313, 320-21
Weslyans (Methodists), 255, 299
West India Regiment, 225
Westmoreland, 60, 69, 82(7), 89, 138-44, 148, 154, 158, 170, 173, 176, 178, 180, 182, 251, 257, 260, 262, 264, 265, 266, 278, 281, 289, 295, 299, 302, 309, 312, 313, 316, 318, 321, 322, 323, 326, 328-30
Whitehall plantation, 151-2
Wiles Town, 54
Windsor Castle, 42, 315
Worthy Park, 3, 28(6), 59(16), 210-11

Yallahs, 244
Yallahs River, 50
York, 275, 281, 316
Y.S. estate, 273 (25), 282-3, 287
Yoruba, 13

Lightning Source UK Ltd.
Milton Keynes UK
UKHW030421041122
411562UK00012B/134